WHO ARE WE?

THE CHALLENGES TO
AMERICA'S NATIONAL IDENTITY

SAMUEL P. HUNTINGTON

SIMON & SCHUSTER PAPERBACKS

NEW YORK LONDON TORONTO SYDNEY

SIMON & SCHUSTER PAPERBACKS
Rockefeller Center
1230 Avenue of the Americas
New York, NY 10020

Copyright © 2004 by Samuel P. Huntington

First Simon & Schuster paperback edition 2005

SIMON & SCHUSTER PAPERBACKS and colophon are registered trademarks
of Simon & Schuster, Inc.

For information regarding special discounts for bulk purchases,
please contact Simon & Schuster Special Sales
at 1-800-456-6798 or business@simonandschuster.com.

Manufactured in the United States of America

10   9   8   7   6   5   4   3   2   1

The Library of Congress has cataloged the hardcover edition as follows:
Huntington, Samuel P.
Who are we? : The Challenges to America's National Identity / Samuel P. Huntington.
p. cm.
Includes bibliographical references and index.
1. National characteristics, American.   2. United States—Civilization—1970–   I. Title.
E169.12.H78 2004   305.8'00973—dc22
2004042902
ISBN-13: 978-0-684-87053-3
ISBN-10:   0-684-87053-3
ISBN-13: 978-0-684-87054-0 (Pbk.)
ISBN-10:   0-684-87054-1 (Pbk.)

ACKNOWLEDGMENTS

This book, like my previous ones, grew out of my teaching. For several years I have taught a course on American national identity. It provided me with the opportunity and the imperative to formulate and present my thoughts on this subject in a reasonably coherent fashion. The questions, comments, and criticisms I received from the undergraduate and graduate students caused me to rethink, refine, elaborate, and occasionally reject my ideas and approaches. Whatever its merits now, this book is far better than it would have been without their contributions.

In the early phases of manuscript preparation, Tammy Frisby, Marius Hentea, and John Stephenson provided valuable assistance by running down materials, organizing data, writing memos summarizing their research, and making many useful comments on what I was trying to do. In this same phase, Carol Edwards and Jeana Flahive typed drafts of the first chapters of the manuscript.

The bulk of the book, however, emerged in a second phase when I was extraordinarily lucky to be helped by an outstanding team of assistants: Beth Baiter, Todd Fine, and James Perry. Without the help of this Book Team, the manuscript would not have been completed when it was and might never have seen the light of day. James Perry's help was indispensable in assembling and analyzing quantitative data, applying his superb computer skills to the many problems we faced, drawing on his background in law, and, most importantly, offering me wise counsel on how to set forth my arguments clearly, accurately, and in balanced fashion. James is a master of the ability to write succinct memos setting forth authoritative facts and persuasive interpretations of them.

Todd Fine, with persistence and imagination, pursued, located, and exhumed from the multiple caverns of the Harvard library system huge numbers of books, documents, data sets, and other materials. His major contribution, however, was his effort to ensure accuracy. Conscientiously, comprehensively, and relentlessly, he checked and rechecked facts, figures, quotations, and citations, even to the point of resisting, for example, my inclination to round off percentages and insisting they be specified to at least one-tenth of one percent. In a book like this one, with many thousands of pieces of information, the probability of errors creeping in is huge. Todd has done everything humanly possible to reduce them to the absolute minimum.

The third member of the Book Team, Beth Baiter, was the hub around whom we all circulated. She was our communications center and the coordinator of our activities, ensuring that each of us knew what we should do and what the others should do and were doing. With buoyant humor, she kept reminding us of deadlines, while simultaneously fueling us with coffee and cookies. Indispensably for me, she also sorted out, disposed of, or deflected the requests for my time and services, other than from students and colleagues, that came into the office each day. She also typed draft after draft of all the chapters in this book.

In the past I have had many first-rate assistants. Never before, however, have I been helped by such a diversely talented Book Team, whose members worked together so harmoniously, enthusiastically, and constructively. This was for me a truly wonderful experience.

My friends Lawrence Harrison, Peter Skerry, and Tony Smith read a draft of the manuscript and provided extremely valuable comments and criticisms that greatly improved the final version of this book. In addition, I owe a special debt to Larry Harrison for all the ideas and suggestions and the constant encouragement he has given me during the many years this book has been in preparation.

My work on this book and that of the Book Team was made possible by funding from the Smith Richardson Foundation, the Bradley Foundation, the Weatherhead Foundation, Harvard University, and the Weatherhead Center for International Affairs at Harvard.

From the initial conception of this book to its final stage, Denise Shannon went far beyond an agent's normal responsibilities by being comforting, bolstering, and most effective in ensuring that the published book is what I wanted. Throughout this process, Bob Bender, my editor at Simon and Schuster, did everything he could to move the book along on schedule, all the while stoically coping with my penchant for missing deadlines. He was cheerfully assisted by Johanna Li.

To all these individuals and institutions, I can only express my deepest thanks. All of them, in various ways, made this book possible. Clearly, however, I am solely responsible for the text, what it says and what it does not say, and hence any deficiencies of commission or omission are mine alone.

Finally and most importantly, I met my wife, Nancy, in 1956 and we were married a year later. At that point, I had just finished my first book, *The Soldier and the State*, and had not started a new one. Over the course of a dozen subsequent books, she has frequently commented that our marriage might not have taken place if she had known what it was like to live with an anguished, frantic, over-burdened academic confronted with the agonies, frustrations, and incredible time demands involved in producing serious scholarly works. She has, however, soldiered on right through this book, and our marriage has not only survived, but thanks to her efforts, has also been extraordinarily happy and rewarding. For making that happen, I can only add my deepest admiration and gratitude to almost a half-century of my deepest love.

S.P.H.

To

CANDACE, MAX, ELIZA

And

THEIR AMERICAN FUTURES

CONTENTS

LIST OF ILLUSTRATIONS

TABLES

FIGURES

FOREWORD

This book deals with the changes occurring in the salience and substance of American national identity. Salience is the importance that Americans attribute to their national identity compared to their many other identities. Substance refers to what Americans think they have in common and distinguishes them from other peoples. This book advances three central arguments.

First, the salience of their national identity for Americans has varied through history. Only in the late eighteenth century did the British settlers on the Atlantic coast begin to identify themselves not only as residents of their individual colonies but also as Americans. Following independence, the idea of an American nation took hold gradually and haltingly in the nineteenth century. National identity became preeminent compared to other identities after the Civil War, and American nationalism flourished during the following century. In the 1960s, however, subnational, dual-national, and transnational identities began to rival and erode the preeminence of national identity. The tragic events of September 11 dramatically brought that identity back to the fore. So long as Americans see their nation endangered, they are likely to have a high sense of identity with it. If their perception of threat fades, other identities could again take precedence over national identity.

Second, through the centuries Americans have, in varying degrees, defined the substance of their identity in terms of race, ethnicity, ideology, and culture. Race and ethnicity are now largely eliminated: Americans see their country as a multiethnic, multiracial society. The "American Creed," as initially formulated by Thomas Jefferson and elaborated by many others, is widely viewed as the crucial defining element of American identity. The Creed, however, was the product of the distinct Anglo-Protestant culture of the founding settlers of America in the seventeenth and eighteenth centuries. Key elements of that culture include: the English language; Christianity; religious commitment; English concepts of the rule of law, the responsibility of rulers, and the rights of individuals; and dissenting Protestant values of individualism, the work ethic, and the belief that humans have the ability and the duty to try to create a heaven on earth, a "city on a hill." Historically, millions of immigrants were attracted to America because of this culture and the economic opportunities it helped to make possible.

Third, Anglo-Protestant culture has been central to American identity for three centuries. It is what Americans have had in common and, as countless foreigners have observed, what has distinguished them from other peoples. In the late twentieth century, however, the salience and substance of this culture were challenged by a new wave of immigrants from Latin America and Asia, the popularity in intellectual and political circles of the doctrines of multiculturalism and diversity, the spread of Spanish as the second American language and the Hispanization trends in American society, the assertion of group identities based on race, ethnicity, and gender, the impact of diasporas and their homeland governments, and the growing commitment of elites to cosmopolitan and transnational identities. In response to these challenges, American identity could evolve in the direction of: (1) a creedal America, lacking its historic cultural core, and united only by a common commitment to the principles of the American Creed; (2) a bifurcated America, with two languages, Spanish and English, and two cultures, Anglo-Protestant and Hispanic; (3) an exclusivist America, once again defined by race and ethnicity and that excludes and/or subordinates those who are not white and European; (4) a revitalized America reaffirming its historic Anglo-Protestant culture, religious commitments, and values and bolstered by confrontations with an unfriendly world; (5) some combination of these and other possibilities. How Americans define their identity, in turn, affects the extent to which they conceive of their country as being cosmopolitan, imperial, or national in its relations with the rest of the world.

This book is shaped by my own identities as a patriot and a scholar. As a patriot, I am deeply concerned about the unity and strength of my country as a society based on liberty, equality, law, and individual rights. As a scholar, I find that the historical evolution of American identity and its present state pose fascinating and important issues for in-depth study and analysis. The motives of patriotism and of scholarship, however, may conflict. Recognizing this problem, I attempt to engage in as detached and thorough an analysis of the evidence as I can, while warning the reader that my selection and presentation of that evidence may well be influenced by my patriotic desire to find meaning and virtue in America's past and in its possible future.

All societies face recurring threats to their existence, to which they eventually succumb. Yet some societies, even when so threatened, are also capable of postponing their demise by halting and reversing the processes of decline and renewing their vitality and identity. I believe that America can do that and that Americans should recommit themselves to the Anglo-Protestant culture, traditions, and values that for three and a half centuries have been embraced by Americans of all races, ethnicities, and religions and that have been the source of their liberty, unity, power, prosperity, and moral leadership as a force for good in the world.

This is, let me make clear, an argument for the importance of Anglo-Protestant culture, not for the importance of Anglo-Protestant people. I believe one of the greatest achievements, perhaps the greatest achievement, of America is the extent to which it has eliminated the racial and ethnic components that historically were central to its identity and has become a multiethnic, multiracial society in which individuals are to be judged on their merits. That has happened, I believe, because of the commitment successive generations of Americans have had to the Anglo-Protestant culture and the Creed of the founding settlers. If that commitment is sustained, America will still be America long after the WASPish descendants of its founders have become a small and uninfluential minority. That is the America I know and love. It is also, as the evidence in these pages demonstrates, the America most Americans love and want.

PART I

The Issues of Identity

CHAPTER 1

The Crisis of National Identity

SALIENCE: ARE THE FLAGS STILL THERE?

Charles Street, the principal thoroughfare on Boston's Beacon Hill, is a comfortable street bordered by four-story brick buildings with apartments above antique stores and other shops on the ground level. At one time on one block American flags regularly hung over the entrances to the United States Post Office and the liquor store. Then the Post Office stopped displaying the flag, and on September 11, 2001, the liquor store flag flew alone. Two weeks later seventeen flags flew on this block, in addition to a huge Stars and Stripes suspended across the street a short distance away. With their country under attack, Charles Street denizens rediscovered their nation and identified themselves with it.

In their surge of patriotism, Charles Streeters were at one with people throughout America. Since the Civil War, Americans have been a flag-oriented people. The Stars and Stripes has the status of a religious icon and is a more central symbol of national identity for Americans than their flags are for peoples of other nations. Probably never in the past, however, was the flag as omnipresent as it was after September 11. It was everywhere: homes, businesses, automobiles, clothes, furniture, windows, storefronts, lampposts, telephone poles. In early October, 80 percent of Americans said they were displaying the flag, 63 percent at home, 29 percent on clothes, 28 percent on cars.[1] Wal-Mart reportedly sold 116,000 flags on September 11 and 250,000 the next day, "compared with 6,400 and 10,000 on the same days a year earlier." The demand for flags was ten times what it had been during the Gulf War; flag manufacturers went overtime and doubled, tripled, or quintupled production.[2]

The flags were physical evidence of the sudden and dramatic rise in the salience of national identity for Americans compared to their other identities, a transformation exemplified by the comment on October 1 of one young woman:

> When I was 19, I moved to New York City. . . . If you asked me to describe myself then, I would have told you I was a musician, a poet, an artist and, on a somewhat political level, a woman, a lesbian and a Jew. Being an American wouldn't have made my list.
>
> [In my college class Gender and Economics my] girlfriend and I were so frustrated by inequality in America that we discussed moving to another country. On Sept. 11, all that changed. I realized that I had been taking the freedoms I have here for granted. Now I have an American flag on my backpack, I cheer at the fighter jets as they pass overhead and I am calling myself a patriot.[3]

Rachel Newman's words reflect the low salience of national identity for some Americans before September 11. Among some educated and elite Americans, national identity seemed at times to have faded from sight. Globalization, multiculturalism, cosmopolitanism, immigration, subnationalism, and anti-nationalism had battered American consciousness. Ethnic, racial, and gender identities came to the fore. In contrast to their predecessors, many immigrants were ampersands, maintaining dual loyalties and dual citizenships. A massive Hispanic influx raised questions concerning America's linguistic and cultural unity. Corporate executives, professionals, and Information Age technocrats espoused cosmopolitan over national identities. The teaching of national history gave way to the teaching of ethnic and racial histories. The celebration of diversity replaced emphasis on what Americans had in common. The national unity and sense of national identity created by work and war in the eighteenth and nineteenth centuries and consolidated in the world wars of the twentieth century seemed to be eroding. By 2000, America was, in many respects, less a nation than it had been for a century. The Stars and Stripes were at half-mast and other flags flew higher on the flagpole of American identities.

The challenges to the salience of American national identity from other-national, subnational, and transnational identities were epitomized in several events of the 1990s.

Other-National Identities. At a Gold Cup soccer game between Mexico and the United States in February 1998, the 91,255 fans were immersed in a "sea of red, white, and green flags"; they booed when "The Star-Spangled Banner" was played; they "pelted" the U.S. players "with debris and cups of what might have been water, beer or worse"; and they attacked with "fruit and cups of beer" a few fans who tried to raise an American flag. This game took place not in Mexico City but in Los Angeles. "Something's wrong when I can't even raise an American flag in my own country," a U.S. fan commented, as he ducked a lemon going by his head. "Playing in Los Angeles is not a home game for the United States," a *Los Angeles Times* reporter agreed.[4]

Past immigrants wept with joy when, after overcoming hardship and risk, they saw the Statue of Liberty; enthusiastically identified themselves with their new country that offered them liberty, work, and hope; and often became the most intensely patriotic of citizens. In 2000 the proportion of foreign-born was somewhat less than in 1910, but the proportion of people in America who were also loyal to and identified with other countries was quite possibly higher than at any time since the American Revolution.

Subnational Identities. In his book *Race Pride and the American Identity*, Joseph Rhea quotes the poetry recited at two presidential inaugurations. At President John F. Kennedy's in 1961, Robert Frost hailed the "heroic deeds" of America's founding that with God's "approval" ushered in "a new order of the ages":

> *Our venture in revolution and outlawry*
> *Has justified itself in freedom's story*
> *Right down to now in glory upon glory.*

America, he said, was entering a new "golden age of poetry and power."

Thirty-two years later, Maya Angelou recited a poem at President Bill Clinton's inauguration that conveyed a different image of America. Without ever mentioning the words "America" or "American," she identified twenty-seven racial, religious, tribal, and ethnic groups—Asian, Jewish, Muslim, Pawnee, Hispanic, Eskimo, Arab, Ashanti, among others—and denounced the immoral repression they suffered, as a result of America's "armed struggles for profit" and its "bloody sear" of "cynicism." America, she said, may be "wedded forever to fear, yoked eternally to brutishness."[5] Frost saw America's history and identity as glories to be celebrated and perpetuated. Angelou saw the manifestations of American identity as evil threats to the well-being and real identities of people with their subnational groups.

A similar contrast in attitudes occurred in a 1997 telephone interview by a *New York Times* reporter with Ward Connerly, then the leading proponent of an initiative measure in California prohibiting affirmative action by the state government. The following exchange occurred:

REPORTER: "What are you?"
CONNERLY: "I am an American."
REPORTER: "No, no, no! What *are* you?"
CONNERLY: "Yes, yes, yes! I am an American."
REPORTER: "That is not what I mean. I was told that you are African American. Are you ashamed to be African American?"
CONNERLY: "No, I am just proud to be an American."

Connerly then explained that his ancestry included Africans, French, Irish, and American Indians, and the dialogue concluded:

REPORTER: "What does that make you?"
CONNERLY: "That makes me all-American!"[6]

In the 1990s, however, Americans like Rachel Newman did not respond to the question "What are you?" with Ward Connerly's passionate affirmation of his national identity. They instead articulated subnational racial, ethnic, or gender identities, as the *Times* reporter clearly expected.

Transnational Identities. In 1996 Ralph Nader wrote to the chief executive officers of one hundred of the largest American corporations pointing to the substantial tax benefits and other subsidies (estimated at $65 billion a year by the Cato Institute) they received from the federal government and urging them to show their support for "the country that bred them, built them, subsidized them, and defended them" by having their directors open their annual stockholders meeting by reciting the Pledge of Allegiance to the flag and the republic for which it stands. One corporation (Federated Department Stores) responded favorably; half the corporations never responded; others rejected it brusquely. The respondent for Ford explicitly claimed transnational identity: "As a multinational . . . Ford in its largest sense is an Australian country in Australia, a British company in the United Kingdom, a German company in Germany." Aetna's CEO called Nader's idea "contrary to the principles on which our democracy was founded." Motorola's respondent condemned its "political and nationalistic overtones." Price Costco's CEO asked, "What do you propose next—personal loyalty oaths?" And Kimberly-Clark's executive asserted that it was "a grim reminder of the loyalty oaths of the 1950s."[7]

Undoubtedly the vociferous reaction of American corporate leaders was in part because Nader had been hounding them for years and they could not resist the opportunity to castigate him as a latter-day Joe McCarthy. Yet they were not alone among American elites in downgrading or disavowing identification with their country. Prominent intellectuals and scholars attacked nationalism, warned of the dangers of inculcating national pride and commitment to America in students, and argued that a national identity was undesirable. Statements like these reflected the extent to which some people in American elite groups, business, financial, intellectual, professional, and even governmental, were becoming denationalized and developing transnational and cosmopolitan identities superseding their national ones. This was not true of the

American public, and a gap consequently emerged between the primacy of national identity for most Americans and the growth of transnational identities among the controllers of power, wealth, and knowledge in American society.

September 11 drastically reduced the salience of these other identities and sent Old Glory back to the top of the national flag pole. Will it stay there? The seventeen flags on Charles Street declined to twelve in November, nine in December, seven in January, and five in March, and were down to four by the first anniversary of the attacks, four times the number pre–September 11 but also one-fourth of those displayed immediately afterward. As an index of the salience of national identity, did this represent a modified post–September 11 normalcy, a slightly revised pre–September 11 normalcy, or a new, post–post–September 11 normalcy? Does it take an Osama bin Laden, as it did for Rachel Newman, to make us realize that we are Americans? If we do not experience recurring destructive attacks, will we return to the fragmentation and eroded Americanism before September 11? Or will we find a revitalized national identity that is not dependent on calamitous threats from abroad and that provides the unity lacking in the last decades of the twentieth century?

SUBSTANCE: WHO ARE WE?

The post–September 11 flags symbolized America, but they did not convey any meaning of America. Some national flags, such as the tricolor, the Union Jack, or Pakistan's green flag with its star and crescent, say something significant about the identity of the country they represent. The explicit visual message of the Stars and Stripes is simply that America is a country that originally had thirteen and currently has fifty states. Beyond that, Americans, and others, can read into the flag any meaning they want. The post–September 11 proliferation of flags may well evidence not only the intensified salience of national identity to Americans but also their uncertainty as to the substance of that identity. While the salience of national identity may vary sharply with the intensity of external threats, the substance of national identity is shaped slowly and more fundamentally by a wide variety of long-term, often conflicting social, economic, and political trends. The crucial issues concerning the substance of American identity on September 10 did not disappear the following day.

"We Americans" face a substantive problem of national identity epitomized by the subject of this sentence. Are we a "we," one people or several? If we are a "we," what distinguishes us from the "thems" who are not us? Race, religion, ethnicity, values, culture, wealth, politics, or what? Is the United States, as some have argued, a "universal nation," based on values common to all humanity and in principle embracing all peoples? Or are we a Western nation with our identity defined by our European heritage and institutions? Or are we unique with a distinctive civilization of our own, as the proponents of "American exceptionalism" have argued throughout our history? Are we basically a political community whose identity exists only in a social contract embodied in the Declaration of Independence and other founding documents? Are we multicultural, bicultural, or unicultural, a mosaic or a melting pot? Do we have any meaningful identity as a nation that transcends our subnational ethnic, religious, racial identities? These questions remain for Americans in their post–September 11 era. They are in part rhetorical questions, but they are also questions that have profound implications for American society and American policy at home and abroad. In the 1990s Americans engaged in intense debates over immigration and assimilation, multiculturalism and diversity, race relations and affirmative action, religion in the public sphere, bilingual education, school and college curricula, school prayer and abortion, the meaning of citizenship and nationality, foreign involvement in American elections, the extraterritorial application of American law, and the increasing political role of diasporas here and abroad. Underlying all these issues is the question of national identity. Virtually any position on any one of these issues implies certain assumptions about that identity.

So also with foreign policy. The 1990s saw intense, wide-ranging, and rather confused debates over American national interests after the Cold War. Much of this confusion stemmed from the complexity and novelty of that world. Yet that was not the only source of uncertainty about America's role. National interests derive from national identity. We have to know who we are before we can know what our interests are.

If American identity is defined by a set of universal principles of liberty and democracy, then presumably the promotion of those principles in other countries should be the primary goal of American foreign policy. If, however, the United States is "exceptional," the rationale for promoting human rights and democracy elsewhere disappears. If the United States is primarily a collection of cultural and ethnic entities, its national interest is in the promotion of the goals of those entities and we should have a "multicultural foreign policy." If the United States is primarily defined by its European cultural heritage as a Western country, then it should direct its attention to strengthening its ties with Western Europe. If immigration is making the United States a more Hispanic nation, we should orient ourselves primarily toward Latin America. If neither European nor Hispanic culture is central to American identity, then presumably America should pursue a foreign policy divorced from cultural ties to other countries. Other definitions of national identity generate different national interests and policy priorities. Conflicts over what we should do abroad are rooted in conflicts over who we are at home.

The United Kingdom of Great Britain and Ireland was created in 1801, the United States of America in 1776, and the Union of Soviet Socialist Republics in 1918. As their names indicate, they were all unions "of" entities brought together through processes of federation and conquest. In the early 1980s, all three seemed like reasonably cohesive and successful societies, whose governments were relatively effective and in varying degrees accepted as legitimate, and whose peoples had strong senses of their British, American, and Soviet identities. By the early 1990s the Soviet Union was no more. By the late 1990s, the United Kingdom was becoming less united, with a new regime struggling to be born in Northern Ireland, devolution well under way in Scotland and Wales, many Scots looking forward to eventual independence, and the English increasingly defining themselves as English rather than British. The Union Jack was being disassembled into its separate crosses, and it seemed possible that sometime in the first part of the twenty-first century the United Kingdom could follow the Soviet Union into history.

Few people anticipated the dissolution of the Soviet Union and the movement toward possible decomposition of the United Kingdom a decade before they got under way. Few Americans now anticipate the dissolution of or even fundamental changes in the United States. Yet the end of the Cold War, the collapse of the Soviet Union, the 1990s East Asian economic crisis, and September 11 remind us that history is replete with surprises. The greatest surprise might be if the United States in 2025 were still much the same country it was in 2000 rather than a very different country (or countries) with very different conceptions of itself and its identity than it had a quarter century earlier.

The American people who achieved independence in the late eighteenth century were few and homogeneous: overwhelmingly white (thanks to the exclusion of blacks and Indians from citizenship), British, and Protestant, broadly sharing a common culture, and overwhelmingly committed to the political principles embodied in the Declaration of Independence, the Constitution, and other founding documents. By the end of the twentieth century, the number of Americans had multiplied almost one hundred times. America had become multiracial (roughly 69 percent white, 12 percent Hispanic, 12 percent black, 4 percent Asian and Pacific Islander, 3 percent other), multiethnic (with no majority ethnic group), and 63 percent Protestant, 23 percent Catholic, 8 percent other religions, and 6 percent no religion. America's common culture and the principles of equality and individualism central to the American Creed were under attack by many individuals and groups in American society. The end of the Cold War deprived America of the evil empire against which it could define itself. We Americans were not what we were, and uncertain who we were becoming.

No society is immortal. As Rousseau said, "If Sparta and Rome perished, what state can hope to endure forever?" Even the most successful societies are at some point threatened by internal disintegration and decay and by more vigorous and ruthless external "barbarian" forces. In the end, the United States of America will suffer the fate of Sparta,

Rome, and other human communities. Historically the substance of American identity has involved four key components: race, ethnicity, culture (most notably language and religion), and ideology. The racial and ethnic Americas are no more. Cultural America is under siege. And as the Soviet experience illustrates, ideology is a weak glue to hold together people otherwise lacking racial, ethnic, and cultural sources of community. Reasons could exist, as Robert Kaplan observed, why "America, more than any other nation, may have been born to die."[8] Yet some societies, confronted with serious challenges to their existence, are also able to postpone their demise and halt disintegration, by renewing their sense of national identity, their national purpose, and the cultural values they have in common. Americans did this after September 11. The challenge they face in the first years of the third millennium is whether they can continue to do this if they are not under attack.

THE GLOBAL IDENTITY CRISIS

America's identity problem is unique, but America is not unique in having an identity problem. Debates over national identity are a pervasive characteristic of our time. Almost everywhere people have questioned, reconsidered, and redefined what they have in common and what distinguishes them from other people: Who are we? Where do we belong? The Japanese agonize over whether their location, history, and culture make them Asian or whether their wealth, democracy, and modernity make them Western. Iran has been described as "a nation in search of an identity," South Africa as engaged in "the search for identity" and China in a "quest for national identity," while Taiwan was involved in the "dissolution and reconstruction of national identity." Syria and Brazil are each said to face an "identity crisis," Canada "a continuing identity crisis," Denmark an "acute identity crisis," Algeria a "destructive identity crisis," Turkey a "unique identity crisis" leading to heated "debate on national identity," and Russia "a profound identity crisis" reopening the classic nineteenth-century debate between Slavophiles and Westernizers as to whether Russia is a "normal" European country or a distinctly different Eurasian one. In Mexico questions are coming to the fore "about Mexico's identity." The people who had identified with different Germanies, democratic and Western European vs. communist and Eastern European, struggle to recreate a common German identity. The inhabitants of the British Isles have become less sure of their British identity and uncertain as to whether they were primarily a European or a North Atlantic people.[9] Crises of national identity have become a global phenomenon.

The identity crises of these and other countries vary in form, substance, and intensity. Undoubtedly each crisis in large part has unique causes. Yet their simultaneous appearance in the United States and so many other countries suggests that common factors are also likely to be at work. The more general causes of these quests and questionings include the emergence of a global economy, tremendous improvements in communications and transportation, rising levels of migration, the global expansion of democracy, and the end both of the Cold War and of Soviet communism as a viable economic and political system.

Modernization, economic development, urbanization, and globalization have led people to rethink their identities and to redefine them in narrower, more intimate, communal terms. Subnational cultural and regional identities are taking precedence over broader national identities. People identify with those who are most like themselves and with whom they share a perceived common ethnicity, religion, traditions, and myth of common descent and common history. In the United States this fragmentation of identity manifested itself in the rise of multiculturalism and racial, ethnic, and gender consciousness. In other countries it takes the more extreme form of communal movements demanding political recognition, autonomy, or independence. These have included movements on behalf of Quebecois, Scots, Flemings, Catalonians, Basques, Lombards, Corsicans, Kurds, Kosovars, Berbers, Chiapans, Chechens, Palestinians, Tibetans, Muslim Mindanaoans, Christian Sudanese, Abkhazians, Tamils, Acehans, East Timorese, and others.

This narrowing of identities, however, has been paralleled by a broadening of identity as people increasingly interact with other people of very different cultures and civilizations and at the same time are able through modern means of communication to identify with people geographically distant but with similar language, religion, or culture. The emergence of a broader supranational identity has been most obvious in Europe, and its emergence there reinforces the simultaneous narrowing of identities. Scots increasingly think of themselves as Scottish rather than British because they can also think of themselves as European. Their Scottish identity is rooted in their European identity. This is equally true for Lombards, Catalonians, and others.

A related dialectic has been occurring between mixing and huddling, the interaction and separation, of communal groups. Massive migrations, both temporary and permanent, have increasingly intermingled peoples of various races and cultures: Asians and Latin Americans coming to the United States, Arabs, Turks, Yugoslavs, Albanians entering Western Europe. As a result of modern communications and transportation, these migrants have been able to remain part of their original culture and community. Their identity is thus less that of migrants than of diasporans, that is, members of a transnational, trans-state cultural community. They both mix with other peoples and huddle with their own. For the United States, these developments mean the high levels of immigration from Mexico and elsewhere in Latin America could have quite different consequences for assimilation than previous waves of immigration.

In the nineteenth and twentieth centuries, nationalism was intensely promoted by intellectual, political, and, on occasion, economic elites. These elites developed sophisticated and emotionally charged appeals to generate among those whom they saw as their compatriots a sense of national identity and to rally them for nationalist causes. The last decades of the twentieth century, on the other hand, witnessed a growing denationalization of elites in many countries, as well as the United States. The emergence of a global economy and global corporations plus the ability to form transnational coalitions to promote reforms on a global basis (women's rights, the environment, land mines, human rights, small arms) led many elites to develop supranational identities and to downgrade their national identities. Previously, mobile individuals pursued their careers and fortunes within a country by moving from farms to cities and from one city to another. Now they increasingly move from one country to another, and just as intracountry mobility decreased their identity with any particular locale within that country, so their intercountry mobility decreases their identity with any particular country. They become binational, multinational, or cosmopolitan.

In the early stage of European nationalism, national identity was often defined primarily in religious terms. In the nineteenth and twentieth centuries, nationalist ideologies became largely secular. Germans, British, French, and others defined themselves increasingly in terms of ancestry, language, or culture, rather than religion, which often would have divided their societies. In the twentieth century, people in Western countries (with the notable exception of the United States) generally became secularized, and churches and religion played decreasing roles in public, social, and private life.

The twenty-first century, however, is dawning as a century of religion. Virtually everywhere, apart from Western Europe, people are turning to religion for comfort, guidance, solace, and identity. "La revanche de Dieu," as Gilles Kepel termed it, is in full swing.[10] Violence between religious groups is proliferating around the world. People are increasingly concerned with the fate of geographically remote co-religionists. In many countries powerful movements have appeared attempting to redefine the identity of their country in religious terms. In a very different way, movements in the United States arc recalling America's religious origins and the extraordinary commitment to religion of the American people. Evangelical Christianity has become an important force, and Americans generally may be returning to the self-image prevalent for three centuries that they are a Christian people.

The last quarter of the twentieth century saw transitions from authoritarian to democratic regimes in more than fifty countries scattered throughout the world. It also witnessed efforts to broaden and deepen democracy in the United States and other developed countries. Individual authoritarian governments may rule and often have ruled over people of diverse nationalities and cultures. Democracy, on the other hand, means that at a minimum people choose their rulers and that more broadly they participate in government in other ways. The question of identity thus becomes central: Who are the people? As Ivor Jennings observed, "the people cannot decide until someone decides who are the people."[11] The decision as to who are the people may be the result of long-standing tradition, war and conquest, plebiscite or referendum, constitutional provision, or other causes, but it cannot be avoided. Debates over how to define that identity, who is a citizen and who is not, come to the fore when autocracies democratize and when democracies confront many new claimants on citizenship.

Historically, the emergence of nation-states in Europe was the result of several centuries of recurring wars. "War made the state, and the state made war," as Charles Tilly said.[12] These wars also made it possible and necessary for states to generate national consciousness among their peoples. The primary function of the state was to create and defend the nation, and the need to perform that function justified the expansion of state authority and the establishment of military forces, bureaucracies, and effective tax systems. Two world wars and a cold war reinforced these trends in the twentieth century. By the end of that century, however, the Cold War was over, and interstate wars had become rare; in one estimate only seven of one hundred and ten wars between 1989 and 1999 were not civil wars.[13] War is now more often the breaker of states than the maker of states. More generally, the erosion of the national security function reduced the authority of states and the reason for people to identify with their state, and instead promoted identification with subnational and transnational groups.

The relative significance of national identity has varied among cultures. In the Muslim world, the distribution of identities has tended to be U-shaped: the strongest identities and commitments have been to family, clan, and tribe, at one extreme, and to Islam and the *ummah* or Islamic community, at the other. With a few exceptions, loyalties to nations and nation-states have been weak. In the Western world for over two centuries, in contrast, the identity curve has been more an upside-down U, with the nation at the apex commanding deeper loyalty and commitment than narrower or broader sources of identity. Now, however, that may be changing, with transnational and subnational identities gaining salience and the European and American patterns flattening and coming more to resemble the Muslim one. The notions of nation, national identity, and national interest may be losing relevance and usefulness. If this is the case, the question becomes: What, if anything, will replace them and what does that mean for the United States? If this is not the case and national identity still is relevant, the question then becomes: What are the implications for America of changes in the content of its national identity?

PROSPECTS FOR AMERICAN IDENTITY

The relative importance of the components of national identity and the salience of national identity compared to other identities have varied over the years. In the last half of the eighteenth century the peoples of the colonies and states developed a common American identity that coexisted with other, primarily state and local, identities. The struggles first with Britain, then France, and then again Britain strengthened this sense of Americans as a single people. After 1815 the threats to the nation's security disappeared, and the salience of national identity declined. Sectional and economic identities emerged and increasingly divided the country, leading to the Civil War. That war solidified America as a nation by the end of the nineteenth century. American nationalism became preeminent as the United States emerged on the world scene and in the following century fought two world wars and a cold war.

The ethnic component of American identity gradually weakened as a result of the assimilation of the Irish and Germans who came in the mid-nineteenth century and the southern and eastern Europeans who came between 1880 and 1914. The racial component was first marginally weakened by the outcome of the Civil War and then drastically eroded by the civil rights movement in the 1950s and 1960s. In the following decades, America's core Anglo-Protestant culture and its political Creed of liberty and democracy faced four challenges.

First, the dissolution of the Soviet Union eliminated one major and obvious threat to American security and hence reduced the salience of national identity compared to subnational, transnational, binational, and other-national identities. Historical experience and sociological analysis show that the absence of an external "other" is likely to undermine unity and breed divisions within a society. It is problematic whether intermittent terrorist attacks and conflicts with Iraq or other "rogue states" will generate the national coherence that twentieth-century wars did.

Second, the ideologies of multiculturalism and diversity eroded the legitimacy of the remaining central elements of American identity, the cultural core and the American Creed. President Clinton explicitly set forth this challenge when he said that America needed a third "great revolution" (in addition to *the* American Revolution and the civil rights revolution) to "prove that we literally can live without having a dominant European culture."[14] Attacks on that culture undermined the Creed that it produced, and were reflected in the various movements promoting group rights against individual rights.

Third, America's third major wave of immigration that began in the 1960s brought to America people primarily from Latin America and Asia rather than Europe as the previous waves did. The culture and values of their countries of origin often differ substantially from those prevalent in America. It is much easier for these immigrants to retain contact with and to remain culturally part of their country of origin. Earlier waves of immigrants were subjected to intense programs of Americanization to assimilate them into American society. Nothing comparable occurred after 1965. In the past, assimilation was greatly facilitated because both waves substantially tapered off due to the Civil War, World War I, and laws limiting immigration. The current wave continues unabated. The erosion of other national loyalties and the assimilation of recent immigrants could be much slower and more problematic than assimilation has been in the past.

Fourth, never before in American history has close to a majority of immigrants spoken a single non-English language. The impact of the predominance of Spanish-speaking immigrants is reinforced by many other factors: the proximity of their countries of origin; their absolute numbers; the improbability of this flow ending or being significantly reduced; their geographical concentration; their home government policies promoting their migration and influence in American society and politics; the support of many elite Americans for multiculturalism, diversity, bilingual education, and affirmative action; the economic incentives for American businesses to cater to Hispanic tastes, use Spanish in their business and advertising, and hire Spanish-speaking employees; the pressures to use Spanish as well as English in government signs, forms, reports, and offices.

The elimination of the racial and ethnic components of national identity and the challenges to its cultural and creedal components raise questions concerning the prospects for American identity. At least four possible future identities exist: ideological, bifurcated, exclusivist, and cultural. The America of the future is in reality likely to be a mixture of these and other possible identities.

First, America could lose its core culture, as President Clinton anticipated, and become multicultural. Yet Americans could also retain their commitment to the principles of the Creed, which would provide an ideological or political base for national unity and identity. Many people, particularly liberals, favor this alternative. It assumes, however, that a nation can be based on only a political contract among individuals lacking any other commonality. This is the classic Enlightenment-based, civic concept of a nation. History and psychology, however, suggest that it is unlikely to be enough to sustain a nation for long. America with only the Creed as a basis for unity could soon evolve into a loose confederation of ethnic, racial, cultural, and political groups, with little or nothing in common apart from their location in the territory of what had been the United States of America. This could resemble the collections of diverse groups that once constituted the Austro-Hungarian, Ottoman, and Russian empires. These conglomerations were held together by the emperor and his bureaucracy. What central institutions, however, would hold together a loose American assemblage of groups? As the experiences of America in the 1780s and Germany in the 1860s suggest, past confederations normally have not lasted long.

Second, the massive Hispanic immigration after 1965 could make America increasingly bifurcated in terms of language (English and Spanish) and culture (Anglo and Hispanic), which could supplement or supplant the black-white racial bifurcation as the most important division in American society. Substantial parts of America, primarily in southern Florida and the Southwest, would be primarily Hispanic in culture and language, while both cultures and languages would coexist in the rest of America. America, in short, would lose its cultural and linguistic unity and become a bilingual, bicultural society like Canada, Switzerland, or Belgium.

Third, the various forces challenging the core American culture and Creed could generate a move by native white Americans to revive the discarded and discredited racial and ethnic concepts of American identity and to create an America that would exclude, expel, or suppress people of other racial, ethnic, and cultural groups. Historical and contemporary experience suggest that this is a highly probable reaction from a once dominant ethnic-racial group that feels threatened by the rise of other groups. It could produce a racially intolerant country with high levels of intergroup conflict.

Fourth, Americans of all races and ethnicities could attempt to reinvigorate their core culture. This would mean a recommitment to America as a deeply religious and primarily Christian country, encompassing several religious minorities, adhering to Anglo-Protestant values, speaking English, maintaining its European cultural heritage, and committed to the principles of the Creed. Religion has been and still is a central, perhaps the central, element of American identity. America was founded in large part for religious reasons, and religious movements have shaped its evolution for almost four centuries. By every indicator, Americans are far more religious than the people of other industrialized countries. Overwhelming majorities of white Americans, of black Americans, and of Hispanic Americans are Christian. In a world in which culture and particularly religion shape the allegiances, the alliances, and the antagonisms of people on every continent, Americans could again find their national identity and their national purposes in their culture and religion.

CHAPTER 2

Identities:
National and Other

THE CONCEPT OF IDENTITY

The "concept of identity," it has been said, "is as indispensable as it is unclear." It "is manifold, hard to define and evades many ordinary methods of measurement." The twentieth century's leading scholar of identity, Erik Erikson, termed the concept "all-pervasive" but also "vague" and "unfathomable." The infuriating inescapability of identity is well demonstrated in the work of the distinguished social theorist Leon Wieseltier. In 1996 he published a book, *Against Identity*, denouncing and ridiculing the fascination of intellectuals with that concept. In 1998, he published another book, *Kaddish*, an eloquent, passionate, and explicit affirmation of his own Jewish identity. Identity, it appears, is like sin: however much we may oppose it, we cannot escape it.[1]

Given its unavoidability, how do we define it? Scholars have various answers, which nonetheless converge on one central theme. Identity is an individual's or a group's sense of self. It is a product of self-consciousness, that I or we possess distinct qualities as an entity that differentiates me from you and us from them. A new baby may have elements of an identity at birth in terms of a name, sex, parentage, and citizenship. These do not, however, become part of his or her identity until the baby becomes conscious of them and defines itself in terms of them. Identity, as one group of scholars phrased it, "refers to the images of individuality and distinctiveness ('selfhood') held and projected by an

21

actor and formed (and modified over time) through relations with significant 'others.' "[2] So long as people interact with others, they have no choice but to define themselves in relation to those others and identify their similarities with and differences from those others.

Identities are important because they shape the behavior of people. If I think of myself as a scholar, I will try to act like a scholar. But individuals also can change their identities. If I begin to act differently—as a polemicist, for instance—I will suffer "cognitive dissonance" and am likely to try to relieve the resulting anguish by stopping that behavior or by redefining myself from a scholar to a political advocate. Similarly, if a person inherits a partisan identity as a Democrat but increasingly finds him- or herself voting for Republican candidates, that person may well redefine him- or herself as a Republican.

Several key points concerning identities need to be made.

First, both individuals and groups have identities. Individuals, however, find and redefine their identities in groups. As social identity theory has shown, the need for identity leads them even to seek identity in an arbitrarily and randomly constructed group. An individual may be a member of many groups and hence is able to shift identities. Group identity, on the other hand, usually involves a primary defining characteristic and is less fungible. I have identities as a political scientist and a member of the Harvard Department of Government. Conceivably, I could redefine myself as a historian or become a member of the Stanford Department of Political Science, if they were willing to accept this change in my identity. The Harvard Department of Government, however, cannot become a history department or move as an institution to Stanford. Its identity is much more fixed than mine. If the basis for the defining characteristic of a group disappears, perhaps because it achieves the goal it was created to achieve, the existence of the group is threatened, unless it can find another cause to motivate its members.

Second, identities are, overwhelmingly, constructed. People make their identity, under varying degrees of pressure, inducements, and freedom. In an oft-quoted phrase, Benedict Anderson described nations as "imagined communities." Identities are imagined selves: they are what we think we are and what we want to be. Apart from ancestry (although that can be repudiated), gender (and people occasionally change that), and age (which may be denied but not changed by human action), people are relatively free to define their identities as they wish, although they may not be able to implement those identities in practice. They may inherit their ethnicity and race but these can be redefined or rejected, and the meaning and applicability of a term like "race" changes over time.

Third, individuals and to a lesser extent groups have multiple identities. These may be ascriptive, territorial, economic, cultural, political, social, and national. The relative salience of these identities to the individual or group can change from time to time and situation to situation, as can the extent to which these identities complement or conflict with each other. "Only extreme social situations," Karmela Liebkind observes, "such as battles in war, may temporarily eradicate all other group affiliations but one."[3]

Fourth, identities are defined by the self but they are the product of the interaction between the self and others. How others perceive an individual or group affects the self-definition of that individual or group. If one enters a new social situation and is perceived as an outsider who does not belong, one is likely to think of oneself that way. If a large majority of the people in a country think that members of a minority group are inherently backward and inferior, the minority group members may internalize that concept of themselves, at which point it becomes part of their identity. Alternatively, they may react against that characterization and define themselves in opposition to it. External sources of identity may come from the immediate environment, the broader society, or political authorities. Governments have, indeed, assigned racial or other identities to people.

People can aspire to an identity but not be able to achieve it unless they are welcomed by those who already have that identity. The crucial post–Cold War issue for East European peoples was whether the West would accept their identification of themselves as part of the West. Westerners have accepted Poles, Czechs, and Hungarians. They are less likely to do that with some other Eastern European peoples who also want a Western identity. They have been quite reluctant to do so with the Turks, whose bureaucratic elites desperately want Turkey to be Western. As a result, Turks have been conflicted over whether they should think of themselves primarily as European, Western, Muslim, Middle Eastern, or even Central Asian.

Fifth, the relative salience of alternative identities for any individual or group is situational. In some situations, people stress that aspect of their identity that links them to the people with whom they are interacting. In other situations, people emphasize that aspect of their identity that distinguishes them from others. A female psychologist, it has been argued, in the company of a dozen male psychologists will think of herself as a woman; in the company of a dozen women who are not psychologists, she will think of herself as a psychologist.[4] The salience of people's identity with their homeland typically increases when they travel abroad and observe the different ways of life of foreigners. In attempting to free themselves from Ottoman rule, Serbs stressed their Orthodox religion, while Muslim Albanians stressed their ethnicity and language. Similarly, the founders of Pakistan defined its identity in terms of their Muslim religion to justify independence from India. A few years later the Muslim Bangladeshi emphasized culture and language to legitimate their independence from their Pakistani co-religionists.

Identities may be narrow or broad, and the breadth of the most salient identity changes with the situation people are in. "You" and "I" become "we" when a "they" appears, or, as an Arab saying has it, "My brother and I against our cousins, we and our cousins against the world." As people increasingly interact with people of more distant and different cultures, they also broaden their identities. For French and Germans, their national identity loses salience in relation to their European identity, as Jonathan Mercer says, when there emerges a broader "sense of difference between 'us' and 'them,' or between the European and the Japanese identities."[5] Hence it is only natural that the processes of globalization should lead to the broader identities of religion and civilization assuming greater importance for individuals and peoples.

OTHERS AND ENEMIES

To define themselves, people need an other. Do they also need an enemy? Some people clearly do. "Oh, how wonderful it is to hate," said

Josef Goebbels. "Oh, what a relief to fight, to fight enemies who defend themselves, enemies who are awake," said André Malraux. These are extreme articulations of a generally more subdued but widespread human need, as acknowledged by two of the twentieth century's greatest minds. Writing to Sigmund Freud in 1933, Albert Einstein argued that every attempt to eliminate war had "ended in a lamentable breakdown . . . man has within him a lust for hatred and destruction." Freud agreed: people are like animals, he wrote back, they solve problems through the use of force, and only an all-powerful world state could prevent this from happening. Humans, Freud argued, have only two types of instincts, "those which seek to preserve and unite . . . and those which seek to destroy and kill." Both are essential and they operate in conjunction with each other. Hence, "there is no use in trying to get rid of men's aggressive inclinations."[6]

Other scholars of human psychology and human relations have made similar arguments. There is a need, Vamik Volkan has said, "to have enemies and allies." This tendency appears in early-mid-adolescence when "the other group comes to be definitely viewed as the enemy." The psyche is "the creator of the concept of the enemy. . . . As long as the enemy group is kept at least at a psychological distance, it gives us aid and comfort, enhancing our cohesion and making comparisons with ourselves gratifying." Individuals need self-esteem, recognition, approbation, what Plato, as Francis Fukuyama reminded us, designated *thymos* and Adam Smith termed vanity. Conflict with the enemy reinforces these qualities in the group.[7]

The need of individuals for self-esteem leads them to believe that their group is better than other groups. Their sense of self rises and falls with the fortunes of the groups with which they identify and with the extent to which other people are excluded from their group. Ethnocentrism, as Mercer puts it, is "the logical corollary to egocentrism." Even when their group may be totally arbitrary, temporary, and "minimal," people still, as social identity theory predicts, discriminate in favor of their group as compared to another group. Hence in many situations people choose to sacrifice absolute gains in order to achieve relative gains. They prefer to be worse off absolutely but better off compared to someone they see as a rival rather than better off absolutely but not as well off as that rival: "beating the outgroup is more important than sheer profit." This preference has been repeatedly supported by evidence from psychological experiments and public opinion polls, not to mention common sense and everyday experience. To the bafflement of economists, Americans say that they would prefer to be worse off economically but ahead of the Japanese rather than better off and behind the Japanese.[8]

Recognition of difference does not necessarily generate competition, much less hate. Yet even people who have little psychological need to hate can become involved in processes leading to the creation of enemies. Identity requires differentiation. Differentiation necessitates comparison, the identification of the ways in which "our" group differs from "their" group. Comparison, in turn, generates evaluation: Are the ways of our group better or worse than the ways of their group? Group egotism leads to justification: Our ways are better than their ways. Since the members of the other group are engaged in a similar process, conflicting justifications lead to competition. We have to demonstrate the superiority of our ways to their ways. Competition leads to antagonism and the broadening of what may have started as the perception of narrow differences into more intense and fundamental ones. Stereotypes are created, the opponent is demonized, the other is transmogrified into the enemy.

While the need for enemies explains the ubiquity of conflict between and within human societies, it does not explain the forms and locales of conflict. Competition and conflict can only occur between entities that are in the same universe or arena. In some sense, as Volkan put it, "the enemy" has to be "like us."[9] A soccer team may view another soccer team as its rival; it will not view a hockey team that way. The history department in one university will see history departments in other universities as its rivals for faculty, students, prestige within the discipline of history. It will not see the physics department in its own university in that light. It may, however, see the physics department as a rival for funding within their university. Competitors have to be playing on the same chessboard and most individuals and groups compete on several different chessboards. The chessboards have to be there but the players may change, and one game is succeeded by another. Hence, the likelihood of general or lasting peace among ethnic groups, states, or nations is remote. As human experience shows, the end of a hot or cold war creates the conditions for another. "A part of being human," as a committee of psychiatrists put it, "has always been the search for an enemy to embody temporarily or permanently disavowed aspects of our selves."[10] Late-twentieth-century distinctiveness theory, social identity theory, sociobiology, and attribution theory all lend support to the conclusion that the roots of hate, rivalry, the need for enemies, personal and group violence, and war are ineluctably located in human psychology and the human condition.

SOURCES OF IDENTITY

People have an almost infinite number of possible sources of identity. These include ones that are primarily:

1. *Ascriptive*, such as age, ancestry, gender, kin (blood relatives), ethnicity (defined as extended kin), and race;
2. *Cultural*, such as clan, tribe, ethnicity (defined as a way of life), language, nationality, religion, civilization;
3. *Territorial*, such as neighborhood, village, town, city, province, state, section, country, geographical area, continent, hemisphere;
4. *Political*, such as faction, clique, leader, interest group, movement, cause, party, ideology, state;
5. *Economic*, such as job, occupation, profession, work group, employer, industry, economic sector, labor union, class;
6. *Social*, such as friends, club, team, colleagues, leisure group, status.

Any individual is likely to be involved in many of these groupings, but that does not necessarily mean that they are sources of his or her identity. A person may, for instance, find either his job or his country loathsome and totally reject it. In addition, relations among identities are complex. A differentiated relation exists when the identities are compatible in the abstract but at times, such as family identity and job identity, may impose conflicting demands on the individual. Other identities, such as territorial or cultural identities, are hierarchical in terms of their scope. Broader identities are inclusive of narrower identities, and the less inclusive identity, to a province, for instance, may or may not conflict with the more inclusive identity to a country. In addition, identities of the same sort may or may not be exclusive. People may, for instance, assert dual nationality and claim to be both American and Italian, but it is difficult for them to assert dual religiosity and claim to be both Muslim and Catholic.

Identities also differ in their intensity. Intensity often varies inversely with scope; people identify more intensely with their family than with their political party, but this is not always the case. In addition, the salience of identities of all types varies with the interactions between the individual or group and its environment.

Narrower and broader identities in a single hierarchy may either reinforce or conflict with each other. In a famous phrase, Edmund Burke argued that "To be attached to the subdivision, to love the little platoon we belong to in society, is the first principle (the germ, as it were) of public affections. The love to the whole is not extinguished by this subordinate partiality." The "little platoon" phenomenon is key to military success. Armies win battles because their soldiers intensely identify with their immediate comrades in arms. Failure to promote small unit cohesion, as the U.S. Army learned in Vietnam, can lead to military disaster. At times, however, subordinate loyalties conflict with and perhaps displace broader ones, as with territorial movements for autonomy or independence. Hierarchical identities coexist uneasily with each other.

THE FALSE DICHOTOMY

Nations, nationalism, and national identity are, in large part, the product of the tumultuous course of European history from the fifteenth to the nineteenth centuries. War made the state and it also made nations. "No Nation, in the true sense of the word," the historian Michael Howard argues, "could be born without war . . . no self-conscious community could establish itself as a new and independent actor on the world scene without an armed conflict or the threat of one."[11] People developed their sense of national identity as they fought to differentiate themselves from other people with different language, religion, history, or location.

The French and the English and then the Dutch, Spanish, French, Swedes, Prussians, Germans, and Italians crystallized their national identities in the crucible of war. To survive and to succeed in the sixteenth to eighteenth centuries, kings and princes increasingly had to mobilize the economic and demographic resources of their territories and eventually to create national armies to replace mercenary ones. In the process they promoted national consciousness and the confrontation of nation against nation. By the 1790s, as R. R. Palmer put it, "The wars of kings were over; the wars of peoples had begun."[12] Only in the mid-eighteenth century do the words "nation" and *"patrie"* enter into European languages. The emergence of British identity was prototypical. English identity was defined in wars against the French and the Scots. British identity subsequently emerged as "an invention forged above all by war. Time and time again, war with France brought Britons, whether they hailed from Wales or Scotland or England, into confrontation with an obviously hostile Other and encouraged them to define themselves collectively against it. They defined themselves as Protestants struggling for survival against the world's foremost Catholic power."[13]

Scholars generally posit two types of nationalism and national identity, which they variously label: civic and ethnic, political and cultural, revolutionary and tribalist, liberal and integral, rational-associational and organic-mystical, civic-territorial and ethnic-genealogical, or simply patriotism and nationalism.[14] In each pairing, the first is seen as good, and the second as bad. The good, civic nationalism, assumes an open society based, at least in theory, on a social contract to which people of any race or ethnicity are able to subscribe and thus become citizens. Ethnic nationalism, in contrast, is exclusive, and membership in the nation is limited to those who share certain primordial, ethnic, or cultural characteristics. In the early nineteenth century, scholars argue, nationalism and efforts in European societies to create national identities were primarily of the civic variety. Nationalist movements affirmed the equality of citizens, thereby undermining class and status distinctions. Liberal nationalism challenged authoritarian multinational empires. Subsequently, romanticism and other movements generated illiberal ethnic nationalism, glorifying the ethnic community over the individual, and reaching its apotheosis in Hitler's Germany.

The dichotomy between civic and ethnic nationalism, whatever the labels, is overly simple and cannot stand. In most of these pairings, the ethnic category is a catch-all for all forms of nationalism or national identity that are not clearly contractual, civic, and liberal. In particular, it combines two very different conceptions of national identity: ethnic-racial, on the one hand, and cultural, on the other. The reader may or may not have noted that "nation" is missing from the list of some forty-eight possible sources of identity on p. 27. The reason is that while national identity was at times in the West the highest form of identity, it also has been a derived identity whose intensity comes from other sources. National identity usually but not always includes a territorial element and may also include one or more ascriptive (race, ethnicity), cultural (religion, language), and political (state, ideology) elements, as well as occasionally economic (farming) or social (networks) ones.

The principal theme of this book is the continuing centrality of Anglo-Protestant culture to American national identity. The term "culture," however, has many meanings. Probably most often, it is used to refer to the cultural products of a society, including both its "high" culture of art, literature, and music and its "low" culture of popular entertainments and consumer preferences. Culture in this book means something different. It refers to a people's language, religious beliefs, social and political values, assumptions as to what is right and wrong, appropriate and inappropriate, and to the objective institutions and behavioral patterns that reflect these subjective elements. To cite one example, discussed in Chapter 4: Overall, more Americans are in the labor force and work longer hours, have shorter vacations, get less in unemployment, disability, and retirement benefits, and retire later, than people in comparable societies. Overall, Americans also take greater pride in their work, tend to view leisure with ambivalence and at times guilt, disdain those who do not work, and see the work ethic as a key element of what it means to be an American. It thus seems reasonable to conclude that this objective and subjective emphasis on work is one distinguishing characteristic of American culture, compared to those of other societies. This is the sense in which culture is used in this book.

The simple civic-ethnic duality conflates culture and ascriptive elements, which are very different. In developing his theory of ethnicity in the United States, Horace Kallen argued that however an immigrant may change, "he cannot change his grandfather." Hence ethnic identities are relatively permanent.[15] Intermarriage undermines that argument, but even more important is the distinction between ancestry and culture. One cannot change one's grandparents, and in that sense one's ethnic heritage is given. Similarly, one cannot change one's skin color, although the perceptions of what that color means may change. One can, however, change one's culture. People convert from one religion to another, learn new languages, adopt new values and beliefs, identify with new symbols, and accommodate themselves to new ways of life. The culture of a younger generation often differs along many of these dimensions from that of the previous generation. At times the cultures of whole societies can change dramatically. Both before and after World War II, Germans and Japanese defined their national identities overwhelmingly in ascriptive, ethnic terms. Their defeat in that war, however, changed one central element of their cultures. The two most militaristic countries in the world in the 1930s were transformed into two of the most pacifist countries. Cultural identity is fungible; ethnic-ancestral identity is not. Hence a clear distinction has to be maintained between the two.

The relative importance of the elements of national identity varies with the historical experiences of the people. Often one source will tend to be preeminent. German identity includes linguistic and other cultural elements but was defined by a 1913 law ascriptively in terms of descent. Germans are people who have German parents. As a result, contemporary descendants of eighteenth-century German migrants to Russia are considered German. If they migrate to Germany, they automatically receive German citizenship although the German they speak, if they speak any, may be unintelligible to their compatriots, and their customs may seem alien to native Germans. In contrast, before 1999 third-generation descendants of Turkish immigrants to Germany, who grew up and were educated in Germany, worked in Germany, and spoke fluent colloquial German, faced serious obstacles to becoming German citizens.

In the former Soviet Union and Yugoslavia, national identity was defined politically by their communist ideologies and communist regimes. These countries included peoples of different nationalities, which were defined culturally and accorded official recognition. For a century and a half after 1789, on the other hand, the French were divided politically into "two Frances" of *mouvement* and *l'ordre établi*, who differed fundamentally on whether France should accept or reject the results of the French Revolution. French identity was instead defined culturally. Immigrants who adopted French mores and ways of life and, most importantly, spoke French perfectly were accepted as French. In contrast to German law, French law provided that anyone born in France of foreign parents was automatically a French citizen. By 1993, however, the French had become concerned about whether children of Muslim North African immigrants were being absorbed into French culture and changed the law to require French-born children of immigrants to apply for citizenship before their eighteenth birthday. This restriction was eased in 1998 to allow children born in France to foreign parents automatically to become French citizens at age eighteen if they had lived in France for five of the previous seven years.

The relative salience of different components of national identity may change. In the late twentieth century both Germans and French generally rejected the authoritarian components that had been part of their history and made democracy part of their self-concept. In France, the Revolution triumphed; in Germany, Nazism was expurgated. With the end of the Cold War, Russians became divided over their identity, with only a minority continuing to embrace communist ideology, some wanting a European identity, others espousing a cultural definition involving elements of Orthodoxy and pan-Slavism, and still others giving primacy to a territorial concept of Russia as primarily a Eurasian society. Germany, France, and the Soviet Union/Russia thus historically emphasized different components in their national identity, and the relative salience of some components shifted over time. The same is true for other countries, including America.

PART II

American
Identity

CHAPTER 3

Components of American Identity

CHANGE, CONTINUITY, AND PARTIAL TRUTHS

Partial truths or half-truths are often more insidious than total falsehoods. The latter can be easily exposed for what they are by citing exceptions to their claims; hence they are less likely to be accepted as the total truth. A partial truth, on the other hand, is plausible because some evidence does support it, and it is, consequently, easy to assume that it is the total truth. Thinking about American identity has involved the wide acceptance of two propositions that are true but only partially true and yet often are accepted as the whole truth. These are the claims, first, that America is a nation of immigrants, and second, that American identity is defined solely by a set of political principles, the American Creed. These two concepts of America are often linked together. The common Creed is said to unify the diverse ethnicities produced by immigration. It is, in Gunnar Myrdal's phrase, "the cement in the structure of this great and disparate nation." America's identity, Stanley Hoffmann has similarly argued, is the unique product of a "material feature," its ethnic diversity produced by immigration, and an "ideological feature," its liberal democratic Creed.[1]

There is much truth in these claims. Immigration and the Creed are key elements of American national identity. They are not mistaken identities; they are partial identities. Neither one nor both is the whole truth concerning America. They do not tell us anything about the society that attracted the immigrants or the culture that produced the Creed.

America is a founded society created by seventeenth- and eighteenth-century settlers almost all of whom came from the British Isles. Their values, institutions, and culture provided the foundation for and shaped the development of America in the following centuries. They initially defined America in terms of race, ethnicity, culture, and most importantly religion. Then in the eighteenth century they also had to define America ideologically to justify their independence from their home-countrymen. These four components remained part of American identity for most of the nineteenth century. By the latter years of that century, the ethnic component had been broadened to include Germans, Irish, and Scandinavians. By World War II and the assimilation into American society of large numbers of southern and eastern European immigrants and their offspring, ethnicity virtually disappeared as a defining component of national identity. Following the achievements of the civil rights movement and the immigration act of 1965, so did race. As a result, by the 1970s American identity was defined in terms of culture and Creed. At this point, the core Anglo-Protestant culture that had existed for three centuries came under attack, raising the prospect that American identity might come to be equated solely with ideological commitment to the Creed. Table 3.1 sets forth in highly simplified fashion the changing roles of these four components of American identity.

SETTLERS BEFORE IMMIGRANTS

For most of their history, most Americans did not hold favorable views of immigrants and did not celebrate their country as a "nation of immigrants." After the prohibition of large-scale immigration in 1924, however, attitudes toward America's immigrant heritage began to change. That change was dramatized by President Franklin Roosevelt's famous challenge to the Daughters of the American Revolution in 1938: "Remember, remember always, that all of us, and you and I especially, are descended from immigrants and revolutionists." President Kennedy quoted this remark in his book *A Nation of Immigrants*,

Table 3.1

Components of American Identity

	Ethnic	Racial	Cultural	Political
1607–1775	Y	Y	Y	N
1775–1940	Y	Y	Y	Y (except 1840–1865)
1940–1965	N	Y	Y	Y
1965–1990	N	N	Y	Y
1990–	N	N	?	Y

published posthumously. Before and since, that phrase has been constantly invoked by scholars and journalists. The leading historian of American immigration, Oscar Handlin, claimed "the immigrants *were* American history." The leading sociologist Robert Bellah echoed FDR: "All Americans except the Indians are immigrants or the descendants of immigrants."[2]

These claims are valid partial truths, but false total truths. Roosevelt was partly wrong when he suggested that all Americans were descended from "revolutionists"; he was totally wrong when he suggested that he and his DAR audience were (at least in their name line) descendants of "immigrants." Their ancestors were not immigrants but settlers, and in its origins America was not a nation of immigrants, it was a society, or societies, of settlers who came to the New World in the seventeenth and eighteenth centuries. Its origins as an Anglo-Protestant settler society have, more than anything else, profoundly and lastingly shaped American culture, institutions, historical development, and identity.

Settlers and immigrants differ fundamentally. Settlers leave an existing society, usually in a group, in order to create a new community, a city on a hill, in a new and often distant territory. They are imbued with a sense of collective purpose. Implicitly or explicitly they subscribe to a compact or charter that defines the basis of the community they create and their collective relation to their mother country. Immigrants, in contrast, do not create a new society. They move from one society to a different society. Migration is usually a personal process, involving individuals and families, who individually define their relation to their old and new countries. The seventeenth- and eighteenth-century settlers came to America because it was a *tabula rasa*. Apart from Indian tribes, which could be killed off or pushed westward, no society was there; and they came in order to create societies that embodied and would reinforce the culture and values they brought with them from their origin country. Immigrants came later because they wanted to become part of the society the settlers had created. Unlike settlers, they experienced "culture shock" as they and their offspring attempted to absorb a culture often much at odds with that which they brought with them.[3] Before immigrants could come to America, settlers had to found America.

Americans commonly refer to those who produced independence and the Constitution in the 1770s and 1780s as the Founding Fathers. Before there could be Founding Fathers, however, there were founding settlers. America did not begin in 1775, 1776, or 1787. It began with the first settler communities of 1607, 1620, and 1630. What happened in the 1770s and 1780s was rooted in and a product of the Anglo-American Protestant society and culture that had developed over the intervening one and a half centuries.

The distinction between settlers and immigrants was well recognized by those who led America to independence. Before the Revolution, as John Higham has observed, English and Dutch colonists "conceived of themselves as founders, settlers, or planters—the formative population of those colonial societies—not as immigrants. Theirs was the polity, the language, the pattern of work and settlement, and many of the mental habits to which the immigrants would have to adjust."[4] The term "immigrant" came into the English language in the America of the 1780s to distinguish current arrivals from the founding settlers.

America's core culture has been and, at the moment, is still primarily the culture of the seventeenth- and eighteenth-century settlers who founded American society. The central elements of that culture can be defined in a variety of ways but include the Christian religion, Protestant values and moralism, a work ethic, the English language, British traditions of law, justice, and the limits of government power, and a legacy of European art, literature, philosophy, and music. Out of this culture the settlers developed in the eighteenth and nineteenth centuries the American Creed with its principles of liberty, equality, individualism, representative government, and private property. Subsequent generations of immigrants were assimilated into the culture of the founding settlers and contributed to and modified it. But they did not change it fundamentally. This is because, at least until the late twentieth century, it was Anglo-Protestant culture and the political liberties and economic opportunities it produced that attracted them to America.

In its origin and its continuing core, America is thus a colonial society, in the strict and original sense of the word "colony," that is, a settlement created by people who leave a mother country and travel elsewhere to establish a new society on distant turf. A colony, in this original and strict sense, is entirely different from a colony in the later meaning given the term, that is, a territory and its indigenous people ruled by the government of another people. Historical counterparts to the English, French, and Dutch North American settler colonies of the seventeenth century are the Athenian, Corinthian, and other colonies in Sicily founded in the eighth and seventh centuries B.C. The processes of settlement and the patterns of development of the former broadly parallel those of the latter more than two millennia earlier.[5]

The settlers who create a colony have a decisive and lasting impact on the culture and institutions of that society. They are, the historian John Porter argues, the "charter group," which "as the effective possessor, has the most to say" on that society's subsequent development. The cultural geographer Wilbur Zelinsky terms this phenomenon the "Doctrine of First Effective Settlement." In new territories, "the specific characteristics of the first group able to effect a viable, self-perpetuating society are of crucial significance for the later social and cultural geography of the area, no matter how tiny the initial band of settlers may have been. . . . In terms of lasting impact, the activities of a few hundred, or even a few score, initial colonizers can mean much more for the cultural geography of a place than the contributions of tens of thousands of new immigrants a few generations later."[6]

The initial settlers bring their own culture and institutions with them. These are perpetuated in the new territory, while change takes place in the homeland. "A new nation is not new in all respects," Ronald Syme has observed of early Roman colonies in Spain. "It is an observable phenomenon in other ages that colonists preserve habits of life or speech no longer current at home; and the Spanish language in fact goes back to a form of Latin more archaic than does French. The Spanish Romans (it might seem) parade and exploit their loyalty to the old Roman traditions. On the other hand, their resplendent success proves them eager, ambitious and innovatory." Quebec stimulated a similar comment from Tocqueville:

> The physiognomy of a government may best be judged in its colonies, for there its features are magnified and rendered more conspicuous. When I wish to study the merits and faults of the administration of Louis XIV, I must go to Canada; its deformity is there seen as through a microscope. . . . Everywhere we were received . . . like children of Old France, as they say here. To my mind the epithet is badly chosen. Old France is in Canada, the new is with us.[7]

In America, the British settlers of the seventeenth and eighteenth centuries, as David Hackett Fischer argues in his monumental study, fall into four groups in terms of their places of origin in England, their socioeconomic status, their specific religious affiliations, and their time of settlement. Virtually all of them, however, spoke English, were Protestant, adhered to British legal traditions, and valued British liberties. This common culture and its four distinct subcultures were perpetuated in America. "In a cultural sense," Fischer observes, "most Americans are Albion's seed, no matter who their own forebears may have been. . . . [T]he legacy of four British folkways in early America remains the most powerful determinant of a voluntary society in the United States today." The Wisconsin historian J. Rogers Hollingsworth agrees: "The most important fact to keep in mind when studying political change in America is that the United States is a product of a settler society." The way of life of the initial English settlers "developed into a whole society" and "gave rise to the dominant political culture, the political institutions, the language, the pattern of work and settlement, and many of the mental habits to which subsequent immigrants had to adjust."[8]

The initial American settlers, like other settlers elsewhere, were not representative of the homeland population as a whole but rather came from particular segments or fragments, to use Louis Hartz's term, of that population. They leave their homeland and move elsewhere to establish a new community because they suffer oppression at home and/or see opportunity in the new land. Each group of European settlers in North and South America, South Africa, and the South Pacific brought with it the ideas or ideologies of its social class in the home country: feudal aristocracy, liberalism, working-class socialism. In the new venue, however, the European class ideology lacked class antagonism, and was transmuted into the nationalism of the new society. As fragments of the more complicated society of origin, settlement societies do not have the change dynamics of that society and hence preserve the institutions and culture from their original society in their new society.[9]

As founded societies, settler societies also have a clear beginning at a specific time and place. Their founders hence feel the need to define their institutions with charters, compacts, and constitutions and to lay out plans for their development. The first Greek law codes were produced not in mainland Greece but in the Greek colonies in Sicily in the seventh century B.C. The earliest systematic codes in the English-speaking world were drawn up in Virginia (1606), Bermuda (included in the third charter of the Virginia Company in 1612), Plymouth (1636), and Massachusetts Bay (1648). The "first written constitution of modern democracy" was the Fundamental Orders of Connecticut, adopted by the citizens of Hartford and neighboring towns in 1638.[10] Settlement societies tend to be explicitly planned societies, but their plans incorporate and perpetuate the experience, values, and goals of their founders at the time of the settlement.

The process by which British and a few other northern European settlers created societies in the New World was replicated for two and a half centuries as Americans moved westward and created new settlements on the frontier. Settlement is central not only to the creation of America but to its development until the end of the nineteenth century.

"Up to our own day," Frederick Jackson Turner said in 1892, "American history has been in a large degree the history of the colonization of the Great West." He signaled the end of that process with his famous quotation from the 1890 census: "Up to and including 1880, the country had a frontier of settlement, but at present the unsettled area has been so broken into by isolated bodies of settlement that there can hardly be said to be a frontier line."[11] The American frontier, unlike other frontiers in Canada, Australia, or Russia, lacked a significant governmental presence. It was populated in its first phase by individual hunters, trappers, prospectors, adventurers, and traders, who were then followed by settlers who founded communities along waterways and later along prospective railways. The peopling of the American frontier involved a combination of settlement and migration. Communities of settlers from easterly parts of the country moved westward to found new societies, and migrants from both America and Europe moved westward as individuals and families to participate in this settlement process.

In 1790 the total population of the United States, excluding Indians, was 3,929,000, of whom 698,000 were slaves and not viewed by the others as part of American society. The white population was ethnically 60 percent English, 80 percent British (the remainder being largely German and Dutch), and 98 percent Protestant. Excluding blacks, America was a highly homogeneous society in terms of race, national origin, and religion. "Providence has been pleased," John Jay observed in *The Federalist*, "to give this one connected country to one united people—a people descended from the same ancestors, speaking the same language, professing the same religion, attached to the same principles of government, very similar in their manners and customs, and who, by their joint counsels, arms, and efforts, fighting side by side throughout a long and bloody war, have nobly established liberty and independence."

Between 1820 and 2000 approximately 66 million immigrants came to America, making its people highly heterogeneous in terms of ancestry, ethnicity, and religion.[12] The demographic impact of the immigrants, however, only marginally exceeded that of the seventeenth- and eighteenth-century settlers and their slaves. The end of the eighteenth century witnessed an American population explosion, possibly unique in history, with extraordinarily high birth rates and, for the times, an extremely large proportion of children in the Northern states reaching adulthood. The crude birth rate for America in 1790 has been estimated at 55 per 1,000 population compared to a rate of about 35 per 1,000 in European countries. American women married when they were four or five years younger than their European contemporaries. The total fertility rate in America is estimated at 7.7 children per woman in 1790 and 7.0 in 1800, far above the 2.1 necessary to maintain a stable population.* Fertility remained above 6.0 until the 1840s and then gradually declined to about 3.0 by the onset of the Great Depression. Overall the American population increased by 35 percent between 1790 and 1800, 36 percent between 1800 and 1810, and 82 percent between 1800 and 1820. During these years, the Napoleonic wars kept immigration to a trickle, and four fifths of this increase was from natural causes, or what one congressman called "the American Multiplication Table."[13] In a careful analysis, the statistical demographer Campbell Gibson concludes that in 1990, 49 percent of the American population was attributable to the settler and black populations of 1790 and 51 percent to immigration after that date. With no immigration after 1790, the 1990 American population would have been about 122 million instead of 249 million.[14] In short, toward the end of the twentieth century, America was demographically roughly half the product of early settlers and slaves and half that of immigrants who joined the society the settlers had created.

In addition to immigrants and the descendants of settlers, immigrants, and slaves, some contemporary Americans are the descendants of people whom Americans conquered. These include Indians, Puerto Ricans, Hawaiians, and those with Mexican ancestors living in Texas and the southwest territories taken from Mexico in the mid-nineteenth century. The distinctive character of the Indians and Puerto Ricans as *in* but not fully *of* the American republic is reflected in the arrangements nego-

---

* Some examples: Ebenezer Huntington and Elizabeth Strong married in 1806, had ten children, nine of whom then had children, producing a total of seventy-four grandchildren for Ebenezer and Elizabeth; in the same generation, Harry Huntington had sixteen children with two wives while his brother James had seventeen children with one wife! *Huntington Family Association Newsletter,* May 1999, p. 5.

tiated with them for reservations and tribal government, on the one hand, and commonwealth status, on the other. Residents of Puerto Rico are American citizens, but they do not pay federal taxes, do not vote in national elections, and conduct their affairs in Spanish, not English.

Large-scale immigration has been an intermittent feature of American life. Immigration did not become significant in absolute and relative terms until the 1830s, declined in the 1850s, increased dramatically in the 1880s, declined in the 1890s, became very high in the decade and a half before World War I, declined drastically after passage of the 1924 immigration act, and stayed low until the 1965 immigration act generated a massive new wave. Over the years, immigrants have played a central and, in some respects, more than proportionate role in American development. Between 1820 and 2000, however, the foreign-born averaged only slightly over 10 percent of the American population. To describe America as a "nation of immigrants" is to stretch a partial truth into a misleading falsehood, and to ignore the central fact of America's beginning as a society of settlers.

MORE THAN THE CREED

Americans, it is often said, are a people defined by and united by their commitment to the political principles of liberty, equality, democracy, individualism, human rights, the rule of law, and private property embodied in the American Creed. Foreign observers from Crèvecoeur to Tocqueville, Bryce, and Myrdal, to the present have pointed to this distinctive characteristic of America as a nation. American scholars have generally agreed. Richard Hofstadter provided the most succinct formulation: "It has been our fate as a nation not to have ideologies but to be one." The most appropriate formulation to quote here, however, comes from a different scholar: " 'We hold these truths to be self-evident,' says the Declaration. Who holds these truths? Americans hold these truths. Who are Americans? People who adhere to these truths. National identity and political principle are inseparable." "The political ideas of the American Creed have been the basis of national identity."[15]

In fact, however, they have been only one of several components of that identity.

Until the middle of the eighteenth century Americans defined themselves in terms of race, ethnicity, and culture, particularly religion. The creedal component of American identity only began to emerge as relations with Britain deteriorated over issues of trade, taxes, military security, and the extent of Parliament's power over the colonies. Conflicts over these issues fostered the belief that independence was probably the only solution to the problems of the colonies. Independence could not, however, be justified on the grounds that most subsequent independence movements would use: the illegitimacy of the rule of one people by another people. In terms of race, ethnicity, culture, and language, Americans and British were one people. Hence American independence required a different rationale, an appeal to political ideas. This took two forms. Americans first argued that the British government was itself deviating from English concepts of liberty, law, and government by consent. Americans were defending these traditional English values against the efforts of the British government to subvert them. "It was a resistance," Benjamin Franklin said, "in favor of a British constitution, which every Englishman might share . . . a resistance in favor of the liberties of England."[16] As their debates over their relations with Britain intensified, Americans also began to invoke more universalistic, Enlightenment self-evident truths concerning liberty, equality, and individual rights. Combined, these two sources generated the creedal definition of American identity embodied most notably in the Declaration of Independence, but also expressed in many other documents, sermons, pamphlets, writings, and speeches in the 1770s and 1780s.

Identifying America with the ideology of the Creed enables Americans to claim that they have a "civic" national identity as contrasted with the ethnic and ethno-cultural identities of other countries. America is said to be more liberal, more principled, more civilized than those tribally defined societies. The creedal definition allows Americans to hold that theirs is an "exceptional" country because unlike other nations its identity is defined by principle rather than ascription and, at the same time, to claim that America is a "universal" nation because its principles are applicable to all human societies. The Creed makes it possible to speak of "Americanism" as a political ideology or set of beliefs, comparable to socialism or communism, in a way in which one would never speak of Frenchism, Britishism, or Germanism. It also gives Americanism, as many foreign commentators have observed, the characteristics of a religion and makes America, in G. K. Chesterton's oft-quoted phrase, "a nation with the soul of a church." Beginning with the expulsion of the loyalists and the confiscation of their property, Americans have not hesitated to persecute, exclude, and discriminate against those they see as not adhering to the American faith.

Americans have regularly perceived their enemies and friends in creedal terms. In 1745 the Georgian monarchy was challenged by the Stuart uprising of the Young Pretender rooted in the traditional issues of family, ethnicity, and religion. Thirty years later the entirely different American challenge introduced ideology into modern politics. "In 1776," as the German historian Jürgen Heideking argues, "ideology, not ethnicity, language, or religion, had become the touchstone of national identity," and "the American image of an English enemy was the first ideological enemy image in modern history." [17] For most of its first century of independence, America was the only country with a continuing republican government and many of the institutions of modern democracy. Americans identified their enemies with tyranny, monarchy, aristocracy, the suppression of liberty and individual rights. George III was indicted for trying to establish "an absolute Tyranny." In the first decades of the republic, Federalists and Jeffersonians debated whether the French revolutionary and Napoleonic regimes or the British monarchy was the greater threat to American liberty. During the nineteenth century, Americans enthusiastically endorsed the efforts of Latin Americans, Hungarians, and others to free themselves from foreign monarchical rule.

Their perceptions of the extent to which the political systems of foreign countries resembled their own shaped American policies toward those countries and influenced decisions on war and peace. As John Owen has shown, the evolution of British government in a more liberal and democratic direction made it easier to resolve differences with

Britain in the nineteenth century. By the Venezuelan boundary dispute of 1895–1896, leading Americans were invoking the common British-American political tradition as insuring amity between the two countries. In a major crisis with Spain in 1873, senators argued that war was not an option because Spain, at that moment, had a republican government. In 1898, on the other hand, Spain was a monarchy and its portrayal as engaged in brutal tyranny in Cuba helped America justify declaring war. An 1891 incident involving attacks on American sailors in Chile escalated to the brink of war, but "many American elites were loath to fight their fellow republic" and in the end Chile agreed to most American demands.[18] In the twentieth century, Americans defined themselves as the global champions of democracy and liberty against German and Japanese militarism, Nazism, and Soviet communism.

The Creed has thus been one element of American identity since the Revolution. But as Rogers Smith says, the argument that American identity is defined only by the Creed "is at best a half-truth." For much of their history, Americans enslaved and then segregated blacks, massacred and marginalized Indians, excluded Asians, discriminated against Catholics, and obstructed immigration by people from outside northwestern Europe. The early American republic, in Michael Lind's words, was a "nation-state, based upon an Anglo-American Protestant nationalism that was as much racial and religious as it was political."[19] American identity has thus had several components. Historically, however, territory has not been one of them.

"NO ATTACHMENT TO PLACE"

For peoples throughout the world, national identity is often linked to a particular piece of earth. It is associated with places of historical or cultural significance (the Île de France, Kosovo, the Holy Land), cities (Athens, Rome, Moscow), insularity (Britain, Japan), places where the people can claim to be the original inhabitants ("sons of the soil" or *bumiputra*), or lands where they believe their ancestors have lived since time immemorial (Germany, Spain). These peoples speak of their "fatherland" or "motherland" and "sacred soil," loss of which would be tantamount to the end of their identity as a people. For Israelis and Palestinians, as with other peoples, Herbert Kelman has pointed out, "the threat to collective identity . . . is integrally related to the struggle over territory and resources. Both peoples and their national movements claim the same territory . . . as the basis of an independent state that gives political expression to its national identity."[20]

People identify deeply with the localities where they have been born and lived their lives, which, in accord with the "little platoon" phenomenon, then reinforces their identity with their country as a whole. People may also see some specific locale as the historical, cultural, and symbolic heart of the nation. More broadly they may identify with the general geographic and physical characteristics of the land they inhabit.

All three of these manifestations of territorial identity have been weak or missing in America. Individual Americans have from the first generally not developed intense attachments to particular localities. This reflects their consistently high level of geographical mobility, a phenomenon that has been commented on by foreign and native observers throughout American history. Americans, Lord Dunmore observed in the 1770s, "acquire no attachment to Place: But wandering about Seems engrafted in their Nature." "Americans were noted as early as 1800," the historian Gordon S. Wood has said, "for moving four or five times in their lifetime . . . no other culture has ever had so much movement as ours." At the end of the twentieth century 16 percent to 17 percent of Americans were moving their homes every year. Between March 1999 and March 2000, 43 million Americans changed their residence. "Americans," Stephen Vincent Benét said, "are always moving on."[21] As a result, few Americans have had an intense personal identification with any particular geographical locale.

Nor have Americans linked themselves as a people with any particular national site as the unique embodiment of their identity. To be sure, certain places have a special place in American historical memories: those associated with triumph over hardship (Plymouth Rock, Valley Forge), with critical battles (Lexington and Concord, Yorktown, Gettysburg), major steps toward nationhood (the Liberty Bell and Independence

Hall), or central aspects of national character (the Statue of Liberty). These and others have resonance for Americans, but no one of them is crucial to their identity. Any one of them could disappear and Americans would mourn the loss but not feel their nationality had been threatened. Certainly few Americans would place Washington, D.C., at the center of their identity, since, despite its national monuments, it is also the location of a central government for which many Americans often manifest little enthusiasm. Most Americans would not think of either of their two largest cities, New York (at least before it was attacked) and Los Angeles, as the embodiment of the American spirit.

Nor have Americans to the same extent as other peoples identified themselves with the overall territory they inhabit. They have, to be sure, celebrated the scope and beauty of their land, but it has normally been land in the abstract. Americans may sing "Oh beautiful for spacious skies," "The land we belong to is grand," or "This land was made for you and me," but what they celebrate is an abstraction, not a particularity, and, as these examples illustrate, the connection to the land is often expressed in terms of belonging or possession, not in terms of identity. Americans have been settlers, immigrants, and their descendants, all of whose forefathers ultimately came from elsewhere, and hence, however patriotic they may be, they have not called America their fatherland or motherland. The government's focus on "homeland security" after September 11 even generated uneasiness among some Americans and suggestions that the concept of "homeland" was in some way un-American.

This attitude reflects the extent to which Americans identify their country not with place but with political ideas and institutions. In 1849 a European visitor, Alexander Mackey, observed that an American "exhibits little or none of the local attachments which distinguish the European. His feelings are more centered upon his institutions than his mere country. He looks upon himself more in the light of a republican than in that of a native of a particular territory. . . . Every American is thus, in his own estimation, the apostle of a particular political creed." When asked over a hundred years later what aspects of their nation they were most proud of, only 5 percent of Americans mentioned the physical characteristics of their country, compared to 10 percent of Britons, 17 percent of Germans, 22 percent of Mexicans, and 25 percent of Italians. Eighty-five percent of Americans, on the other hand, cited their "governmental, political institutions" as that aspect of their country of which they were the most proud, compared with 46 percent of Britons, 30 percent of Mexicans, 7 percent of Germans, and 3 percent of Italians.[22] For Americans, ideology trumps territory.

The low salience of their national territory as part of the national identity of Americans has two roots. First, land has been plentiful and cheap. It could be acquired for little or nothing, settled, developed, exploited, and abandoned. A resource far more available than labor or capital, it was not something to be cherished, infused with sacred meaning, and preserved and enshrined in people's memory. Second, the land that was America was ever changing. Throughout American history it expanded and hence it was impossible to ascribe any special sanctity to what might be included within its borders at any particular time. The stars in the flag were always increasing and being rearranged, and at the start of the twenty-first century, some Americans were arguing that a fifty-first star should be added for Puerto Rico.

In a similar vein, for over 250 years the frontier was a central element in American identity, but the frontier was always moving. It was not permanently identified with any one place. The frontier was a phase through which American communities evolved. The myth of the frontier in the national consciousness provoked continual migration: the most desirable land and opportunity were not where Americans were but the "virgin land" to the west. Frederick Jackson Turner did his first work on the frontier by studying the seventeenth-century suburbs of Boston. The "oldest West," as he said, "was the Atlantic Coast." It was, Lord Dunmore said, "a weakness" of Americans "that they should forever imagine the Lands further off, are Still better than those upon which they have already Settled."[23] And so the frontier continually receded westward, but it left as its legacy "the moving American," lacking sustained territorial passion, loyalty, or commitment.

RACE AND ETHNICITY

Americans have, in contrast, felt passionate about race and ethnicity. For much of its history the United States, as Arthur Schlesinger, Jr., says, "has been a racist nation."[24] Historically white Americans have sharply distinguished themselves from Indians, blacks, Asians, and Mexicans, and excluded them from the American community. American relations with these other races are symbolized in one defining event early in American history.

In the decades following the Plymouth and Massachusetts Bay settlements of 1620 and 1630, relations between the colonies and Indians were generally cooperative. In the mid-seventeenth century a " 'golden age' of mutual prosperity" existed for Indian tribes and English settlers in New England. People from both groups intermingled and benefited from the growing commerce.[25] In the 1660s, however, commercial relations deteriorated, and the settlers' expanding demands for land and Indian fears that coexistence was giving way to domination led to King Philip's War in 1675–1676. This was proportionately the bloodiest war in American history: the death rate of the colonists was almost twice that of Americans in the Civil War and seven times that in World War II. The Indians attacked fifty-two of the ninety settler towns in New England, pillaged twenty-five, and razed seventeen. The settlers were driven back to the coast and their economy devastated, the effects of which lasted for decades. In the end, however, the Indian tribes were decimated, their leaders killed, and large numbers of men, women, and children enslaved and shipped to the West Indies. As a result of the war, according to Jill Lapore, the Puritans drew "sharp new boundaries on the land and in their minds" between the Indians and themselves. The "English colonists became Americans." Increase Mather argued that God had inflicted the war on the settlers because "Christians in this Land have become too like unto the Indians," and the settlers concluded that expulsion and/or extermination were the only policies to follow in the future.[26] The possibility of a multicultural society in America was extinguished and was not to be revived for three hundred years.

King Philip's War was, as Richard Slotkin said, "in many ways an archetype of all the wars which followed." For well over two centuries after it, Americans defined themselves against the Indians whom they generally viewed as savage, backward, and uncivilized. The relation between settlers and Indians became one of intermittent but continuing warfare, and for fifty years after the Constitution was adopted, the War Department was in charge of dealing with the Indians. The interaction of Americans with them involved bloodshed, coercion, dispossession, and corruption. In the 1830s President Andrew Jackson persuaded Congress to pass the Indian Removal Act and the principal tribes in six Southern states were forcibly moved west of the Mississippi, which led to the Second Seminole War of 1835–1843. These removals would today be termed "ethnic cleansing." They appalled Tocqueville: "It is impossible to conceive the frightful sufferings that attend these forced migrations. They are undertaken by a people already exhausted and reduced; and the countries to which the new-comers betake themselves are inhabited by other tribes, which receive them with jealous hostility. Hunger is in the rear, war awaits them, and misery besets them on all sides."[27] In connection with the Indian removals, the Supreme Court, in an opinion by Chief Justice John Marshall, held that the tribes were "domestic dependent nations" and that individual Indians owed allegiance to their tribe and hence were not eligible for American citizenship unless they explicitly detached themselves from the tribe and integrated themselves into American society.[28]

While Indians were expelled and/or exterminated, blacks were imported until 1808, and enslaved and suppressed. The Founding Fathers assumed that the survival of republican government required relatively high levels of racial, religious, and ethnic homogeneity. The first naturalization statute in 1790 opened citizenship only to "free white persons." At that time, blacks, overwhelmingly slaves, constituted 20 percent of the total population. They were not, however, viewed by Americans as members of their community. Slaves, as the first attorney general, Edmund Randolph, put it, are not "constituent members of our society." Free blacks were viewed similarly and were almost universally denied the right to vote. Thomas Jefferson, along with other Founding Fathers, believed whites and blacks "equally free, cannot live in the same government."

Jefferson, James Madison, Henry Clay, John Randolph, Abraham Lincoln, and other leading political figures supported the efforts of the American Colonization Society to promote emigration of free blacks to Africa. These efforts led to the creation of Liberia in 1821, to which eventually eleven to fifteen thousand free blacks were transported. (To what extent they went voluntarily seems to be in doubt.) In 1862 President Lincoln told the first group of free blacks ever to visit the White House that they should migrate to Africa.[29]

Chief Justice Roger B. Taney's opinion for the Court in the Dred Scott case (1857) held that the Constitution assumed that not just slaves but all blacks were "a subordinate and inferior class of beings" unentitled to "the rights and liberties" of citizens, and hence not part of the "people of the United States." This decision was abrogated by the Fourteenth Amendment in 1868, which declared that all persons born or naturalized in the United States were citizens of the United States. Blacks remained nonetheless subject to extreme forms of segregation and discrimination, including denial of the right to vote, for another century. The principal obstacles to equality for blacks and their political participation only began to disappear with *Brown v. Board of Education* in 1954 and the Civil Rights and Voting Rights Acts of 1964 and 1965.

In the early nineteenth century, the concept of race played an increasingly important role in scientific, intellectual, and popular thinking in both Europe and America. By the middle of the century, "the inherent inequality of races was simply accepted as a scientific fact in America."[30] Americans also came to believe that the qualitative differences among races were innate rather than environmentally determined. Humans, it was widely held, were divided into four major races, which in descending order of quality were Caucasian, Mongolian, Indian, and African. A further differentiation among Caucasians placed Anglo-Saxon descendants of Germanic tribes at the top. This racial concept of national identity was invoked by both sides in nineteenth-century debates over territorial expansion. On the one hand, the superiority of the "Anglo-American race" justified its members conquering and ruling Mexicans, Indians, and others. On the other hand, the desirability of maintaining the racial purity of an Anglo-American society was an important argument of those opposed to the annexation of Mexico, the Dominican Republic, Cuba, and the Philippines.[31]

The building of the railroads after the Civil War led to the immigration of substantial numbers of Chinese workers. These were allegedly followed by substantial numbers of Chinese prostitutes, and in 1875 the United States "passed its first law directly restricting immigration" prohibiting the immigration of prostitutes and criminals.[32] In 1882 popular pressure from California and elsewhere led to the Chinese Exclusion Act, suspending all Chinese immigration for ten years, a suspension that eventually became permanent. In 1889 the Supreme Court upheld the constitutionality of excluding Chinese on the grounds, as stated by Justice Stephen J. Field, that the Chinese were of a different race, that it seemed "impossible for them to assimilate," and that they "remained strangers in the land, residing apart by themselves, and adhering to the customs and usages of their own country." If not restricted, this "Oriental invasion" would constitute "a menace to our civilization."[33] At the turn of the century, Japanese immigration also became an issue, and in 1908 President Theodore Roosevelt negotiated the Gentlemen's Agreement with Japan under which Japan agreed to prevent such immigration. In 1917 Congress passed a law barring immigration from virtually all the rest of Asia. These barriers to Asian immigration were not lifted until 1952. For all practical purposes America was a white society until the mid-twentieth century.

Ethnicity is a more limited category than religion or race. Yet historically it also played a central role in the definition of American identity. Until the late nineteenth century the huge majority of immigrants came from northern Europe. Among the original British settlers antagonism existed toward German-Americans, focused largely on the efforts of the latter to continue to use their language in churches, schools, and other public institutions and events. Opposition to the Irish, on the other hand, was primarily on religious and political grounds rather than ethnic ones.

The issue of ethnicity came to the fore with the large increases in immigration from southern and eastern Europe, beginning in the 1880s, exploding in 1900, and rising even higher in the years up to 1914. Between 1860 and 1924, Philip Gleason observes, "ethnicity assumed greater salience as an element of national identity than it has had at any other time before or since."[34] As in the 1840s and 1850s, the dramatic increases generated anti-immigration intellectual and political movements. The opponents of immigration drew no sharp line between race and ethnicity and much of the argument against southern and eastern Europeans was that they belonged to inferior races. The Immigration Restriction League, founded in 1894, defined the issue as whether America should "be peopled by British, German and Scandinavian stock, historically free, energetic, progressive, or by Slav, Latin and Asiatic races, historically downtrodden, atavistic, and stagnant."[35] The league promoted a literacy test for admission to the United States, which Congress eventually passed over President Wilson's veto in 1917. Immigration restrictions were furthered by the ideology of "Anglo-Saxonism" articulated by writers and social scientists such as Edward Ross, Madison Grant, Josiah Strong, and Lothrop Stoddard.

Congress approved temporary limits on immigration in 1921 and in 1924 a permanent ceiling of 150,000 immigrants a year and country quotas based on the national origins of the U.S. population in 1920. As a result, 82 percent of the slots were assigned to northern and western European countries and 16 percent to southern and eastern Europe. This produced a drastic change in the ethnic background of immigrants. The average annual immigration for the years 1907–1914 from northern and western Europe had been 176,983 and from southern and eastern Europe 685,531. Under the act, 125,266 immigrants could come annually from the former and 23,235 from the latter.[36] This system remained basically in place until 1965.

The effective shutting off of significant immigration from eastern and southern Europe paradoxically contributed to the virtual elimination of ethnicity as a defining component of American identity. The children of the pre-1914 immigrants filled American armies in World War II and the needs of the war effort dictated that America be portrayed for what it was, a truly multiethnic society. "The typical war movie," Philip Gleason points out, "featured an Italian, a Jew, an Irishman, a Pole, and assorted 'old American' types from the Far West, the hills of Tennessee, and so on, and this motif was not confined to Hollywood."[37] Posters appeared with the names of men of various ethnicities and the caption, "They died together so that we can live together." American identity as a multiethnic society dates from and, in some measure, was a product of World War II.

In the 1830s Tocqueville referred to Americans as "Anglo-Americans." A hundred years later that was no longer possible. Anglo-Americans were still the dominant group and possibly the largest group in American society, but ethnically America was no longer an Anglo-American society. Anglo-Americans had been joined by Irish-, Italian-, Polish-, German-, Jewish-, and other-Americans. This shift in status was signaled by a shift in terminology. No longer the only Americans, Anglo-Americans were now WASPs, one group among many in the American ethnic landscape. Yet while Anglo-Americans declined as a proportion of the American population, the Anglo-Protestant culture of their settler forebears survived for three hundred years as the paramount defining element of American identity.

CHAPTER 4

Anglo-Protestant
Culture

THE CULTURAL CORE

Most countries have a core or mainstream culture shared to varying degrees by most people in their society. In addition to this national culture, subordinate cultures usually exist involving subnational or, on occasion, transnational groups defined by religion, race, ethnicity, region, class, or other categories that people feel give them something in common. America has always had its full share of subcultures. It also has had a mainstream Anglo-Protestant culture in which most of its people, whatever their subcultures, have shared. For almost four centuries this culture of the founding settlers has been the central and the lasting component of American identity. One has only to ask: Would America be the America it is today if in the seventeenth and eighteenth centuries it had been settled not by British Protestants but by French, Spanish, or Portuguese Catholics? The answer is no. It would not be America; it would be Quebec, Mexico, or Brazil.

America's Anglo-Protestant culture has combined political and social institutions and practices inherited from England, including most notably the English language, together with the concepts and values of dissenting Protestantism, which faded in England but which the settlers brought with them and which took on new life on the new continent. This culture thus included both elements of general British culture and elements peculiar to those fragments of English society from which the settlers came. At the beginning, as Alden T. Vaughan has said, "almost everything was fundamentally English: the forms of land ownership and cultivation, the system of government and the basic format of laws and legal procedures, the choices of entertainment and leisure-time pursuits, and innumerable other aspects of colonial life." Arthur Schlesinger, Jr., concurs: "the language of the new nation, its laws, its institutions, its political ideas, its literature, its customs, its precepts, its prayers, primarily derived from Britain."[1]

With adaptations and modifications, this original culture persisted for three hundred years. Two hundred years after John Jay in 1789 identified six central elements Americans had in common, one of these, common ancestry, no longer existed. Several of the five others— language, religion, principles of government, manners and customs, war experience—had been modified or diluted (e.g., by the "same religion," Jay undoubtedly meant Protestantism, which two hundred years later would have to be modified to Christianity). Yet in their fundamentals Jay's components of American identity, although challenged, still were central to American culture in the twentieth century. Protestant values have been of primary and continuing importance. With respect to language, the efforts of eighteenth-century German settlers in Pennsylvania to make German the equal of English infuriated Benjamin Franklin, among others, and did not succeed. The efforts of nineteenth-century German immigrants to maintain German-speaking enclaves in Wisconsin and to use German in schools eventually came to naught as a result of pressures for assimilation and the Wisconsin legislature in 1889 requiring schools to use English as their language of instruction.[2] Until the appearance of large concentrations of Spanish-speaking immigrants in Miami and the Southwest, America was unique as a huge country of more than 200 million people virtually all speaking the same language.

The political and legal institutions the settlers created in the seventeenth and eighteenth centuries embodied in large part the institutions and practices of England's late-sixteenth-century and early-seventeenth-century "Tudor constitution." These included: the concept of a fundamental law superior to and limiting government; the fusion of executive, legislative, and judicial functions, and the division of power among separate institutions and governments; the relative power of the legislature and chief executive; the merger of "dignified" and "efficient" functions in the chief executive; a two-house legislature; the responsibility of legislators to their local constituencies; a legislative committee system; and primary reliance for defense on militia rather than a standing army. These Tudor patterns of governance were subsequently fundamentally changed in the United Kingdom, but their central elements persisted in the United States well into the twentieth century.[3]

During the nineteenth century and until the late twentieth century, immigrants were in various ways compelled, induced, and persuaded to adhere to the central elements of the Anglo-Protestant culture. Twentieth-century cultural pluralists, multiculturalists, and spokesmen for ethnic and racial minorities testify to the success of these efforts. Southern and eastern European immigrants, Michael Novak poignantly commented in 1977, were pressured to become "American" by adapting to Anglo-American culture: Americanization "was a process of vast psychic repression." In similar language, Will Kymlicka in 1995 argued that prior to the 1960s, immigrants "were expected to shed their distinctive heritage and assimilate entirely to existing cultural norms," which he labeled the "Anglo-conformity model." If they were thought incapable of assimilation, like the Chinese, they were excluded. In 1967 Harold Cruse declared that "America is a nation that lies to itself about who and what it is. It is a nation of minorities ruled by a minority of one—it thinks and acts as if it were a nation of white Anglo-Saxon Protestants."[4]

These critics are right. Throughout American history, people who were not white Anglo-Saxon Protestants have become Americans by adopting America's Anglo-Protestant culture and political values. This benefited them and the country. American national identity and unity, as Benjamin C. Schwarz has said, derived "from the ability and willingness of an Anglo elite to stamp its image on other peoples coming to this country. That elite's religious and political principles, its customs and social relations, its standards of taste and morality, were for 300 years, America's, and in basic ways they still, are—despite our celebration of 'diversity.' Whatever freedom from ethnic and nationalist conflict this country has enjoyed (and it has been considerably less than our national mythology would have us believe) has existed thanks to a cultural and ethnic predominance that would not tolerate conflict or confusion regarding the national identity."[5] Millions of immigrants and their children achieved wealth, power, and status in American society precisely because they assimilated themselves into the prevailing American culture. Hence there is no validity to the claim that Americans have to choose between a white, WASPish ethnic identity, on the one hand, and an abstract, shallow civic identity dependent on commitment to certain political principles, on the other. The core of their identity is the culture that the settlers created, which generations of immigrants have absorbed, and which gave birth to the American Creed. At the heart of that culture has been Protestantism.

"THE DISSIDENCE OF DISSENT"

America was founded as a Protestant society, and for two hundred years almost all Americans were Protestant. With the substantial Catholic immigration first from Germany and Ireland and then Italy and Poland, the proportion of Protestants declined fairly steadily. By 2000, about 60 percent of Americans were Protestants. Protestant beliefs, values, and assumptions, however, had been the core element, along with the English language, of America's settler culture, and that culture continued to pervade and shape American life, society, and thought as the proportion of Protestants declined. Because they are central to American culture, Protestant values deeply influenced Catholicism and other religions in America. They have shaped American attitudes toward private and public morality, economic activity, government, and public policy. Most importantly, they are the primary source of the American Creed, the ostensibly secular political principles that supplement Anglo-Protestant culture as the critical defining element of what it means to be American.

In the early seventeenth century, as Adrian Hastings has said, Christianity was the "shaper of nations, even of nationalisms," and states and countries explicitly defined themselves as Protestant or Catholic. In Europe existing societies accepted or rejected the Protestant Reformation. In America, the Reformation created a new society. Unique among countries, America is the child of that Reformation. Without it there would be no America as we have known it. The origins of America, another scholar has argued, "are to be found in the English Puritan Revolution. That revolution is, in fact, the single most important formative event of American political history." In America, the nineteenth-century European visitor Philip Schaff observed, "every thing had a Protestant beginning."[6] America was created as a Protestant society just as and for some of the same reasons Pakistan and Israel were created as Muslim and Jewish societies in the twentieth century.

Its Protestant origins make America unique among nations and help explain why even in the twentieth century religion is central to American identity in a way not as true of other Protestant people (see Chapter 5). Throughout most of the nineteenth century, Americans thought of their country as a Protestant country, America was seen as a Protestant country by others, and America was identified as Protestant in textbooks, maps, and literature.

America, said Tocqueville in an oft-quoted phrase, "was born equal and hence did not have to become so." More significantly, America was born Protestant and did not have to become so. America was thus not founded, as Louis Hartz argued, as a "liberal," "Lockeian," or "Enlightenment" fragment of Europe.[7] It was founded as a succession of Protestant fragments, a process under way in 1632 when Locke was born. The bourgeois, liberal ethos that subsequently emerged was not so much imported from Europe as it was the outgrowth of the Protestant societies established in North America. Scholars who attempt to identify the American "liberal consensus" or Creed solely with Lockeian ideas and the Enlightenment are giving a secular interpretation to the religious sources of American values.

The settling of America was, of course, a result of economic and other motives, as well as religious ones. Yet religion still was central. Although less important in New York and the Carolinas, religion was a predominant motive in the creation of the other colonies. Virginia had "religious origins."[8] Quakers and Methodists settled in Pennsylvania.

Catholics established a beachhead in Maryland. Religious intensity was undoubtedly greatest among the Puritans, especially in Massachusetts. They took the lead in defining their settlement based on "a Covenant with God" to create "a city on a hill" as a model for all the world, and people of other Protestant faiths soon also came to see themselves and America in a similar way. In the seventeenth and eighteenth centuries, Americans defined their mission in the New World in biblical terms. They were a "chosen people," on an "errand in the wilderness," creating "the new Israel" or the "new Jerusalem" in what was clearly "the promised land." America was the site of a "new Heaven and a new earth, the home of justice," God's country. The settlement of America was vested, as Sacvan Bercovitch put it, "with all the emotional, spiritual, and intellectual appeal of a religious quest." This sense of holy mission was easily expanded into millennarian themes of America as "the redeemer nation" and "the visionary republic."[9]

American Protestantism differs from European Protestantism, particularly those denominations, Anglican or Lutheran, that have involved established churches. This difference was noted by Edmund Burke, who contrasted the fear, awe, duty, and reverence Englishmen felt toward political and religious authorities with the "fierce spirit of liberty" among Americans. This spirit, he argued, was rooted in the distinctively American brand of Protestantism. The Americans "are Protestants, and of that kind which is the most averse to all implicit submission of mind and opinion. All Protestantism, even the most cold and passive, is a sort of dissent. But the religion most prevalent in our northern colonies is a refinement on the principle of resistance: it is the dissidence of dissent, and the protestantism of the Protestant religion."[10]

This dissidence was manifest from the first with the settlements of the Pilgrims and the Puritans in New England. The Puritan message, style, and assumptions, if not doctrines, spread throughout the colonies and became absorbed into the beliefs and outlooks of other Protestant groups. In some measure, as Tocqueville said, "the entire destiny of America" was shaped by the Puritans. The "religious zeal and the religious conscience" of New England, James Bryce agreed, in "large measure passed into the whole nation." Qualified, modified, diffused, the

Puritan legacy became the American essence. While "England had a Puritan Revolution without creating a Puritan society, America created a Puritan society without enduring a Puritan revolution."[11] The permeation of Puritan ideas and styles among the American colonies was in some measure a result of the distinctive characteristics of the East Anglian settlers. Unlike the settlers in the three other waves of English settlement identified by David Hackett Fischer, the East Anglians were predominantly urban artisans rather than farmers and came overwhelmingly in family groups. Virtually all were literate. Many had attended Cambridge. They were also devoutly religious and committed to spreading the word of God. Their ideas, values, and culture diffused throughout the new land, especially in the "Greater New England" of the Middle West, and decisively shaped the way of life and political development of the new nation.[12]

The dissidence of American Protestantism, manifested first in Puritanism and congregationalism, reappeared in subsequent centuries in Baptist, Methodist, pietist, fundamentalist, evangelical, Pentecostal, and other types of Protestantism. These movements differed greatly. They were, however, generally committed to an emphasis on the individual's direct relation to God, the supremacy of the Bible as the sole source of God's word, salvation through faith and for many the transforming experience of being "born again," personal responsibility to proselytize and bear witness, and democratic and participatory church organization.[13] Beginning in the eighteenth century, American Protestantism became increasingly populist and less hierarchical and increasingly emotional and less intellectual. Doctrine gave way to passion. Sects and movements multiplied constantly, the dissenting sects of one generation then being challenged by the new dissidents of the next generation. "Dissidence of dissent" describes the history as well as the character of American Protestantism.

Religious enthusiasm was a distinctive trait of many American sects in the seventeenth and eighteenth centuries, and evangelism, in various manifestations, has been central to American Protestantism. From the beginning, America was, in the phrase of the University of Chicago historian Martin Marty, an "evangelical empire." Evangelical Protestantism, according to George Marsden, was "the dominant force in American life" in the nineteenth century, and, according to Garry Wills, has always constituted "the mainstream of American religion."[14] In the early nineteenth century, sects, preachers, and adherents exploded in number. Religious dissidence or insurgency was the name of the game. "Young men of relentless energy," as the historian Nathan Hatch has said, "went about movement-building as self-conscious outsiders. They shared an ethic of unrelenting toil, a passion for expansion, a hostility to orthodox belief and style, a zeal for religious reconstruction, and a systematic plan to realize their ideals. . . . They all offered common people, especially the poor, compelling visions of individual self-respect and collective self-confidence." "The history of American Evangelicism is then more than a history of a religious movement," William McLoughlin, the leading scholar of Great Awakenings, agrees. "To understand it is to understand the whole temper of American life in the nineteenth century."[15]

Much the same could be said of the late twentieth century. In the 1980s slightly less than one third of Americans said they were "born-again" Christians, including a majority of Baptists, about one third of Methodists, and more than a quarter of Lutherans and Presbyterians. In 1999 roughly 39 percent of Americans said they were born again. "Contemporary evangelicalism," it was reported, "has been gaining momentum among Americans since the early 1970s." Evangelicalism was also winning many converts among America's largest immigrant group, Latin American Catholics. Evangelical students were also becoming increasingly numerous at elite universities, with the membership of the evangelical association at Harvard, for example, doubling from five hundred to one thousand between 1996 and 2000.[16] As the new millennium began, dissenting Protestantism and evangelicalism were continuing to play central roles in meeting the spiritual needs of Americans.

THE AMERICAN CREED

The term "the American Creed" was popularized by Gunnar Myrdal in 1944 in *The American Dilemma*. Pointing to the racial, religious, ethnic, regional, and economic heterogeneity of the United States, he argued that Americans had "something in common: a social *ethos*, a political creed," which he labeled the American Creed in capitals. His term has been accepted as the common label for a phenomenon that had been noted by many earlier commentators, and which both foreign and American observers have identified as a key element of American identity and often as the only significant determinant of that identity.

Scholars have defined the concepts of the Creed in various ways, but they almost universally agree on its central ideas. Myrdal spoke of "the essential dignity of the individual human being, of the fundamental equality of all men, and of certain inalienable rights to freedom, justice, and a fair opportunity." Jefferson wrote the equality of man, inalienable rights, and "life, liberty, and the pursuit of happiness" into the Declaration of Independence. Tocqueville found people throughout America agreeing on "liberty and equality, the liberty of the press, the right of association, the jury, and the responsibility of the agents of government." In the 1890s Bryce summed up the political beliefs of Americans as including the sacred rights of the individual, the people as the source of political power, government limited by law and the people, a preference for local over national government, majority rule, and "the less government the better." In the twentieth century, Daniel Bell pointed to "individualism, achievement and equality of opportunity" as central values of the Creed and highlighted the extent to which in America, "the tension between liberty and equality, which framed the great philosophical debates in Europe, was dissolved by an individualism which encompassed both." Seymour Martin Lipset identified five key principles as its core: liberty, egalitarianism (of opportunity and respect, not result or condition), individualism, populism, and laissez-faire.[17]

The principles of the Creed have three outstanding characteristics. First, they have remained remarkably stable over time. There has been, as Lipset said, "more continuity than change with respect to the main elements in the national value system."[18] From the late eighteenth century to the late twentieth century, descriptions of the Creed have not varied significantly. Second, until the late twentieth century, the Creed also commanded the widespread agreement and support of the American people, however practice might deviate from it. The only major exception was the effort in the South to formulate a justification for slavery. Otherwise, the general principles of the Creed have been overwhelmingly endorsed by the American people, according to both nineteenth-century observers and twentieth-century public opinion surveys.

Third, almost all the central ideas of the Creed have their origins in dissenting Protestantism. The Protestant emphasis on the individual conscience and the responsibility of individuals to learn God's truths directly from the Bible promoted American commitment to individualism, equality, and the rights to freedom of religion and opinion. Protestantism stressed the work ethic and the responsibility of the individual for his own success or failure in life. With its congregational forms of church organization, Protestantism fostered opposition to hierarchy and the assumption that similar democratic forms should be employed in government. It also promoted moralistic efforts to reform society and to secure peace and justice at home and throughout the world.

Nothing like the Creed was created in continental European societies apart from revolutionary France, or in French, Spanish, or Portuguese colonies, or even in subsequent British colonies in Canada, South Africa, Australia, and New Zealand. Muslim, Buddhist, Orthodox, Confucian, Hindu, Jewish, Catholic, and even Lutheran and Anglican cultures have produced nothing comparable. The American Creed is the unique creation of a dissenting Protestant culture. The extent, the fervor, and the continuity with which Americans have embraced the Creed testify to its place as an indispensable part of their national character and national identity.

The sources of the Creed include the Enlightenment ideas that became popular among some American elites in the mid-eighteenth century. These ideas, however, found receptive ground in the Anglo-Protestant culture that had already existed in America for over a century. Of central importance in that culture were long-standing English ideas of natural and common law, the limits of government authority, and the rights of Englishmen going back to Magna Carta. To these the more radical Puritan sects of the English Revolution added equality and the responsiveness of government to the people. Religion in America, as William Lee Miller has observed, "helped to make the creed and was compatible with it. . . . Here liberal Protestantism and political liberalism, democratic religion and democratic politics, American faith and Christian faith, penetrated each other and exerted a profound influence upon each other." Protestant beliefs and the American political Creed encompassed similar and parallel ideas and came together, John Higham has argued, forging "the strongest bonds that united the American people during the nineteenth century." Or as Jeff Spinner observed, "It's difficult to disentangle what is Protestant from what is liberal in the United States."[19] The American Creed, in short, is Protestantism without God, the secular credo of the "nation with the soul of a church."

INDIVIDUALISM AND THE WORK ETHIC

Protestantism in America generally involves a belief in the fundamental opposition of good and evil, right and wrong. Americans are far more likely than Canadians, Europeans, and Japanese to believe that "There are absolutely clear guidelines about what is good and evil" applicable "whatever the circumstances" rather than to believe that no such guidelines exist and what is good or evil depends on circumstances.[20] Americans are thus continually confronted by the gap between the absolute standards that should govern their individual behavior and the nature of their society, and the failure of themselves and their society to live up to those standards.

Most Protestant sects emphasize the role of the individual in achieving knowledge of God directly from the Bible without intermediation by clerical hierarchy. Many denominations also emphasize that the individual achieves salvation or is "born again" as a result of the grace of God, also without clerical intermediation. Success in this world places on the individual the responsibility to do good in this world. "Protestantism, republicanism, and individualism are all one," as F. J. Grund observed of America in 1837.[21]

Their Protestant culture has made Americans the most individualistic people in the world. In Geert Hofstede's comparative analysis of 116,000 employees of IBM in thirty-nine countries, for instance, the mean individualism index was 51. Americans, however, were far above that mean, ranking first with an index of 91, followed by Australia, Britain, Canada, the Netherlands, and New Zealand. Eight of the ten countries with the highest individualism indices were Protestant. A survey of cadets in military academies in fourteen countries produced comparable results, with those from the United States, Canada, and Denmark ranking highest in individualism. The 1995–97 World Values Survey asked people in forty-eight countries whether individuals or the state should be primarily responsible for their welfare. Americans (with Swedes) came in close seconds to Swiss in emphasizing individual responsibility. In a survey of fifteen thousand managers in several countries, the Americans scored the highest on individualism, Japanese the lowest, with Canadians, British, Germans, and French between them in that order. The authors of the study concluded: "American managers are by far the strongest individualists in our national samples. They are also more inner-directed. Americans believe you should 'make up your mind' and 'do your own thing' rather than allow yourself to be influenced too much by other people and the external flow of events."[22]

The American Protestant belief in individual responsibility gave rise to the gospel of success and the concept of the self-made man. "It was Anglo-Saxon Protestants," as Robert Bellah says, "who created the gospel of wealth and the ideal of success." The concept of the self-made man came to the fore in the Jacksonian years, Henry Clay first using the phrase in a Senate debate in 1832. Americans, countless opinion surveys have shown, believe that whether or not one succeeds in life depends overwhelmingly on one's own talents and character. This central element of the American dream was perfectly expressed by President Clinton:

The American dream that we were all raised on is a simple but powerful one—if you work hard and play by the rules you should be given a chance to go as far as your God-given ability will take you.[23]

In the absence of rigid social hierarchies, one is what one achieves. The horizons are open, the opportunities boundless, and the realization of them depends on an individual's energy, system, and perseverance, in short, the capability for and willingness to work.

The work ethic is a central feature of Protestant culture, and from the beginning America's religion has been the religion of work. In other societies, heredity, class, social status, ethnicity, and family are the principal sources of status and legitimacy. In America, work is. In different ways both aristocratic and socialist societies tend to demean and discourage work. Bourgeois societies promote work. America, the quintessential bourgeois society, glorifies work. When asked "What do you do?" almost no American dares answer "Nothing." As Judith Shklar has pointed out, throughout American history social standing has depended on working and earning money by working. Employment is the source of self-assurance and independence. "Be industrious and FREE," as Benjamin Franklin put it. This glorification of work came to the fore during the Jacksonian era, when people were classified as "do-somethings" or "do-nothings." "The addiction to work," Shklar comments, "that this [attitude] induced was noted by every visitor to the United States in the first half of the nineteenth century."[24] In the America of the 1830s, the Swiss-German Philip Schaff observed, prayer and work were linked together and idleness was sinful. The Frenchman Michel Chevalier, who also visited America in the 1830s, commented,

> The manners and customs are those of a working, busy society. A man who has no profession and—which is nearly the same thing—who is not married enjoys little consideration; he who is an active and useful member of society, who contributes his share to augment the national wealth and increase the numbers of the population, he only is looked upon with respect and favor. The American is brought up with the idea that he will have some particular occupation and that if he is active and intelligent he will make his fortune. He has no conception of living without a profession, even when his family is rich. The habits of life are those of an exclusively working people. From the moment he gets up, the American is at his work, and he is absorbed in it till the

hour of sleep. Even mealtime is not for him a period of relaxation. It is only a disagreeable interruption of business which he cuts short as much as possible.[25]

The right to labor and to the rewards of labor was part of the nineteenth-century arguments against slavery, and the central right espoused by the new Republican Party was the "right to labor productively, to pursue one's vocation and reap its rewards." The concept of "the self-made man" is a distinctive product of this American environment and culture.[26]

In the 1990s Americans remained people of work. They worked longer hours and took shorter vacations than people in other industrialized democracies. The hours of work in other industrialized societies were decreasing. In America, if anything, they were increasing. Among industrialized countries the average hours a worker worked in 1997 were: America—1,966, Japan—1,889, Australia—1,867, New Zealand—1,838, Britain—1,731, France—1,656, Sweden—1,582, Germany—1,560, Norway—1,399. On average Americans worked 350 more hours per year than Europeans. In 1999, 60 percent of American teenagers worked, three times the average of other industrialized countries. Historically Americans have had an ambivalent attitude toward leisure, often feeling guilty about it, and attempting to reconcile it with their work ethic. As Cindy Aron argued in her book *Working at Play*, Americans in the twentieth century remained prisoners of the "persistent and continuing American suspicion of time spent away from work."[27] Americans often tend to feel they should devote their vacations not only to unproductive leisure but to good works and self-improvement.

Americans have not only worked more than other peoples, but they have found satisfaction in and identified themselves with their work more than others have. In a 1990 International Values Survey of ten countries, 87 percent of Americans reported that they took a great deal of pride in their work, with only the British reporting a comparable number. In most countries, less than 30 percent of workers expressed that view (see Figure 4.1). Americans have consistently believed that hard work is the key to individual success. In the early 1990s, some 80

Figure 4.1

Pride in Work

Question to jobholders: "How much pride, if any, do you take in the work that you do? Would you say 'a great deal,' 'some,' 'little,' or 'none'?"

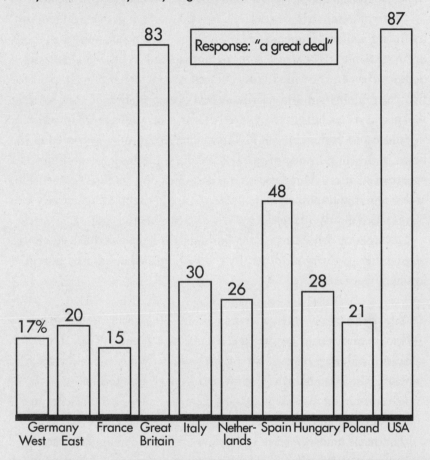

Response: "a great deal"

Germany West	East	France	Great Britain	Italy	Nether-lands	Spain	Hungary	Poland	USA
17%	20	15	83	30	26	48	28	21	87

Source: International Values Study 1990; figure from Institut für Demoskopie Allensbach, *The Allensbach Institute* (Allensbach, 1998), p. 71.

percent of Americans said that to be an American it is necessary to sub-scribe to the work ethic. Ninety percent of Americans said they would work harder if necessary for the success of their organization and 67 percent said they would not welcome social change that would lead to less emphasis on hard work. In their attitudes Americans see society as divided between people who are productive and people who are not.[28]

This work ethic has, of course, shaped American policies on employ-ment and welfare. Dependence on what are often referred to as "gov-ernment handouts" carries a stigma unmatched in other industrialized democracies. In the late 1990s, unemployment benefits were paid for five years in Britain and Germany, two years in France, one year in Japan, and six months in the United States. The 1990s move in America to reduce and, if possible, eliminate welfare programs was rooted in the belief in the moral value of work. "Getting something for nothing" is a source of shame. "Workfare," as Shklar points out, "is about citizenship, and whether able-bodied adults who do not earn anything actively can be regarded as full citizens."[29]

Throughout American history immigrants have faced the challenge of adapting to the work ethic. In 1854 Philip Schaff advised potential immigrants to America:

Only one thing must we say to immigrants: Prepare for all sorts of pri-vations; trust not to fortune and circumstances, but to God and un-wearied industry. If you wish a calm and cheerful life, better stay at home. The good old advice: Pray and work, is nowhere more to the point than in the United States. The genuine American despises noth-ing more than idleness and stagnation; he regards not enjoyment, but labor, not comfortable repose, but busy unrest, as the proper earthly lot of man; and this has unspeakable importance for him, and upon the whole a most salutary influence on the moral life of the nation.

In the 1890s Polish immigrants to America were overwhelmed by the amount of work that they were expected to perform. This was a domi-nant theme in their letters back to Poland: "In America," as one wrote, "one has to sweat more during a day than during a whole week in

Poland." In 1999 a Cuban-American, Alex Alvarez, warned new Cuban immigrants of what they would confront in America:

> Welcome to the capitalist system. Each one of you is responsible for the amount of money you have in your pocket. The Government is not responsible for whether you eat, or whether you're poor or rich. The Government doesn't guarantee you a job or a house. You've come to a rich and powerful country, but it is up to you whether or not you continue living like you did in Cuba.[30]

MORALISM AND THE REFORM ETHIC

American politics, like the politics of other societies, has been and remains a politics of personality and faction, class and region, interest group and ethnic group. To an extraordinary degree, however, it has also been and remains a politics of moralism and moral passion. American political values are embodied in the Creed, and efforts to realize those values in political behavior and institutions are a recurring theme in American history. Individually Americans have the responsibility to pursue the American dream and achieve what they can through their talents, character, and hard work. Collectively Americans have the responsibility to insure that their society is indeed the promised land. In theory, success in the reform of the individual could remove any need for the collective reform of society, and several great evangelists opposed social and political reforms precisely because they were not directed to the regeneration of the individual soul. In practice, however, the Great Awakenings in American history have been closely related to great periods of political reform in American history. These manifestations of "creedal passion" have been fundamentally shaped by the dissenting, evangelical nature of American Protestantism. Robert Bellah neatly summarizes its role:

> Most of what is good and most of what is bad in our history is rooted in our public theology. Every movement to make America more fully

realize its professed values has grown out of some form of public theology, from the abolitionists to the social gospel and the early socialist party to the civil rights movement under Martin Luther King and the farm workers' movement under César Chávez. But so has every expansionist war and every form of oppression of racial minorities and immigrant groups.

Garry Wills concurs: "Religion has been at the center of our major political crises, which are always moral crises—the supporting and opposing of wars, of slavery, of corporate power, of civil rights, of sexual codes, of 'the West,' of American separatism and claims to empire."[31]

Historians identify four Great Awakenings in the history of American Protestantism, each of which was associated with and immediately followed by major efforts at political reform. Many political, economic, and ideational factors came together to create the American Revolution. Among the latter were Lockeian liberalism, Enlightenment rationalism, and Whig republicanism. Also of central importance were the Revolution's religious sources, most notably the Great Awakening of the 1730s and 1740s. Led by George Whitefield and other revivalist preachers and provided with doctrine and justification by Jonathan Edwards, the Awakening swept across the colonies mobilizing thousands of Americans to commit themselves to a new birth in Christ. This religious upheaval laid the basis for the political upheaval that immediately followed. Although a revolution might well have occurred without the Awakening, the Revolution that did occur was grounded in the Awakening and significantly shaped by it. "The evangelical impulse," as the Harvard scholar Alan Heimert said, "was the avatar and instrument of a fervent American nationalism. In the evangelical churches of pre-Revolutionary America was forged that union of tribunes and people that was to characterize the early American Democracy." Substantial proportions of Congregationalists, Presbyterians, and Baptists, involving close to half of the American people, "entertained millennial ideas," and these "millennialist denominations were also those that most solidly backed the American Revolution."[32]

Although Americans varied in the degree to which they supported or opposed it, the Awakening was the first popular movement to engage people from virtually all sects and denominations throughout the colonies. The Awakening's charismatic evangelist, Whitefield, preached from Georgia to New Hampshire and was the first truly *American* public figure. It thus created the experience and the environment for the trans-colony political movements that led to independence. It was the first unifying experience for Americans, generating a sense of national, distinct from provincial, consciousness. "The Revolution," John Adams observed in 1818, "was effected before the war commenced. The Revolution was in the minds and hearts of the people; a change in their religious sentiments of their duties and obligations." Echoing Adams, William McLoughlin concluded in 1973 that the Great Awakening was "the beginning of America's identity as a nation and the starting point of the Revolution."[33]

The Second Great Awakening of the 1820s and 1830s was, as Robert Bellah says, "evangelical and revivalist," in effect the "second American revolution."[34] It was marked by the tremendous expansion of the Methodist and Baptist churches and by the formation of many new sects and denominations, including the Church of the Latter Day Saints. In the Second Great Awakening the counterpart to Whitefield was Charles G. Finney, who recruited tens of thousands of people into American churches and preached the need to "work as well as believe" and as a result generated a "mighty influence toward reform." Religious revivalism gave rise to multitudinous efforts at social and political improvement. As William Sweet describes it: "Societies were formed to advance the cause of temperance; to promote Sunday Schools; to save sailors at the ports and along the canals; to fight the use of tobacco; to improve the diet; to advance the cause of peace; to reform prisons; to stop prostitution; to colonize Negroes in Africa; to support education."[35] The most important child of the Awakening, however, was the abolitionist movement, which in the early 1830s took on new life, placed the slavery issue squarely on the national agenda, and for the next quarter century aroused and mobilized people in the cause of emancipation. When war came over that issue, soldiers from both North and South marched off to fight sure that their cause was God's cause. The depth of the religious dimension in that conflict is reflected in the immense popularity in the North of the "Battle Hymn" crafted by Julia Ward Howe, which begins with a vision of "the glory of the coming of the Lord" and ends with the invocation of Christ: "As He died to make men holy, let us die to make men free. While God is marching on."

The third Great Awakening got under way in the 1890s and was intimately linked with the populist and Progressive drives for social and political reform. The latter were suffused with Protestant morality and, as in the previous reform periods, the reformers stressed the moral necessity of eliminating the gap between institutions and ideals and creating a just and equitable society. The reformers attacked the concentrated power of corporate monopolies and big city machines and, in varying degrees, advocated antitrust measures, women's suffrage, the initiative, referendum, and recall, prohibition, regulation of railroads, the direct primary. Support for these reforms was strongest in the Midwest and far West, the areas of "Greater New England" to which the descendants of the Puritans had migrated and where the intellectual, social, and religious legacy of the Puritans predominated. The participants in the Progressive movement, Alan Grimes observes, generally believed in: "the superiority of native-born, white Americans; the superiority of Protestant, indeed Puritan, morality; and the superiority of a kind of populism, of some degree of direct control over the state and city machines, which, it was alleged, were dominated by the 'interests.' "[36]

The fourth Great Awakening originated in the 1950s and 1960s with the growth of evangelical Protestantism. This "Great Awakening," Sidney Ahlstrom argues, "left the human landscape [at least in America] profoundly changed."[37] It is associated with two reform movements in American politics. The first, beginning in the late 1950s, focused on the most obvious gap between American values and American reality, the legal and institutional discrimination against and segregation of America's black minority. It then led on to the general challenging of the institutions of established authority in the 1960s and 1970s, focused on the conduct of the Vietnam War and the abuse of power in the Nixon administration. In some cases, Protestant leaders and organizations, such as the Southern Christian Leadership Conference, played central roles.

In other instances, as with New Left organizations, the movement w
entirely secular in definition but equally intense in its moralism. The
New Left, as one of its leaders said, in the early 1960s, "begins from
moral values which are held as absolute."[38] The second and later manifestation was the conservative drive for reform in the 1980s and 1990s
focusing on the need to reduce governmental authority, social welfare
programs, and taxes while at the same time attempting to expand government restrictions on abortion.

Dissenting Protestantism has marked American foreign policy as well
as its domestic politics. In conducting their foreign policy, most states
give overwhelming priority to what are generally termed the "realist"
concerns of power, security, and wealth. When push comes to shove, the
United States does this too. Americans also, however, feel the need to
promote in their relations with other societies and within those societies
the moralistic goals they pursue at home. In the new republic before
1815, America's Founding Fathers debated and conducted its foreign
relations overwhelmingly in realist terms. They led an extremely small
republic bordered by possessions of the then great powers, Britain,
France, and Spain, which were for most of these years fighting each
other. In the course of fighting indecisive wars with Britain and France,
intervening militarily in Spain's possessions, and doubling the size of
their country by the Louisiana Purchase from Napoleon, America's
leaders proved themselves adept practitioners of European-style power
politics. With the end of the Napoleonic era, America was able to downgrade its realist concerns with power and security and pursue largely
economic objectives in its foreign relations while concentrating its energies on the expansion and development of its own territory. In this
phase, as Walter McDougall has argued, the purpose of Americans was
indeed to make their country the promised land.

At the end of the nineteenth century, however, America emerged as a
global power. This produced two conflicting developments. On the one
hand, as a great power, America could not ignore the realities of power
politics. To maintain its status and security it would presumably have to
compete in a hard-nosed manner with the other great powers in the
world, as it had not had to do and had been unable to do during most of

the nineteenth century. At the same time, its emergence as a great power also made it possible for America to promote abroad the moral values and principles on which it had aspired to build its society at home and which its weakness and isolation in the nineteenth century had prevented it from promoting abroad. The relation between realism and moralism thus became the central issue of American foreign policy in the twentieth century, as Americans, in McDougall's words, redefined their country from "promised land" to "crusader state." [39]

CHAPTER 5

Religion and Christianity

GOD, THE CROSS, AND AMERICA

In June 2002, a three-judge panel of the Ninth Circuit Court of Appeals in San Francisco decided by a 2-to-1 vote that the words "under God" in the Pledge of Allegiance were a violation of the separation of church and state. These words, the judges said, constituted "an endorsement of religion" and "a profession of religious belief . . . in monotheism." Hence the 1954 act of Congress adding them to the Pledge was unconstitutional, and public school teachers, as state employees, could not recite them in class. The dissenting judge argued that the First Amendment simply required governmental neutrality toward religion and that the threat the two words posed to "our First Amendment freedoms is picayune at most."

The court's decision stimulated vigorous controversy on an issue central to America's identity. Supporters of the decision argued that the United States is a secular country, that the First Amendment prohibited governmental rhetorical and material support for religion, and that people should be able to pledge allegiance to their country without implicitly also affirming a belief in God. Critics pointed out that the phrase was perfectly consonant with the views of the framers of the Constitution, that Lincoln had used these words in the Gettysburg Address, that the Supreme Court had long held that no one could be compelled to say the Pledge, and that President Eisenhower was correct when he described the words as simply "reaffirming the transcendence of religious faith in America's heritage and future."

The supporters of the court were an articulate but very small minority. The critics were an outraged and overwhelming majority of all political persuasions. President Bush termed the decision "ridiculous." The Democratic Senate majority leader, Tom Daschle, called it "nuts"; Governor George Pataki of New York said it was "junk justice." The Senate passed a resolution, 99 to 0, urging that the decision be reversed, and members of the House of Representatives gathered on the steps of the Capitol to recite the Pledge and sing "God Bless America." A *Newsweek* poll found that 87 percent of the public supported inclusion of the words while 9 percent opposed. Eighty-four percent also said they approved of references to God in public settings, including schools and government buildings, so long as no "specific religion" was mentioned.[1]

The court's decision sharply posed the issue of whether America is a secular or religious nation. The support for "under God" reflected the extent to which Americans are one of the most religious people in the world, particularly compared to the peoples of other highly industrialized democracies. Americans nonetheless tolerate and respect the rights of atheists and nonbelievers. Dr. Michael Newdow, however, according to the *New York Times*, planned "to ferret out all insidious uses of religion in daily life." "Why should I be made to feel like an outsider?" he asked. The court agreed that the words "under God" sent "a message to unbelievers that they are outsiders, not full members of the political community."[2] Dr. Newdow and the court majority got it right: atheists are "outsiders" in the American community. As unbelievers they do not have to recite the Pledge or to engage in any religiously tainted practice of which they disapprove. They also, however, do not have the right to impose their atheism on all those Americans whose beliefs now and historically have defined America as a religious nation.

Is America also a Christian nation? The statistics say yes; 80 percent to 85 percent of Americans regularly identify themselves as Christians. Yet there is a difference between government support for religion in general, which occurs in many ways, and government support exclusively or especially for any particular religion, including Christianity.

This issue came to the fore in 1999 in Boise, Idaho, in a challenge to a sixty-foot cross that had stood for forty-three years on publicly owned land. In this and other cases involving tall crosses (forty-three and 103 feet high) on public land in San Diego and San Francisco, backers of the cross attempted to preserve it by transferring ownership of the land to private groups, thus implicitly recognizing problems involved in the blatant government display of the symbol of only one religion. As Brian Cronin, the challenger of the Boise cross, argued, "For Buddhists, Jews, Muslims and other non-Christians in Boise, the cross only drives home the point that they are strangers in a strange land."[3] Like Dr. Newdow and the Ninth Circuit judges, Mr. Cronin was on target. America is a predominantly Christian nation with a secular government. Non-Christians may legitimately see themselves as strangers because they or their ancestors moved to this "strange land" founded and peopled by Christians, even as Christians become strangers by moving to Israel, India, Thailand, or Morocco.

A RELIGIOUS PEOPLE

Americans have been extremely religious and overwhelmingly Christian throughout their history. The seventeenth-century settlers, as we have seen, founded their communities in America in large part for religious reasons. Eighteenth-century Americans and their leaders saw their Revolution in religious and largely biblical terms. In America, "the Bible played a role in shaping the culture for which there was no European parallel. . . . American Protestants were united behind the principle of *Scriptura sola.*" The Revolution reflected their "covenant with God" and was a war between "God's elect" and the British "Antichrist." Jefferson, Paine, and other Deists or nonbelievers felt it necessary to invoke religion to justify the Revolution.[4] The Continental Congress declared days of fasting to implore the forgiveness and help of God and days of thanksgiving for what He had done to promote their cause. Well into the nineteenth century, Sunday church services were held in the chambers of the Supreme Court as well as the House of Representatives. The

Declaration of Independence appealed to "Nature's God," the "Creator," "the Supreme Judge of the World," and "divine Providence" for approval, legitimacy, and protection.

The Constitution includes no such references. Its text is strictly secular. Yet its framers firmly believed that the republican government they were creating could only last if it was deeply rooted in morality and religion. "A Republic can only be supported by pure religion or austere morals," John Adams said. The Bible offers "the only system that ever did or ever will preserve a republic in the world." "Our constitution was made only for a moral and religious people." Washington agreed: "Reason and experience both forbid us to expect that national morality can prevail in exclusion of religious principles." The happiness of the people, good order, and civil government, the Massachusetts constitution of 1780 declared, "essentially depend on piety, religion, and morality." Fifty years after the Constitution was adopted, Tocqueville reported that all Americans held religion "to be indispensable to the maintenance of republican institutions. This opinion is not peculiar to a class of citizens or to a party, but it belongs to the whole nation and to every rank of society."[5]

The words "separation of church and state" do not appear in the Constitution, and, as Sidney Mead has pointed out, Madison spoke not of "church" and "state," European concepts with little relevance to America, but of "sects" and "Civil authority," and the "line" not the "wall" between them.[6] Religion and society were coterminous. The prohibition of an established national religion and the gradual disestablishment of state religions promoted the growth of religion in society. "As the state's authority in religion faded," Jon Butler notes, "denominational authority expanded," leading to "the single most important institutional development of post-revolutionary Christianity: the shift of religious authority away from the state and toward the 'voluntary' institutional bodies. Out of this shift came an extraordinary expansion of denominational institutions, new means to reach great numbers of individuals and groups, and a new confidence to shape society and its values."[7]

Some people cite the absence of religious language in the Constitution and the provisions of the First Amendment as evidence that America is fundamentally a secular country. Nothing could be further from the truth. At the end of the eighteenth century, religious establishments existed throughout European countries and in several American states. State control of the church was a key element of state power, and the established church, in turn, provided legitimacy to the state. The framers of the American Constitution prohibited an established national church in order to limit the power of government and to protect and strengthen religion. The "separation of church and state" is the corollary to the identity of religion and society. Its purpose, as William McLoughlin has said, was not to establish freedom *from* religion but to establish freedom *for* religion. It was spectacularly successful. In the absence of a state religion, Americans were not only free to believe as they wished but also free to create whatever religious communities and organizations they wished. As a result, Americans have been unique among peoples in the diversity of sects, denominations, and religious movements to which they have given birth, almost all embodying some form of Protestantism. When substantial numbers of Catholic immigrants arrived, it was eventually possible to accept Catholicism as one more denomination within the broad framework of Christianity. The proportion of the population who were "religious adherents," that is church members, increased fairly steadily through most of American history.[8]

European observers repeatedly commented on the high levels of religious commitment of Americans compared to that of their own peoples. As usual, Tocqueville said it most eloquently: "On my arrival in the United States the religious aspect of the country was the first thing that struck my attention, and the longer I stayed there, the more I perceived the great political consequences resulting from this new state of things." In France religion and liberty opposed each other. The Americans, in contrast, "have succeeded . . . combining admirably . . . the *spirit of religion* and the *spirit of liberty.*" Religion in America "must be regarded as the first of their political institutions." Tocqueville's Swiss-German contemporary Philip Schaff similarly noted the centrality of religion in America and approvingly quoted a Jewish observer: "The United States is by far the most religious and Christian country in the world; and that, just because religion is there most free." The number and variety of churches, religious schools, missionary activities, "Bible and Tract Societies," and revivals, along with the high levels of church attendance, all were "expressions of the general Christian character of the people, in which the Americans are already in advance of most of the old Christian nations of Europe." [9]

A half century after Tocqueville and Schaff, James Bryce came to similar conclusions. The Americans are "a religious people"; religion "influences conduct . . . probably more than it does in any other modern country, and far more than it did in the so-called ages of faith." And again, "the influence of Christianity seems to be . . . greater and more widespread in the United States than in any part of western Continental Europe, and I think greater than in England." A half century after Bryce, the eminent Swedish observer Gunnar Myrdal judged that "America probably is still the most religious country in the Western world." And a half century after him, the English historian Paul Johnson described America as "a God-fearing country, with all it implies." America's religious commitment "is a primary source—*the* primary source, I think—of American exceptionalism." He went on to quote Lincoln on how God shapes events and how Lincoln hoped God was supporting the Union cause and then commented: "It is impossible to imagine Lincoln's European contemporaries, Napoleon III, Bismarck, Marx, or Disraeli, thinking in these terms. Lincoln did so in the certainty that most of his fellow Americans could and did think along similar lines." [10]

Overwhelming majorities of Americans affirm religious beliefs. When asked in 1999 whether they believed in God or a universal spirit, or neither, 86 percent of those polled said they believed in God, 8 percent in a universal spirit, and 5 percent in neither. When asked in 2003 simply whether they believed in God or not, 92 percent said yes. In a series of 2002–2003 polls, 57 percent to 65 percent of Americans said religion was very important in their life, 23 percent to 27 percent said fairly important, and 12 percent to 18 percent said not very important. Seventy-two percent to 74 percent said they believed in life after death, while 17 percent said they did not. In 1996, 39 percent of Americans said they believed the Bible is the actual word of God and should be taken literally; 46 percent said they believed the Bible is the word of God but not everything in it should be taken literally word for word; 13 percent said it is not the word of God.[11]

Large proportions of Americans also appear to be active in the practice of their religion. In 2002–2003, 63 percent to 66 percent of Americans claimed membership in a church or synagogue. Thirty-eight percent to 44 percent said they had attended church or synagogue in the last seven days. Twenty-nine percent to 37 percent said they went to church at least once a week, 8 percent to 14 percent almost every week, 11 percent to 18 percent about once a month, 24 percent to 30 percent seldom or a few times a year, and 13 percent to 18 percent never. In 2002–03, 58 percent to 60 percent of Americans said they prayed one or more times a day, 20 percent to 23 percent once or more a week, 8 percent to 11 percent less than once a week, and 9 percent to 11 percent never. Given human nature, these claims of religious practice were undoubtedly overstated, but even discounting for this, the level of religious activity was still high; and the extent to which Americans believe the right response is to affirm their religiosity is itself evidence of the centrality of religious norms in American society. More than twice as many Americans belong to religious organizations as to any other type of organization; Americans direct 42.4 percent of their charitable giving to religious organizations, three times as much as to any other category; and reportedly in any one week more Americans go to church than go to sporting events.[12]

Reflecting on the depth of American religiosity, the Swedish theologian Krister Stendhal remarked that "Even the atheists in America speak in a religious key." That may be the case, but only 10 percent or less of Americans espouse atheism, and most Americans do not approve of it. In 1992, 68 percent of Americans said that a belief in God is very important or extremely important for a true American, with blacks and Hispanics holding this view more strongly than whites. Americans view atheists more unfavorably than most other minorities. A 1973 poll asked: "Should a socialist or an atheist be allowed to teach in a college or university?" The community leaders surveyed approved of both teaching. The American public as a whole agreed that socialists could teach

(52 percent yes, 39 percent no), but decisively rejected the idea of atheists on college or university faculties (38 percent yes, 57 percent no). Since the 1930s, the willingness of Americans to vote for presidential candidates from minorities has increased dramatically, with over 90 percent of those polled in 1999 saying they would vote for a black, a Jew, or a woman for president, while 59 percent were willing to vote for a homosexual. Only 49 percent, however, were willing to vote for an atheist for president.[13] In 2001, 66 percent of Americans viewed atheists unfavorably, while 35 percent viewed Muslims this way. Similarly, 69 percent of all Americans said they would be bothered by or could not accept the marriage of a member of their family to an atheist, compared with 45 percent of white Americans who said the same about a family member marrying a black person. Americans seem to agree with the Founding Fathers that their republican government requires a religious base, and hence they find it difficult to accept the explicit rejection of God and religion.

These high levels of religiosity would be less significant if they were the norm for other countries. Americans rank, however, among the most religious people in the world and differ dramatically in their high level of religiosity from the people of other economically developed countries. This religiosity is conclusively revealed in three cross-national surveys. First, in general, the level of religious commitment of countries varies inversely with their level of economic development: people in poor countries are highly religious, those in rich countries are not. America is a glaring exception, as can be seen by Figure 5.1, which compares economic development with the proportion of people saying their religious beliefs are very important to them for fifteen countries at varied levels of economic development. The regression line would lead one to expect that 5 percent of Americans would think religion very important; in fact in this poll, 51 percent do, slightly less than in the previously cited polls.[14]

Second, an International Social Survey Program survey in 1991 asked people in seventeen countries seven questions concerning their belief in God, life after death, heaven, and other religious concepts. Reporting the results, George Bishop ranked the countries according to the per-

Figure 5.1

The Relationship Between Economic Development and Religious Beliefs

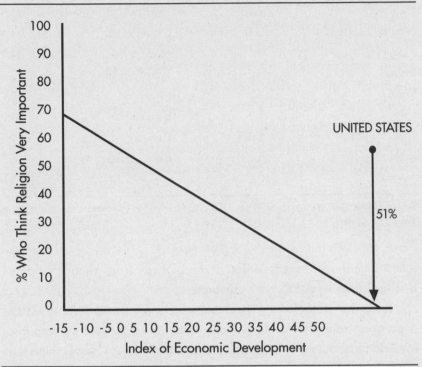

Source: Kenneth D. Wald, *Religion and Politics in the United States* (New York: St. Martin's Press, 1987), p. 7. Reprinted with permission of Rowman and Littlefield, 2003.

centage of their population that affirmed these religious beliefs.[15] The average country rankings are set forth in Table 5.1. The United States was far ahead in its overall level of religiosity, ranking first on four questions, second on one, and third on two, for an average ranking of 1.7. It was followed by Northern Ireland (2.4), where religion is obviously of crucial importance to both Protestants and Catholics, and then by four Catholic countries. After them came New Zealand, Israel, five Western European countries, and four former communist countries, with East Germany last, the least religious on six of the seven questions. According to this poll, Americans are more deeply religious than even the people of countries like Ireland and Poland, where religion has been the

Table 5.1

Extent of Belief in Religion: Average Ranking in Response to Seven Questions

United States	1.7	Norway	11.0
Northern Ireland	2.4	Great Britain	11.6
Philippines	3.3	Netherlands	11.9
Ireland	4.1	West Germany	12.1
Poland	5.2	Russia	12.7
Italy	5.9	Slovenia	13.9
New Zealand	8.0	Hungary	14.3
Israel	8.3	East Germany	16.3
Austria	10.6		

Source: George Bishop, "What Americans Really Believe and Why Faith Isn't As Universal as They Think," *Free Inquiry*, 19 (Summer 1999), pp. 38–42.

core of national identity differentiating them from their traditional British, German, and Russian antagonists.

Third, the 1990–1993 World Values Survey asked nine questions concerning religiosity in forty-one countries.[16] The average responses for individual countries are displayed in Figure 5.2.* Overall these data show the United States to be one of the most religious countries in the world. Apart from the Poles and the Irish, Americans are much more religious than the people of European countries. Most striking is the high religiosity of America in comparison to other Protestant countries. The top fifteen countries in religiosity include Nigeria, India, and Turkey (the only African and predominantly Hindu and Muslim countries in the sample), eight predominantly Catholic countries, one Orthodox country (Romania), sharply divided Northern Ireland, and two predominantly Protestant countries, the United States in fifth place and Canada

* These surveys involve a common questionnaire but are carried out by different organizations in different countries. Hence the reliability of the data may vary. In addition, the extent to which respondents give "sincere" answers expressing their own views or "strategic" answers may vary. Three types of strategic answers are: (1) those that express what the respondent thinks is the preferred or expected answer in his society or social group; (2) those where he gives the answer he thinks will please the interviewer; and (3) those where his answer is designed to keep him out of trouble with governmental authorities. A Type I strategic answer, however, may be evidence of the extent of or intensity with which an attitude is held in a society.

Figure 5.2
Religiosity in the World

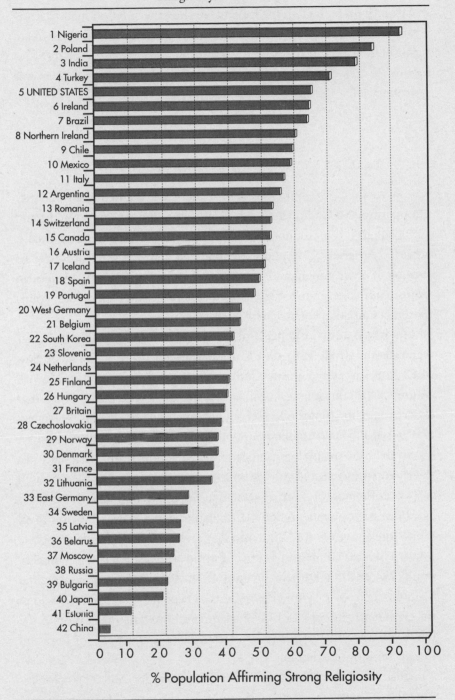

1 Nigeria
2 Poland
3 India
4 Turkey
5 UNITED STATES
6 Ireland
7 Brazil
8 Northern Ireland
9 Chile
10 Mexico
11 Italy
12 Argentina
13 Romania
14 Switzerland
15 Canada
16 Austria
17 Iceland
18 Spain
19 Portugal
20 West Germany
21 Belgium
22 South Korea
23 Slovenia
24 Netherlands
25 Finland
26 Hungary
27 Britain
28 Czechoslovakia
29 Norway
30 Denmark
31 France
32 Lithuania
33 East Germany
34 Sweden
35 Latvia
36 Belarus
37 Moscow
38 Russia
39 Bulgaria
40 Japan
41 Estonia
42 China

0 10 20 30 40 50 60 70 80 90 100

% Population Affirming Strong Religiosity

Source: Graph prepared by James Perry from data in *Human Values and Beliefs: A Cross-Cultural Sourcebook—Political, Religious, Sexual, and Economic Norms in 43 Societies, Findings from the 1990–1993 World Values Survey* (Ann Arbor: University of Michigan Press, 1998).

in fifteenth place. Except for Iceland, all the other predominantly Protestant countries fall well into the lower half of the countries surveyed in terms of their religiosity. America is thus by a large margin the most religious Protestant country. The legacy of its Reformation origins was alive and well at the end of the twentieth century.

PROTESTANT AMERICA AND CATHOLICISM

For more than two hundred years Americans defined their identity in opposition to Catholicism. The Catholic other was first fought and excluded and then opposed and discriminated against. Eventually, however, American Catholicism assimilated many of the features of its Protestant environment and was, in turn, assimilated into the American mainstream. These processes changed America from a Protestant country into a Christian country with Protestant values.

The initial anti-Catholicism of Americans derived both from their Reformation struggles against Catholicism and from the English view of Catholicism as a major threat during the seventeenth and eighteenth centuries. Britain defined itself largely by the Protestant culture that differentiated it from the French and Spanish. Fears of papist conspiracies and of alleged Catholic sympathies or hidden Catholicism of Stuart monarchs were recurring themes in seventeenth-century England. In the eighteenth century, anti-Catholicism was reinforced by the repeated wars with France. The British were determined to maintain their purity as a Protestant people. In 1609 Parliament "denied naturalization to all non-Protestants." In 1673 the Test Act excluded Catholics from public office, a ban that remained in effect for the armed services and judiciary until 1793 and for Parliament until 1828. Persecution by continental Catholic regimes led many Protestants to become refugees in Britain in the eighteenth century. In 1740 Parliament limited naturalization in the home country and colonies to Protestants with exemptions for Jews and Quakers but not Catholics.[17]

British attitudes and actions were replicated in its American colonies. Americans, particularly dissenting Protestants, saw the papacy and

Catholicism as the Antichrist. The wars of Britain with France and Spain led the colonists to view the Catholics in their midst as potential traitors. Colonial governments allowed naturalization of Jews but not Catholics, and by 1700, aside from Maryland, "restrictions on Catholic worship were nearly universal in the colonies, remaining relatively light only in Rhode Island and Pennsylvania."[18] Their anti-Catholicism also helped to turn the colonists against the mother country. In 1774 Parliament passed an act decreeing toleration for the Catholic Church in Quebec. The American reaction was intensely critical. Alexander Hamilton denounced it as "popery"; others used more colorful language. In one of its first actions the Continental Congress vigorously protested against this law, which Americans ranked with the tax on tea as a threat to their civil and religious liberty.[19]

As the Revolution began, Americans denounced George III for his "popery," and he responded in kind by describing the rebellion as a "Presbyterian war." For Americans "popist" became a label like "communist" in the twentieth century, often applied to antagonists with little regard for its accuracy. Political considerations, however, soon led to the moderation of anti-Catholic attitudes. Jefferson made only oblique reference to the Quebec Act in the Declaration, since the Americans now hoped to persuade Canadian Catholics to join them in the struggle against the Crown. The alliance with France in 1778 produced a major change in elite, if not popular, opinion, and, despite some intense opposition, the prohibition on religious qualifications for federal office was incorporated into the Constitution. This was followed by the gradual elimination of such restrictions from state constitutions, although well into the nineteenth century, the North Carolina constitution barred from office anyone who denied "the truths of the Protestant religion."[20]

The anti-Catholic colonial laws severely restricted Catholic organizations and activities and reduced the attractions of America to potential Catholic migrants. The small numbers of Catholics led to high rates of intermarriage, and the proportion of Catholics in the American population may have declined during the eighteenth century. In 1789, about one percent of Americans were Catholic, while one tenth of one percent were Jewish. America was the prototypical Protestant country and was seen as such by both Americans and Europeans. The prevailing attitude was well expressed by Philip Schaff, who, after coming to America in the mid-1840s, concluded that the Protestant sects "have given the country its spirit and character. Its past course and present condition are unquestionably due mainly to the influence of Protestant principles."[21]

After 1815 accelerating immigration from Ireland and Germany began to moderate America's exclusively Protestant character. In the 1820s, 62,000 immigrants entered the United States from Ireland and Germany. In the 1840s almost 800,000 arrived from Ireland, and in the 1850s, 952,000 came from Germany and 914,000 from Ireland. Ninety percent of the Irish and a substantial portion of Germans were Catholic. This huge influx rekindled anti-Catholic fears and passions. Americans had defined themselves as an anti-Catholic people, and they were now being invaded by the enemy. This coincided with the Second Great Awakening, and as Perry Miller notes, "fear of Catholicism became a morbid obsession of the Revival."[22] This anti-Catholicism was often formulated in political rather than religious terms. The Catholic Church was seen as an autocratic, anti-democratic organization and Catholics as people accustomed to hierarchy and obedience who lacked the moral character required for citizens of a republic. Catholicism was a threat to American democracy as well as to American Protestantism.

Anti-Catholic actions and movements intensified in the 1830s and 1840s, including the burning of a convent in Charlestown, Massachusetts, in 1834. The immigration explosion of the 1840s led to the formation in 1850 of a secret organization, the Order of the Star-Spangled Banner, which became known as the Know-Nothing movement. In the mid-1850s, the Know-Nothings elected six state governors, secured control of nine state legislatures, and had forty-three representatives in Congress. Millard Fillmore, the Know-Nothing presidential candidate in 1856, received 22 percent of the popular vote and eight electoral votes. The intensifying controversy over the extension of slavery, however, displaced immigration as an issue, and the Know-Nothings faded away as a political force. The Civil War marked the end of explicit anti-Catholic political movements, and governmental restrictions on the rights of Catholics had virtually all disappeared by then. For decades, however, anti-Catholic social and political prejudices remained strong in many segments of American society, and in 1898 Americans were urged to go to war to liberate Cuba from "Pope-ridden Spain."[23]

The fading of overtly anti-Catholic attitudes and activities was paralleled by and directly related to the Americanization of Catholicism. This was a complex and often convoluted process. At one level, it involved the creation of a vast, intricate network of Catholic institutions—churches, seminaries, convents, charities, associations, political clubs, and schools—which, in the short term, provided a community where new immigrants could feel at home and, in the longer term, provided institutional stepping-stones for their movement and, more importantly, the movement of their children into the broader reaches of American society. At another level, it involved the adaptation of Catholicism to its American, that is, Protestant, environment, including changes in Catholic attitudes, practices, organization, and behavior—in effect, the transformation of a Roman Catholic Church into an American Catholic Church.

The pros and cons of "Americanization" were intensely debated within the Catholic hierarchy throughout the nineteenth century. The leading American bishops generally, but not unanimously, made great efforts to reconcile Americanism and Catholicism and to legitimate the Catholic presence in American society in the eyes of Protestant Americans. The Americanists argued, in the words of Archbishop John Ireland, that "There is no conflict between the Catholic Church and America . . . the principles of the Church are in thorough harmony with the interests of the Republic."[24] Their opponents saw Americanization as a path of corruption leading to the worst forms of modernism, individualism, materialism, and liberalism. These debates culminated in and came to an end with Pope Leo XIII's papal letter, *Testem Benevolentiae*, in January 1899 to Cardinal Gibbons denouncing the false doctrine of "Americanism." The letter was widely seen as a severe rebuke to Gibbons, Archbishop Ireland, and other "Americanists," but was also criticized for defining and attacking a set of beliefs no one had.

Some groups, German Catholics in particular, resisted Americanization, and strove to maintain their language, culture, and religion unchanged. Assimilation, however, could not be halted. In due course the "de-Romanization" of the Church occurred as Catholics increasingly thought of themselves less as Roman Catholics and more as American Catholics.[25] By the mid-twentieth century, Catholic leaders such as Bishop Fulton J. Sheen and Cardinal Francis Spellman had become fervent American nationalists, and the Irish-American Catholic became the prototype of the patriotic American. Peter Steinfels describes one aspect of this shift:

> In three consecutive years, 1943, 1944 and 1945, movies centering on Roman Catholicism—"Song of Bernadette," "Going My Way," "The Bells of St. Mary's" and "The Keys of the Kingdom"—were nominated for 34 Oscars and won 12. The Catholic priest, once a sinister figure in the American imagination, actually became a cinematic model of American manhood. From Spencer Tracy's Father Flanagan in "Boys Town"; Bing Crosby's crooning ex-baseball player, Father Chuck O'Malley; Karl Malden's labor priest in "On the Waterfront"; and assorted roles by Pat O'Brien, there emerged the "superpadre": virile, wise, good-humored, compassionate and, in emergencies, possessed of a remarkable knockout punch.[26]

And in 1960 John F. Kennedy was elected president.

Catholics are proud of their American identity, the Americanization of their church, and its emergence as a central and influential institution of American society. For understandable reasons, however, they do not like people referring to the "Protestantization" of their religion. Yet in some degree that is precisely what Americanization involves. Given the Protestant origins of America, the overwhelming predominance of Protestantism for over two centuries, the central and pervasive role of Protestant values and assumptions in American culture and society, how could it be otherwise for this later arrival on the American scene? Nor is Protestantization unique to America. As Ronald Inglehart's careful analysis of data from the World Values Survey shows, Catholics in societies that have historically been shaped by Protestantism—Germany, Switzerland, the Netherlands, and the United States—typically have values more similar to those of their Protestant countrymen than to Catholics in other countries. "Catholics and Protestants *within* these societies do not show markedly different values: Dutch Catholics today are about as Calvinist as the members of the Dutch Reformed Church."[27]

In Europe, Protestantism was a revolt against a long-established and universally dominant Catholicism. In America, in contrast, Catholicism, as Schaff put it, came into a Protestant society "as one sect among the others," "found an adopted home," and was "everywhere surrounded by purely Protestant institutions." Lord Baltimore's early Catholic colony of Maryland "was founded expressly on the thoroughly anti-Roman, and essentially Protestant, principles of religious toleration." In the early nineteenth century, as Will Herberg remarks, Catholics "established a pattern of church government very much along the lines of the ubiquitous Protestant model." Known as "lay trusteeism," this asserted the rights and powers of the laity at the congregational level. This movement was rejected by the first provincial council in Baltimore in 1829 and the authority of the bishops reasserted. It was, however, illustrative of the pressures for the Church to adapt itself to the Protestant ways of America. By the late nineteenth and early twentieth centuries, Dorothy Dohen reports, "Archbishop Ireland and Cardinal Gibbons, in their writings and speeches, urged on the faithful the acceptance of the Protestant ethic (insofar as they stressed, as virtues to be developed, the 'American' traits of sobriety, thrift and initiative)."[28]

One striking dimension of Protestantization was the way in which and the extent to which Catholic prelates reconciled Catholic universalism with American nationalism. Echoing the tones, ideas, and words of evangelical Protestants, they argued divine legitimacy for America's mission in the world. "We cannot but believe," Archbishop Ireland said in 1905, "that a singular mission is assigned to America . . . the mission of bringing about a new social and political order. . . . The Church triumphing in America, Catholic truth will travel on the wings of American influence, and encircle the universe." In the mid-twentieth century, Bishop Sheen similarly spoke of America as a chosen nation, and Cardinal Spellman, as one scholar said, was "overt in identifying the judgments and action of the American nation with those of God. . . . Cardinal Spellman's acceptance of the messianic mission of America has been complete."[29] "American Catholics," an observer from Africa noted in the 1990s, "are a nuisance for Rome just because they are . . . well, so Protestant." In this respect Catholicism does not differ from Judaism or other religions. "American religion, whatever its formal sectarian designation, is decidedly Protestant."[30]

A CHRISTIAN PEOPLE

Along with their general religiosity, the Christianity of Americans has also impressed foreign observers. "There is no country in the world," Tocqueville said, "where the Christian religion retains a greater influence over the souls of men than in America. . . . Christianity, therefore, reigns without obstacle, by universal consent." Christianity, Bryce similarly observed, is "the national religion" of Americans.[31] Americans have also affirmed their Christian identity. "We are a Christian people," the Supreme Court declared in 1811. "We are a Christian people," the Senate Judiciary Committee said in 1853, "almost our entire population belong to or sympathise with some one of the Christian denominations." In the midst of the Civil War, Lincoln also described Americans as "a Christian people." In 1892 the Supreme Court again declared that "This is a Christian nation." In 1908, a House of Representatives committee said that the United States is "a Christian nation" and that "the best and only reliance for the perpetuation of the republican institution is upon a Christian patriotism." In 1917 Congress passed legislation declaring a day of prayer in support of the war effort and invoking America's status as a Christian nation. In 1931 the Supreme Court reaffirmed its earlier view: "We are a Christian people, according to one another the equal right of religious freedom, and acknowledging with reverence the duty of obedience to the will of God."[32] Posing the question in 1873, "In what sense can this country then be called a *Christian* country?" Theodore Dwight Woolsey, former president of Yale, provided an accurate answer. "In this sense certainly, that the vast majority

of the people believe in Christianity and the Gospel, that Christian influences are universal, that our civilization and intellectual culture are
built on that foundation, and that the institutions are so adjusted as, in
the opinion of almost all Christians, to furnish the best hope for spreading and carrying down to posterity our faith and our morality."[33]

While the balance between Protestants and Catholics shifted over the
years, the proportion of Americans identifying themselves as Christian
has remained relatively constant. In three surveys between 1989 and
1996, between 84 percent and 88 percent of Americans said they were
Christians.[34] The proportion of Christians in America rivals or exceeds
the proportion of Jews in Israel, of Muslims in Egypt, of Hindus in India, and of Orthodox believers in Russia. America's Christian identity
has, nonetheless, been questioned on two grounds. First, it is argued
that America is losing that identity because non-Christian religions are
expanding in numbers, and thus Americans are becoming a multireli-
gious and not simply a multidenominational people. Second, it is argued
that Americans are losing their religious identity and are becoming secular, atheistic, materialistic, and indifferent to their religious heritage.
Neither of these propositions comes close to the truth.

The argument that America is losing its Christian identity due to the
spread of non-Christian religions was advanced by several scholars in
the 1980s and 1990s. They pointed to the growing numbers of Muslims,
Sikhs, Hindus, and Buddhists in American society. Adherents of these
religions have become more numerous. Hindus in America increased
from 70,000 in 1977 to 800,000 in 1997. Muslims amounted to at least
3.5 million in 1997, while Buddhists numbered somewhere between
750,000 and two million. From these developments, the proponents of
de-Christianization argue, in the words of Professor Diana Eck, that
"religious diversity" has "shattered the paradigm of America" as an
overwhelmingly Christian country with a small Jewish minority.[35] Another scholar suggested that public holidays should be adjusted to accommodate this increasing religious diversity and that, for a start, it
would be desirable to "have one Christian holiday (say, Christmas), but
replace Easter and Thanksgiving with a Muslim and Jewish holiday." In
some measure, however, the holiday trend was in the opposite direction.

Hanukkah, "traditionally a minor Jewish holiday," has, according to Professor Jeff Spinner, been elevated into the "Jewish Christmas" and displaced Purim as a holiday, so as "to fit in better with the dominant culture."[36]

The increases in the membership of some non-Christian religions have not, to put it mildly, had any significant effect on America's Christian identity. As a result of assimilation, low birth rates, and intermarriage, the proportion of Jews dropped from 4 percent in the 1920s to 3 percent in the 1950s to slightly over 2 percent in 1997. If the absolute numbers claimed by their spokesmen are correct, by 1997 about 1.5 percent of Americans were Muslim, while Hindus and Buddhists were each less than one percent. The numbers of non-Christian, non-Jewish believers undoubtedly will continue to grow, but for years to come they will remain extremely small. Some increases in the membership in non-Christian religions come from conversions, but the largest share is from immigration and high birth rates. The immigrants of these religions, however, are far outnumbered by the huge numbers of immigrants from Latin America and the Philippines, almost all of whom are Catholic and have high birth rates. Latin American immigrants are also converting to evangelical Protestantism. In addition, Christians in Asia and the Middle East are more likely than non-Christians to migrate to America. As of 1990, a majority of Asian-Americans were Christian rather than Buddhist or Hindu. Among Korean-Americans, Christians outnumber Buddhists by at least ten to one. Roughly one third of Vietnamese immigrants are Catholics. About two thirds of Arab-Americans have been Christian rather than Muslim, although the number of Muslims was growing rapidly before September 11.[37] While a precise judgment is impossible, at the start of the twenty-first century the United States was probably becoming more rather than less Christian in its religious composition.

The increases in the small numbers of non-Christians in America unavoidably raise questions concerning their status in a country with an overwhelmingly Christian people and a secular government. These include such practical issues as when Muslim women may wear Muslim headdress and Sikh men their beards and turbans. Americans have generally attempted to tolerate and accommodate the practices of non-Christian groups. America's Christianity, Protestant values, and constitutional guarantees of freedom of religion mean that non-Christian groups should be and, in general, have been freely allowed to practice and promulgate their beliefs. Americans tend to have a certain catholicity toward religion: all deserve respect. In 1860 Anthony Trollope observed that in America, "Everybody is bound to have a religion, but it does not matter much what it is." Almost a hundred years later President Eisenhower expressed the same view: "Our government makes no sense unless it is founded on a deeply felt religious faith. And I don't care what it is."[38] Given this general tolerance of religious diversity, non-Christian faiths have little alternative but to recognize and accept America as a Christian society. They are tiny minorities among a people overwhelmingly devoted to the Christian God and His Son. "Americans have always thought of themselves as a Christian nation," Irving Kristol argues, "equally tolerant of all religions so long as they were congruent with traditional Judeo-Christian morality. But equal toleration . . . never meant perfect equality of status in fact." Christianity is not legally established, "but it is established informally, nevertheless."[39] And, Kristol warns his fellow Jews, that is a fact they must accept. Americans are still a Christian people, as they have been throughout their history.

But are they believing and practicing Christians? Has not any earlier religiosity been diluted and even dissolved over time and supplanted by a culture that is pervasively secular and irreligious if not anti-religious? These terms describe segments of American intellectual, academic, and media elites. As we have seen, they do not describe the bulk of the American people.[40] American religiosity could still be high by absolute measures and high relative to that of comparable societies, yet the secularization thesis would still be valid if the commitment of Americans to religion declined over time. Little or no evidence exists of such a decline either historically or in the late twentieth century. The one significant shift that does appear to have occurred is a drop in the 1960s and 1970s in the religious commitment of Catholics. An overall fall-off in church attendance in the 1960s was due to a decline in the proportion of Catholics attending mass every Sunday. In 1952, 83 percent of Catholics said that religion was very important in their lives; in 1987, 54 percent of Catholics said this. This shift brought Catholic attitudes on religion more into congruence with those of Protestants.[41]

In general, few other changes occurred in the religious attitudes and behavior of Americans in the last half of the twentieth century. Ninety-six percent of Americans in 1944 and 98 percent in 1968 said they believed in God, while 96 percent in 1995 said they believed in God or a universal spirit.* The proportion of Americans saying that religion was very important in their lives dropped from 70 percent in 1965 to 52 percent in 1978 and then increased to 61 percent to 65 percent in late 2002. The 1970s decline was, however, primarily among Catholics. In 1940, 37 percent of Americans said they had attended a church or synagogue in the past seven days; in 2002, 43 percent said they had. In 1940, 72 percent of Americans said they were members of a church or synagogue; in 2002, 66 percent said they were, with the decline again concentrated among Catholics in the 1970s. In an exhaustive survey of the polling data, Andrew Greeley concludes, "Only three indicators show a decline—church attendance, financial contributions, and belief in the literal interpretation of the scripture. All three declines are limited to Catholics." The causes of these Catholic declines probably include the impact of the Second Vatican Council and the unyielding position of the Church on birth control.[42]

Over the course of American history, fluctuations did occur in levels of American religious commitment and religious involvement. In some measure, these fluctuations were related to the Great Awakenings of the mid-eighteenth century, the early nineteenth century, and late nineteenth–early twentieth centuries. Little or no evidence exists, however, of a downward trend in American religiosity. The multiplication of sects and especially the explosive growth of the Methodists and Baptists in the nineteenth century significantly expanded religious involvement. Between 1775 and 1845, an almost tenfold increase occurred in the

---

* The words "or universal spirit" were added to this question in the 1970s. It is possible, although not certain, that if the original wording referring only to God had been retained, the proportion of people affirming that belief might have declined up to 13 percent. Richard Morin, *Washington Post Weekly Edition*, 1 June 1998, p. 30.

American population, while at the same time the number of Christian ministers per capita tripled, from one per fifteen hundred inhabitants to one per five hundred inhabitants. A comparable increase occurred in the number of congregations, and according to another careful study of census and denominational membership data, the percentage of Americans who were formal members of a church increased from 17 percent in 1776 to 37 percent in 1860 and then rose steadily in the twentieth century to 62 percent in 1980.[43] At the start of the twenty-first century, Americans were no less committed and quite possibly were more committed to their Christian identity than at any time in their history.

CIVIL RELIGION

"In the United States," Tocqueville said, "religion . . . is mingled with all the habits of the nation and all the feelings of patriotism, whence it derives a peculiar force." The mingling of religion and patriotism is evident in America's civil religion. Writing in the 1960s, Robert Bellah defined civil religion, "at its best" as a "genuine apprehension of universal and transcendent religious reality as seen in or, one could almost say, as revealed through the experience of the American people."[44] Civil religion enables Americans to bring together their secular politics and their religious society, to marry God and country, so as to give religious sanctity to their patriotism and nationalist legitimacy to their religious beliefs, and thus to merge what could be conflicting loyalties into loyalty to a religiously endowed country.

America's civil religion provides a religious blessing to what Americans feel they have in common. It is perfectly compatible with each American belonging to his or her own denomination, believing in a Christian or non-Christian god, or being Deist, as were several of the Founding Fathers. It is not compatible, however, with being atheist, for it is a religion, invoking a transcendental Being apart from the terrestrial human world.

The American civil religion encompasses four major elements.

First, central to it is the proposition that the American system of government rests on a religious base. It presupposes a Supreme Being. The views of the framers of the Constitution that the republican government they were creating could survive only among a people imbued with religion and morality have been endorsed and repeated by subsequent generations of American leaders. Our institutions "presuppose a Supreme Being," as Justice William O. Douglas put it, and President Eisenhower similarly declared that "Recognition of the Supreme Being is the first, the most basic expression of Americanism. Without God there could be no American form of government, nor an American way of life."[45] To deny God is to challenge the fundamental principle underlying American society and government.

A second core element of the civil religion is the belief that Americans are God's "chosen," or, in Lincoln's phrase, "almost chosen" people, that America is the "new Israel," with a divinely sanctioned mission to do good in the world. The core of the civil religion, as Conrad Cherry has said, is "the sense of America's special destiny under God."[46] Two of the three Latin phrases the Founding Fathers chose for the republic they were creating sum up this sense of mission: *Annuit Coeptis* (God smiles on our undertakings), and *Novus Ordo Seclorum* (New order for the ages).*

A third element of America's civil religion is the prevalence of religious allusions and symbols in American public rhetoric, rituals, and ceremonies. Presidents have always taken their oath of office on a Bible and, with other officials, formally assume their offices when, at the conclusion of their oaths, they utter the words, "So help me God." Except for Washington in his two-paragraph second inaugural remarks, all presidents have invoked God in their inaugural addresses and in most other major addresses as well. The speeches of some presidents, most notably Lincoln, are filled with religious resonance and biblical references. Eight words, and only eight words, appear on every piece of American currency, bills and coins: "United States of America" and "In God We Trust." Americans pledge allegiance to "one Nation under God." Major public ceremonies begin with an invocation by a clergy-

* The third was *E pluribus unum* (From many one).

man from one denomination and end with a benediction by a clergyman of a different denomination. The military services have a substantial corps of chaplains, and the daily sessions of Congress open with prayer.

Fourth, national ceremonies and activities themselves take on a religious aura and perform religious functions. Historically, as Lloyd Warner argues, celebration of Memorial Day was "an American sacred ceremony."[47] So also is the celebration of Thanksgiving, as well as presidential inaugurations and funerals. The Declaration of Independence, the Constitution, the Bill of Rights, the Gettysburg Address, Lincoln's second inaugural, Kennedy's inaugural, Martin Luther King's "I have a dream" speech have all become sacred texts defining America's identity.

The marriage of religion and politics in America's civil religion is well caught in Peter Steinfels's account of the inauguration of Bill Clinton in 1993:

> At its core [was] the solemn administration of an oath on the Bible, preceded and followed by prayers and accompanied by hymns as well as patriotic music. . . .
>
> The week was rich with religious gestures alongside moments when the religious overtones, though not explicit, were unmistakable. The inaugural week officially began with a nationwide ringing of church bells. At Howard University, Bill Clinton invoked the memory of the Rev. Dr. Martin Luther King Jr., echoing his lessons and quoting the verse from Scripture that would also close the Inaugural Address. . . .
>
> The President was surrounded throughout the day by an array of religious leaders.[48]

This was not the ceremony of a secular, much less atheistic, society or polity. As the British scholar D. W. Brogan pointed out, in the past when children recited daily the "American's Creed"* in schools, they

---

* "I believe in the United States of America as a Government of the people, by the people, for the people; whose just powers are derived from the consent of the governed; a democracy in a republic; a sovereign Nation of many sovereign States; a perfect union, one and inseparable; established upon those principles of freedom, equality, justice, and humanity for which American patriots sacrificed their lives and fortunes. I therefore believe it is my duty to my

performed a religious exercise as truly as if they began their day by saying, "I believe in God the Father Almighty" or "There is no God but God."[49] Civil religion converts Americans from religious people of many denominations into a nation with the soul of a church.

But, apart from its being American, what is that church? It is a church that has included Protestants, Catholics, Jews, other non-Christians, and even agnostics. It is, however, a church that is profoundly Christian in its origins, symbolism, spirit, accoutrements, and, most importantly, its basic assumptions about the nature of man, history, right and wrong. The Christian Bible, Christian references, biblical allusions and metaphors, permeate expressions of the civil religion. "Behind the civil religion at every point lie Biblical archetypes," Bellah has said: "Exodus, Chosen People, Promised Land, New Jerusalem, Sacrificial Death and Rebirth." Washington becomes Moses, Lincoln becomes Christ. "The deepest source of the symbols, beliefs and rituals of the [civil] religion," Conrad Cherry agrees, "lies in the Old and New Testaments."[50] America's civil religion is a nondenominational, national religion and, in its articulated form, not expressly a Christian religion. Yet it is thoroughly Christian in its origins, content, assumptions, and tone. The God in whom their currency says Americans trust is implicitly the Christian God. Two words, nonetheless, do not appear in civil religion statements and ceremonies. They are "Jesus Christ."* While the American Creed is Protestantism without God, the American civil religion is Christianity without Christ.

---

country to love it; to support its Constitution; to obey its laws; to respect its flag, and to defend it against all enemies."

* The violation of this prohibition by the Reverend Franklin Graham at the inauguration of President George W. Bush provoked much criticism. Bush explicitly proclaimed his faith in Christ during his presidential campaign (see Chapter 12). Perhaps in response to the criticism of Graham, he quite consciously did not do this in his many expressions of faith as president (*New York Times*, 9 February 2003, sect. 4, p. 4).

CHAPTER 6

Emergence, Triumph, Erosion

THE FRAGILITY OF NATIONS

Nations and nationalism have been key features of the West since the eighteenth century. In the twentieth century they became central to peoples throughout the world. "The supreme claims of his nation upon the individual," as Isaiah Berlin summarized the nationalist case, "are based on the fact that its life and ends and history alone give life and meaning to all he is and does." In a similar vein, John Mack noted: "There are but a few commitments for which men will kill others or will voluntarily surrender their own lives. The defence of the nation, if it is felt to be threatened, is one of them."[1] Yet the identity of nations is not fixed and permanent, and nationalism is not a uniformly pervasive force overriding all else. A nation exists only when a group of people think of themselves as a nation, and their conceptions of themselves may be highly fungible. In addition, the significance of their national commitment as compared to other commitments may vary greatly. As described in Chapter 2, European governments at times had to expend great efforts to mold the people they governed into a cohesive entity and create a sense of common national identity. National identities, like other identities, are constructed and deconstructed, upgraded and downgraded, embraced and rejected. Different peoples rate national identity differently compared to their other identities, and the relative salience and intensity of national identity for any one people changes over time.

As late-twentieth-century history amply demonstrates, there is nothing fixed about nations and nation-states; they come and go. More than many European nations, the American nation is a fragile and recent human construction.

From the seventeenth century to the end of the twentieth, the salience for Americans of their national identity compared to other identities evolved through four phases. In only one of these phases did Americans clearly elevate their national identity over other identities. In the seventeenth and early eighteenth centuries, the free people living in Britain's North American colonies had much in common in terms of race, ethnicity, political values, language, culture, and religion, which they shared in large part with the people of the British Isles. Until the mid-eighteenth century their identities and loyalties were to their individual settlements and colonies, to Virginia, Pennsylvania, New York, or Massachusetts, and at a broader level to the British Crown. A collective sense of American identity emerged only in the decades leading up to the Revolution. Second, with independence and the emigration of the loyalists, the claims of a British identity disappeared, but state identities remained preeminent. Competing local, sectional, and partisan identities became more salient, and particularly after 1830, national identity was increasingly contested and problematical. Third, after the Civil War the supremacy of national identity became firmly established, and the era from the 1870s to the 1970s was for America the century of nationalism triumphant. In the 1960s and 1970s the primacy of national identity came under challenge. Massive new numbers of immigrants were able to maintain close ties with their country of origin, sustaining dual loyalties, dual nationalities, and often dual citizenship. Subnational racial, ethnic, gender, and cultural identities took on new importance for many Americans. Elements of America's intellectual, political, and business elites increasingly downgraded their commitment to their nation and gave privilege to transnational and subnational claims on their loyalties.

September 11 brought this fourth phase to a sharp halt and dramatically restored the primacy of national identity over other identities for virtually all Americans. Two years later this new preeminence of national identity was subsiding. Conceivably this process could continue and the phase four pattern of identities reappear. Or the revelation of America's new vulnerability to attack, the need for massive efforts to insure the security of the homeland, and the realization that America exists in a largely unfriendly world, could generate a new and different phase in the salience of their nation for Americans.

CREATING AN AMERICAN IDENTITY

In January 1760 Benjamin Franklin hailed Wolfe's defeat of the French on the Plains of Abraham and proudly proclaimed, "I am a Briton."[2] In July 1776, Franklin signed the Declaration renouncing his British identity. In a few years Franklin transformed himself from a Briton into an American. He was not alone. Between the 1740s and the 1770s a large proportion of the settlers in North America also changed their identity from British to American while maintaining even more intense loyalties to their states and localities. This was a quick and dramatic shift in collective identities. The causes of this rapid emergence of an American identity are complex. The following are among the more important ones.

First, the Great Awakening of the 1730s and 1740s, as was pointed out in Chapter 4, for the first time in their history brought people from all the colonies together in a common social, emotional, and religious experience. It was a truly American movement and promoted a sense of a transcolony consciousness, ideas, and themes, which were subsequently transferred from a religious to a political context.

Second, for half of the seventy-four years between 1689 and 1763 Americans fought with the British in five wars against the French and their Indian allies. Even when France and Britain were at peace Americans engaged in shorter, localized but still bloody conflicts with the Indians. These wars did not, in themselves, promote or retard the development of American consciousness. American symbols in colonial newspapers, according to Richard Merritt's analysis, peaked at the start of the War of Jenkins' Ear (1739–1742) and the French and Indian or

Seven Years War (1756–1763), declined during the course of these wars, and turned up slightly at the end. The wars were, nonetheless, a shared experience for the colonists. Their settlements were raided and on occasion seized, pillaged, and destroyed. War and the threat of war were the continuing reality for American colonists. In these wars, the colonists learned the ways of successful combat and developed the ability to organize militia forces. They also acquired military self-confidence, comparing their performance to that of their enemies and their English allies. War makes nations, and, as S. M. Grant has observed, "Warfare lies at the heart of the American national experience."[3]

Third, as a consequence of these wars, particularly the Seven Years War (which lasted nine years, 1754–1763, in America), the British government felt it had to levy new taxes on its colonists to cover the past, present, and future costs of defending them, to improve and centralize revenue collection and other aspects of colonial governance, and to quarter troops in some colonies, which it expected them to support financially. These measures provoked protests and opposition in individual colonies and then collective action. Massachusetts initiated the first effort at joint political protest in 1764, which was followed by the Sons of Liberty and the Stamp Act Congress in 1765, the committees of correspondence in 1773, and the First Continental Congress in 1774. The sense of grievance and opposition to the British was furthered by the actions of British troops, most famously the Boston Massacre (1770).

Fourth, the expansion of intercolonial communication facilitated the growth of one colony's knowledge of and interest in the affairs of other colonies. The "amount of intercolonial news carried by the newspapers" in five cities surveyed by Merritt "increased sixfold and more from the late 1730s to the early 1770s." The reactions of the colonists to the early actions of the British government "were isolated, and hence to a large measure ineffective. As the facilities for intercolonial communication improved, however, and as the colonists began to focus more and more of their attention upon the American community, such tones of dissatisfaction could find echoes throughout the continent."[4]

Fifth, the abundance of fertile land, rapid population growth, and the dynamic expansion of trade created new agricultural and commercial elites and a widespread sense of the opportunity for future wealth among the colonists, particularly compared with what they saw as the extensive poverty in their class-ridden home country. While still thinking of themselves as British they also became convinced that America would be the future center of the British Empire.

Finally, outsiders are likely to perceive people who share something in common as a collective entity before those people do and even if major differences exist among them. Looking at their North American colonies from London, the British saw them as a whole before the colonists did. "The British worried about the whole," John M. Murrin states, "because they did not understand the parts, and they reified their concerns into a totality they called America. . . . In a word, America was Britain's idea." Merritt's study of the colonial press documents this judgment. In five major newspapers in Boston, New York, Philadelphia, Williamsburg, and Charleston between 1735 and 1775, articles by English writers "preceded American writers in identifying both the land and its people as 'American.' "[5]

These developments stimulated emergence of an American identity distinct from British, imperial, or colonial identity. Before 1740 the term "America" described a territory not a society. Beginning then, however, the colonists and others began to speak of Americans collectively. Participants in the War of Jenkins' Ear called each other "Europeans" and "Americans." Development of an American consciousness proceeded rapidly. The "evidence," according to E. McClung Fleming, "suggests that the identification of an American community distinct from the British had taken place by 1755 and was widely accepted by 1766."[6] In the century's third quarter Americans thus became increasingly aware of their collective identity. According to Merritt, about 6.5 percent of American place-name symbols in the colonial press between 1735 and 1761 referred to the colonies as a single unit, while 25.8 percent did between 1762 and 1775. In addition, after 1763, "symbols of American origin more often identified the colonies as American than British in every year save two, 1765 and 1766." The explosion in American consciousness in 1763 is dramatically illustrated in Figure 6.1 (reproduced from Merritt), which shows the distribution over time of three key sets of symbols.[7]

Nation building in America differed from that in Europe, where po-

Figure 6.1

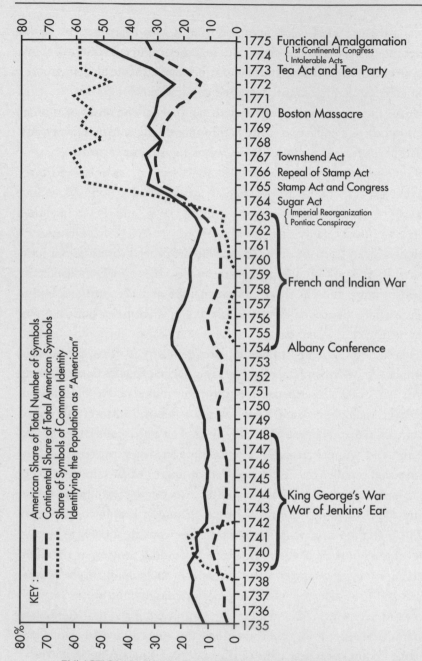

KEY:

— American Share of Total Number of Symbols
‒ ‒ Continental Share of Total American Symbols
······ Share of Symbols of Common Identity
  Identifying the Population as "American"

1775	Functional Amalgamation
1774	{ 1st Continental Congress / Intolerable Acts
1773	Tea Act and Tea Party
1772	
1771	
1770	Boston Massacre
1769	
1768	
1767	Townshend Act
1766	Repeal of Stamp Act
1765	Stamp Act and Congress
1764	Sugar Act
1763	{ Imperial Reorganization / Pontiac Conspiracy
1762	
1761	
1760	
1759	French and Indian War
1758	
1757	
1756	
1755	
1754	Albany Conference
1753	
1752	
1751	
1750	
1749	
1748	
1747	
1746	
1745	
1744	King George's War
1743	War of Jenkins' Ear
1742	
1741	
1740	
1739	
1738	
1737	
1736	
1735	

FUNCTIONAL AMALGAMATION, FORMATIVE EVENTS,
CURVES OF AMERICAN COMMUNITY AWARENESS, 1735–1775
A Comparison, Using "Moving Averages"

Source: Richard L. Merritt, *Symbols of American Community 1735–1775* (New Haven: Yale University Press, 1966), p. 144. Copyright Richard L. Merritt. Reprinted with permission.

litical leaders created a state and then tried to create a nation out of the people they were attempting to rule. In America, in contrast, collective experiences, together with the leadership of widely dispersed elites, created a common consciousness among people, who fought for and won their independence, and then created minimal central political institutions, which, as European visitors throughout the nineteenth century observed, did not really constitute a state in the European sense.

NATIONAL VS. OTHER IDENTITIES

American victory in the Revolution had two major consequences for American identity. First, it removed conclusively the possibility of the Atlantic seaboard settlers identifying themselves as Britons, British colonists, or subjects of His Britannic Majesty. The Revolution, however, was, as Adams recognized, a revolution in the hearts and minds of only some of the people. A substantial minority, Adams estimated a third, of the colonial population maintained their loyalty to the Crown. When the Crown lost, these people had to either abandon their British identity or emigrate. Many were not given a choice and were forced to leave. All told, perhaps 100,000 loyalists went to Canada, Britain, and the West Indies, their properties confiscated by state governments. This process removed any possibility of a reunification of Britain and America. Second, victory in the war also removed the enemy against whom Americans had been fighting. It ended the major reason for elevating national identity over other identities and for making ideology the central component of that identity. It thus initiated a prolonged period in which national identity was under recurring challenge from the proponents of subnational, sectional, state, and partisan identities.

The Revolution made colonists Americans, but it did not make them a nation. Whether they were was until 1865 a debatable issue. The Declaration of Independence makes no reference to an American nation but rather to "Free and Independent States." Early in their work, the members of the Constitutional Convention voted unanimously to delete the word "national" from the document they were drafting and to substitute "the United States" for "national government."* Elbridge Gerry summed up the uncertainty when he said that "We were neither the same nation nor different nations." In 1792 Fisher Ames went further: "Instead of feeling as a Nation, a State is our country." Jefferson agreed with this sentiment and often referred to Virginia as his "nation" although he did, when secretary of state, also argue that France and America were both "nations" with a continuing existence apart from their systems of government. In the debates leading up to the Civil War, Southerners rejected this contention. "I never use the word 'Nation' in speaking of the United States," John C. Calhoun declared in 1849; "I always use the word 'Union' or 'Confederacy.' We are not a Nation, but a Union, a Confederacy of equal and sovereign States." Even a strong proponent of national authority, John Marshall, qualified his use of the term: "America has chosen to be, in many respects and to many purposes, a nation." In the controversies over states' rights and nullification, people on all sides commonly referred to their country by the neutral and ambiguous term "the Union." Those opposing national authority emphasized that it was a "union of *States,*" created by the mutual agreement of these independent entities and hence quite distinct from a homogeneous or integrated nation. Nationalists like Andrew Jackson and Daniel Webster, on the other hand, hailed "*the Union,*" without specifying what it was a union of but also not calling it a nation.[8]

In its early decades many people including its creators viewed the sustained existence of the Union as highly uncertain. Despite Madison's argument to the contrary, most people believed that only small countries could be republics. The United States was a huge country and hence it would have to become a monarchy or subdivide into smaller entities. Jefferson saw the likelihood of the emergence, at the very least, of a federation of the Atlantic and a federation of the Mississippi. There was, as Henry Steele Commager argued, "nothing foreordained about this triumph of nationalism and consolidation." English-speaking America could have become divided as Spanish-speaking America did.[9]

---

* This deletion mired Americans in a semantic inaccuracy. They typically refer to the government in Washington as "the federal government," whereas it is technically the national government in a federal system of government that also includes state governments.

Between the Revolution and the Civil War, national identity competed with state, sectional, and partisan identities. Before 1830 nationalist sentiments achieved some success in this competition. While alive,
Washington was a commanding national presence and a charismatic
symbol of national unity.[10] After his death, he remained the most revered
and in some respects the only unanimously revered figure among the
Founding Fathers. The victory of the "war hawks" in the 1810 elections,
anticipation of the conquest of Canada, and outrage at the British interference with American shipping, generated a surge of nationalism, outside of New England, leading to the War of 1812. The outcome of the
war, particularly Jackson's victory at New Orleans, renewed these nationalist sentiments. A final wave of nationalism occurred in 1824–1826,
prompted by Lafayette's extraordinary tour of the country, "which occa-
sioned," one scholar has argued, "an orgy of celebration unsurpassed
before or since for sheer scale and excitement."[11] This wave culminated
in the fiftieth anniversary of the Declaration of Independence on July 4,
1826, and the deaths that day of both John Adams and Thomas Jefferson. Awed by the statistical improbability of these three events coincid-
ing, Americans easily concluded that this could only be a definitive
message from on high that they were indeed God's Chosen People.

More generally, other identities competed vigorously with and often
surpassed the identification of Americans with the broader union. In
1803 and again in 1814–1815, representatives of the New England
states met to talk confederation and possible secession. In 1807 Aaron
Burr purportedly conspired to promote the secession of at least some of
trans-Appalachia. From the Kentucky and Virginia Resolutions of
1799–1800 until the Civil War, state governments often asserted the
right to "nullify" or otherwise prevent the enforcement of laws enacted
by the national government. Until 1815, partisan loyalties and rivalries
also were intense, in part because Federalists and Republicans, representing different economic interests, identified with different sides in
the French revolutionary wars. Symptomatic of the salience of partisan
over national identities were the separate celebrations of July 4th by the
two parties.

A nation, as Benedict Anderson said, is an imagined community, but
it is more specifically a remembered community, a community with an

imagined history, and it is defined by its historical memory of itself. No nation exists in the absence of a national history, enshrining in the minds of its people common memories of their travails and triumphs, heroes and villains, enemies and wars, defeats and victories. By this criterion, for much of the early nineteenth century the United States was not a nation because it did not have a national history. "For at least a half-century after the Declaration of Independence," Daniel Boorstin observes, "it was generally assumed that a history of the United States would consist of a history in turn of each of the states. The history of states and regions seemed primary; the history of the United States seemed contrived and derivative." State and local historical societies were created to perpetuate, to glorify, and to promote the importance of their respective states and localities, while efforts to create a national historical society came to naught.[12] Scholars who wished to turn to the national past wrote biographies of local heroes promoting them as national heroes.

The only important and comprehensive pre–Civil War history of America by an American was George Bancroft's great work *A History of the United States*, which appeared in ten volumes from 1834 to 1874. The first nine volumes dealt with American history from the earliest European settlements to the Revolution. America's mission in the world, Bancroft argued, was to promote human freedom. His work was immensely popular, and he became, Boorstin reports, the "high priest of American nationality" precisely because of the "very weaknesses of the American national spirit in the early decades of national life, the prevalence of conflicting localisms, the vagueness and confusion about the meaning and purpose of the nation." Despite Bancroft's impact, however, "Not until after the Civil War would a national perspective on American history begin to seem normal." This "great pioneer 'national' history," Boorstin comments, "described the country before it had become the nation."[13]

Following 1830, nationalism gave way to sectionalism and renewed partisanship. A "singleminded focus on patriotism and national unity," John Bodnar argues, "reached a peak in 1825." Wilbur Zelinsky agrees that nationalism hit a high point in 1824–1826, after which it declined rapidly. By the 1830s national politics was characterized, Bodnar says, by "the exacerbation of class, ethnic, and regional tensions caused by economic growth and the rise of a strong Democratic Party." National loyalty "now had increased competition. More commemorative attention was given to local, state, and regional pasts, so much so that . . . parochial attitudes made it difficult to muster sufficient public support for an appropriate celebration of the centennial of Washington's birth in 1832." In the years before the Civil War, Lyn Spillman similarly argues, "Regional and local concerns overdetermined most expressions of nationality. Fragmentation and localization were encouraged." Even in the Civil War, "troops on both sides viewed their national army service in fundamentally local terms."[14]

The declining salience of national identity in the three decades before the Civil War was encouraged by two profound changes in the American environment. First, of course, the emergence of the abolitionist movement, increasing conflict of economic interests between North and South, and the dynamic expansion westward all brought slavery to the top of the national agenda. Second, before the 1820s the United States faced threats to its security from the three great powers of Europe: the British to the north and east, the French to the west, and the Spanish to the south. By purchasing and seizing the French and Spanish territories and reaching accommodation with the British in the Rush-Bagot agreement and the Monroe Doctrine, America moved into a long century in which it faced no significant foreign threats to its territory, security, or survival. It did, however, as Commager points out, have two enemies. The Indians engaged Americans almost continuously in violent warfare until the 1890s. They were "a focus for fear" for Americans moving westward on the frontier. They were not, however, a significant threat to the American people as a whole. Americans were confident that their superior numbers, technology, social and intellectual skills, economic resources, and civilization guaranteed their eventual triumph. The Indians, as Commager says, were the perfect enemy for Americans because they seemed so vicious and yet also were so weak.

The second nineteenth-century enemy for Americans was the European old order. Americans viewed with contempt and disgust the lack of liberty, equality, democracy, and the rule of law in most European states characterized by monarchy, aristocracy, and the remnants of feudalism.

America, in contrast, was the epitome and citadel of republican virtue. The ideological component that had been added to American identity by the Revolution made this distinction of crucial importance. The European old order was the relevant other for Americans, who believed they represented the bright, open, prosperous, democratic future. Americans sympathized with efforts to promote democratic change in Europe, manifest most notably in the 1848 revolutions following which they gave the Hungarian patriot Lajos Kossuth a hero's welcome. Most importantly, however, they wanted to take advantage of distance and maintain their virtues and advantages uncorrupted by Europe.

The Indians were near but weak. The Europeans were strong but distant. Each was an enemy, but neither was a credible threat. In addition, American victory in the Mexican War of 1846–1848 removed the possibility of considering that country a potential threat. America was safe and secure with a continental territory to occupy, exploit, and develop without interference by foreign powers. The lack of an external threat allowed Americans to focus on their sectional, economic, and policy differences, rooted in the controversy over slavery and its possible extension to these new territories. In 1837 Abraham Lincoln presciently warned of the potential consequences of the loss of an external foe. Reflecting on American memories of their revolutionary struggle for independence and security against foreign powers, he argued that through their "powerful influence" the

> jealousy, envy, and avarice incident to our nature, and so common to a state of peace, prosperity, and conscious strength, were for the time in a great measure smothered and rendered inactive, while the deep-rooted principles of hate, and the powerful motive of revenge, instead of being turned against each other, were directed exclusively against the British nation. And thus, from the force of circumstances, the basest principles of our nature were either made to lie dormant, or to become the active agents in the advancement of the noblest of causes—that of establishing and maintaining civil and religious liberty.
>
> But this state of feeling must fade, is fading, has faded, with the circumstances that produced it.[15]

With that fading, Americans directed their hatred, jealousy, envy, and avarice against each other and moved down the road to civil war. And on April 14, 1861, the flag that had waved through the night over Fort McHenry was hauled down at Fort Sumter.

NATION AND PATRIOTISM TRIUMPHANT

National Consciousness. The Civil War, James Russell Lowell said as it concluded, was "costly stuff whereof to make a nation!" But make a nation it did. The American nation was born in the war and came into its full being in the decades after the war. So also did American nationalism, patriotism, and the unqualified identification of Americans with their country. American patriotism before the war, Ralph Waldo Emerson observed, had been a sometime, summertime thing. The "deaths of thousands and the determination of millions of men and women" in the war, however, showed that American patriotism now "is real."[16] Before the war Americans and others referred to their country in the plural: "These United States are . . ." After the war they used the singular. The Civil War, Woodrow Wilson said in his 1915 Memorial Day address, "created in this country what had never existed before—a national consciousness." That consciousness manifested itself in a variety of ways in the decades following the war. "The late nineteenth century," Lyn Spillman affirms, "was the period of greatest innovation in American national identity. . . . Most patriotic practices, organizations, and symbols familiar today date from or became institutionalized at that time."[17]

The years immediately following the war saw a surge of nationalist sentiment. "Publicists, intellectuals, and politicians," Morton Keller observes, "indulged in a rhetoric of triumphant nationalism." When former abolitionists wanted to establish a successor to Garrison's *Liberator*, they quite naturally named it *The Nation*. Virtually everyone identified the United States as their nation. In the debates over adoption of the Fifteenth Amendment, a few opponents, such as Senator Willard Saulsbury of Delaware, argued to the contrary; they were, however, decisively and overwhelmingly rebuffed, by an overwhelming majority, whose views were reflected in Indiana senator Oliver Morton's response:

> The Senator told us to-day frankly that we are not one people. He said . . . after the culmination of a war that cost this nation six hundred thousand lives, that we are not a nation. . . . He gave us to understand that he belonged to the tribe of the Delawares, an independent and sovereign tribe living on a reservation . . . near the city of Philadelphia. . . . I assert that we are one people . . . we are one nation.[18]

Before the war secession was a possible option not just in the South; after 1865 it becomes unthinkable and unmentioned. Nationalism subsided somewhat in the 1870s and early 1880s but then reappeared with renewed force in the late 1880s and 1890s. There was, as John Higham said, an "intensification of nationalism in the period from 1886 to 1924."[19] During the Great Depression, nationalist sentiments gave way to economic and political preoccupations. They came back, however, in their fullest force in the rallying and mobilization of Americans in World War II. The ideological and security threat Americans perceived from the Soviet Union sustained the salience of national identity until the 1960s when social, economic, and cultural divisions created and reinforced other identities. The diminution and eventual disappearance of the Soviet threat in the 1980s further lowered the salience of national identity. The century from the 1860s to the 1960s was, thus, the century of American nationalism, that period in American history when national identity was strongest compared to other identities and when Americans of all classes, regions, and ethnic groups competed in expressing their nationalism and demonstrating their patriotism.

Economic Development and National Organizations. Union victory in the Civil War made America a nation, and after that victory many factors combined to make nationalism preeminent. Of primary importance were rapid industrialization and economic growth. Nationalist assertion and expansion have gone with intense economic development and industrialization in many societies, including Britain, France, Germany, Japan, China, Russia, and the Soviet Union. It is not surprising that this also occurred in the United States. The multiplication of economic activities and wealth creates pride in one's country, a sense of growing power, and the felt need to establish the rightful place of the country in the world of nations and to secure recognition of this new status. Improvements in transportation and communication, particularly completion of the transcontinental railroad in 1869, and the rapid introduction of the telephone following its invention in 1876, enhanced the ability of Americans to interact with each other and promoted their development of a national consciousness.

The emergence of an integrated national economy was accompanied by the dramatic increase in the number, size, and activities of corporations operating on a national scale. The heads of these organizations had to think in national terms and to subordinate attachments to individual states and localities. Coincidentally Americans also created, as Robert Putnam and Theda Skocpol have separately demonstrated, an unprecedented number of national voluntary associations. Half of all the mass membership organizations that ever enrolled one percent of the adult male or female American people were created between 1870 and 1920.[20] These national organizations quite naturally directed the attention and interests of their members to national issues and concerns. The development of national identity was a popular, not a governmental, enterprise. Governments, particularly the national government, played little or no role in it. The initiative came from a myriad of private and local individuals and groups. As Professor Cecilia O'Leary says:

> Beginning in the 1880s, organized patriots initiated campaigns to establish new national anniversaries; lobbied for additions to the nation's pantheon of heroes; urged the teaching of U.S. history and civics in the public schools; agitated for flag reverence and the daily pledge of allegiance; ushered in the greatest era in monument building, established national shrines and mapped out historical pilgrimages; and organized petition drives and congressional hearings to legislate patriotism.[21]

The first and probably the most important nationalist organization was the Grand Army of the Republic, formed in 1866. As Wilbur Zelinsky says, it "quickly grew into a powerful force in the political and symbolic life of the nation . . . and more than any other single group was responsible for the propagation of nationalistic ritual on a mass scale." It was followed by the Veterans of Foreign Wars, organized after the Spanish-American War, and the American Legion, after World War I. These were truly mass organizations with branches in communities throughout the country. They devoted much of their programs to promoting national identity and patriotism. In addition in the 1890s, "great numbers of patriotic-hereditary organizations materialized or came to the fore," including the Daughters of the American Revolution, the Sons of the American Revolution, the Colonial Dames of America, and the Mayflower Descendants (all formed between 1889 and 1897). Subsequently the Boy Scouts, Girl Scouts, and Camp Fire Girls came into being, committed, among other things, to encouraging devotion to America among its youth. Many fraternal organizations also were formed during these years, with a variety of purposes and activities. Their "common characteristic," however, Zelinsky emphasizes, ". . . was the promotion of national loyalty through rituals, publications, and civic activities." [22]

Before the Civil War the national government was a relatively weak and minuscule institution. The war started a sustained expansion of its activities. New departments were added: Agriculture (1862), Justice (1870), Commerce (1903), and Labor (1913). The federal (or national) government asserted its control over immigration in the 1870s and created the Interstate Commerce Commission to regulate the railroads in 1890. This accretion of functions continued steadily and then accelerated during the Great Depression. World War II left an even more expanded government; and the Cold War added an unprecedented, large defense establishment. Beginning with Theodore Roosevelt, the presidency also took on new status, authority, and importance as the nation's central political institution.

These years saw not only an enhanced role of the national government in the nation but also the increased role of the nation and its government in the world. In the 1880s the United States, for the first time in its history, began to acquire colonial territories with substantial non-

American populations, which were, hence, unlikely to become states of the Union. The United States also began expanding its navy which in three decades would become the equal of Britain's. The Spanish-American War was a nationalist fiesta, extending American presence in East Asia, and adding significantly to the budding colonial empire. The completion of the huge engineering project involved in building the Panama Canal, following the American separation of Panama from Colombia, further reinforced the new position of the United States in world affairs. Beginning with what Higham termed the "minor international controversies" of the 1880s and 1890s, American public opinion took on a distinct nationalist and jingoist cast, enhanced by the spectacular and quick victory in the war with Spain, the completion of the Canal, and the voyage of the Great White Fleet around the world in 1908.[23]

North-South Reconciliation. A central component of post–Civil War nationalism had to be and was the reconciliation of North and South in a common commitment to a unified nation. Following the end of Reconstruction, the withdrawal of federal troops from the South, and the Grand Compromise of 1877 over the presidency, this reconciliation proceeded forward at the price of effectively excluding the freed slaves from the nation. The process of reintegration was at first slow and halting and during the 1870s and 1880s "nearly all of the [Southern] animus against outsiders centered on the northern Yankee." In the 1870s, however, Confederate veterans volunteered to fight in the Indian wars so as to demonstrate that "we who are soldiers of the 'lost cause' are not deficient in patriotism." By 1897 the annual encampment of the Grand Army of the Republic was reaching out to Confederate veterans with the slogan, "one country, one flag, one people, one destiny." The next year the Spanish-American War brought the country together. "The War of 1898," Higham argues, "completed a stage in sectional reconciliation by turning the martial ardor of the Confederate tradition into a patriotic crusade, by linking all parts of the country in a common purpose, and by giving the South an opportunity to demonstrate a passionate national loyalty." President William McKinley made a point of offering high-level commissions to former Confederate officers, a move that "enthused the South" with the result that "applications poured into recruitment offices for the newly organized volunteer army. Regiments from all the Southern states filled their quotas quickly."[24]

In the aftermath, the contributions of black soldiers to the war were generally ignored, white Southern soldiers were hailed for their valor, and Congress returned to the Southerners their Confederate battle flags. Localities began to erect joint monuments to the Blue and the Gray, and in 1910 the commander of the Grand Army of the Republic saluted the contributions of the Southerners to the war with Spain for their "loyalty and devotion" to their country. As a result of the war, he said, "we had a new union. No Northerners, no Southerners, but Americans all." The reconciliation culminated in the celebration of the fiftieth anniversary of the battle of Gettysburg in 1913 in which fifty thousand Union and Confederate veterans participated together with patriotic groups from all over the country, saluting the heroism of both sides, and joining together, President Wilson said, "as brothers and comrades in arms, enemies no longer."[25]

National History. The writing and teaching of American history, fragmentary and neglected before the Civil War, blossomed in the nationalist era. "American historiography," Zelinsky notes, "did not become fully institutionalized until the 1880s with the creation of the university chairs and departments and a nationwide professional association with erudite journals and annual conventions." Educators and politicians promoted the teaching of American history. Before the Civil War only six states required the teaching of history in public schools. By 1900 twenty-three did.[26] Schools were explicitly directed to teach patriotism, and manuals of patriotism were prepared and circulated to serve this end. In the words of Merle Curti, educators "emphasized the importance of presenting vividly and attractively to children the glorious deeds of American heroes, the sacrifices and bravery of our soldiers and sailors in wartime, the personalities of the presidents, who might properly be regarded as symbols of the nation in the manner in which royal personages of Europe were regarded. By the 1890s, state after state was requiring by law that subjects deemed peculiarly fitted to inculcating patriotism, such as American history and civics, be taught on every educational level below the college."[27] From the 1880s onward, according to Zelinsky, American schools were "obliged to assume an even greater burden than ever for ideological indoctrination and preserving national unity. . . . The newly formed patriotic-hereditary and veterans organizations went to some pains to make certain that American history and ideals were being properly taught in the schools. In addition to imbibing nationalism from their history, civics, geography, and literary textbooks, the pupils also learned flag etiquette and the Pledge of Allegiance." In classes, textbooks, and ceremonies, children were indoctrinated as they had not been before in the glories of the *Mayflower*, the Minute Men, the Founding Fathers, pioneers, and the great presidents. This tradition continued into the interwar period. The vast majority of almost four hundred textbooks published between 1915 and 1930 were nationalistic, according to one scholar's analysis. "The American is taught to respect and to venerate his forebears and the institution which they designed and developed."[28]

Patriotic Rituals and Symbols. During the post–Civil War decades people also inaugurated, developed, and increasingly engaged in a wide range of patriotic symbols, rituals, and ceremonies. The nationalist surge was greatly promoted by and to some extent triggered by the centennial celebrations starting in 1875. The high point of these was the Centennial Exhibition in 1876 in Philadelphia: a financial disaster but in every other way "a smashing triumph" with almost 10 million admissions to it from a country with a total population of 46 million. The dedication of the Statue of Liberty in 1886 and the Columbian Exposition in Chicago in 1893 generated renewed pride in, enthusiasm for, and rhetoric on the virtues and achievements of the great American nation. These ceremonials, particularly those related to 1876, "served to remind the American people of their past and of the nation's achievements."[29] They helped to stimulate the formation, particularly in the 1890s, of over five hundred new patriotic societies.

Before the Civil War only July 4th and Washington's birthday had been celebrated on anything like a national basis, with the latter observed only sporadically and intermittently by various political subdivisions, and celebration of the former often undertaken by competing philanthropic, partisan, and interest groups. After the war, Independence Day was celebrated on a more national and a more united basis by local communities. A national day of Thanksgiving was first proclaimed by President Lincoln in 1863. In the decades after the war, Thanksgiving became an occasion for a deep national-religious ritual. "School children listened to Pilgrim lore, ministers preached special sermons associating religion and patriotism in the traditional manner, and the appropriate dinner became a national institution."[30] Memorial Day was created immediately after the Civil War. Zelinsky reports that, "Several localities in both the North and South invented the holiday almost simultaneously and quite independently in 1866 or thereabouts; but it was especially popular in the former, and by 1891 it had become a legal holiday in every northern state. . . . For some years, Americans observed the day with fitting solemnity and care, and, in a manner replicating the earlier Independence Days, parades, orations, military maneuvers, graveyard decorations, and the dedication of monuments were all in order."[31]

Most nations have several symbols of their identity and the United States is no exception: Uncle Sam, Brother Jonathan, the Statue of Liberty, the Liberty Bell, Yankee Doodle, the bald eagle, *Novus Ordo Seclorum, E Pluribus Unum*, In God We Trust. The United States is an exception, however, in the extent to which its flag predominates over all other symbols and has been pervasively present in the American landscape. In most countries the national flag is displayed at public buildings and national monuments, but not often elsewhere. In the United States, in contrast, the national flag is flown before homes and businesses, in concert halls and sports stadiums, in clubs and classrooms. Wilbur Zelinsky reports that on his personal observations in ten states in 1981 and 1982, he found the flag displayed at all government buildings, "well over" 50 percent of factories and warehouses, 25 percent to 30 percent of shops and office buildings, and at 4.7 percent of private homes.[32] Although no exact comparative statistics exist, it seems probable that in almost no other country is the flag so pervasively present and so central to national identity. The national anthem is a salute to the flag. Americans pledge allegiance "to the flag of the United States of America and to the Republic for which it stands . . ." That is, first to the symbol of the country and then to the country. The proper use of the flag is prescribed by an elaborate code of etiquette, formulated in the early twentieth century. Americans even have a special holiday, Flag Day, to honor their flag.

This cult of the flag was a major product of the Civil War and the subsequent patriotic era. Before the Civil War, as M. M. Quaife says, "the vast majority of Americans . . . seldom, if ever, saw the Stars and Stripes, and never, until the Mexican War of 1846–48, fought under it" and hence "did not possess the sentiment of love for the Flag which today is shared by all Americans." That sentiment first erupted when, to the surprise and shock of Northerners, the flag came down on Fort Sumter. The Civil War encouraged for the first time the display of the national flag. "The cult of the national flag, as it has endured to this day, was a direct outcome of the Great Rebellion." The first Flag Day was celebrated in 1877, and Woodrow Wilson proclaimed it a national holiday in 1916. "From the late 1880s onward, and especially during the 1890s, organized zeal on behalf of the flag attained fever pitch." The Grand Army of the Republic and many other groups campaigned to have flags flying at every schoolhouse, and by 1905 nineteen states had passed laws requiring this.[33]

The flag, as many scholars have pointed out, became essentially a religious symbol, the equivalent of the cross for Christians. It was revered. It was central to all public and many private ceremonies. People were expected to stand in its presence, remove their hats, and, when appropriate, salute it. Schoolchildren in almost all states were required daily to pledge allegiance to it. During the nationalist era, many states passed laws prohibiting the "desecration of the flag," reflecting its quasi-religious status for Americans. In 1907 the United States Supreme Court upheld the constitutionality of one such law, sustaining the judgment of the Supreme Court of Nebraska that the flag must be protected just as religious symbols are kept sacred. "The flag is the emblem of national authority," the Nebraska court said. "To the citizen it is an object of patriotic adoration, emblematic of all for which his country stands— her institutions, her achievements, her long roster of heroic dead, the story of her past, the promise of her future."[34]

The Assimilation Debate. In 1908 Israel Zangwill's play *The Melting Pot* provoked widespread discussion and an enthusiastic endorsement from President Theodore Roosevelt. The play brought to the fore a confused debate that had been developing over the ways and the possibility of assimilating the new immigrants flooding into the country. Did assimilation mean that immigrants would and should absorb and be absorbed into the Anglo-Protestant culture of the founding settlers? Or did it mean that they would and should join with the descendants of settlers, slaves, conquerees, and prior immigrants to create a new American culture and "the new American man"? Or was the creation of a common culture either undesirable or impossible, and should or must America be a conglomeration of peoples with different cultures? These questions went to the heart of America's ethnic and cultural identity. The three concepts developed in response to these questions framed debates over assimilation for the following century. In keeping with the prevalence of metaphors, particularly culinary ones, in the debates over assimilation,* they can be labeled the melting pot, tomato soup, and salad concepts of assimilation.

The melting pot concept had been initially set forth by Hector St. John de Crèvecoeur in the 1780s. In America, he argued, "individuals of

---

* Since Zangwill, the temptation to phrase discussions of assimilation in metaphorical terms has seemed irresistible. In his classic essay on the melting pot, Philip Gleason lists more than a dozen other metaphors analysts have used to make vivid assimilation or the lack of it in America: pressure cooker, stew, salad, mixing bowl, mosaic, kaleidoscope, rainbow, irradiation, orchestra, dance, weaving machine, pipeline dumping ground, village pound, catch basin, cul-de-sac. Culinary metaphors, however, seem to abound; and as Gleason comments, "It is probably indicative of something about our national character that culinary symbolism supplies more replacements for the melting pot than any other source." Perhaps even more indicative is the fact that the melting pot in its original meaning had nothing to do with food; it was a synonym for a crucible, that is, a place for the fusing of metals. Philip Gleason, "The Melting Pot: Symbol of Fusion or Confusion?" *American Quarterly*, 16 (Spring 1964), p. 32.

all nations are melted into a new race of men." This new American man is a "mixture of English, Scotch, Irish, French, Dutch, Germans, and Swedes." The new American, he also says, leaves "behind him all his ancient prejudices and manners, receives new ones from the new mode of life he has embraced, the new government he obeys, and the new rank he holds." Crèvecoeur thus appears to view America not just as a new nationality produced by the intermarriage of people from old ones, but also as a society with a new culture produced by this amalgamation of peoples on its shores. Zangwill broadened the blend beyond northwestern Europeans to include "Celt and Latin, Slav and Teuton, Greek and Syrian, black and yellow—Jew and Gentile . . ." For him, like Crèvecoeur, this "melting and re-forming" also appears to involve not just the intermarriage of ethnicities and races but also the creation of a new common culture in which all will unite to build the Republic of Man and the Kingdom of God.[35]

In contrast, the "Anglo-conformity" model focuses on cultural assimilation. It is based on the premise that "immigrants and their descendants duly adopt the standard Anglo-Saxon cultural patterns," in Milton Gordon's words, and "should adapt to the cultural history of the Anglo-American part of the population," in Michael Novak's. It assumes, in short, the centrality and durability of the culture of the founding settlers. The culinary metaphor is an Anglo-Protestant tomato soup to which immigration adds celery, croutons, spices, parsley, and other ingredients that enrich and diversify the taste, but which are absorbed into what remains fundamentally tomato soup. Explicitly and even more pervasively implicitly this Anglo-conformity model, "in various guises," as Gordon remarks, "has probably been the most prevalent ideology of assimilation in the American historical experience."[36] More accurately than the other models, it describes the cultural absorption of immigrants until the 1960s.

The melting pot and tomato soup concepts in different ways expressed American nationalism and portrayed a coherent American identity. In 1915 they were challenged by Horace Kallen's vigorously setting forth a salad image of America, which he labeled "cultural pluralism." That name has stuck, but in fact it was more a theory of ethnic pluralism. For him groups were based on ancestry not culture. In an oft-quoted statement, he argued: "Men change their clothes, their politics, their wives, their religions, their philosophies to a greater or lesser extent; they cannot change their grandfathers. An Irishman is always an Irishman, a Jew always a Jew. . . . Irishman and Jew are facts of nature; citizen and church-member are artifacts of civilization." In short, people can change their culture, they cannot change their ethnicity. Biology is destiny, identities are "ancestrally determined," and these identities represent "permanent group distinctions." Immigration, according to Kallen, dissolved any earlier American nationality and changed America into a "federation of nationalities," "a democracy of nationalities."[37] The model he saw for America was Europe where many nationalities coexist within the framework of a common civilization. Kallen's argument for biological determinism reflects the racial concepts of national identity pervasive in American thinking in his time. His racist assumptions are not very different from the racism of the image of a pure Anglo-Saxon America, which he attacked.[38]

Kallen's stress on the overpowering role of ancestry in shaping identity leaves ambiguous what he meant by "cultural pluralism." If people can change their religion, language, politics, and philosophy, cultural identity must be divorced from unchangeable ethnic or ancestral identity. What then, however, is left of the ancestral identity that Kallen sees as permanent? In what sense is an Irishman or a Jew who changes his language, religion, philosophy, and politics still an Irishman or a Jew? Kallen's contemporary and admirer Randolph Bourne attempted to formulate a less extreme and more fluid critique of the melting pot and Anglo-conformity theories. He nonetheless still saw America in European terms, "a cosmopolitan federation of national colonies, of foreign cultures, from whom [unlike Europe] the sting of devastating competition has been removed." The result would not be an American "nationality, but a trans-nationality, a weaving back and forth, with the other lands, of many threads of all sizes and colors."[39]

The ideas of Kallen and Bourne were a reaction against the popularity of the two nationalist concepts of America. "Very much on the defensive," Arthur Mann observes, "Kallen proposed cultural pluralism as an alternative to both the melting-pot concept and the doctrine of Anglo-Saxon supremacy." Kallen's ideas aroused some interest in intellectual circles but had little impact on public attitudes and the pervasive nationalism. Kallen was roundly denounced by establishment figures for advocating the "Balkanization" of America. His supporters, Mann argues, were "of two sorts: Zionists and non-Jewish but philo-Semitic intellectuals fascinated by the ethnic diversity of American urban life."[40] Many years later Kallen conceded his failure to have an impact. In the early twentieth century, Americans were determined to maintain an America that might eventually become a melting pot through ethnic intermarriage but would staunchly remain tomato soup in its Anglo-Protestant cultural identity.

Theodore Roosevelt expressed the prevailing nationalist view when, after initially endorsing Zangwill's melting pot, he then questioned its relevance and embraced the tomato soup concept of American culture. The "crucible in which all the new types are melted into one," he said, "was shaped from 1776 to 1789, and our nationality was definitely fixed in all its essentials by the men of Washington's day."[41] American determination to maintain the "essentials" of that "nationality" manifested itself in immense efforts to Americanize immigrants before and during World War I.

Americanizing the Immigrant. Americans created the term and the concept of Americanization in the late eighteenth century when they also created the term and the concept of immigrant. They saw the need to make Americans of the new arrivals on their shores. "We must," John Jay said in 1797, "see our people more Americanized," and Jefferson spoke in similar fashion.[42] Efforts to achieve this goal peaked in the late nineteenth and early twentieth centuries. Americanization, Justice Louis Brandeis declared in 1919, meant that the immigrant "adopts the clothes, the manners, and the customs generally prevailing here . . . substitutes for his mother tongue the English language," insures that "his interests and affections have become deeply rooted here," and comes "into complete harmony with our ideals and aspirations, and cooperate[s] with us for their attainment." When he has done all this he will have "the national consciousness of an American." To this definition, other exponents of Americanization added the acquisition of American citizenship, the renunciation of foreign allegiances, and the rejection of dual loyalties and nationalities.[43]

The perceived need to Americanize the immigrants generated a major social movement devoted to that end. It produced many different, overlapping, and at times conflicting efforts by local, state, and national governments, private organizations, and businesses, with the public schools playing a central role. "The extent of the [Americanization] movement is difficult to exaggerate," one historian concludes. It was a "social crusade" and a key element in the Progressive phase of American politics. Settlement house workers, educators, reformers, businessmen, and political leaders, including Theodore Roosevelt and Woodrow Wilson, all promoted or actively participated in this crusade. A "list of movement organizers," another historian noted, "reads like a combination of *Who's Who* and the *Social Register.*"[44]

The new large industrial corporations needed masses of immigrant workers and established schools at their factories to train immigrants in the English language and American values. In almost every city with a significant immigrant population, the chamber of commerce had an Americanization program. Henry Ford was a leader in efforts to make immigrants into productive American workers because, he said, "these men of many nations must be taught American ways, the English language, and the right way to live." The Ford Motor Company instituted many Americanization activities including a six- to eight-month English language course that immigrant employees were compelled to attend and graduates of which received diplomas qualifying them for citizenship. U.S. Steel and International Harvester sponsored similar programs, and "a good many businessmen inaugurated factory classes, distributed civics lessons in pay envelopes, and even subsidized public evening schools."[45]

Progressive era businessmen were concerned with the need to educate their immigrant workers in the English language, American culture, and the American private enterprise system, both to increase their productivity and to inoculate them against unionism and socialism.

Their special interests overlapped with what was seen as a broad national interest. Dramatizing the goal to be achieved, in 1916 Ford organized a gala patriotic pageant, centered on a gigantic melting pot, in which a large stream of immigrant workers "descended into the pot from backstage, clad in outlandish garb and flaunting signs proclaiming their fatherlands. Simultaneously from either side of the pot another stream of men emerged, each prosperously dressed in identical suits of clothes and each carrying a little American flag."[46]

A huge number of private nonprofit organizations became involved in Americanization activities. They included both established organizations as well as new organizations specifically created for that purpose. The YMCA organized classes to teach immigrants English. The Sons of the American Revolution and the Colonial Dames had Americanization programs. American International College, designed especially for immigrants, was created in Springfield, Massachusetts. Ethnic and religious organizations with ties to incoming immigrants actively promoted their Americanization. Liberal reformers, conservative businessmen, and concerned citizens founded organizations such as the Committee on Information for Aliens, the North American Civic League for Immigrants, the Chicago League for the Protection of Immigrants, the Educational Alliance of New York City, the Baron de Hirsch Fund (aimed at Jewish immigrants), the Society for Italian Immigrants, and many similar organizations. These groups counseled immigrants, provided evening classes in the English language and American ways, and helped them find jobs and homes. Much of the Americanization work and many of the people active in it, like Frances Kellor, came out of the settlement houses that began in the urban slums of the 1890s, such as Jane Addams's Hull House in Chicago. The urban political machines wanted the votes of immigrants and hence actively helped to get them settled in America, provided them with jobs and economic support, and, of course, sped them down the road to citizenship and voting.[47]

Before World War I Protestant, Catholic, and Jewish groups pushed for the integration of their immigrant faithful into American society. "The Roman Catholic Church used its clergy, schools, press, charity institutions, and fraternal organizations to persuade immigrants to give up their foreign cultural patterns and conform to American customs. Archbishop John Ireland . . . an Irish immigrant, was a leader among the Americanizing bishops. . . . He struggled against the efforts of immigrant Catholics to preserve their languages and traditions." In addition, "Jewish settlement houses developed in many cities to encourage Jewish immigrant children to learn American ways, to attend public school, and to preserve their identity within American parameters." [48]

The Americanization movement began with private organizations at the grass roots. They then pressured local and state governments to support and participate in these efforts. In due course over thirty states passed laws establishing Americanization programs; Connecticut even created a Department of Americanization. Eventually the federal government also became active, with the Bureau of Naturalization in the Labor Department and the Bureau of Education in the Interior Department competing vigorously to raise funds and further their own assimilation efforts. By 1921 some 3,526 states, cities, towns, and communities were participating in Bureau of Naturalization programs. [49] English language education was the most extensive activity of the Americanization movement, and governments played a key role in sponsoring and supporting these programs.

Until the mid-twentieth century the central institution for Americanization was the public school system. Its creation and expansion in the mid-nineteenth century was, indeed, in part dictated by and shaped by the perceived need for Americanization. According to Carl Kaestle, "Education for assimilation became one of the central preoccupations of nineteenth-century school officials." The schools insisted on the immigrants accepting "Anglo-American Protestant traditions and values." Particularly in New England, with its large immigrant population, "people looked to education as the best way to transmit Anglo-American Protestant values and to prevent the collapse of republican institutions." [50] In the longer term, Stephen Steinberg observes, "More than any other single factor, the public school undermined the capacity of immigrant groups to transmit their native cultures to their American-born children." [51] The pervasive Protestant atmosphere and values in the schools quite naturally led to a countermovement by the Catholic

Church and the creation of a large Catholic school system, which, in due course, also became a channel for the propagation of American values and American nationalism.

Schools were central to the pre–World War I efforts to Americanize the immigrants from southern and eastern Europe. "The Progressive believed in education," Joel M. Roitman says. "He would use it as a basic tool in attempting to assimilate (Americanize) the millions of people who came to the United States in the period 1890–1924." Schools were encouraged to offer Americanization and English classes for adult immigrants. A leading Americanization organization, the North American Civic League, published in 1913 a plan for *Education of the Immigrant*. The Federal Bureau of Education promoted these efforts, and in 1919 urged the transformation of schools from simply a place for daytime learning by children into community centers with evening programs for the Americanization of adults. In 1921–1922 between 750 and one thousand communities conducted "special public school programs to Americanize the foreign-born." Between 1915 and 1922, over one million immigrants enrolled in (but did not always complete) these programs. In the first decades of the twentieth century, Reed Ueda reports, teachers "tried to inculcate in the children of immigrants a sense of American national identity. The literature and social studies textbooks students read focused on the institutions and political history of the nation and an iconographic gallery of great men and women who served as heroic models of national character." Throughout the country, school systems "had been shaped by successive generations of reformers from Horace Mann to John Dewey who saw public education as an instrument to create a unified society out of the multiplying diversity created by immigration and its attendant social changes."[52]

The later phases of the Americanization movement have been criticized for applying undue pressure to immigrants and becoming nativist and anti-immigrant, leading to the dramatic 1924 reduction in immigration. Without the Americanizing activities starting in the early 1890s, however, that cut in immigration would in all likelihood have come much earlier. Americanization made immigration acceptable to Americans. The success of the movement was manifest when the immigrants and their children rallied to the colors and marched off to fight their country's wars.

World Wars. World War I stimulated patriotism and enhanced the salience of national identity over other identities. National identity reached its peak, however, in World War II, when racial, ethnic, and class identities were subordinated to national loyalty. Although some black organizations and unions did not support America's becoming involved in the war, the attack on Pearl Harbor, Paul Stern argues "shifted their identification at least temporarily from their racial or class groups to the nation, so that it was the nation that provided the identity in whose name people took action."[53] In similar fashion, Japanese-Americans affirmed their loyalty to their country and volunteered for military service. The mobilization of over 10 million men and women into the armed forces, the most national of national institutions, was a homogenizing experience that "left a new residue of shared values and traditions."[54]

World War II, as we have seen, heightened the significance of the ideological component of American identity and paved the way for the end of the ethnic and racial legal definitions of that identity. The war, as Philip Gleason said, "enhanced national unity and a common sense of national belongingness." The American people had one overriding purpose; almost all shared, although not equally, in the dangers and hardships of the war; and, as often happens in major wars, economic inequalities were reduced. World War II was "a great common experience" that shaped "Americans' understanding of their national identity for the next generation."[55] The identification of Americans with their country reached its highest point in history during World War II.

This experience was not limited to Americans. German nationalism, much to the subsequent regret of Germans, also reached an intensity rivaled perhaps only by that of the French in their revolutionary wars. Russians fondly remember the war as a time of great national effort and cohesion. When in the mid-1970s Hedrick Smith asked Russians what had been the best period in Russian history, they agreed it was "the war." People, he reported, "spoke of the war not only as a time of suffering and sacrifice, but also a time of belonging and solidarity. The war had meant death and destruction but it had also demonstrated indestructible unity and invincible power. And the memory of the shared ordeal and triumph in what the Soviet people call The Great Patriotic War is a primary source of the unblushing patriotism they feel today."[56] "The Great Patriotic War" for the Russians, "their finest hour" for the British, "the good war" for Americans, World War II was both the expression of and the stimulant to the most intense nationalism ever experienced by countries of the European world, the culmination of the nationalist era in the West.

FADING NATIONALISM

The century in which national identity dominated other identities and in which Americans were enthusiastically nationalist and patriotic began to fade in the 1960s. A decline in the centrality of national identity was noted by many observers in the 1990s. In 1994, nineteen scholars of American history and politics were asked to evaluate the level of American integration in 1930, 1950, 1970, and 1990. Using a scale of 1 to 5, with 1 representing the highest level of integration, the panelists rated 1930 at 1.71, 1950 at 1.46, 1970 at 2.65, and 1990 at 2.60. The year 1950, the authors of this study said, was "the perceived zenith of American national integration." Since then "cultural and political fragmentation has increased" and "conflict emanating from intensified ethnic and religious consciousness poses the main current challenge to the American national myth."[57] Similar views were expressed by individual scholars both sympathetic to and regretful of what they were describing. Robert Kaplan spoke of "the eclipse of nationhood." Diana Schaub argued that America was facing the "circumstance of faded patriotism." George Lipsitz, attacking Ronald Reagan's "new patriotism," highlighted what he termed the "dilemmas of beset nationhood." Walter Berns deplored the oncoming "end of patriotism," and Peter Schuck traced "the devaluation of American citizenship."[58]

This erosion of national identity in the later decades of the twentieth century had four principal manifestations: the popularity of the doctrines of multiculturalism and diversity among some elite elements, and special interests that elevated racial, ethnic, gender, and other subnational identities over national identity; the weakness or absence of the factors that previously promoted immigrant assimilation combined with the increased tendency of immigrants to maintain dual identities, loyalties, and citizenships; the dominance among immigrants of speakers, largely Mexican, of a single non-English language (a phenomenon without precedent in American history), with the resulting tendencies toward Hispanization and the transformation of America into a bilingual, bicultural society; and the denationalization of important segments of America's elites, with a growing gap between their cosmopolitan and transnational commitments and the still highly nationalist and patriotic values of the American public.

PART III

Challenges to American Identity

CHAPTER 7

Deconstructing America: The Rise of Subnational Identities

THE DECONSTRUCTIONIST MOVEMENT

American national identity peaked politically with the rallying of Americans to their country and its cause in World War II. It peaked symbolically with President Kennedy's 1961 summons: "Ask not what your country can do for you—ask what you can do for your country." In the intervening decade and a half, the unifying impact of World War II, the confrontations of the early Cold War, the successful incorporation into American society of the pre–World War I immigrants and their children, the slow but steady progress toward ending racial discrimination, and unprecedented economic prosperity all combined to reinforce Americans' identification with their country. Americans were one nation of individuals with equal rights, who shared a primarily Anglo-Protestant core culture, and were dedicated to the liberal-democratic principles of the American Creed. This, at least, was the prevailing image Americans had of what their country should be, and the goal toward which, in some measure, it seemed to be moving.

In the 1960s powerful movements began to challenge the salience, the substance, and the desirability of this concept of America. America for them was not a national community of individuals sharing a common culture, history, and creed but a conglomerate of different races, ethnicities, and subnational cultures, in which individuals were defined by their group membership, not common nationality. The proponents of this view castigated the melting pot and tomato soup concepts of America that had prevailed earlier in the century and argued that America was instead a mosaic or salad of diverse peoples. Acknowledging his previous defeat, Horace Kallen claimed victory on his ninetieth birthday in 1972: "It takes about 50 years for an idea to break through and become vogue. No one likes an intruder, particularly when he is upsetting the commonplace." President Clinton hailed the liberation of Americans from their dominant European culture. Vice President Gore interpreted the nation's motto, *E pluribus unum* (chosen by Franklin, Jefferson, and Adams), to mean "out of one, many," and political theorist Michael Walzer, citing Kallen's vision of a "nation of nationalities," argued it should mean "Within one, many."[1]

The deconstructionists promoted programs to enhance the status and influence of subnational racial, ethnic, and cultural groups. They encouraged immigrants to maintain their birth country cultures, granted them legal privileges denied to native-born Americans, and denounced the idea of Americanization as un-American. They pushed the rewriting of history syllabi and textbooks so as to refer to the "peoples" of the United States in place of the single people of the Constitution. They urged supplementing or substituting for national history the history of subnational groups. They downgraded the centrality of English in American life and pushed bilingual education and linguistic diversity. They advocated legal recognition of group rights and racial preferences over the individual rights central to the American Creed. They justified their actions by theories of multiculturalism and the idea that diversity rather than unity or community should be America's overriding value. The combined effect of these efforts was to promote the deconstruction of the American identity that had been gradually created over three centuries and the ascendance of subnational identities.

The resulting controversies over racial preferences, bilingualism, multiculturalism, immigration, assimilation, national history standards, English as the official language, "Eurocentrism," were in effect all battles in a single war over the nature of American national identity. On one side were substantial elements of America's political, intellectual, and institutional elites, plus the leaders or aspiring leaders of the subnational groups whose interests were being promoted. Of central importance in this deconstruction coalition were governmental officials, particularly bureaucrats, judges, and educators. In the past, imperial and colonial governments provided resources to minority groups and encouraged people to identify with them, so as to enhance the government's ability to divide and rule. The governments of nation-states, in contrast, attempted to promote the unity of their people, the development of national consciousness, the suppression of subnational regional and ethnic loyalties, the universal use of the national language, and the allocation of benefits to those who conform to the national norm. Until the late twentieth century, American political and governmental leaders acted similarly. Then in the 1960s and 1970s they began to promote measures consciously designed to weaken America's cultural and creedal identity and to strengthen racial, ethnic, cultural, and other subnational identities. These efforts by a nation's leaders to deconstruct the nation they governed were, quite possibly, without precedent in human history.

Substantial elements of America's elites in academia, the media, business, and the professions joined governmental elites in these efforts. The deconstructionist coalition, however, did not include most Americans. In poll after poll and in several referenda, majorities of Americans rejected ideas and measures for weakening national identity and promoting subnational identities. They were often joined by substantial minorities, at times pluralities, and even majorities of the subnational groups these measures were designed to benefit. Overall, the American people remained deeply patriotic, nationalistic in their outlook, and committed to their national culture, creed, and identity. A major gap thus developed between portions of America's elite, on the one hand, and the bulk of the American people, on the other, over the fundamental issues of what America is and what America should be.

Several factors were responsible for the emergence of the deconstructionist movements. First, in some measure, they were the American manifestation of the global rise of more limited subnational identities that were creating crises of national identity in countries throughout the world. These were, as we have seen, related to economic globalization and the expansion of transportation and communication, which generated in people the need to seek identity, support, and assurance in smaller groups. Second, the rise of subnational identities preceded the end of the Cold War but the easing of that conflict in the later decades of the century and its abrupt end in 1989 eliminated one powerful reason for giving preeminence to national identity and thus opened the way for people to find greater salience in other identities. Third, political calculations at times undoubtedly motivated elected officials and would-be elected officials to promote measures they assumed would appeal to significant political constituencies. President Nixon, for instance, endorsed Congressman Roman Pucinski's legislation on ethnic groups before the 1972 election and allegedly encouraged affirmative action in employment to promote conflict between blacks and working-class whites within the Democratic Party. Fourth, it clearly was in the interests of the leaders and aspiring leaders of minority groups to promote measures that would provide benefits for and enhance the status of their groups. Fifth, bureaucratic imperatives led government officials to interpret acts of Congress in ways that would make it easier for them to implement those acts, to expand the activities, power, and resources of their agencies, and to promote their own policy goals.

Sixth, liberal political beliefs fostered among academics, intellectuals, journalists, and others feelings of sympathy and guilt concerning those whom they saw as the victims of exclusion, discrimination, and oppression. Racial groups and women became the focus of late-twentieth-century liberal activism much as the working class and the labor movement had been for early-twentieth-century liberals. The cults of multiculturalism and diversity took the place of left-wing, socialist, and working-class ideologies and sympathies.

Finally, and perhaps most importantly, the formal de-legitimation of race and ethnicity as components of national identity in the civil rights, voting rights, and immigration acts of 1964–1965 paradoxically legitimated their reappearance in subnational identities. So long as race and ethnicity were key components defining America, those who were not white and not northern European could challenge that definition only by seeming to be un-American. "Becoming white" and "Anglo-conformity" were the ways in which immigrants, blacks, and others made themselves Americans. With race and ethnicity formally exorcised, and culture downgraded, the way opened for minority groups to assert their own identities within a society now defined largely by its creed. No longer the means by which Americans differentiated themselves from other peoples, race, ethnicity, and, to some extent, culture became the grounds by which Americans differentiated themselves from each other.

The deconstructionist movement generated much controversy, political and intellectual. By the 1990s commentators were awarding victory to the deconstructionists. In 1992 Arthur Schlesinger, Jr., warned that the "ethnic upsurge," which had begun "as a gesture of protest against the Anglocentric culture," had become "a cult, and today it threatens to become a counter-revolution against the original theory of America as 'one people,' a common culture, a single nation." And in 1997 Harvard sociologist Nathan Glazer concluded "we are all multiculturists now."[2] Yet opposition to the counterrevolution quickly developed, and vigorous movements emerged committed to a more traditional concept of American identity. In the 1990s, bureaucrats and judges, including Supreme Court justices, who had earlier backed racial categorization and racial preferences, began to moderate and even reverse their views. Led by energetic entrepreneurs, movements developed forcing referenda votes on ending affirmative action and bilingual education. The efforts to rewrite American history and educational curricula were countered by new organizations of scholars and teachers.

September 11 gave a major boost to the supporters of America as one people with a common culture. Yet the deconstruction war did not end and it remained unresolved as to whether America was, would be, or should be a nation of individuals with equal rights and a common culture and creed or an association of racial, ethnic, and cultural subnational groups held together by the hopes for the material gains that can be provided by a healthy economy and a compliant government. Major battles in this war involved challenges to America's Creed, its language, and its core culture.

THE CHALLENGE TO THE CREED

The core of the American Creed, as Myrdal said, involves the "ideals of the essential dignity of the individual human being, of the fundamental equality of all men, and of certain inalienable rights to freedom, justice, and a fair opportunity."[3] Throughout America's history, American political and social institutions and practices have fallen short of these goals. A gap has existed between ideal and reality. At times some Americans have found this gap intolerable and launched social and political movements promoting major reforms in institutions and practices so as to bring them more in accord with the values on which most Americans agree and which are, indeed, central to American national identity. "The history of reform" in America, as Ralph Waldo Emerson said, "is always identical; it is the comparison of the idea with the fact."[4]

Myrdal described and invoked the Creed in order to highlight "an American dilemma," the gap between its principles and the inequality, lack of civil rights, discrimination, and segregation to which black Americans were still subjected in the 1930s. Slavery and its legacies have historically been *the* American dilemma, the most blatant, profound, and evil violation of America's values. Following the compromise of 1877, Americans attempted to ignore, deny, and explain away this dilemma. In the mid-twentieth century, however, several developments made this no longer possible: urbanization of blacks and their massive migration north; the impact of World War II and then the Cold War, which made racial discrimination a foreign policy liability; the changing attitudes of white Americans about race as they attempted to resolve the cognitive dissonance between their beliefs and reality; the efforts by the federal judiciary in the 1940s and 1950s to bring laws and institutions affecting blacks into accord with the Fourteenth Amendment; the emergence in the late 1950s and 1960s of the boomer generation as a source of reform activists; and new assertiveness by the leaders of black organizations trying to achieve the equality that had been denied African-Americans.

As had been the case with previous reform movements, the principles of the American Creed were the single greatest resource of those push-

rhetoric?

ing for the end of racial segregation and discrimination. The dignity of the individual, the right of all individuals to equal treatment and opportunity, regardless of race, were the recurring themes of the campaign. Without the principles of the Creed embedded in American identity, the campaign for equal treatment of blacks would, arguably, have gone nowhere. The case for eliminating race as a consideration in the actions of governments and other institutions rested squarely on the Creed's concept of equal rights for all. "Classifications and distinctions based on race or color," the leading black attorney Thurgood Marshall argued in 1948, "have no moral or legal validity in our society." Supreme Court justices in the early 1960s described the Constitution as "color-blind." The U.S. Commission on Civil Rights in 1960, in a statement on higher education, concluded that "questions as to the applicant's race or color are clearly irrelevant and improper. They serve no legitimate purpose in helping the college to select its students."[5]

The Civil Rights Act of 1964 and the Voting Rights Act of 1965 were expressly designed to make American reality reflect American principles. Title VII of the former made it unlawful for an employer "(1) to fail or refuse to hire . . . any individual . . . because of such individual's race, color, religion, sex or national origin; or (2) to . . . classify his employees . . . in any way which would deprive or tend to deprive any individual of employment opportunities . . . because of such individual's race, color, religion, sex, or national origin." Senator Hubert Humphrey, the floor manager of the bill, assured the Senate that nothing in the bill gave courts or executive agencies the power "to require hiring, firing, or promotion of employees in order to meet a racial 'quota' or to achieve a certain racial balance. . . . Title VII prohibits discrimination . . . [and] is designed to encourage hiring on the basis of ability and qualifications, not race or religion."[6] The bill required a showing of intent to discriminate to make a practice unlawful, authorized employers to make appointments on the basis of seniority and merit, and gave employers the right to use ability tests, provided they were not designed to discriminate on the basis of race. Courts could provide relief only if they found that an employer intentionally engaged in an unlawful practice. The following year, the Voting Rights Act made it illegal to deny a citizen the right to vote because of race or color in the jurisdictions (mostly Southern states) covered by the act. The combined effect of these acts was to prohibit discrimination among races in employment, voting, public accommodations, public facilities, federal programs, and federally supported public education.[7] The language of the laws and the intentions of their framers could not have been clearer. In America's historic pattern, reformers had produced changes in institutions and practices so as to bring them into greater accord with the principles of America's Creed.

Yet almost immediately this momentous development was reversed. As soon as the Civil Rights Act was passed, black leaders such as Bayard Rustin stopped demanding rights common to all American citizens and instead began demanding governmental programs to provide material benefits to blacks as a distinct racial group, toward the goal of "achieving the fact of [economic] equality" with whites. To reach this goal as quickly as possible, federal administrators, later joined by judges, interpreted the reform statutes to mean the opposite of what they said and through these interpretations launched a frontal assault on the Creed's principle of equal rights for all that had made the new laws possible. The common theme of these actions was to replace the prescription of nondiscrimination in those laws with "affirmative discrimination" (in Nathan Glazer's phrase) in favor of blacks.[8]

By 1967, as Hugh Davis Graham observes in his exhaustive study *The Civil Rights Era*, the chairman, a majority of the commissioners, and the staff of the Equal Employment Opportunity Commission created by the Civil Rights Act were "prepared to defy Title VII's restrictions and attempt to build a body of case law that would justify its [the commission's] focus on effects and its disregard of intent." The administrators, as Glazer put it, "took statistical disparities as evidence of discrimination, and tried to pressure employers, public and private, into overcoming them by hiring on the basis of race, color, and national origin—exactly what the original Civil Rights Act of 1964 had forbidden." Officials in the Department of Labor also acted to reverse the directives of presidents and Congress. In March 1961 President Kennedy issued Executive Order 10,925 ordering government contractors to hire and treat employees "without regard to their race, creed, color, or national origin."* President Johnson reaffirmed this requirement. In 1968–1970, however, the Department of Labor issued orders requiring government contractors when hiring workers to take into account the proportion of races in their geographic area of their business. Businesses were told to establish "a set of specific and result-oriented procedures" keyed to the problems and needs of members of minority groups. As Andrew Kull points out in his analysis *The Color-Blind Constitution:* "An executive order whose language required nondiscrimination—its literal command was still that government contractors 'ensure that applicants be employed without regard to their race' . . . had been formally interpreted by the Labor Department to require the contrary." The Labor Department's actions also ran afoul of the nondiscrimination language of Title VII. "The policy of the U.S. Department of Labor by 1969 was thus to require what Congress had prohibited scarcely five years before."[9]

In *Griggs v. Duke Power Co.* (401 U.S. 424, 1971), the first Title VII case to come before it, the Supreme Court similarly disregarded the statute's language requiring proof of intent. It found that the employer in question had no "intention to discriminate against Negro employees," but then it still outlawed the company's employment requirement of either a high school diploma or passing a standard general intelligence test. "As is clear both from the language of the statute and from some particularly unambiguous legislative history," Kull comments, "the Court derived from Title VII a legal requirement that the proponents of the law had expressly disclaimed." This decision was of far-reaching importance. As Herman Belz argues in his book *Equality Transformed*, it "shifted civil rights policy to a group-rights, equality-of-result rationale that made the social consequences of employment practices, rather than their purposes, intent, or motivation, the decisive consideration in determining their lawfulness. The decision supplied a

---

* The executive order also called for "affirmative action" in its original meaning: "The employer will not discriminate against any employee or applicant for employment because of race, creed, color, or national origin. The contractor will take *affirmative action* to ensure that applicants are employed and that employees are treated during employment, *without regard* to their race, creed, color or national origin." Emphasis added.

theoretical basis for preferential treatment as well as a practical incentive for extending race-conscious preference." Under the court's decision, "minority preference was practically required in order to protect against charges of disparate impact discrimination. The logical premise of disparate impact theory was group rights and equality of result. . . . Contrary to the traditional concept of justice, under disparate impact theory employers were held accountable for societal discrimination, although they were not responsible for it." The court, Belz concludes, adopted "a theory of discrimination entirely contradictory to the requirements and intent of the Civil Rights Act."[10]

Something similar happened to the Voting Rights Act, which had been designed to prevent Southern states from denying or restricting the right of blacks to vote. In 1969, however, the Supreme Court interpreted that act not simply to protect the rights of individuals but to mandate systems of representation that would insure the election of minority candidates. It thus gave judicial endorsement to what became the widespread practice of "racial gerrymandering" with district boundaries drawn to provide safe seats for blacks and Hispanics. "By the early 1970s," Kull notes, "the federal government was thus in the anomalous position, by the standards of a decade before, of requiring state and local governments to gerrymander their election districts on racial lines."[11]

The elites in most major American institutions—government, business, the media, education—are white. In the last decades of the twentieth century substantial elements of these elites rejected the color-blind values of the American Creed and endorsed discrimination among races. "For many years," Jack Citrin observed in 1996, "the white establishment embraced affirmative action and downplayed the moral costs of deviation from difference-blind principles." The leading sociologist Seymour Martin Lipset reported in 1992 that "the heaviest support for preferential treatment seems to come from the liberal intelligentsia, the well-educated, the five to six percent of the population who have gone to graduate school, plus those who have majored in liberal arts in college. Support is also strong among the political elite, particularly Democrats but including many Republicans (though not many prominent officeholders)."[12] In the 1970s and 1980s, the principal newspapers and journals of opinion enthusiastically endorsed affirmative action and related programs to give racial minorities preference over whites. The Ford Foundation and other foundations provided tens of millions of dollars to encourage racial preference. With the approval of their faculties, colleges and universities competed for minority students through lower admission standards, race-designated scholarships, and other benefits.

Of central importance in the establishment of race-based programs was American business, motivated by marketing concerns and the desire to head off lawsuits and avoid bad publicity from boycotts organized by black and other minority groups. The "dirty little secret of affirmative action politics," Richard Kahlenberg noted in 1996, "is that corporate America actually supports affirmative action." That, however, was a fast-dissolving secret as corporations publicized their commitment to affirmative action policies and the hiring and promotion of minorities and women. In the early 1980s, Du Pont announced that 50 percent of its new appointments to professional and managerial positions would be minorities or women. Other corporations took comparable actions. In the major controversies, business corporations lined up in support of racial preferences, opposed the 1996 California initiative, Proposition 209, banning state racial preferences and the comparable initiative, Proposition I-200, in the state of Washington in 1998, while supporting the University of Michigan's appeal of a district court's order banning racial preference in its law school admissions.[13]

The differences between elites and the public over racial preferences were dramatically evident in the two state referenda. California's Proposition 209, echoing the language of the Civil Rights Act, provided: "The state shall not discriminate against, or grant preferential treatment to, any individual or group on the basis of race, sex, color, ethnicity, or national origin in the operation of public employment, public education, or public contracting." When asked his view on it, Senator Joseph Lieberman said: "I can't see how I could be opposed to it, because it is basically a statement of American values . . . and says . . . we shouldn't discriminate in favor of somebody based on the group they represent."

The bulk of the California establishment, however, rejected these "American values."[14] Most political leaders (except for Governor Pete Wilson), college and university presidents, Hollywood celebrities, newspapers, TV stations, union leaders, and many business leaders opposed the ban on racial preferences. They were joined by the Clinton administration, the Ford Foundation, and many national organizations. The opponents of the proposition spent far more than its supporters. Yet the California public approved it by a vote of 54 percent to 46 percent.

Two years later in the state of Washington, the effort to ban racial preferences was also almost unanimously opposed by the state establishment, including the governor and other top political figures, the state's major businesses, the principal media, including the *Seattle Times*, which provided free space for ads opposing the proposition, the heads of educational institutions, large numbers of intellectuals and commentators, and outside political figures such as Vice President Al Gore and the Reverend Jesse Jackson. Business was particularly prominent. The opposition campaign was led by Bill Gates, Sr., father of the Microsoft founder, and supported by Boeing, Starbucks, Weyerhaeuser, Costco, and Eddie Bauer. "The most significant obstacle we faced in the Washington campaign," observed Ward Connerly, the leading supporter of the proposition, "was not the media, or even the political personalities who attacked us . . . but the corporate world."[15] The proposition's opponents spent three times as much as its supporters. Washington voters approved it by a margin of 58 percent to 42 percent.

Public opinion surveys show that the public generally approves of affirmative action in the original sense used in the directives of Presidents Kennedy and Johnson to mean actions to prevent discrimination and to help minorities to compete better for jobs and higher education by improving their family situations, schools, housing, and job training. The polls also have consistently shown a large majority of Americans opposing racial preferences in hiring, promotion, and college admissions, even if these are explicitly designed to correct the effects of past discrimination. Five times between 1977 and 1989, Seymour Martin Lipset reports, the Gallup Organization asked the question:

Some people say that to make up for past discrimination, women and minorities should be given preferential treatment in getting jobs and places in college. Others say that ability, as determined by test scores, should be the main consideration. Which point of view comes close to how you feel on the subject?

In these surveys 81 percent to 84 percent chose test-based ability and 10 percent to 11 percent chose preferential treatment. In two other polls in 1987 and 1990, Gallup asked whether people supported or opposed the proposition: "We should make every effort to improve the position of blacks and other minorities even if it means giving them preferential treatment." In these two polls, 71 percent and 72 percent of the public opposed this proposition, while 24 percent supported it, with blacks voting 66 percent against and 32 percent in favor.[16] Similarly, a 1995 poll asking whether "hiring, promotion, and college admissions should be based strictly on merit and qualifications other than race or ethnicity" produced agreement from 86 percent of whites, 78 percent of Hispanics, 74 percent of Asians, and 68 percent of blacks. In another series of five polls between 1986 and 1994, asking people whether they were for or against "preferential hiring and promotion of blacks," from 69 percent to 82 percent of the public said they were opposed. In a 1995 survey by *USA Weekend Magazine*, 90 percent of 248,000 American teenagers said they opposed "affirmative action in hiring and college admissions to make up for past discrimination." Reviewing the evidence in 1996, Jack Citrin concludes that "In sum, with the issue framed as a choice between group equality or individual merit, affirmative action loses. A majority of Americans rejects explicit preferences, regardless of the particular group they are intended to assist."[17]

In these polls, black attitudes on racial preferences varied with the nature of the question asked. In the 1989 Gallup poll on whether preferential treatment was warranted for women and minorities in hiring and college admissions or whether these should be determined by ability as revealed in tests, 56 percent of blacks chose ability and 14 percent racial preferences. In the five American National Election Studies polls between 1986 and 1994, asking people whether they were for or against "preferential hiring and promotion of blacks," from 23 percent to 46 percent of blacks expressed opposition.[18] Overall, blacks and other minorities appeared to be ambivalent about racial preferences. This ambivalence disappears, however, in situations of intense political controversy, such as referenda contests, when leaders of racial organizations vigorously try to mobilize their voters in favor of preferences. In March 1995, for instance, 71 percent of whites, 54 percent of Asians, 52 percent of Hispanics, and 45 percent of blacks said they approved the proposed California Civil Rights Initiative. The initiative was voted on in November 1996 after eighteen months of an extraordinarily vigorous, massive, and at times vitriolic campaign to mobilize minority voters against it. According to exit polls, only 27 percent of blacks and 30 percent of Hispanics voted in favor of it, decreases of 18 percent and 22 percent from the views expressed eighteen months earlier.[19] Working together, the leaders of the white establishment and of black organizations persuaded large majorities of black people to support racial preferences.

In the late 1980s broader opposition developed against preferences. Public disapproval, lawsuits by white job seekers and university applicants charging "reverse discrimination," and a decade of Republican presidents nominating federal judges produced a shift in judicial decisions. The courts began to narrow the room for preferential treatment of blacks and other minorities. "Nineteen eighty-nine," as Stephan and Abigail Thernstrom say, "was a year of second thoughts." That year in *Richmond v. J. A. Croson* (488 U.S. 469), the Supreme Court reviewed a minority contract set-aside plan of the sort that at least thirty-six states and more than 190 local governments had adopted. Writing for a six-justice majority, Justice Sandra Day O'Connor ruled against the Richmond ordinance, affirming the principles of the American Creed. Classifications based on race, she said, created "a danger of stigmatic harm. Unless they are strictly reserved for remedial settings, they may in fact promote notions of racial inferiority and lead to a politics of racial hostility." The court rejected the argument that "past societal discrimination alone can serve as the basis for rigid racial preferences" and declared that "the dream of a Nation of equal citizens in a society where race is irrelevant to personal opportunity and achievement would be lost in a mosaic of shifting preferences based on inherently unmeasurable claims of past wrongs."[20] The same year in another case, *Wards Cove Packing Co. v. Antonio* (490 U.S. 642), the Supreme Court revised the disparate-impact test it had set forth in the *Griggs* case, which prompted Congress, controlled by Democrats, to pass legislation limiting the decision's impact.

The tide, however, was moving in the opposite direction. In 1993, in *Shaw v. Reno* (509 U.S. 657), Justice O'Connor on behalf of a 5-to-4 majority remanded to the district court a case concerning a North Carolina congressional district, running across the state along an interstate highway, so as to produce a majority black district. "Racial classifications of any sort," she wrote, "pose the risk of lasting harm to our society. They reinforce the belief, held by too many for too much of our history, that individuals should be judged by the color of their skin." Race-conscious districts "may balkanize us into competing racial factions . . . and carry us further from the goal of a political system in which race no longer matters." Then, in 1995, in *Adarand Contractors v. Pena* (515 U.S. 200), the court held that government regulations prescribing favorable treatment for minority contractors were inherently suspect. Writing for a 5-to-4 majority, Justice Antonin Scalia declared, "In the eyes of government we are just one race here. It is American." Thirty years after Congress by huge majorities had written that principle into American law, the Supreme Court finally accepted it by a narrow majority. The Clinton administration, however, did not accept this affirmation of the American Creed. It devised various schemes to limit the court's holding in *Adarand*, and as a result by 1996, as the Thernstroms put it, "a remarkable state of affairs had emerged: the Supreme Court and the U.S. Department of Justice were at war."[21]

That "war" continued in the next administration, but the participants changed sides. In 2003 the Bush administration argued that race should be eliminated as a factor in admission to the University of Michigan undergraduate college and law school and that the goal of racial diversity should be pursued through other means. By a 6-to-3 vote the Supreme Court invalidated the automatic awarding of 20 points (out of a possible

150) to minority applicants to the college. In its most important decision on race and higher education since the Bakke case in 1978, however, the court approved the use of race in the law school admissions.
Endorsing the reasoning of Justice Lewis F. Powell, Jr., in *Bakke*, the
court by a 5-to-4 vote argued in an opinion by Justice O'Connor that
the law school admission process "bears the hallmarks of a narrowly tai-
lored plan" and that "student body diversity is a compelling state interest that can justify the use of race in university admissions." It also said
that "a university admissions program must remain flexible enough to
ensure that each applicant is evaluated as an individual and not in a way
that makes an applicant's race or ethnicity the defining feature of his
or her application." The court added that "Race-conscious admissions
policies must be limited in time" and it expected "that twenty-five years
from now, the use of racial preferences will no longer be necessary to
further the interest approved today."

Opponents of affirmative action had promoted the suits against the
University of Michigan in the hope that, given the increasing judicial
restraints on racial preferences in the 1990s, the court would outlaw any
role for race in university admissions. The supporters of preferences
feared that this could well be the case. The court's law school decision,
however, marked a pause in if not a reversal of the recent trend. It did
not affirm the goal of a race-blind society, and it did not ban racial preferences but defined how they must be applied. Overall, it was judged, as
a *New York Times* editorial hailed it, "A Win for Affirmative Action." It
was also a win for the American establishment. Hundreds of organizations filed briefs supporting Michigan, including major corporations
such as General Motors, Microsoft, Boeing, American Express, and
Shell, plus more than two dozen retired military officers and defense officials. Their views, of course, contrasted with those of the majorities of
Americans consistently opposed to racial preferences, which were reit-
erated in the lead-up to the court's decision. In 2001, 92 percent of the
public, including 88 percent of Hispanics and 86 percent of blacks, said
race should not be used as a factor in college admissions or job hirings
so as to give minorities more opportunity. A few months before the
Supreme Court's decision, 68 percent of the public, including 56 per-

cent of minorities, opposed preferences for blacks, with larger majorities opposing them for other minorities.[22] Five justices thus sided with the establishment, four justices and the Bush administration with the public.

As the Michigan case demonstrated, Americans remain deeply divided over whether America should be race-blind or race-conscious and organized on the basis of equal rights for all or special rights for particular racial, ethnic, and cultural groups. It would be hard to overestimate the importance of this issue. For over two hundred years the creedal principle of equal rights for all without regard to race had been ignored and flouted in practice in American society, politics, and law. In the 1940s, the president, federal courts, and then Congress began to make federal and state law color-blind and used whatever powers they had to eliminate racial discrimination in America, culminating in the Civil Rights and Voting Rights acts. Yet nonelected officials immediately launched a counterreform, if not a counterrevolution (and, as President Clinton said, the civil rights effort was in some sense a revolution), to reintroduce racial discrimination into American practice. The justification for this momentous reversal, as Herman Belz says, "was the belief that group rights, racial proportionalism, and equality of result are correct principles of social organization that deserve to be established as the basis of civil rights policy." This replacement of individual rights by ✳ group rights and of color-blind law by color-conscious law was never approved by the American people and received only intermittent, passive, and partial acceptance by American legislators. "What is extraordinary about this change," the distinguished sociologist Daniel Bell commented, "is that, without public debate, an entirely new principle of rights has been introduced into the polity." "Group rights and equality of condition," Belz agrees, "were introduced into public opinion as a new public philosophy that distinguishes among individuals on racial and ethnic grounds and that ultimately denies the existence of a common good." The implications of this view were cogently stated by the Thernstroms: "Racial classifications deliver the message that skin color matters—profoundly. They suggest that whites and blacks are not the same, that race and ethnicity are the qualities that really matter. They imply that individuals are defined by blood—not by character, social class, religious sentiments, age, or education. But categories appropriate to a caste system are a poor basis on which to build that community of equal citizens upon which democratic government depends."[23]

THE CHALLENGE TO ENGLISH

During the 1988 campaign to have English declared the official language of Florida, the Republican governor, Bob Martinez, declared his opposition: "We don't select a religion for Americans. We don't select a race for Americans. And we have not selected a language for Americans."[24] He was wrong. Three hundred years of history had selected English as the language for Americans, and on election day 83.9 percent of Florida's voters endorsed that choice. The presence of this language proposal on the Florida ballot (as it was in two other states that year) was symptomatic of the extent to which, during the 1980s and 1990s, language became a central issue of American identity. Controversies arose over bilingual education, businesses requiring their employees to speak English, government documents in languages other than English, ballots and election materials in districts with significant non-English-speaking minorities, the designation of English as the official language of national and state governments. The role of English in schools and other contexts had come up before in the United States, but the profusion and intensity of controversies at the national as well as state and local levels were unprecedented. In terms of both symbol and substance, the battles over English were a major front in the broader war over American identity. The question in this conflict, one scholar said, is "whether the United States should reflect a dominant English-speaking majoritarianism or encourage a multilingual culture."[25] The real issue, however, is not multilingualism but bilingualism.

Only a few questioned the importance of English in American culture and the desirability of Americans being proficient in English. The language controversies did, however, raise two key issues. First, to what extent should the U.S. government promote the knowledge and use of languages other than English and restrict the ability of governments, private businesses, and other institutions to require the use of English? In most instances, the other language is Spanish, which gives rise to the second and much more important issue: Should the United States become a bilingual society, with Spanish on an equal footing with English?

"Language," Miguel de Unamuno said, "is the blood of the spirit." It is also something much more down-to-earth. It is the basis of community. In this respect, despite Governor Martinez, it differs fundamentally from race and religion. People of different races and different religions have often fought each other, but if they have the same language they can still speak to each other and read what each writes. Nations, as Karl Deutsch showed in his classic work *Nationalism and Social Communication*, are groups of people who communicate more extensively and intensely with each other than they do with other people.[26] Without a common language, communication becomes difficult if not impossible, and the nation becomes the arena for two or more language communities whose members communicate far more intensely with the members of their group than with those of the other group. Countries where almost everyone speaks the same language, such as France, Germany, and Japan, differ significantly from countries with two or more linguistic communities, such as Switzerland, Belgium, and Canada. In the latter countries divorce is always a possibility, and historically these countries have in large part held together by fear of more powerful neighbors. Efforts to make each group fluent in the other's language seldom succeed. Few Anglo-Canadians have been fluent in French. Few Flemish and Walloons are at home in the other's language. German-speaking and French-speaking Swiss communicate with each other in English.

Throughout American history English has been central to American national identity. Immigrant groups have at times attempted to maintain the use of a different language but, except for some small, isolated, rural communities, English has triumphed in the second and third generations. Teaching new immigrants English, as we have seen, has been a central concern of American governments, corporations, churches, and social welfare organizations.

At least that was the case until the late twentieth century. The promotion of minority languages and the downgrading of English then became key elements in the efforts by governments and other institutions to encourage subnational identities. Central to these efforts was the interpretation of the Civil Rights Act (1964), the Voting Rights Act (1965), and the Bilingual Education Act (1967). Title VI of the Civil Rights Act prohibited discrimination on the basis of "national origin" in federally assisted programs of state and local governments and private institutions. Title VII prohibited discrimination in employment on the basis of national origin in firms employing fifteen or more workers. The Voting Rights Act included a provision sponsored by Senator Robert F. Kennedy requiring New York election authorities to provide election materials in Spanish to Puerto Rican voters. The Bilingual Education Act was designed by Senator Ralph Yarborough of Texas to provide help to Mexican-American children who were poor and educationally disadvantaged because of their weak knowledge of English. The initial appropriation was $7.5 million.

From these humble and limited beginnings emerged a complex structure of federal regulations, court decisions, and further legislation in a process somewhat similar to that by which the race-blind civil rights acts gave birth to racial preferences. Federal administrators interpreted the laws so as to authorize and require government support for non-English languages. Their interpretations were generally upheld by federal judges. Congress then enacted new laws expanding support for non-English languages and limiting the use of English. These moves in turn stimulated organized opposition and popular reaction manifested most notably in a dozen referenda in which, with one exception, the pro-English forces always won.

The lineup in these battles also paralleled that on racial preferences. Large numbers of government officials, judges, intellectuals, and liberals, a fair number of elected legislators and executives, and the leaders of Hispanic and other minority organizations were on one side. On the other side were many legislators, a small number of private individuals and groups, and, as with racial preferences, large majorities of the American public. They were regularly joined by substantial numbers of people from the language minority groups.

The language battles between opposing coalitions on the roles of English and other languages occurred with respect to elections, government, business, and schools. Only citizens may vote in American elections. People become citizens by birth or naturalization. Citizens by birth (with the possible exception of Puerto Ricans) may be presumed to have a rudimentary knowledge of English. People who wish to be naturalized are required to demonstrate "an understanding of the English language, including an ability to read, write, and speak . . . simple words and phrases . . . in ordinary usage in the English language."[27] Only the disabled and elderly persons who have resided in the United States for fifteen or more years are exempt from this requirement. It thus seems reasonable to assume that virtually all those with the right to vote know or should know at least enough English to read a ballot and related voting materials.

In 1975, however, Congress amended the 1965 Voting Rights Act so as to prohibit state and local governments from imposing any voting qualification, prerequisite, or procedure that would "deny or abridge the right of any citizen of the United States to vote because he is a member of a language minority group." The act required local governments to provide bilingual ballots in voting districts where: (1) either the English literacy rate was below the national average or fewer than 50 percent of potential voters voted in the 1972 election where election materials were only in English; and (2) five percent or more of the population belonged to a language minority group, defined as American Indian, Asian, Alaskan native, or "of Spanish heritage." In 1980, in response to a federal lawsuit, the San Francisco registrar of voters agreed to provide ballots, voter pamphlets, poll watchers, and to conduct voter registration drives in Spanish and Chinese as well as English. By 2002 some 335 jurisdictions in thirty states had to provide written materials, and oral assistance in languages other than English, of which 220 were required to do so in Spanish. These requirements often affected very small language minorities. In 1994, for example, Los Angeles County spent over $67,000 on voting services for 692 Tagalog speakers.[28]

Federal agencies and the courts interpreted "national origin" in the Civil Rights Act to include language and the prohibition against discrimination to prevent the covered institutions from requiring participants in their programs to speak English. In addition, these institutions were mandated to provide service and support to non-English speakers to make them equal to English speakers. Courts also ruled that state and local laws requiring the use of English in certain circumstances were unconstitutional because they violate the First Amendment guarantee of free speech. The First Amendment was thus extended to cover not just freedom of expression and the content of speech but also the language used to express that content. In short, governments may not be able to require the use of English when they determine that to be necessary.

The influx of Asian and Hispanic immigrants in the 1980s prompted many California localities to adopt ordinances requiring store signs to be at least partly in English for public safety reasons. An Asian American Business Group challenge to such a rule in Pomona was upheld in 1989 by Federal District Court Judge Robert Takasugi on the grounds that the signs were "an expression of national origin, culture, and ethnicity" and hence regulation of them violated the First and Fourteenth amendments. In another case, in 1994 the Department of Housing and Urban Development challenged an Allentown, Pennsylvania, ordinance directing the mayor to issue all documents exclusively in English and threatened to withhold its $4 million annual grant to Allentown. After considerable furor, the mayor said he would not implement the ordinance and HUD did not suspend the payments. In 1999 the 11th Circuit Court of Appeals ruled that Alabama could not give driver's license tests only in English because Title VI's provision against "national origin" discrimination prohibited actions that had disparate impact on non-English speakers. The U.S. Supreme Court, however, held that the private parties to this suit would have to prove not just disparate impact but also discriminatory intent, which they had not done.[29]

In 1988 Arizona voters narrowly approved an amendment to the constitution making English the state's official language and requiring that all state officials and employees "act" only in English in performing government business. The Arizona Supreme Court recognized the validity of the requirement in the act of Congress admitting Arizona to the union that English be the only language of instruction in Arizona schools and that all Arizona officials and employees must be able to use and understand English. It invalidated the constitutional amendment, however, for violating the First Amendment "because it adversely impacts the constitutional rights of non-English-speaking persons with regard to their obtaining access to their government and limits the political speech of elected officials and public employees."[30] The U.S. Supreme Court declined to review this decision.

In a parallel series of cases, the Equal Employment Opportunity Commission interpreted the "national origin" provision of Title VII so as to challenge rules of employers requiring employees to speak only English while at work. The EEOC filed thirty-two such suits in 1996 and ninety-one in 1999. Companies may impose such restrictions only in situations where it can be justified by a narrowly defined "business necessity." As one attorney opposed to official English has argued, with respect to Titles VI and VII, "the key legal issue is whether the prohibition on national-origin discrimination extends to language discrimination." If it does, he points out, "The failure of private hospitals that receive federal funds to provide adequate translation services for non-English speaking patients" could violate the law.[31]

Following Congress's adoption of Senator Yarborough's proposal to help his poor Mexican-American constituents to get a better education, education in non-English languages spread rapidly throughout the country, even to those seven states whose laws or constitutions prohibited instruction in languages other than English. In 1970 the federal Office for Civil Rights directed that under Title VI of the Civil Rights Act, a school district with "more than five percent national-origin-minority-group children" had to "take affirmative steps to rectify the language deficiency in order to open its instructional program to these students." Two years later, a federal district judge ruled that the equal protection of the laws clause required students in New Mexico to be instructed in their native language and culture. In 1974, in a San Francisco case involving Chinese children, the U.S. Supreme Court interpreted Title VI to mean that schools cannot simply provide non-English-speaking schoolchildren with the same instruction as English speakers and instead must provide some remedy to compensate for this deficiency in their knowledge.[32] By 2001 Congress was appropriating $446 million for bilingual programs, which was supplemented by huge amounts of state funding.

From the beginning of the bilingual program, as one of its supporters commented, "a key question of goals—whether the act was to speed the transition to English or to promote bilingualism—was left unresolved." Initially both goals were pursued, and in 1974 the act was amended to require schools to provide instruction in a student's native language and culture "to the extent necessary to allow a child to progress effectively through the educational system." Both maintenance and transitional programs existed until 1978, when the American Institutes for Research reported that 86 percent of the directors of bilingual education programs said that Spanish-speaking children were kept in such programs after they had become proficient in English. Congress then ended support for maintenance programs, but in 1984 reversed itself and explicitly authorized their funding.[33]

By the mid-1980s much of the instruction in bilingual education was, according to a *Time* magazine survey, "designed to maintain a student's original language indefinitely, bolstering the language with enrichment studies in indigenous art, music, literature and history." "It is very important to us that kids take pride in their own culture," said the director of bilingual programs in San Francisco, meaning, of course, their ancestral culture, not American culture.[34] In 1985 Secretary of Education William Bennett argued that the U.S. Department of Health, Education, and Welfare had previously "increasingly emphasized bilingual education as a way of enhancing students' knowledge of their native language and culture. Bilingual education was no longer seen so much as a means to ensure that students learned English, or as a transitional method until students learned English. Rather, it became an emblem of cultural pride, a means of producing a positive self-image in the student." Congressman James Scheuer, who had been an original sponsor of the Bilingual Education Act, expressed similar views. The program, he said, had become "perverted and politicized," and instead of helping students master English, "the English has been sort of thinned out and stretched out and in many cases banished into the mists and all of the courses tended to be taught in Spanish. That was not the original intent of the program."[35] In 2000 another original sponsor of the bilingual education law, former Congressman Herman Badillo, expressed similar views. In New York City, he pointed out, 85 percent of ninth-grade students in bilingual and ESL—English as a Second Language—programs did not finish the program by the end of high school and 55 percent of those in such programs in the sixth grade had not moved into mainstream classes eight years later. Bilingual education, he said, "has become 'monolingual education,' which doesn't help the students. . . . It's supposed to be English first, and then Spanish. It wasn't supposed to be eight years in a program. It was supposed to be transitional."[36]

The federal government's promotion of non-English languages and opposition to the English-only policies by state governments and private institutions generated a countermovement. In 1981 Senator S. I. Hayakawa introduced a constitutional amendment declaring English the official language of the United States. Two years later he joined with others to form an organization, U.S. English, to promote this goal. And in 1986 another pro-English group, English First, came into being. These organizations launched a broad movement that resulted in nineteen states adopting some sort of official English declaration during the 1980s and 1990s. These decisions were hotly contested by Hispanic and other language minority groups, plus liberal and civil rights organizations, and they got three states to pass alternative "English Plus" resolutions. Several legislatures declined to act on any of these proposals, but nowhere was an official English proposal defeated at the polls.[37]

Those states in which the legislature took pro-English action tended to be Southern and other states with relatively small immigrant, Asian, and Hispanic populations. In states with large minority populations, the legislatures declined to act or defeated these proposals. The four states (Arizona, California, Colorado, Florida) where voters approved the official English proposals (in three by substantial majorities) had, as Jack Citrin et al. observe, "as a group, the highest proportion of non-English speakers, immigrants, Hispanics, and Asians. These four states also experienced the highest rate of growth in their Hispanic and foreign-born populations between 1970 and 1980." In somewhat similar fashion, the 1989 official English referendum in Lowell, Massachusetts, followed a decade of large Hispanic and Southeast Asian inflows into the city, producing a quadrupling of children with limited English proficiency, or LEP, in five years.[38] Rapid expansions of non-English-speaking peoples, the evidence suggests, creates a powerful stimulus for the reassertion of their English language identity by native Americans but not by their legislators.

By every indication the American public is overwhelmingly pro-English. In a careful 1990 public opinion survey, four scholars concluded that "To the mass public, English remains an important symbol of national identity." In 1986, 81 percent of the American public believed that "anyone who wants to stay in this country should have to learn English." In a 1988 poll, 76 percent of Californians rated speaking English as "very important" in making one an American, and 61 percent believed that the right to vote should be limited to English speakers. In a 1998 poll, 52 percent of Americans strongly supported and 25 percent somewhat supported legislation that would require all school instruction to be in English and the placing of LEP students in a one-year English immersion program.[39] The huge majority of Americans who hold English as a key component of their national identity, combined with squeamishness of legislators on language issues, provided a strong incentive for proponents of official English and opponents of bilingual education to resort to initiatives and referenda to get their policies enacted into law.

From 1980 to 2000, twelve referenda were held in three cities and four states on English as the official language and on bilingual education. (See Table 7.1.) These referenda were all initiated by pro-English groups. In all except one, the voters approved the pro-English or anti-bilingual-education proposal. The average vote in favor of pro-English positions was 65 percent, ranging from a low of 44 percent in Colorado to a high of 85 percent in Florida. In all these cases political elites and establishment institutions overwhelmingly opposed these measures, as did heads of Hispanic and other language minority groups.

In 1980, a measure to reverse an ordinance declaring Dade County, Florida, bilingual and bicultural, to mandate the use of only English in government, and to prohibit the use of public money for "promoting

Table 7.1

Language Referenda, 1980–2002

Year	Jurisdiction	Purpose	% in favor
1980	Dade County, Florida	Reversing 1973 bilingual ordinance	59
1983	San Francisco, California	Opposing federal law requiring non-English ballots	62
1984	California	Urging federal authorization for English-only voting materials	71
1986	California	Making English official language	73
1988	Florida	Making English official language	85.5
1988	Colorado	Making English official language	64
1988	Arizona	Making English official language	50.5
1989	Lowell, Massachusetts	Making English official language and urging approval of English Language Amendment to U.S. Constitution	67
1998	California	Ending bilingual education	61
2000	Arizona	Ending bilingual education	63
2002	Massachusetts	Ending bilingual education	68
2002	Colorado	Ending bilingual education	44

any culture other than that of the United States," was vigorously opposed by Hispanic groups, the *Miami Herald*, and the Greater Miami Chamber of Commerce, which alone spent $50,000 trying to defeat it. Those in favor of the proposal spent about $10,000 on their campaign. Dade county voters approved the proposal by a 59.2 percent majority.[40]

In 1986 a proposed amendment to California's constitution making English the official language was opposed by all the state's top political figures (except then Senator Pete Wilson), including the governor, attorney general, the other U.S. senator, the state Senate president, the speaker of the Assembly, the mayors of San Francisco and San Diego, the city councils of Los Angeles and San Jose, all the major television and radio stations, all the major newspapers except the *San Francisco Examiner*, the California Labor Federation (AFL-CIO), and the California

Catholic Bishops Conference. On election day, 73.2 percent of California voters approved the amendment with majorities for it in every county.[41]

In 1988 presidential candidates George H. W. Bush and Michael Dukakis opposed the official English measures on the ballot in Florida, Arizona, and Colorado. So also did the political, social, and economic elites in these states. In Florida the proposed constitutional amendment was opposed by the governor, the attorney general, the secretary of state, the *Miami Herald*, the Greater Miami Chamber of Commerce, plus many Hispanic organizations, others of which, however, abstained in deference to the overwhelming popularity of the measure. It was approved by 85.5 percent of the voters and carried every county.

Also in 1988, in a bitter contest in Arizona, an official English initiative was opposed by the governor, two former governors, both United States senators, the mayor of Phoenix, the Arizona Judges Association, the League of Arizona Cities and Towns, Jewish leaders, and the Arizona Ecumenical Council composed of eleven Christian denominations. The proposal suffered from the disclosure in the midst of the campaign of a memo by John Tanton, the head of U.S. English, the campaign's principal funder, that proposed a moratorium on immigration, included allegedly derogatory remarks on Catholics, and hence was labeled "the Nazi memo" by the proposal's opponents. These circumstances produced the only close vote among the official English referenda, with 50.5 percent of Arizonans approving it. In Colorado, the official English measure was opposed by the governor, the lieutenant governor, the attorney general, the mayor of Denver, one United States senator, the leading Catholic bishops, the *Denver Post*, the state Democratic Party (the Republicans taking no position), and Jesse Jackson. It was approved by 64 percent of Colorado's voters.[42]

In 1989, looking back on the previous year's referenda, a Stanford University linguist commented sadly but accurately, "By and large, the successes of the [Official English] movement have been achieved without the support of establishment politicians and organizations. . . . The U.S. English leadership is probably justified in claiming that 'no one is for us but the people.' "[43]

The following decade the same lineup appeared in referenda on bilingual education. In 1998 in California several Hispanic leaders and many Hispanic voters supported Proposition 227 to end bilingual education. All the state's elected Democratic officials and President Clinton opposed it, as, with some qualification, did Texas Governor George W. Bush. Sixty-one percent of the state's voters approved it, as did majorities in every county except San Francisco. Two years later, a similar proposal in Arizona was opposed by the state Republican leadership, all the state's top elected officials from the governor on down, all the major newspapers, Governor Bush and Vice President Gore, with the opposition spending many times that spent by the supporters. It was approved by 63 percent of the Arizona voters. In 2002 in Massachusetts, the Republican gubernatorial candidate, Mitt Romney, backed an initiative to end bilingual education, but it was opposed by Democratic leaders, prominent academics including the deans of eight schools of education, other establishment figures, major media including the *Boston Globe*, and a "coalition of teachers, unions, immigrants' rights activists, and community groups."[44] Sixty-eight percent of the voters approved it.

In more than two decades, the only defeat by popular vote of a pro-English or anti-bilingual-education measure occurred in Colorado in 2002 when an initiative to end bilingual education lost by 56 percent to 44 percent. This result was brought about by a last-minute huge expenditure of funds provided by a pro-bilingual-education millionairess. These were used for an appeal to the anti-Hispanic sentiments of Colorado voters by warning them that the end of bilingual education would create "chaos in the classroom" and "bedlam if thousands of ill-prepared immigrant children flooded mainstream classrooms."[45] Faced with this prospect, the Colorado voters chose to endorse educational apartheid.

The attitudes of Hispanics on language issues partly paralleled but also differed somewhat from those of blacks on racial preferences. Hispanics tended to oppose the largely symbolic official English proposals. In exit polls in 1988 in California and Texas, for instance, on average only 25 percent of Hispanics supported declaring English the official language of the United States as compared with 60 percent of Anglos. The 1980 Dade County English only initiative was endorsed by 71 percent of whites and 44 percent of blacks, but only 15 percent of Hispanics. In 1986, 41 percent of Hispanics voted in favor of the official English proposal in California. Two years later, only 25 percent of Florida Hispanics voted for a similar measure.[46]

Hispanics have tended to be more ambivalent, and often favorable, toward measures to end or limit bilingual education, which have immediate and powerful consequences for their children. A 1998 national poll showed 66 percent of Hispanic parents wanting their children to learn English "as quickly as possible, even if this means they fall behind in other subjects."[47] Hispanic parents surveyed in 1996 in Houston, Los Angeles, Miami, New York, and San Antonio said that teaching their children English was by far the most important thing that schools do. In the 1998 national poll on whether all instruction in schools should be in English with a special one-year immersion program for those deficient in English, 38 percent of Hispanics expressed strong support and 26 percent somewhat supported this position. The impetus for the California anti-bilingual-education proposal came from Hispanic parents in Los Angeles who pulled their ninety children out of school to protest the inferior education they were receiving in bilingual classes. As the Reverend Alice Callaghan, an Episcopal priest and director of a Hispanic community center, observed: "Parents do not want their children working in sweatshops or cleaning downtown office buildings when they grow up. They want them to get into Harvard and Stanford, and that won't happen unless they are truly fluent and literate in English." In one 1997 poll in Orange County, 83 percent of Hispanic parents "said they wanted their children to be taught in English as soon as they started school." In a different October 1997 *Los Angeles Times* poll, 84 percent of California Hispanics said they favored limiting bilingual education. Alarmed by these figures, Hispanic politicians and leaders of Hispanic organizations duplicated their efforts against the Civil Rights Initiative and launched a massive campaign to convince Hispanics to oppose the bilingual education initiative. Again they succeeded. On election day in June 1998, after what the *New York Times* called "a blitz against the measure by almost every elected Hispanic official in the state," less than 40 percent of Hispanics voted for it.[48]

THE CHALLENGE TO THE CORE CULTURE

When President Clinton in 1997 said that America needed a third "great revolution" to prove it could exist without a dominant European culture, that revolution was well under way. The multiculturalist movement to replace America's mainstream Anglo-Protestant culture with other cultures linked primarily to racial groups began in the 1970s. It achieved its greatest success and prominence in the 1980s and early 1990s, and then was challenged by an aroused opposition in the cultural wars of the 1990s. Whether and to what extent the revolution had succeeded was unclear as the twenty-first century began.

Multiculturalism is in its essence anti-European civilization. It is, as one scholar said, a "movement opposed to the monocultural hegemony of Eurocentric values, which has generally resulted in the marginalization of other ethnic cultural values. . . . [It is opposed to] narrow Eurocentric concepts of American democratic principles, culture, and identity."[49] It is basically an anti-Western ideology. Multiculturalists advance several propositions. First, America is composed of many different ethnic and racial groups. Second, each of these groups has its own distinctive culture. Third, the white Anglo elite dominant in American society has suppressed these cultures and compelled or induced those belonging to other ethnic or racial groups to accept the elite's Anglo-Protestant culture. Fourth, justice, equality, and the rights of minorities demand that these suppressed cultures be liberated and that governments and private institutions encourage and support their revitalization. America is not and should not be a society with a single pervasive national culture. The melting pot and tomato soup metaphors do not describe the true America. America is instead a mosaic, a salad, or even a "tossed salad."[50]

The emergence of the multiculturalists in the 1970s coincided with the appearance of a very different group, "the new ethnics," who propounded somewhat parallel views. They focused on non-British European immigrant groups and expressed what they saw as the resentment of "white ethnic working-class communities" against WASP elites for their suppression of ethnic cultures, their patronizing attitudes, and their promotion of the causes of blacks and other racial minorities. America was not a melting pot, but in the words of Senator Barbara Mikulski, a leader of the new ethnicity, it was a "sizzling cauldron." Jews and Catholics, Mikulski argued, should go ethnic against "phony white liberals, pseudo black militants, and patronizing bureaucrats." "The point about the melting pot is that it did not happen," Nathan Glazer and Daniel Patrick Moynihan famously declared in their seminal 1963 study *Beyond the Melting Pot.* They recognized that "the distinctive language, customs and culture are lost . . . largely . . . in the second generation, and even more fully in the third generation." Yet they also argued that ethnicity is re-created as "a new social form by new experiences in America."[51] To further this ethnic revival Congressman Roman Pucinski from Chicago introduced in 1970 the Ethnic Studies Act, which authorized government funding for ethnic activities. In vigorous language he denounced the melting pot concept and enthusiastically embraced the idea of America as a mosaic. Pucinski's bill passed but without much popular support.[52] Little was done to implement it in the following decade, and in 1981 it expired.

The end of the Ethnic Studies Act symbolized the failure of the ethnic revival movement, which occurred for two reasons. First, white ethnics were increasingly intermarrying and hence their identification with any one ethnic group was fading (see Chapter 11). In addition, third- or fourth-generation Americans, many of whom had fought for their country in World War II, had become substantially assimilated into America's mainstream culture. The 1970s "ethnic revival was," as Stephen Steinberg argues, " 'a dying gasp' on the part of ethnic groups descended from the great waves of immigration of the nineteenth and early twentieth centuries."[53] The multiculturalists, strongly denouncing European civilization, could hardly embrace white ethnics whose cultures were part of that civilization. The latter responded accordingly. "Most Polish Americans," one of their leaders said of multiculturalism in 1997, "would tend to oppose its anti-Western orientation: its attitude of denouncing Western civilization with its past imperialism as the source of all evil and glorifying non-Western civilizations and cultures for their goodness. . . . [It is necessary] to emphasize the fact that Europe is the birthplace of the United States of America, that European ideas of individual liberty, political democracy, rule of law, human rights, and cultural freedom formed the American Republic."[54] While the proponents of the new ethnicity thus emphasized the difference between the ethnicity of second-wave immigrants and the WASP elite and its culture, the multiculturalists viewed them both as parts of a European civilization whose dominance had to be destroyed.

The multiculturalists directly challenged the "Anglo-conformist" image of America. They look forward, as one scholar put it, to a time the United States "may never again be culturally 'united,' if 'united' means 'unified' in beliefs and practices," and to a time when Americans will be less "a culturally definable group."[55] This transformation would, indeed, as President Clinton said, be a dramatic change in America's national identity. The multiculturalists included many intellectuals, academics, and educators. They thus had their principal impact on the educational practices of schools and colleges. As we have seen, historically the public schools were the great channel through which the children and grandchildren of immigrants were brought into American society and culture. The goal of the multiculturalists was to do exactly the opposite. Instead of schools giving priority to educating children in the English language and the common American culture, they want teachers, as one of them said, to engage in the "transforming of schools into authentic culturally democratic sites" by giving primary emphasis to the cultures of subnational groups.[56]

"A major goal of multicultural education," according to James Banks, a leading contributor to multicultural studies, "is to reform the school and other educational institutions so that students from diverse racial, ethnic, and social-class groups will experience educational equality."[57] "Educational equality," in one sense, can refer to the equal access of students from all groups and classes to education of similar quality, a goal from which few Americans are likely to dissent. In the multiculturalist sense, however, it also meant equal treatment in the educational curriculum of the cultures of different races, ethnic groups, and social classes. Achieving this goal came at the expense of teaching the values and culture that Americans have had in common. The multiculturalists' teaching manuals ignore the mainstream culture of America because for them there is no such thing. As two of them affirmed, "We believe that multicultural teaching should permeate the entire school curriculum," and that "multicultural education is integral to teaching and learning at all levels." [58]

Multiculturalism represented the culmination of a long erosion of the emphasis on national identity in American education. National and patriotic themes declined in school readers in the middle and late twentieth century and reached a low point by its end. In one comprehensive study, Charlotte Iiams analyzed the content of readers from 1900 to 1970, using a five-point scale ranging from "no mention of nation" through "neutral," "patriotic," and "nationalistic" to "chauvinistic." Between 1900 and 1940, the content of the intermediate-grade readers ranged from patriotic to nationalistic, while the primary-grade readers had little or no patriotic content. "By the 1950s and 1960s," however, "most textbooks ranged from neutral to barely patriotic in both the primary and intermediate grades." This change was manifest in "the gradually diminishing presence of war-related stories designed to give children a common history and common political ideals." [59]

A study by Paul Vitz of twenty-two readers for grades three and six published in the 1970s and early 1980s and used in California, Texas, and many other states revealed that only five out of 670 stories and articles in these readers had "any patriotic theme." Seventeen of the twenty-two textbooks did not contain any story with a patriotic theme. All five patriotic stories dealt with the Revolution; none had "anything to do with American history since 1780." In four of the five stories the principal person is a girl, in three the same girl, Sybil Ludington. The twenty-two books lack any story "featuring Nathan Hale, Patrick Henry, Daniel Boone, or Paul Revere's ride." "Patriotism," Vitz concludes, "is close to nonexistent" in these readers. In another study of six 1970s high school history textbooks, Harvard professor Nathan Glazer and Tufts professor Reed Ueda found that "not one of the new histories claims as a principal objective inculcating patriotism, a function embraced by the history texts that appeared during and soon after World War I. Moralism and nationalism are both out of date." In the 1970s histories "the central processes that integrated American society are trivialized."[60]

An analysis by Sandra Stotsky of twelve grade four and grade six readers published in the 1990s concluded that "the trends Iiams and Vitz detected have continued, if not accelerated." In these readers, "selections about national symbols and songs are almost nonexistent." The emphasis is instead on ethnic and racial groups. From 31 percent to 73 percent of all the selections dealing with America dealt with ethnic and racial groups, and in 90 percent of these selections with ethnic content the groups referred to were blacks, Asian-Americans, American Indians, and Hispanic-Americans. As a result, a 1987 study of high school students found that more knew who Harriet Tubman was than knew that Washington commanded the American army in the Revolution or that Abraham Lincoln wrote the Emancipation Proclamation. "The net effect," Stotsky concludes, "is the disappearing of an American culture as a whole." Summing up the situation in 1997, Nathan Glazer highlighted "how complete has been the victory of multiculturalism in the public schools of America."[61]

That victory was paralleled by a comparable movement in colleges and universities leading to not just inclusion in the curriculum of courses on minority groups but the requiring of students to take such courses. At Stanford, as Glazer points out, a required course on Western civilization was replaced by "courses with a focus on minorities, Third World peoples, and women." This was followed by "the establishment of required courses on American minorities at the University of California, Berkeley, at the University of Minnesota, at Hunter College, and elsewhere." In the early 1990s Arthur Schlesinger observed, "students could graduate from 78 percent of American colleges and universities without taking a course in the history of Western civilization. A number of institutions—among them Dartmouth, Wisconsin, Mt. Holyoke— require courses in third world or ethnic studies but not in Western civilization. The mood is one of divesting Americans of the sinful European inheritance and seeking redemptive infusions from non-Western cultures." At the turn of the century, none of fifty top American colleges and universities required a course in American history.[62]

With the downgrading of American and Western history in the curriculum, college students remained ignorant of many central events and people in the nation's past. In one early 1990s poll, 90 percent of Ivy League students could identify Rosa Parks but only 25 percent could identify the author of the words "government of the people, by the people, and for the people." A 1999 survey of seniors at fifty-five top colleges produced similar results:

> *More than a third . . . did not know the Constitution* established the *division of powers in American government.*
>
> Forty percent could not say within a half-century *when the Civil War was fought.*
>
> *More students named the Civil War general, Ulysses S. Grant, than George Washington . . .* as the man who defeated the British at *Yorktown, the final battle of the Revolutionary War.*
>
> *Only 22 percent could identify the Gettysburg address* as the source of the phrase "government of the people, by the people, for the people."[63]

Before the Civil War, as we have seen, American history was primarily the histories of individual states and localities. National history emerged after that war and for a hundred years was central to defining American identity. Then in the late twentieth century, the histories of subnational racial and cultural groups rose to a new prominence comparable to that of pre-1860 state and local histories, and national history was downgraded. If, however, a nation is a remembered as well as an imagined community, people who are losing that memory are becoming something less than a nation.

The deconstructionist challenges to the Creed, the primacy of English, and the core culture were overwhelmingly opposed by the American public. In addition, as with the other two, the multicultural challenge generated countermovements in the 1980s and 1990s. Books appeared with titles such as *Illiberal Education: The Politics of Race and Sex on Campus; Culture of Complaint: The Fraying of America; Dictatorship of Virtue: Multiculturalism and the Battle for America's Future; The Diversity Myth: Multiculturalism and Political Intolerance on Campus.* Opposition to changes in school and college curricula increased and in some cases were successful. Organizations such as the American Council of Trustees and Alumni and the National Association of Scholars came into being to fight the downgrading of American and Western history and the lowering of standards in America's colleges and universities. In due course, political leaders responded. In 2000 Congress unanimously approved a resolution urging educational authorities to take actions to correct American historical illiteracy. In 2001 tens of millions of dollars were added to the Department of Education's budget to improve the teaching of American history. In 2002 President Bush proposed measures to address this problem to a gathering of two hundred education leaders. In 2003 Senator Lamar Alexander introduced a bill to create summer academies in American history and civics for schoolteachers and high school students.

The battles over the racial, bilingual, and multiculturalist challenges to the Creed, English, and America's core culture had become key elements of the American political landscape by the early years of the twenty-first century. The outcomes of these battles in the deconstructionist war will undoubtedly be substantially affected by the extent to which Americans suffer repeated terrorist attacks on their homeland and their country engages in overseas wars against its enemies. If external threats subside, deconstructionist movements could achieve renewed momentum. If America becomes continuously engaged with foreign enemies, their influence is likely to subside. If the external threats to America are modest, intermittent, and ambiguous, Americans may well remain divided over the appropriate roles of their Creed, language, and core culture in their national identity.

CHAPTER 8

Assimilation: Converts, Ampersands, and the Erosion of Citizenship

IMMIGRATION WITH OR WITHOUT ASSIMILATION

Between 1820 and 1924 about 34 million Europeans came to the United States. Those who stayed were partially assimilated and their children and grandchildren almost totally assimilated into American society and culture. Between 1965 and 2000, 23 million new immigrants arrived in the United States, mostly from Latin America and Asia.[1] The central issue this poses for America is not immigration but immigration with or without assimilation. To what extent will these immigrants, their successors, and descendants follow the path of earlier immigrants and be successfully assimilated into American society and culture, become committed Americans forswearing other national identities, and adhere through belief and action to the principles of the American Creed?

America is not the only nation with this problem. All wealthy, industrialized countries face it. In the last decades of the twentieth century, global migration reached extraordinarily high levels. Much involved the movement of people from one less-developed country to a neighboring less-developed country. Unprecedented numbers of people also entered and sought to enter wealthy countries. Legal immigration was supplemented by illegal movements. About one quarter of the immigrants to the United States in the 1990s were illegal, and in 2000 the British government's Immigration and Nationality Directorate estimated that about 30 million people were smuggled into countries worldwide each year.[2] In different ways, both poverty and economic development promote immigration, and the plethora and relative cheapness of transportation modes make it feasible for more and more people both to migrate and to maintain ties with their country of origin. In 1998, foreign-born people were 19 percent of the population in Switzerland, 9 percent in Germany, 10 percent in France, 4 percent in Britain, 17 percent in Canada, 23 percent in Australia, and 10 percent in the United States.[3]

The rising levels of immigration and the continuing desire of more people to migrate to Western countries coincide with major declines in fertility rates in most of those countries. In almost all wealthy countries, except the United States, total fertility rates are significantly below the 2.1 rate necessary to maintain a stable population. Between 1995 and 2000, the total fertility rate in the United States was 2.04, but in Germany it was 1.33, in Britain 1.70, in France 1.73, in Italy 1.20, in Japan 1.41, and in Canada 1.60.[4] Continuation of these low rates means an aging and eventually declining population. Unless increases occur in either its fertility or immigration, Japan's 2000 population of 127 million will decline to 100 million by 2050 and to 67 million by 2100.[5] At that time, about one third of the population will be sixty-five or over and will have to be supported by a much smaller workforce. Populations and labor forces in Europe will also shrink dramatically, in the absence of significant changes in fertility or immigration. Population decline will not necessarily reduce the overall prosperity of individuals in these countries. Even with increases in productivity, however, it will eventually reduce a country's gross economic product and its economic, political, and military power, with a corresponding loss of influence in world affairs. In the long term, population decline could be avoided by an increase in fertility rates, but that requires major changes in social and economic behavior, and past government efforts to raise fertility have not been notably successful.

This combination of immigrant pressure and prospective population decline creates incentives for the affected countries to admit more immigrants. In the short term, immigrants help to meet crucial labor needs, even in European countries, which generally had high levels of unemployment throughout the 1990s. In the United States, economic growth, low unemployment, and a labor shortage in the late 1990s created even greater need for immigrant labor. Most potential immigrants, however, come from societies with cultures significantly different from those of the wealthy countries. Immigration, consequently, raises the problem of how to accommodate large numbers of Africans, Arabs, Turks, Albanians, and others in European societies, Asians and Latin Americans in the United States, and Asians in Japan, Australia, and Canada. The substantial benefits from immigration in terms of economic growth, demographic revitalization, and maintenance of international status and influence may be countered by the costs of higher spending on government services, fewer jobs, lower wages, and reduced benefits for native workers, social polarization, cultural conflict, decline in trust and community, and erosion of traditional concepts of national identity. The immigration issue may produce serious divisions among elite groups, arouse popular opinion against immigrants and immigration, and offer opportunities to nationalist and populist politicians and parties to exploit these sentiments.

In the 1990s, the perceived threats from immigration led a group of European scholars to develop the concept of "societal security." National security involves the preservation of the independence, sovereignty, and territory of a state from military attack and political domination by another state. It focuses on political control. Societal security, in contrast, as defined by Ole Waever and his associates in the "Copenhagen school," involves "the ability of a society to persist in its essential character under changing conditions and possible or actual threats." It is about "the sustainability, within acceptable conditions for evolution, of traditional patterns of language, culture, association, and religious and national identity and custom."[6] Thus, while national security is concerned, above all, with sovereignty, societal security is concerned above all with identity, the ability of a people to maintain their culture, institutions, and way of life.

In the contemporary world, the greatest threat to the societal security of nations comes from immigration. Countries can respond to that
threat in one or some combination of three ways. Crudely put, the options are: little or no immigration, immigration without assimilation, or
immigration with assimilation. All three have been tried.

The restriction of immigration may involve limiting the number allowed in, setting criteria for admission that have that effect, such as
skills, education, or source (as the United States did in 1924), or allowing immigrants in for only limited periods of time, as in the "guest
worker" programs of European countries and the bracero and H-1B
programs of the United States. Japan has historically discouraged immigration, and in 2000 only one percent of the Japanese population was
foreign-born. The prospective aging and decline of Japan's population
have forced the government reluctantly to consider adopting a more
pro-immigration stance, but that has engendered intense opposition.
With the partial exception of France, European countries historically
also have not thought of themselves as "immigrant societies." In the
early and mid-1990s, some French leaders called for "zero immigration," and France adopted several measures restricting and discouraging
immigration. At the same time, some German leaders took similar
stances, and Germany toughened its laws governing refugees and asy-
lum. These actions had mixed results. Immigrants into France declined
from over 100,000 annually in the early 1990s to about 75,000 in 1995
and 1996, before rising to 138,000 by 1998. In Germany immigrants declined from a peak of 1.2 million in 1992 to just over half that number in
the late 1990s.[7] In contrast to other wealthy countries, the United States
in 1990 raised the limit on legal immigrants from 270,000 to 700,000,
and total legal immigration (including categories exempt from numerical limits) in the 1990s amounted to 9,095,417 compared to 7,338,062
in the 1980s.[8]

The second option is a permissive policy toward immigration and little effort at assimilation. When combined with large numbers of immigrants from cultures very different from that of the host country, this
can lead to immigrant communities isolated and insulated in varying degrees from the broader society. This has happened with North Africans

in France and Turks in Germany, as well as immigrant groups in other European countries, and was responsible for the broad consensus in those countries that immigration must be reduced. Immigration without assimilation thus generates countervailing pressures and usually cannot be sustained indefinitely.

The final option is for a country to accept substantial immigration and also to promote the assimilation of immigrants into its society and culture. European countries with little history of immigration found this difficult to accomplish with their late-twentieth-century immigrants and hence turned to restriction. Until World War I, however, immigration plus assimilation was the prevailing practice in the United States, with immigrants often subjected to intense pressure and major programs to integrate them into American society. The restrictions on immigration enacted in 1924 lessened the concern over Americanization and removed the perceived need for programs to achieve it.

The increase in immigration that began in the 1960s again brought these issues to the fore. The choices are real, difficult, and reasonably clear-cut. Should America drastically reduce current immigration, or accept roughly the current level and composition of immigrants without additional efforts to promote assimilation, or accept roughly the current level and composition of immigrants and make major efforts promoting their assimilation, and if so, assimilation to what? Which option or combination of options would best promote the culture and values, the social and communal cohesion, the economic development and prosperity, the international power and influence of America? Which options or combinations of options are feasible given contemporary American social, economic, political, and international environments?

ASSIMILATION: STILL A SUCCESS?

America has been in part an immigrant nation, but much more importantly, it has been a nation that assimilated immigrants and their descendants into its society and culture. As Milton Gordon showed in his incisive study, immigrants became assimilated to the extent they adopted the cultural patterns of the host society (acculturation), entered into the "network of groups and institutions, or social structure" of the host society, intermarried with members of the host society (which he labels "amalgamation"), and developed an exclusive "sense of people-hood" with the host society. In addition, assimilation required three steps in American acceptance of immigrants: movement toward the absence of discrimination, absence of prejudice, and absence of value-power conflicts.[9]

The assimilation of different groups into American society has varied and has never been complete. Yet overall, historically assimilation, particularly cultural assimilation, has been a great, possibly the greatest, American success story. It enabled America to expand its population, occupy a continent, and develop its economy with millions of dedicated, energetic, ambitious, and talented people, who became overwhelmingly committed to America's Anglo-Protestant culture and the values of the American Creed, and who helped to make America a major force in global affairs. At the heart of this achievement, unmatched by any other society in history, was an implicit contract, which Peter Salins has termed "assimilation, American style." According to this implicit understanding, he argues, immigrants would be accepted into American society if they embraced English as the national language, took pride in their American identity, believed in the principles of the American Creed, and lived by "the Protestant ethic (to be self-reliant, hardworking, and morally upright)."[10] While one may differ with the exact formulation of this "contract," its principles catch the core of what was involved in the Americanization of millions of immigrants until the 1960s.

The critical first phase of assimilation was the acceptance by the immigrants and their descendants of the culture and values of American society. Immigrants, Gordon argues, became involved in an "immersion in a subsocietal network of groups and institutions which was already fixed in essential outline with an Anglo-Saxon, general Protestant stamp. The prior existence of Anglo-Saxon institutional forms as the norm, the pervasiveness of the English language, and the numerical dominance of the Anglo-Saxon population made this outcome inevitable . . . Rather than an impartial melting pot of the divergent cultural patterns from all immigrant sources, what has actually taken place has been more of a transforming of the later immigrant's specific cultural contributions into the Anglo-Saxon mold." Second-generation immigrants, except for "a few rigidly enclosed enclaves," experience "virtually complete acculturation (although not necessarily structural assimilation) to native American cultural values at selected class levels." [11]

Writing in 1955, Will Herberg came to the same conclusion. It is a mistake, he argued, to believe "that the American's image of himself— and that means the ethnic group member's image of himself as he becomes American—is a composite or synthesis of the ethnic elements that have gone into the making of the American. It is nothing of the kind: the American's image of himself is still the Anglo-American ideal it was at the beginning of our independent existence. . . . Our cultural assimilation has proceeded in essentially the same way as has our linguistic development—a few foreign words here and there, a few modifications of form, but still thoroughly and unquestionably English." The appropriate metaphor is not the melting pot, but in George Stewart's phrase, "the transmuting pot," in which, "as the foreign elements, a little at a time, were added to the pot, they were not merely melted but were largely transmuted, and so did not affect the original material as strikingly as might be expected." [12] Or, in the metaphor previously suggested, they were mixed into the tomato soup, enriching the taste, but not significantly altering the substance. Such has been the history of cultural assimilation in America.

Historically America has thus been a nation of immigration *and* assimilation, and assimilation has meant Americanization. Now, however, immigrants are different; the institutions and processes related to assimilation are different; and, most importantly, America is different. The great American success story may face an uncertain future.

SOURCES OF ASSIMILATION

In the past many factors facilitated the assimilation of immigrants into American society:

Most immigrants came from European societies with cultures similar to or compatible with American culture.

Immigration involved self-selection; immigrants had to be willing to confront its substantial costs, risks, and uncertainties.

Immigrants, generally, *wanted* to be Americans.

Immigrants who did not convert to American values, culture, and way of life returned to their home countries.

Immigrants came from many countries, with no single country or language predominant at any one time.

Immigrants dispersed to ethnic neighborhoods throughout the United States, with no single group of immigrants forming a majority of the population in any region or major city.

Immigration was discontinuous, interrupted by pauses and reductions, both overall and for individual countries.

Immigrants fought and died in America's wars.

Americans shared a common, reasonably clear, and highly positive concept of American identity and created activities, institutions, and policies to promote the Americanization of immigrants.

After 1965, all of these factors are either absent or much more diluted than they were previously. Assimilation of current immigrants is thus likely to be slower, less complete, and different from the assimilation of earlier immigrants. Assimilation no longer necessarily means Americanization. Assimilation is particularly problematic for Mexicans and other Hispanics. Their immigration poses problems unprecedented in America and will be dealt with in detail in the following chapter. This chapter more generally compares pre- and post-1965 immigrants, immigration processes, the responses of American society, and the implications of any differences for assimilation now.

THE IMMIGRANTS

Compatibility. It is natural to assume and it has been widely assumed throughout American history that the ease and the speed with which immigrants assimilate into American culture and society are affected by the compatibility and similarity of their birth society and culture with those of the United States. This assumption is partially valid.

One variation of this assumption focuses on the extent to which the political institutions and values of the immigrants' birth society resemble those of the United States. Jefferson thought that immigrants from societies governed by absolute monarchs posed a major threat to America, in part because from them we could "expect the greatest number of emigrants."* More important, according to Jefferson, these immigrants "will bring with them the principles of the governments they leave, imbibed in their early youth; or, if able to throw them off, it will be in exchange for an unbounded licentiousness, passing, as is usual, from one extreme to another. It would be a miracle were they to stop precisely at the point of temperate liberty. These principles, with their language, they will transmit to their children." Since, as Jefferson recognized, the American political system was virtually unique in the world, implementation of his argument would have prohibited most immigration.[13] In fact, a huge proportion of immigrants did come from countries with political systems antithetical to that of the United States. Most did not, however, "bring with them the principles of the governments" of those countries because they had suffered from those principles and wanted to escape from them.

More substantial arguments concerning assimilability focus on the cultures of immigrant countries. The argument of the nineteenth century Supreme Court that the very different culture of Chinese would prevent their integration into American society has been duplicated for other peoples. Evaluating the validity of such arguments is difficult. Presumably one test would be the proportion of those immigrants from a country who chose not to stay in America and returned to their country of origin. This figure can vary greatly. For the years 1908–1910, for instance, Michael Piore estimates that emigration amounted to about 32 percent of immigration, with the rates varying from 65 percent for Magyars, 63 percent for northern Italians, 59 percent for Slovaks, 57 per-

---

* These observations occur in his *Notes on Virginia*, written in the early 1780s before Americans added the word "immigrant" to the English language.

cent for Croats and Slovenians, and 56 percent for southern Italians, down to 10 percent for Scots, 8 percent for Jews and Welsh, and 7 percent for Irish. Language appears to be one critical factor. Immigrants from English-speaking countries assimilated much more easily than those from other countries.[14]

Nineteenth- and early-twentieth-century Americans believed that immigrants from non-English-speaking northern European countries would assimilate quicker and more easily than people from southern and eastern Europe. This, however, was not necessarily the case. Some nineteenth-century German immigrants in isolated communities resisted assimilation quite successfully for several generations. In effect, they defined themselves as and acted more like settlers than immigrants. These, however, were the exceptions even among German immigrants. Jewish immigrants, mostly from eastern Europe, had extremely low rates of return, and by the second generation, "native-born Jews at various class levels are very similar to native-born non-Jews of the same social class." While a high proportion of Italians went back to Italy, assimilation worked for those who stayed, as it did for southern and eastern Europeans more generally. As Thomas Sowell says: "Although notoriously uneducated and illiterate during the era of mass immigration—and indeed, often resistant to education for their children—Southern and Eastern Europeans eventually became, by 1980, as educated as other Americans and as well-represented in occupations requiring education, such as professional, technical, and managerial positions."[15]

Will the assimilation of post-1965 Latin American and Asian immigrants proceed more or less as it did for the earlier Europeans? Social science and psychoanalytical analyses have shown major and lasting cultural differences among peoples, with societies clustering together in religious-geographical groupings. The limited evidence available on relative assimilation of post-1965 groups indicates that substantial differences may exist, but that these are probably more related to education and occupation before coming to the United States than to other factors. Overall, immigrants from India, Korea, Japan, and the Philippines, whose educational profiles more closely approximate those of native Americans, have generally assimilated rapidly in terms of culture, structural incorporation, and intermarriage. Indians and Filipinos, of course, have also been helped by their knowledge of English. Latin American immigrants, particularly those from Mexico, and their descendants have been slower in approximating American norms. In part this is the result of the large numbers and geographical concentration of Mexicans. The educational levels of Mexican immigrants and of their descendants also have been below that of almost all other immigrant groups, as well as that of native non-Hispanic Americans (see Chapter 9). In addition, Mexican, American, and Mexican-American writers have argued that a major gap exists between American and Mexican cultures, and this may also retard assimilation.

Muslims, particularly Arab Muslims, seem slow to assimilate compared to other post-1965 groups. In part, this may be the result of Christian and Jewish prejudice toward Muslims enhanced in the late 1990s by the highly publicized terrorist incidents perpetrated or thought to have been perpetrated by extremist Muslim groups. The difficulties also may stem from the nature of Muslim culture and its differences from American culture. Elsewhere in the world, Muslim minorities have proved to be "indigestible" by non-Muslim societies.[16] In a 2000 poll of likely Muslim voters in the United States, 66.1 percent said that American society showed "respect toward the Muslim faith," but 31.9 percent disagreed.[17] A study of Los Angeles Muslims found ambivalent attitudes toward America: "a significant number of Muslims, particularly immigrant Muslims, do not have close ties or loyalty to the United States." When asked whether they had "closer ties or loyalty to Islamic countries (perhaps your country of birth) or the United States," 45 percent of the immigrants said Islamic countries, 10 percent the United States, and 32 percent about the same. Among American-born Muslims, 19 percent chose Islamic countries, 38 percent the United States, and 28 percent about the same. Fifty-seven percent of the immigrants and 32 percent of the American-born Muslims said that "if given the choice, [they] would leave the United States to live in an Islamic country." Fifty-two percent of the interviewees said it was very important and 24 percent said it was quite important to replace public schools with Islamic schools.[18]

In some circumstances the desire of Muslims to maintain the purity of their faith and the practices of their religion may lead to conflicts with non-Muslims. Dearborn, Michigan, has a large Muslim population and has been the site of much tension and some violence between Muslims and Christians. Some Muslims there have alleged that the public schools "are taking our youth away from Islam," and that "The public political system in America has failed, and it has become *the* problem." Hence, the only solution is "100% pure Islam, nothing less than the non-violent restoration of the Khilafah, the Islamic superpower!" [19] In the wake of September 11, it remains uncertain to what extent America's assimilation success in the past will extend to its Muslim immigrants.

Selectivity. More important to assimilation than the culture of the society from which immigrants come are their personal motives and character. People who more or less voluntarily choose to move from their home country to a different, often distant, country differ from those who do not choose to leave. There is, so to speak, an immigrant culture that many immigrants share and that distinguishes them from the people in their societies who do not emigrate.

Emma Lazarus's image of America's immigrants as the "wretched refuse" of the earth is, as Senator Daniel Patrick Moynihan argued, an inaccurate myth. Those who historically migrated to America were "extraordinary, enterprising, and self-sufficient folk who knew exactly what they were doing, and [were] doing it quite on their own." [20] Until the late nineteenth century, those who chose to cross the Atlantic usually had to undergo long waits at embarkation ports, voyages of more than a month, and often incredibly crowded and unsanitary conditions aboard ship. Up to 17 percent of those who left Europe died on the crossing. Steamships made the passage shorter, safer, and more predictable, but immigrants still had to risk the possibility that they would be among the 15 percent or so who were turned back at Ellis Island. [21] Those who chose to cross the Atlantic had to have the energy, ambition, initiative, and willingness to take risks, to confront uncertainty and the unknown, to suffer the substantial emotional, fiscal, and physical costs of difficult travel, and to attempt to establish a better life for themselves in a far-off land about which they had little reliable information. The vast majorities of the people in their societies who did not migrate either lacked these qualities or turned their talents and energies to other goals. "Europeans," as one French socialist politician said in 2000, "are Americans who refused to take the boat. We do not take the same risks; we have a need for greater security." [22]

The past difficulties, discomforts, costs, risks, and uncertainties of migrating to the United States have now largely evaporated. Contemporary immigrants may have the grit, determination, and commitment of previous immigrants, but they do not *have* to have them. Ironically, those immigrants who to a much greater extent do need those qualities are those who attempt to enter the United States illegally. To a limited degree this is true of Mexican illegal entrants, who are unlikely to suffer harm from the Border Patrol but may die in the Arizona desert. To a much greater degree, it is true for illegal immigrants from China or elsewhere in Asia, who entrust their savings and their lives to an unscrupulous and possibly criminal gang in exchange for a highly uncomfortable, circuitous, and often dangerous five- to ten-thousand-mile journey. Like those who came to America on sailing ships in the early nineteenth century, they must really want to make it to America. But do they really want to become Americans?

Commitment. Over 60 percent of the 55 million people who left Europe between 1820 and 1924 came to the United States. In part this was undoubtedly because they were attracted by the economic opportunities of a land where the streets were supposedly paved with gold. Similar opportunities, however, existed elsewhere. What distinguished the United States was religious and political freedom, the absence of caste and aristocracy (outside the South), and the Anglo-Protestant culture of the founding settlers. Some immigrants exploited the economic opportunities and returned home. Those who stayed presumably did so because they had a commitment to America, its principles, and its culture, a commitment that often preceded their arrival in America and furnished a central motive for their coming. "The newcomers," as Oscar Handlin observes, "were on the way toward being Americans almost before they stepped off the boat." These immigrants, Arthur Schlesinger, Jr., agreed, "*yearned* to become Americans. Their goals were escape, deliverance, assimilation." John Harles concurs: "In an elementary sense, immigrants are already faithful Americans when they first set foot on American soil. The process of assimilation, widely regarded as the primary means of affecting the immigrant's political metamorphosis, does not so much evangelize the pagan as it preaches to the converted."[23]

For many, but not all immigrants, becoming an American was indeed comparable to conversion to a new religion and with similar consequences. People who inherit their religion are often far more casual about their faith than those who convert to it. The latter involves a conscious and often agonizing choice. Having made a momentous, decisive, and, for many, irrevocable decision, immigrants had to validate and reinforce that decision by wholeheartedly embracing the culture and values of their new homeland. Psychologically, emotionally, intellectually, there was the need to make their action palatable to themselves, their new countrymen, and their former countrymen whom they had left behind. Or, as the distinguished German editor Josef Joffe, reflecting on his own country, said in the 1990s, "People came to America because they wanted to become Americans. The Turks do not come to Germany because they want to become Germans."[24]

In the past, however, the number of immigrants who came to America "because they wanted to become Americans" varied. One relatively objective measure of such commitment is the proportion of those who stay permanently in the United States versus those who emigrate back to their original homeland. Fragmentary evidence suggests that the rate of return among mid-nineteenth-century immigrants was relatively low. By and large, those who came from Ireland, Germany, and Britain stayed. Relatively hard data show that the pre–World War I immigrants were different. As the 1910 Commission on Immigration commented, unlike previous immigrants, these included fewer families and more young single males. After a decade or two earning American wages, many of them, as we have seen, were ready to go back and lead a comfortable life in the familiar surroundings of their birth country. They were sojourners in America, not converts to America.[25]

Like their predecessors, recent immigrants can choose to be converts or sojourners, but unlike earlier immigrants they do not have to make that choice. A third possibility exists: they can become ampersands, that is, they can maintain dual residences, dual attachments, dual loyalties, and often dual citizenships in America and their birth country. This is made possible, first, by modern means of transportation and communication, which provide cheap and easy ways of traveling and communicating between distant countries, and, second, by an American society that does not require the commitment from them that it did of their predecessors. Previously Americans expected immigrants to Americanize, to adopt the ideas, culture, institutions, and ways of life of America's Anglo-Protestant society. Immigrants also felt discriminated against if obstacles were raised to their incorporating themselves into that society. In post-1965 America, however, the pressures for Americanization have been weak or absent, and immigrants have often felt discriminated against if obstacles were raised to their maintaining the cultural identity they brought with them. Thus, while 20 percent to 35 percent of post-1965 immigrants may return home, those who remain do not necessarily "want to become Americans" but may instead want to be ampersands. Previous immigrants maintained an ethnic identity as a subcomponent of their American national identity. Ampersands, in contrast, have two national identities. They eat their cake and have it too, combining the opportunity, wealth, and liberty of America with the culture, language, family ties, traditions, and social networks of their birth country.

THE IMMIGRATION PROCESS

Diversity and Dispersion. Past assimilation was facilitated by the number and diversity of the societies from which immigrants came and the languages they brought with them. Neither Britain, Ireland, nor Germany supplied a majority of mid-nineteenth-century immigrants. In the 1890s, Italy, Russia, Austria-Hungary, and Germany each supplied about 15 percent of the immigrant total, with Scandinavia, Ireland, and Britain each adding another 10 percent.[26] The diversity among post-

1965 non-Hispanic immigrants is, if anything, even greater. This diversity compels immigrants to learn English to communicate not only with native Americans but also with each other. Unlike previous immigrations, however, roughly 50 percent of current migrants to the continental United States speak a single non-English language, and the proportion has been rising steadily.

In the past, assimilation was also helped by the dispersion of members of immigrant groups to many places in the United States. This was a practice that the Founding Fathers thought essential if the deleterious consequences of immigration were to be avoided. Ambivalent about immigration itself, they were united in their conviction that immigrants should not be allowed to concentrate with their own kind in ethnically homogeneous geographical areas. If immigrants settled together, Washington warned, they would "retain the language, habits and principles (good or bad) which they bring with them." If, however, they were intermixed "with our people, they, or their descendants, will get assimilated to our customs, measures and laws: in a word, soon become one people." Jefferson similarly argued that immigrants "should distribute themselves sparsely among the natives for quicker amalgamation." And Franklin urged that it was necessary "to distribute them more equally, mix them with the English, establish English schools where they are now too thick settled."[27] These attitudes received legislative confirmation by Congress in 1818, when it rejected the petition of Irish-American organizations requesting the formal assignment of a piece of the Northwest Territory for settlement by Irish immigrants. Congress did this because it believed such action would fragment the nation, and as Marcus Hansen commented, "Probably no decision in the history of American immigration policy possesses more profound significance." Following through on this, Congress subsequently admitted new states only when they had a majority of English speakers.[28]

American policy has thus been based on the assumption that assimilation requires dispersion. In fact, the immigration of any one group has always involved first the creation of an ethnic beachhead and then as more of their compatriots arrive the expansion of that beachhead into an ethnic enclave. Most immigrant enclaves have been in cities, and large cities also became home to many different immigrant groups. The diversity of and competition among these groups helped prevent any one of them from establishing cultural dominance and stimulated all of them to become proficient in English. In addition, as the immigrant flow slackened and the second generation gave way to the third, upwardly mobile members of the group moved out of the enclave. The result in the large cities of the Northeast and Midwest was what Samuel Lubell termed "the urban frontier," as generation after generation, immigrant group replaced immigrant group in city neighborhoods.[29]

Post-1965 Hispanic immigration has deviated significantly from the historical pattern of dispersion, with Cubans concentrated in the Miami area and Mexicans in the Southwest, particularly Southern California. With few exceptions, diversity followed by dispersion has, however, characterized other post-1965 immigrants. Immigrants come from an extraordinary range of countries. Compatriots cluster together, but ethnic neighborhoods are also intermixed and their composition changes. In 1995–1996, 18 percent of the immigrants in New York City came from the former Soviet Union, 17 percent from the Dominican Republic, and 10 percent from China. In the late 1990s, New York immigrant neighborhoods typically contained people from many different countries, with no ethnicity constituting more than 15 percent to 20 percent of the population (an exception being the Lower East Side, where 51 percent of the people were Chinese).[30] Summarizing this New York experience, James Dao concluded in 1999: "Today's immigrants come from more countries and speak more languages than the last great wave of European immigrants. They are more economically varied, with highly educated and skilled people among their ranks. And more than their predecessors, they are eschewing homogeneous enclaves, scattering to neighborhoods across the city."* This pattern should greatly fa-

---

* One example of a diverse and shifting neighborhood is Astoria, Queens, in New York City. As a child there in the 1930s and 1940s, my friends included WASPs, who like my family came to New York from farm country, Jews, Irish, Italians, Greeks, and one lone French Huguenot. In 2000, according to the *New York Times Magazine* (17 September 2000, p. 44), the principal ethnic groups in Astoria included only the Greeks from my time but now also Bangladeshi, Brazilians, Ecuadorans, Egyptians, and Filipinos. America marches on!

cilitate their assimilation. In 1990 in those counties with the highest concentration of immigrants from a single country, 11 percent of the foreign-born were fluent in English. In diverse counties, 74 percent of the foreign-born were fluent in English.[31] The Founding Fathers were right. Dispersion is key to assimilation.

Discontinuity. The United States, as Nathan Glazer said, has "not always been a country of immigration." In addition to being a nation of immigrants, the pro-immigration Immigration Forum notes, "the United States has also been a nation of nativists."[32] During the century from the 1870s to the 1960s, legislation first limited and then prohibited immigration by Asians and for forty years effectively limited overall immigration to very small numbers. America has been a nation of restricted and interrupted immigration as much as it has been a nation of immigration. Immigration levels have varied and, as Robert Fogel points out, have tended to follow a cyclical pattern.[33] The immigration wave of the 1840s and 1850s came to an end with the Civil War, and immigration did not again reach the same absolute numbers until the 1880s. The rate of immigration per 1,000 population was 8.4 and 9.3 in the 1840s and 1850s, dropped to 6.4 and 6.2 in the 1860s and 1870s, and rose to 9.2 in the 1880s. Irish immigration, which was 780,000 and 914,000 in the 1840s and 1850s, averaged less than 500,000 in the subsequent decades. German immigration, 951,000 in the 1850s, dropped to 767,468 and 718,182 in the following two decades, reviving in the 1880s but then dropping precipitously to 500,000 and less per decade. Overall, the turn-of-the-century immigration wave hit one peak in the 1880s, dropped in the 1890s, in part due to the recession in the United States, then hit new heights until interrupted by World War I, briefly peaked again immediately after the war, but dropped dramatically as a result of the 1924 immigration law.

This decline had a powerful effect on assimilation. After 1924, Richard Alba and Victor Nee point out, "The ensuing, four-decade interruption in steady, large-scale immigration virtually guaranteed that ethnic communities and cultures would be steadily weakened over time. The social mobility of individuals and families drained these communities, especially of native-born ethnics, and undermined the cultures they supported. There were few newcomers available as replacements. Over time, the modal generation shifted from the immigrant to the second and then from the second to the third." Continuation of current high levels of immigration, in contrast, "will create a fundamentally different ethnic context from that faced by the descendants of European immigrants, for the new ethnic communities are highly likely to remain large, culturally vibrant, and institutionally rich." Under existing conditions, Douglas Massey concluded, "new arrivals from abroad will tend to exceed the rate at which new ethnic culture is created through generational success, social mobility, and intermarriage in the United States. As a result, the character of ethnicity will be determined relatively more by immigrants and relatively less by later generations, shifting the balance of ethnic identity toward the language, culture, and ways of life in the sending society."[34]

The current wave got under way slowly in the late 1960s and early 1970s with legal immigration averaging about 400,000 a year compared to less than 300,000 before 1965. In the late 1970s and early 1980s it increased to about 600,000 a year and then in 1989 jumped to over a million. During the 1960s 3.3 million people entered the United States, during the 1980s, seven million people did, and in the 1990s over nine million did. The foreign-born percentage of the American population, which was 5.4 percent in 1960, more than doubled to 11.5 percent in 2002.[35] Immigration varies year to year, but at the start of the new century it showed little sign of decreasing. The United States thus appears to face something new in its history: persistent high levels of immigration.

The two earlier waves subsided as a result of war plus the end of the potato famine in the first case and war plus anti-immigration legislation in the second. A sustained major war in the future could have comparable impact, and a severe recession in the United States could reduce the incentive for immigration and also increase support for restrictions on it. The war on terrorism, the downturn in the U.S. economy, and the reduction in the backlog of visa applications helped to produce a net drop in legal and illegal immigration from an unusual high of 2.4 million between March 2000 and March 2001 to 1.2 million from March 2001 to March 2002. In November 2002, one analyst concluded: "There is no evidence that the economic slowdown that began in 2000 or the terrorist attacks in 2001 have significantly slowed the rate of immigration."[36] Absent a major escalation in the intensity, scope, or number of America's wars, over one million immigrants are likely to continue to enter the United States each year. In which case, assimilation may still occur but it is likely to be slower and less complete than it has been with past waves of immigrants.

Wars. Fighting in America's wars has bolstered the claims of excluded native groups to full citizenship. In the 1820s it was argued that landless white male citizens deserved the vote because they had not "less profusely than others, poured out their blood in defense of their country." The storming of Fort Wagner by the 54th Massachusetts Infantry and comparable actions by the 200,000 blacks who served in the Union armies enabled Frederick Douglass to claim that "the black man deserves the right to vote for what he has done, to aid in suppressing the rebellion, both by fighting and by assisting the Federal soldier wherever he was found. . . . If he knows enough to shoulder a musket and to fight for the flag, fight for the government, he knows enough to vote."[37] This argument was subsequently reinforced by the service of black soldiers in World War II that bolstered the movement toward desegregation and civil rights in the 1950s and 1960s.

In similar fashion, wars have furthered assimilation of immigrants not only by reducing their numbers but also by giving them the opportunity and the impetus to demonstrate their loyalty to America. Readiness to fight and if necessary die in war cemented their attachment to their new home and made it difficult if not impossible for nativist, anti-immigrant groups to oppose their full membership in American society. A Mexican-American, who with several Jewish friends volunteered for the army after Pearl Harbor, later commented: "All of us had to prove ourselves—to show that we were more American than the Anglos."[38] Converts want to validate their faith.

Yet they may also be torn by conflicting loyalties. In the war with

Mexico, some Irish immigrants deserted the American army to join their fellow Catholics and form the San Patricio Battalion in the Mexican army. In the Civil War, the Irish viewed blacks as their rivals, many supported the Confederacy, and Irish immigrants were the core of the rioters against the draft in 1863. Nonetheless, roughly 150,000 Irish immigrants served in the Union armies and the battlefield exploits of the Irish Brigade, including the "Fighting" 69th Regiment and its reckless charge up the slope at Fredericksburg into Confederate cannon fire, sounded the death knell for organized anti-Irish Know-Nothing nativism.[39]

World War I caused trauma for German-Americans. They vigorously supported American neutrality and attempted to counter the pro-British sentiments of American elites. Between 1914 and 1917 they endured the mounting anti-German hysteria in America and suffered from the actions of the German government, which steadily forced them toward making a choice they wished to avoid. By 1917 leading elements of the German-American community had made that choice: while they wanted peace, they "were 100 percent American." Foreign-born Germans rushed to apply for citizenship and accepted conscription. The war convinced German-Americans that they could no longer maintain their hyphenated identity, so they became simply Americans and were accepted as such. In World War II the combat record of the 442nd Regimental Combat Team, "the most decorated unit in American military history," dramatized the patriotism of Japanese-Americans, fanned the guilt of other Americans over the internment camps, and led to abolition of the restrictions on Asian immigration. During both world wars, American leaders and American propaganda continuously emphasized that this was a war of all Americans of every race, ethnicity, and background against major threats to their country and its values.[40]

On July 4, 1918, John J. Miller reminds us, a remarkable parade or, as it was more accurately termed, pageant occurred in New York City. Watched by hundreds of thousands of spectators, over seventy thousand marchers swept up Fifth Avenue, including native Americans and representatives of allied nations (including the first British military unit ever to participate in an American Independence Day ceremony). The cen-

tral elements in the pageant, however, were the more than forty delegations from New York's immigrant communities. They varied in size
from 18 Haitians to 10,000 Italians and 10,000 Jews, who had been win-
nowed from the 35,000 Italians and 50,000 Jews who wanted to participate. Among other delegations were German-Americans whose signs
asserted "America is our fatherland" and "Born in Germany, Made in
America," Greeks, Hungarians, Irish, Serbs, Croatians, Slovenes, Poles,
and Lithuanians, whose banner proclaimed "Uncle Sam is our uncle."
The Russians wore red, white, and blue costumes, the Venezuelans
played the national anthem, the Chinese highlighted a baseball team.
The reporter for the *New York Times* commented, "In this long kaleido-
scopic pageant, now bright with splendid costumes, now drab with long
columns of civilians, marching with a solemnity of spirit that brought its
meaning home impressively to those who looked on, there was slowly
woven a picture of fighting America of today, a land of many bloods but
one ideal."[41]

Following September 11, immigrants of all sorts, including Arabs and
Muslims, proclaimed their loyalty and flew the flag. Resident aliens
made up 5 percent of the armed forces, and Latin American immigrants
figured prominently among the casualties of the fighting in Afghanistan
and Iraq. Without a major war requiring substantial mobilization and
lasting years, however, contemporary immigrants will have neither the
opportunity nor the need to affirm their identity with and their loyalty
to America as earlier immigrants have done.

AMERICAN SOCIETY:
AMERICANIZATION IS UN-AMERICAN

In 1963, Glazer and Moynihan posed the question: "To what does one
assimilate in modern America?" In 1900 the answer was clear: assimilation meant Americanization. In 2000 the answers were complicated,
contradictory, and ambiguous. Many elite Americans were no longer
confident of the virtue of their mainstream culture and instead preached
a doctrine of diversity and the equal validity of all cultures in America.

"Immigrants do not enter a society that assumes an undifferentiated monolithic American culture," Mary Waters observed in 1994, "but rather a consciously pluralistic society in which a variety of subcultures and racial and ethnic identities coexist."[42] To the extent that America has become multicultural, immigrants may choose among the subcultures they encounter or choose to maintain their original culture. They may assimilate into American society without assimilating the core American culture. Assimilation and Americanization are no longer identical.

The massive influx of immigrants before World War I led, as we have seen, to immense efforts to Americanize them by governments, businesses, and charitable organizations. The late-twentieth-century immigration wave generated nothing comparable. Only Congresswoman Barbara Jordan and the Commission on Immigration Reform she chaired made a prominent argument for an "immigrant policy" to promote Americanization, and the commission's modest 1997 recommendations were largely ignored. The prevailing atmosphere was entirely different from what it had been at the beginning of the century. First, debates over immigration focused almost entirely on its economic costs and benefits and its fiscal impact on government. The consequences of immigration without assimilation for American social cohesion and cultural integrity, which were central to earlier discussions, were now largely ignored.

Second, it often was implicitly assumed that assimilation would occur more or less automatically. Immigrants will become Americans simply because they are in America. Hence no need exists for major efforts explicitly to promote Americanization. Third has been the belief that Americanization is undesirable. This is a new phenomenon in American intellectual and political history. "A radical program of Americanization would really be un-American," one prominent political theorist, Michael Walzer, has argued. "America has no singular national destiny." Americanism, another scholar observed, has "connotations of racism, sexism, class domination, religious intolerance, and ethnic purity." "Today," the sociologist Dennis Wrong concluded in 1989, "nobody advocates 'Americanizing' new immigrants, as in the bad old ethnocentric past."[43]

Almost no political leader, apart from Jordan, urged programs for the Americanization of America's newest immigrants.

As a result of this lack, while 21 million immigrants in 2000 said they did not speak English very well, the government programs and funding to meet this need were in short supply. In Massachusetts in 2002, some 460,000 people, 7.7 percent of the population, did not speak English very well, with the proportion rising to over 30 percent in two cities and over 15 percent in several. This challenged "the state's ability to provide English training and other social services." The waiting list for English as a second language courses was two to three years.[44]

The role of business in the 1990s differed from that of the early 1900s. In the late twentieth century, as in the Progressive Era, businesses found it desirable to help their workers learn English, particularly those who interacted with customers and clients. A substantial proportion of the people enrolled in adult education programs have been immigrants studying English as a second language, and many businesses have provided funding for the English language training of their employees.[45] Overall, however, such business efforts have not been on the scale they were before World War I. Businesses have supported English language training to meet their own very immediate needs, not as a result of a more general concern with Americanization or as part of a broader Americanization movement. In some measure, the general lack of interest of businesses in the broader aspects of Americanization undoubtedly reflected their international involvements and the transnational and cosmopolitan identities of their leaders. In the early 1900s Ford was the corporate leader in promoting Americanization. In the 1990s Ford quite explicitly defined itself as a multinational, not an American corporation, and in 2002 several of its top executives were British.

In the earlier phase, businesses were more concerned with making immigrants into efficient producers of their products than making them consumers of those products. In the consumer society of a hundred years later, however, as immigrant numbers and purchasing power expanded, businesses had to appeal to that growing market. In the 1990s the consumer buying power of immigrant and minority groups was estimated at $1 trillion annually, and American corporations were spending "close to $2 billion a year on advertising" to sell products to those "eager to acquire the markers of their cultural heritage." Ethnic products, artifacts, and identities were "now fostered, even promoted, by our mainstream corporate culture."[46] Businesses used foreign languages to sell products to their immigrant workers.

Before World War I a huge number of private nonprofit organizations became involved in Americanization activities. After 1965 many organizations also provided help to immigrants, but the goal of promoting their Americanization was nowhere near as central as it had been earlier. Organizations founded by native Americans with ethnic ties to particular immigrant groups emphasized development of their group identity rather than the fostering of a broader American identity. Leaders of Hispanic and nonwhite organizations encouraged their constituents to define themselves as racial minorities so as to qualify for the special benefits available from government programs. Organizations, such as the Mexican-American Legal Defense Fund, created by and funded by the Ford Foundation and without any membership, were interested in maintaining immigrant group identity, promoting immigrant group consciousness, and asserting immigrant group rights. As Peter Skerry has shown, the contemporary political dynamic tends to isolate Mexican-Americans from other groups, and Michael Jones-Correa has described how one Democratic political machine in New York had little interest in welcoming Latino immigrants into its clubhouses.[47] In effect, minority group politics has displaced political party politics with respect to immigrants.

In the early twentieth century, federal, state, and local governments devoted substantial resources to often competing efforts to Americanize the new immigrants. In the later part of the century, in contrast, government efforts to promote Americanization were relatively weak and often to the contrary effect. The United States government is probably alone in the extent to which it encourages immigrants to hold on to the language, culture, and identity of their birth country. This favorable atmosphere toward group rights and affirmative action programs has made it in the interest of Hispanic and Asian immigrants to maintain their ethnic identities. Roughly 75 percent of the foreign-born population in

2000 and 85 percent of immigrants during the 1990s qualified as "disadvantaged" and hence eligible for affirmative action, although they obviously could not have experienced a history of discrimination in the United States. The "cult of group rights," as John Miller observed, "remains one of the most significant threats to the Americanization of immigrants." In doing this, it has thus privileged new arrivals over native Americans. In somewhat similar fashion, as Skerry has highlighted, the U.S. government has permitted "rotten boroughs" to develop by apportioning congressional districts on the basis of their total population, including legal and illegal residents, instead of citizens only. As a result, the number of voters in these districts is much smaller than it is in other districts. In addition, district lines have been drawn to insure the existence of majority-Hispanic districts, thereby institutionalizing immigrant group interests rather than encouraging their accommodation with those of other groups.[48]

Historically, the public schools were central in the promotion of national identity. In the late twentieth century, in contrast, schools promoted diversity rather than unity and made little effort to inculcate immigrants in American culture, traditions, customs, and beliefs. American education at times had a denationalizing effect. According to one study of San Diego high school students in the early 1990s, after three years of high school the proportion of students identifying themselves as "American" had dropped by 50 percent, the proportion identifying themselves as hyphenated Americans had gone down by 30 percent, and the proportion identifying themselves with a foreign nationality (overwhelmingly Mexican) had gone up 52 percent. The study's results "point to the rapid growth of a reactive ethnic consciousness." The study's author, sociologist Rubén Rumbaut, concludes: "Change over time, thus, has not been toward assimilative mainstream identities (with or without a hyphen), but rather a return to and a valorization of the immigrant identity for the largest groups." If students avoid denationalization in high school, they may still undergo it in college. At the University of California at Berkeley, many minority and immigrant students "describe themselves in high school as having so assimilated into majority Anglo environments that they did not think of themselves as minority group members." At Berkeley, however, these students began to "see themselves differently" and to develop their ethnic and racial identities. He was, one Mexican-American student said, "born again here at Berkeley."[49] In a society that values ethnic and racial diversity, immigrants have powerful incentives to maintain and to reaffirm their ancestral identity.

AMPERSANDS AND DUAL CITIZENSHIP

I do solemnly swear (1) to support the Constitution of the United States; (2) to renounce and abjure absolutely and entirely all allegiance and fidelity to any foreign prince, potentate, state, or sovereignty of whom or which the applicant was before a subject or citizen; (3) to support and defend the Constitution and the laws of the United States against all enemies, foreign and domestic; (4) to bear true faith and allegiance to the same; and (5) (A) to bear arms on behalf of the United States when required by law, or (B) to perform noncombatant service in the Armed Forces of the United States when required by law, or (C) to perform work of national importance under civilian direction when required by the law.

(INA section 337 [2], § U.S. Code section 1448 [a])

In 1795 Congress required this oath of those wanting to become American citizens. Over two hundred years later, it was still required, although federal bureaucrats in 2003 launched a campaign to rewrite and weaken it. In its original form, the oath embodies two central ideas concerning citizenship. First, citizenship is exclusive; individuals can change their citizenship but they cannot have more than one at a time. Second, citizenship is a distinctive status conferred by a country's government, involving rights and obligations that distinguish citizens from noncitizens.

In the late twentieth century, both these concepts of citizenship were eroded by the combined impact of massive immigration and the deconstructionist movement. The exclusivity principle was undermined by the rise of powerful political forces promoting dual loyalties, dual identities, and dual citizenship. The distinctive status of citizenship was eroded by extension of the rights and privileges of citizens to noncitizens and by the claim that citizenship is not a national status conferred by the state on individuals but a transnational right of individuals against states that they carry with them wherever they choose to reside. These trends were at work in both Europe and America. Due to the nature of American national identity, however, their significance and impact has been greater in America than in other Western societies. In recent decades, the proportion of immigrants who become American citizens has declined substantially and the proportion of naturalized citizens who are also citizens of a foreign country has increased substantially. Together these trends suggest a significant devaluation of American citizenship.

Today many immigrants, particularly those from former communist countries, fit the convert model. Others are sojourners, although it would appear a smaller proportion than in the past. A significant number—exactly how many it is impossible to say—are ampersands. "People like us have the best of two worlds," as one said. "We have two countries, two homes. It doesn't make any sense for us to be either this or that. We're both. It's not a conflict. It's just a human fact." Scholars have called them "perpetual in-betweens," "transmigrants," "transnationals," "between two nations," "migrants" but not "emigrants or immigrants because they do not exchange one position for another," people who are "keeping their feet in both worlds."[50] For geographical reasons, the overwhelming bulk of ampersands are from Latin America and the Caribbean. The ability to go home for a weekend or phone a family member anytime means that "time and distance have different values for Latino immigrants than they do for the European newcomers of long ago. . . . The Statue of Liberty stands as a symbol of the European migration because it represents a terminus. There is no terminus for Latino immigrants."[51]

Creating and maintaining a transnational ampersand identity is easier to the extent that the migrants are a substantial portion of the origin country's population. This is clearly the case with many Western Hemisphere countries. In 1990, the proportions of the populations of the following countries living in the United States were:[52]

Jamaica	23.0%
El Salvador	16.8
Trinidad & Tobago	16.0
Cuba	11.3
Mexico	9.4
Barbados	9.2
Dominican Republic	8.5

The size of these migrant communities in relation to their origin country multiplies the opportunities and the incentives for both the migrants and the origin country governments to promote the ties between them.

Historically migrants from a single locality in Country A tended to gather in a single locality in Country B. Now the people of both localities can be parts of a single transnational community. The community of origin is replicated in the United States. Two thirds of the families in Miraflores in the Dominican Republic (a village of four thousand) have relatives in the Boston area. They dominate one neighborhood in the Jamaica Plain area of Boston, where, Peggy Levitt shows, they "have re-created their premigration lives to the extent that their new physical and cultural environment allows," their homes decorated to resemble those in Miraflores. The interactions between Miraflores South and Miraflores North are intense and sustained. "Because someone is always traveling between Boston and the island, there is a continuous, circular flow of goods, news, and information. As a result, when someone is ill, cheating on his or her spouse, or finally granted a visa, the news spreads as quickly in Jamaica Plain as it does on the streets of Miraflores."[53] In similar fashion, "the population of Chinantlá [Mexico], is evenly divided between that tiny town and New York City, but the Chinatecans still consider themselves one community—2,500 here, 2,500 there." During the 1990s more than half the 5,800 residents of Casa Blanca, Mexico, moved to Tulsa, Oklahoma, raising major doubts as to the continuing viability of the former. In 1985, 20 percent of the population of Intipuca, El Salvador, lived in the Adams-Morgan neighborhood in Washington, D.C.[54] In Marshalltown, Iowa, with thirty thousand residents, natives of Villachuato (population fifteen thousand), Mexico, have held nine hundred of the 1,600 jobs in the Swift & Company meat-packing plant, the town's largest employer. "For these workers," Ryan Rippel has pointed out, "it seems as if Iowa represents merely a long commute to work, rather than a new place of residency," and the Marshalltown "meatpacking industry" is "central" to the "sustainability" of Villachuato.[55]

Transnational villages are united by social, religious, and political associations that exist in both parts of the community. Of particular importance are associations formed by those in the host country locality to assist the source country locality. The Mirafloreños in Boston created a Miraflores Development Committee to improve conditions in Miraflores. The committee raised $70,000 for this purpose between 1992 and 1994, the expenditure of which is implemented by a counterpart committee in Miraflores. Transnational Mexican communities have been particularly active in this regard. Possibly two thousand of these hometown associations or *clubes de oriundos* exist with membership probably in the hundreds of thousands. These clubs, as Robert Leiken has shown, provide various services to promote the interests of their members in the United States and also "provide a concrete link to the communities of origin and a way of maintaining ties with their culture, customs, language, and traditions."[56] In some respects, these transnational localities in the United States resemble the transplanted communities of German immigrants in the mid-nineteenth century. There is, however, one crucial difference. The latter were relatively isolated from their roots in Germany. They were truly transplants, "Germans in America" as they defined themselves. Contemporary Latin American ampersands have roots in two communities; they are "Mexicans in America" and "Mexicans in Mexico."

The growing number of ampersands with two languages, two homes, and possibly two loyalties, generated movement toward two citizenships. In the last decades of the twentieth century the number of people with American citizenship who are also citizens of another country increased rapidly for at least two reasons. First, the number of countries authorizing or condoning multiple citizenships is growing. In 1996 seven of seventeen Latin American countries allowed dual citizenship. In 2000, fourteen of the seventeen did. In 2000, Stanley Renshon estimates, some ninety-three countries allowed dual citizenship, informally or formally, to a greater or lesser extent.[57]

Second, a large proportion of the immigrants to the United States come from countries that permit dual citizenship. Between 1994 and 1998, seventeen of the top twenty countries sending immigrants to the United States allowed dual citizenship (the exceptions being China, Cuba, and South Korea). During those five years, over 2.6 million legal immigrants came from these top twenty countries, with more than 2.2 million (86 percent) coming from multiple-citizenship countries. Immigrants from dual-citizenship countries are more likely to acquire American citizenship than those from countries where doing so would jeopardize their existing citizenship. In addition, each year perhaps half a million dual citizens are born in the United States because one parent is a citizen of a country that, on *jus sanguinis* principles, confers citizenship on the children of its citizens, wherever they are born.[58]

The impetus for dual citizenship comes from two sources. First, the ampersands have lobbied the governments of their origin countries to allow them to maintain their citizenship in that country. Among Latin American countries this was notably the case with respect to immigrants from Mexico, Colombia, Ecuador, and the Dominican Republic, who wanted to avoid choice and to be legally involved, economically, politically, and socially, in two national societies. The second source, in Michael Jones-Correa's phrasing, comes not from the bottom up but from the top down, that is, from the governments of the sending countries. Those governments, first, want to encourage their emigrants to maintain contacts with their origin societies and, in particular, to provide remittances to their families and localities in those societies. Second, they want their migrants to become American citizens so they can participate in the American political processes and advance the interests of the sending country. In 2001, it was reported that "Mexican consulates in the United States have been encouraging Mexican nationals in the United States to naturalize as U.S. citizens, while keeping their nationality as Mexicans as well."[59] In Brazil, Costa Rica, El Salvador, Panama, and Peru the push for dual citizenship came from the government.

The adoption of dual citizenship by the sending country has been followed by a doubling of the naturalization rates of their citizens in the United States, with the increases higher among citizens of those countries where the initiative for dual citizenship came from the immigrants themselves.[60] These people thus become American citizens by falsely swearing that they are renouncing their previous allegiance, when in fact they become American citizens because they are able to maintain that previous allegiance. They can do this because the United States has in practice abandoned the exclusivity principle embodied in the renunciation oath. As with affirmative action and bilingual education, this shift in previously mandated policy originated with un-elected judges and administrators, and was subsequently accepted by Congress.

It is virtually impossible to arrive at an exact figure for the number of American dual citizens. In the late 1980s, however, a million people in France were dual nationals of France and Algeria, and the total number of dual nationals in western Europe was estimated at three to four million. Nathan Glazer's estimate of possibly 7.5 million dual citizens in the United States in the late 1990s thus seems plausible. If this was the case, almost three quarters of the 10.6 million foreign-born American citizens in 2000 were also citizens of another country.[61]

The extent to which American dual citizens can participate in the politics of their country of origin varies from country to country. In some cases, such as Brazil and Colombia, they can vote at the source country's consulates in the United States; in other cases they have to return to the source country to vote; and in still other cases, such as Mexico, they may be recognized as Mexican nationals for some purposes but not for voting. The extent to which dual citizens actually do participate in the politics of their source country also varies considerably. Voting is probably least significant. Even when dual citizens can vote at their consulates in the United States, the turnout tends to be extremely low. Three thousand of the 200,000 Colombians living in New York voted in the Colombian presidential election of 1990, and 1,800 or fewer in the senatorial election in 1998. Only a small proportion of about 22,000 eligible Russians in Massachusetts voted in the Russian presidential election in 1996 and still fewer in the Duma election of 1999. Thousands of Dominicans, however, apparently flew back to the Dominican Republic to vote in that country's 2000 presidential election.[62]

Financial contributions to candidates and parties are more important than voting. Candidates for office in Mexico, the Dominican Republic, and other countries regularly make major fund-raising efforts in the United States. As Jones-Correa observes, "Los Angeles, New York, and Miami [are] now required campaign stops for politicians in national and even state and local campaigns across Latin America." Fifteen percent of the funds spent in Dominican elections, it has been estimated, comes from Dominicans abroad, and an official of one major Dominican political party claimed that in 1996, 75 percent of its cash contributions came from overseas. "Dominicans in New York raise amounts in the hundreds of thousands of dollars for Dominican politicians in Dominican election cycles, much of it raised at $150-a-head dinners in Washington Heights, Corona or the Bronx."[63] Dual citizens residing in the United States may also run for political office in their country of origin. Andrés Bermúdez emigrated illegally from Mexico in 1973, became a highly successful entrepreneur in the United States, and in 2001 was elected mayor of the county in which he was born. In 1997 a city councilor in Hackensack, New Jersey, ran for the Colombian Senate and if he had been elected planned to hold both offices simultaneously.[64]

As these actions indicate, dual citizenship serves the interests of both the ampersands and the countries they come from. Whether it serves the interests of the United States is uncertain.[65] It clearly involves a major change in the meaning and practice of American citizenship. Traditionally in Europe, the relation of a subject to his monarch or prince was both exclusive and perpetual. The prevailing view in England, "Once a subject always a subject," was given authoritative formulation in *Calvin's Case* in 1608. Inherent in this view was the assumption that a person could be the subject of only one sovereign. With independence, Americans rejected the principle of perpetuity but not that of exclusivity. They had, after all, asserted a collective right to terminate allegiance. Perpetuity was also against American interests in the controversies over the British impressment of sailors on American ships who had been born British subjects. The 1795 naturalization law, which affirmed exclusivity, also implicitly rejected perpetuity. Having asserted the right of the subjects or citizens of other countries to change allegiance, Americans could hardly deny it to their own. The formal recognition of that right, however, had to wait until after the Civil War. Because the Union denied the collective right of expatriation (that is, secession) to the Confederate states, which the colonies had asserted for themselves in 1776, it was felt necessary to legitimate explicitly that right for individuals, and Congress did so in 1868.[66] The United States thus became the first country to assert, in effect, that expatriation was a "basic human right," a right now accepted by many, although certainly not all, countries.[67]

This rejection of perpetuity, however, did not involve any formal rejection of exclusivity. Well into the twentieth century it was true that "International law and practice generally regard dual citizenship with disfavor."[68] At various times in the early twentieth century, Congress and the State Department also "sought to discourage or prevent dual citizenship." The Supreme Court, however, began to restrict and invalidate these efforts in the 1960s and Congress in 1978 repealed several laws "requiring dual citizens to elect one allegiance."[69] Congress did not, however, repeal the renunciation oath.

In practice it is now virtually impossible for the government to end a person's citizenship, and it is almost as difficult for a person to end it himself. Citizenship has again become inalienable and irrevocable. As Stanley Renshon summarizes it, "No American citizen can lose their citizenship by undertaking the responsibilities of citizenship in one or more other countries. This is true even if those responsibilities include obtaining a second or even a third citizenship, swearing allegiance to a foreign state, voting in another country's elections, serving in the armed forces (even in combat positions) . . . running for office, and if successful, serving." As far as he knows, Renshon adds, "the United States is the only country in the world . . . to allow its citizens, natural or naturalized, to do *all* of these things."[70] America has thus changed from a nation that rejected perpetuity and embraced exclusivity to one that embraces perpetuity and rejects exclusivity.

As with assimilation, metaphors flourish in the discussion of citizenship. They tend, however, to be familial rather than culinary. Some people argue that having two citizenships is like having two parents or having two children: one can be loyal and devoted to both. In terms of the principles of perpetuity and exclusivity, however, marriage is the more appropriate parallel.[71] In Muslim societies, at least for men, neither perpetuity nor exclusivity is required. At one time in Western societies, in contrast, both principles prevailed: marriages were monogamous "till death do us part." In due course, however, divorce became accepted while monogamy remained. With respect to citizenship, however, bigamy is now acceptable. This shift fundamentally changes the meaning and significance of citizenship.

Dual citizenship legitimizes dual identities and dual loyalties. For a person with two or more citizenships, no one citizenship can be as important as his one citizenship is to a person who only has one. The vitality of a democracy depends on the extent to which its citizens participate in civic associations, public life, and politics. Most citizens are stretched to take an interest in and participate in the public affairs of a single community and a single country. Giving them the opportunity and the incentives to be involved in the public life of a second community and a second country means they will either neglect one and focus on the other or only marginally and intermittently participate in both. Citizenship becomes less a matter of identity and more one of utility. One uses one citizenship for some purposes and in some circumstances and the other for different purposes and in other circumstances. The ability to do this is precisely the appeal dual citizenship has for ampersands. The lack of the need to make a choice means the lack of a comparable need for loyalty and commitment.

Dual citizenship has special import for the United States. The renunciation oath reflected the belief that America was different, something special, the city on the hill, devoted to liberty, opportunity, and the future. People became Americans by embracing these distinctive characteristics, abandoning their previous attachment to another nation, culture, and belief, and rejecting the monarchies, aristocracies, class-ridden societies, and repressive regimes of the old world. Immigrants retained deep emotional attachments to their families and associates in their country of origin, but just as one could not become Baptist and remain Catholic or become Jewish and remain Christian, one could not become American and remain committed to a society with a different political, economic, and social system. With dual citizenship, American identity is no longer distinctive and exceptional. American citizenship becomes simply an add-on to another citizenship.

Dual citizenship also has more practical consequences. It encourages ampersands to maintain and possibly expand their commitments to and involvements in their country of origin. Among these are the tens of billions of dollars in remittances that go from them to relatives, localities, businesses, and development projects in their origin counties. These remittances are often the most important form of foreign economic aid these countries receive, and they have, in many respects, much more constructive consequences than official aid funneled through corrupt and inefficient governmental bureaucracies. Yet the billions of dollars that ampersands send abroad are also billions of dollars they do not invest in building homes, establishing businesses, creating jobs, and improving their communities in the United States. Money talks, and, unlike official aid, the remittances flowing out of America do not speak English.

The concept of dual citizenship is foreign to the American Constitution. According to the Fourteenth Amendment, "All persons born or naturalized in the United States, and subject to the jurisdiction thereof, are citizens of the United States and of the State wherein they reside." This clearly implies that Americans can be citizens of only one state and can vote only in that state. Yet many Americans have homes in two states. Under existing law and practice, however, Americans can be citizens of two countries. Dual citizens with residences in Santo Domingo and Boston can vote in both American and Dominican elections, but Americans with residences in New York and Boston cannot vote in both places. In addition, state laws generally require some period of legal residence in order to run for and be elected to state office. Hence a person cannot run for elected office in two states. Dual citizens, however, can run for and serve in elected office in two countries.

CITIZENS AND NONCITIZENS

Dual citizenship ends the exclusivity of citizenship. The decline in differences between citizens and noncitizens ends the distinctiveness of citizenship, a distinction that goes back centuries. In ancient Athens, a class of noncitizen *metics* existed who had been drawn to the city "by economic opportunity." They had the duty to help defend the city, but they did not have political rights, and their children inherited their noncitizen status. Aristotle, who was a *metic*, endorsed this system, arguing that a certain "excellence" was required for citizenship and one does not become a citizen "merely by inhabiting a place."[72] In the Roman Republic a sharp distinction existed between citizens and noncitizens, and citizenship was a much sought after status. With the empire, citizenship became extended to more and more people and gradually lost its distinctiveness. After the collapse of Rome, the idea of citizenship faded in the Dark Ages and early medieval Europe. The concept began a comeback with the gradual emergence of nation-states in Europe, and people becoming identified as the subjects of the kings or princes who governed the territories in which they resided. The American and French revolutions replaced subjecthood with citizenship, and with democratization, citizenship and the distinction between citizens and noncitizens assumed their modern form. "If citizenship is anything," as Peter Schuck has said, "it is membership in a political community with a more or less distinctive political identity—a set of public values about governance and law that are very widely shared by those within it."[73]

Citizenship linked the identity of the individual to the identity of the nation. National governments defined the bases of citizenship such as *jus sanguinis* or *jus soli*, the criteria for who was eligible to become citizens, and the processes by which that happened. In the late twentieth century, however, the idea of national citizenship came under attack, the requirements that had to be met to become a citizen eroded, and the distinction between the rights and responsibilities of citizens and noncitizens shrank significantly. These developments have been legitimated in the name of international agreements on universal human rights and the argument that citizenship is not a product of the nation but inheres in the individual. The link between citizen and nation is broken, undermining, as Yasemin Soysal has said, "the national order of citizenship."[74]

Contemporary criteria for naturalization in America are limited and specific. Somewhat simplified they are:

(1) Five years legal permanent residence in the United States;
(2) "Good moral character," meaning absence of a criminal record;
(3) The ability to speak, read, and write ordinary (eighth-grade) English; and
(4) A general understanding of American government and history, demonstrated by passing the "civics test."

As one critic of these criteria as too restrictive admits, "In comparative perspective, the American requirements for naturalization are relatively modest."[75] The two key requirements are those for an elementary knowledge of English and of American history and politics. These criteria embody and symbolize the two remaining components of American national identity: the English cultural heritage and the liberal democratic principles of their Creed.

In most Western countries, the distinction between citizens and noncitizens eroded in the late twentieth century. "Sweden, the Netherlands, Switzerland, Great Britain, France, and Germany have increasingly extended civil, social, and even political rights to nonnational residents residing in their territory." In the United States, a similar process occurred, led by the courts. A "line of judicial decisions significantly lowered the political and economic value of citizenship by prohibiting government, especially the states, from allocating certain legal rights and economic advantages on the basis of that status."[76]

Three sets of rights and privileges are important for people in America: rights and liberties specified in the Constitution; economic rights, privileges, and benefits provided by government; and rights to participate in politics and government. Only for the latter are there significant differences in availability for citizens and aliens. Almost all the rights and liberties specified by the Constitution are granted to "persons," irrespective of their status within the United States. Hence, at least before September 11, it was accurate to say that "aliens—as well as citizens— are guaranteed due process in criminal and civil proceedings, benefit from the First Amendment's protection of freedom of speech and religion, are entitled to a lawyer at a criminal trial, may assert a right against self-incrimination, and may not be subjected to unreasonable searches and seizures."[77] Following September 11, however, security concerns led to some significant differences in the treatment of citizens and noncitizens, which, in the longer term, could modify or counter the more general trend toward the elimination of distinctions between them.

With respect to economic rights, benefits, and opportunities, the courts have generally invalidated state laws restricting particular occupations or economic benefits to citizens. In the key case, *Graham v. Richardson* (403 U.S. 365) in 1971, the Supreme Court held that "alienage" was a constitutionally "suspect classification" for states to use in making distinctions among their residents. Two efforts to limit economic benefits to aliens were made in the 1990s. Both failed to achieve their objectives. Proposition 187, a California referendum measure passed by a vote of 59 percent to 41 percent, denied health, educational, and welfare benefits to illegal immigrants and their children. Its educational provisions flew in the face of a 1982 Supreme Court decision that invalidated a Texas effort to exclude children of illegal immigrants from public schools. The referendum measure also was challenged as an encroachment on the authority of Congress to regulate immigration. With one minor exception none of Proposition 187's denials of benefits took effect. Two years later in 1996 Congress prohibited welfare payments and food stamps to legal aliens. During the next few years, however, these restrictions also were eviscerated, with the denial of welfare benefits limited to future immigrants.

This success in emasculating the 1996 law was, Peter Spiro, a critic of the law, said, "striking," and that act could be "a mere blip in the long-term trend in which the difference citizenship makes continues to diminish." Another authority, Alexander Aleinikoff, summed up the situation in 2000:

Settled immigrants live lives largely indistinguishable from those of most U.S. citizens. Although they cannot vote and may be ineligible for some government employment, they work, own property, have access to the courts, can be members of most professions, and exercise most constitutional rights on the same terms as native-born and naturalized citizens.[78]

Politics and government remain one area where significant distinctions exist between citizens and aliens. The latter are barred from some government positions requiring security clearances. They generally may not vote, hold elective office, or serve on juries. These restrictions on political participation are important and are under attack. In many states during the nineteenth century, aliens were able to vote. In the 1920s, suffrage became limited to citizens. Noncitizens have, however, acquired the right to vote in local elections in many European countries, including Denmark, Finland, Ireland, the Netherlands, Norway, Sweden, and some cantons in Switzerland. Arguments have been made for similar suffrage rights in many parts of the United States, and some localities have authorized alien voting in their elections. Leaders of the Mexican-American community have been particularly active in urging suffrage for aliens, including illegal aliens, a position advocated by Jorge Castañeda before he became Mexico's foreign minister. As the head of the Los Angeles school board put it: "At one time only white males could vote. My position is that it's time we cross that line in terms of citizenship."[79]

The easing of the requirements that have to be met to become a citizen presumably should increase the number of applicants for citizenship. The reduction in the differences in rights and privileges of citizens and aliens, on the other hand, presumably would decrease the incentives to acquire citizenship. Which of these two trends has had the greater impact? By and large, naturalization rates in both Europe and the United States were low in the late twentieth century. The U.S. naturalization rate is also lower than that of Canada.[80] Although many factors undoubtedly contribute to low rates of naturalization, the relatively modest American requirements certainly suggest no overriding desire by immigrants to America to naturalize. More significantly, in the United States there was a major decline in naturalization rates in the late twentieth century. The overall naturalization rate for all aliens dropped from 63.6 percent in 1970 to 37.4 percent in 2000. For those who had been in the United States for twenty years or more, it went down from 89.6 percent in 1970 to 71.1 percent in 2000. Dual citizenship provides an incentive to naturalize, but an increasing proportion of immigrants do not want to do so.

The exceptions are when naturalization is seen as necessary to acquire or to maintain government economic benefits. Two events have produced at least temporary increases in naturalization. Between 1994 and 1995, applications for citizenship increased by over 75 percent. Applications approved increased by well over 100 percent from 1995 to 1996, and the number denied quintupled from 46,067 in 1995 to 229,842 in 1996. These dramatic changes were primarily the result of two factors. First, under the Immigration Reform and Control Act of 1986, about three million illegal immigrants became eligible for naturalization in 1994. Second, the vulnerability of government economic benefits available to aliens became visible in 1994 with California's Proposition 187 and the debates leading up to Congress's passage of the Welfare Reform Act in 1996. These developments threatened to open a huge gap between the economic benefits available to citizens and noncitizens. A rush to naturalize followed. This "surge in naturalizations," it has been said, "has no parallel in American history." Aliens naturalized in 1996 were often quite explicit about their motives. Proposition 187, according to one Mexican-American immigrant activist, "was the sort of the bell that woke up the sleeping giant." This surge in citizenship was not naturalization by choice but, in Jones-Correa's phrase, "naturalization by intimidation."[81] After 1997, the number of applicants and the number of petitions approved dropped, although they still remained high compared to their pre-1995 levels.

September 11 generated deeper feelings of identity with their new country among many noncitizen immigrants, and the government's subsequent monitoring of and deportations of noncitizens produced a huge increase in citizenship applications. The Department of Homeland Security reported that 700,649 applications for citizenship were filed between July 1, 2001, and June 30, 2002, compared to 501,646 during the previous year. This 40 percent increase was, however, in part countered by a 6 percent decrease in the number of applications approved, presumably a result of their being reviewed more carefully.[82]

The erosion of the differences between citizens and aliens, the overall declining rates of naturalization, and the naturalization spike of the mid-1990s, all suggest the central importance of material government benefits for immigrant decisions. Immigrants become citizens not because they are attracted to America's culture and Creed, but because they are attracted by government social welfare and affirmative action programs. If these are available to noncitizens, the incentive for citizenship fades. Citizenship is becoming, in Peter Spiro's phrase, one more generally available "federal social benefit."[83] If, however, citizenship is not necessary to get benefits, it is superfluous. As Peter Schuck and Rogers Smith argue, it "is welfare state membership, not citizenship, that increasingly counts. . . . Membership in the welfare state, in contrast [to membership in the political community], is of crucial and growing significance; for some, who are wholly dependent upon public benefits, it may literally be a matter of life or death."[84]

From a different perspective, Joseph Carens asks, "What about loyalty, patriotism, and identity? Can't we expect immigrants to become attached to America?" and answers that "as a normative matter, we should not try to impose such an expectation" on them. This outlook pervades much intellectual and academic thinking about citizenship. Immigrants should not, "as a normative matter," be expected to be loyal and patriotic, and to identify with and be "attached" to America.[85] This rejection of citizenship signals a dramatic and symbolic shift about what it means to be American. Those who deny meaning to American citizenship also deny meaning to the cultural and political community that has been America.

ALTERNATIVES TO AMERICANIZATION

By the end of the twentieth century, assimilation no longer only meant Americanization. It could and did take other forms.

For some immigrants, it is segmented assimilation, that is, assimilation not into mainstream American culture and society but into a subnational, often marginal, segment of American society. Haitian immigrants were particularly under pressure to move in this direction. In New York City, Miami, and Evanston, Illinois, for instance, tensions over assimilation existed between Haitian immigrants and American blacks. First-generation Haitian immigrants saw themselves as having a higher status as immigrant blacks than as American blacks and tended to look down on the latter, Mary Waters points out, as "lazy, disorganized, obsessed with racial slights and barriers, with a disorganized and laissez-faire attitude towards family and child raising." Their children, however, were pressured by their peers to adopt the minority subculture of American blacks and to become, according to another scholar, "not so much 'American' as 'Afro-American.' "[86]

A second alternative to Americanization is, in effect, nonassimilation, the perpetuation in the United States of the culture and social institutions the immigrants had brought with them. It was the "in-but-not-of" effort of nineteenth-century German immigrants to be Germans in America rather than German-Americans. Now, however, this would be the choice not of relatively isolated rural villages but of large, regionally concentrated communities like the Cubans in southern Florida and the Mexicans in the Southwest.

The third possibility is the ampersand alternative, to capitalize on modern communications and transportation to maintain dual allegiance, dual nationality, and dual citizenship. One consequence has been the emergence of diasporas, transnational cultural communities cutting across the boundaries between countries.

These alternatives are explored in the following chapters.

CHAPTER 9

Mexican Immigration and Hispanization

THE MEXICAN/HISPANIC CHALLENGE

By the mid-twentieth century, America had become a multiethnic, multiracial society with an Anglo-Protestant mainstream culture encompassing many subcultures and with a common political creed rooted in that mainstream culture. In the late twentieth century, developments occurred that, if continued, could change America into a culturally bifurcated Anglo-Hispanic society with two national languages. This trend was in part the result of the popularity of the doctrines of multiculturalism and diversity among intellectual and political elites, and the government policies on bilingual education and affirmative action that those doctrines promoted and sanctioned. The driving force behind the trend toward cultural bifurcation, however, has been immigration from Latin America and especially from Mexico.

Mexican immigration is leading toward the demographic *reconquista* of areas Americans took from Mexico by force in the 1830s and 1840s, Mexicanizing them in a manner comparable to, although different from, the Cubanization that has occurred in southern Florida. It is also blurring the border between Mexico and America, introducing a very different culture, while also promoting the emergence, in some areas, of a blended society and culture, half-American and half-Mexican. Along with immigration from other Latin American countries, it is advancing Hispanization throughout America and social, linguistic, and economic practices appropriate for an Anglo-Hispanic society.

221

Mexican immigration has these effects because of the characteristics that differentiate it from past and present immigration from other countries and because of the extent to which Mexican immigrants and their progeny have not assimilated into American society as other immigrants did in the past and as many other immigrants are doing now.

WHY MEXICAN IMMIGRATION DIFFERS

Contemporary Mexican immigration is unprecedented in American history. The experience and lessons of past immigration have little relevance to understanding its dynamics and consequences. Mexican immigration differs from past immigration and most other contemporary immigration due to a combination of six factors.

Contiguity. Americans have thought of immigration as symbolized by the Statue of Liberty, Ellis Island, and more recently perhaps Kennedy Airport. Immigrants arrived in the United States after crossing several thousand miles of ocean. American attitudes toward immigrants and American immigration policies have been and, in considerable measure, still are shaped by this image. These assumptions and policies, however, have little or no relevance for Mexican immigration. America is now confronted by a massive influx of people from a poor, contiguous country with more than one third the population of the United States, who come across a two-thousand-mile border marked historically simply by a line in the ground and a shallow river.

This situation is unique for the United States and unique in the world. No other First World country has a land frontier with a Third World country, much less one of two thousand miles. Japan, Australia, New Zealand are islands; Canada is bordered only by the United States; the closest western European countries come to Third World countries are the Strait of Gibraltar between Spain and Morocco and the Straits of Otranto between Italy and Albania. The significance of the long Mexican-American border is enhanced by the economic differences between the two countries. "The income gap between the United States and Mexico," Stanford historian David Kennedy points out, "is the largest between any two contiguous countries in the world."[1] The consequences of migrants crossing two thousand miles of relatively open border rather than two thousand miles of open ocean are immense for policing and controlling immigration, for the blurring of the border with the rise of trans-border communities, for the society, people, culture, and economy of the American Southwest, and for America as a whole.

Numbers. The causes of Mexican, as well as other, immigration are found in the demographic, economic, and political dynamics of the sending country and the economic, political, and social attractions of the United States. Contiguity, however, obviously encourages immigration. The costs, challenges, and risks of immigration for Mexicans are much less than for others. They can easily go back and forth to Mexico and maintain contact with family and friends there. Aided by these factors, Mexican immigration increased steadily after 1965. About 640,000 Mexicans legally migrated to the United States in the 1970s, 1,656,000 in the 1980s, and 2,249,000 in the 1990s. In these three decades, Mexicans accounted for 14 percent, 23 percent, and 25 percent of total legal immigration. These percentages do not equal the percentages of immigrants who came from Ireland between 1820 and 1860 or from Germany in the 1850s and 1860s.[2] Yet they are high compared to the very dispersed sources of immigrants before World War I and compared to other contemporary immigrants. And to them must be added the large numbers of Mexicans who each year enter the United States illegally.

In 1960 the foreign-born people from the five principal countries of origin were relatively dispersed:

Italy	1,257,000
Germany	990,000
Canada	953,000
United Kingdom	833,000
Poland	748,000

In 2000 the foreign-born of the top five countries were distributed very differently:

Mexico	7,841,000
China	1,391,000
Philippines	1,222,000
India	1,007,000
Cuba	952,000

In the course of four decades, the numbers of foreign-born expanded immensely, Asians and Latin Americans replaced Europeans and Canadians, and diversity of source dramatically gave way to the dominance of one source: Mexico. Mexican immigrants constituted 27.6 percent of the total foreign-born population in 2000. The next largest contingents, Chinese and Filipinos, amounted to only 4.9 percent and 4.3 percent of the foreign-born.[3]

In the 1990s, Mexicans also were over one half of the Latin American immigrants to the United States, and Latin American immigrants were about one half the total immigrants to the continental United States between 1970 and 2000. Hispanics, twelve percent of the total U.S. population in 2000 (two-thirds of Mexican origin), increased by almost 10 percent from 2000 to 2002 and became more numerous than blacks. It is estimated they will constitute up to 25 percent of the population by 2040. These changes are driven not just by immigration but also by fertility. In 2002, total fertility rates were estimated at 1.8 for non-Hispanic whites, 2.1 for blacks, and 3.0 for Hispanics. "This is the characteristic shape of developing countries," the *Economist* commented. "As the bulge of Latinos enters peak child-bearing age in a decade or two, the Latinos' share of America's population will soar."[4]

In the mid-nineteenth century, immigration was dominated by English speakers from the British Isles. The pre–World War I immigration was highly diversified linguistically, including many speakers of Italian, Polish, Russian, Yiddish, English, German, and Swedish, as well as others. The post-1965 immigration differs from both these previous waves because now almost half speak a single non-English language. "The

Hispanic domination of the immigrant flow," as Mark Krikorian observes, "has no precedent in our history."[5]

Illegality. Substantial illegal entry into the United States is a post-1965 and Mexican phenomenon. For almost a century after the Constitution was adopted, illegal immigration was virtually impossible: no national laws restricted or prohibited immigration, and only a few states imposed modest limits. During the following ninety years, illegal immigration was minimal: control of immigrants coming by ship was fairly easy, and a good proportion of those arriving at Ellis Island were denied entry. The 1965 immigration law, the increased availability of transportation, and the intensified forces promoting Mexican emigration drastically changed this situation. Apprehensions by the U.S. Border Patrol rose from 1.6 million in the 1960s to 11.9 million in the 1980s, and 12.9 million in the 1990s. Estimates of the Mexicans who successfully enter illegally each year range from 105,000 by a binational Mexican-American commission up to 350,000 per year by the INS for the 1990s. Roughly two thirds of post-1975 Mexican immigrants, it has been estimated, entered the United States illegally.[6]

The 1986 Immigration Reform and Control Act contained provisions to legalize the status of existing illegal immigrants and to reduce future illegal immigration through employer sanctions and other means. The former goal was achieved: some 3.1 million illegal immigrants, about 90 percent from Mexico, became legal "green card" residents of the United States. The latter goal was not achieved. Estimates of the total number of illegal immigrants in the United States rose from four million in 1995 to six million in 1998 and eight to ten million by 2003. Mexicans accounted for 58 percent of the total illegal population in the United States in 1990; by 2000, an estimated 4.8 million illegal Mexicans were 69 percent of that population.[7] In 2003 illegal Mexicans in the United States were twenty-five times as numerous as the next largest contingent, from El Salvador. Illegal immigration is, overwhelmingly, Mexican immigration.

In 1993 President Clinton declared the organized smuggling of people into the United States a "threat to national security." Illegal immigration is even more a threat to America's societal security. The economic and political forces generating this threat are immense and unrelenting. Nothing comparable has occurred previously in the American experience.

Regional Concentration. As we have seen, the Founding Fathers thought dispersion essential to assimilation, and historically that has been the pattern and continues to be for most contemporary non-Hispanic immigrants. Hispanics, however, have tended to concentrate regionally: Mexicans in Southern California, Cubans in Miami, Dominicans and Puerto Ricans, the last of whom are not technically immigrants, in New York City. In the 1990s, the proportions of Hispanics continued to grow in these regions of heaviest concentration. At the same time, Mexicans and other Hispanics were also establishing beachheads elsewhere. While the absolute numbers often are small, the states with the largest percentage increases in Spanish speakers between 1990 and 2000 were, in decreasing order: North Carolina (449 percent increase), Arkansas, Georgia, Tennessee, South Carolina, Nevada, and Alabama (222 percent increase). Hispanics have also established concentrated presences in individual cities and towns in various parts of the country. In 2003 more than 40 percent of the population of Hartford, Connecticut, was Hispanic (primarily Puerto Rican), "the largest concentration among major cities outside California, Texas, Colorado and Florida," outnumbering the city's 38 percent black population. Hartford, its first Hispanic mayor proclaimed, "has become a Latin city, so to speak. It's a sign of things to come," with Spanish increasingly the language of commerce and government.[8]

The biggest concentrations of Hispanics, however, are in the southwest, particularly California. In 2000 nearly two thirds of Mexican immigrants lived in the West, and nearly half in California. The Los Angeles area has immigrants from many countries, and possesses a distinct Koreatown, a substantial Vietnamese community, and in Monterey Park a city that is reported to be the first continental U.S. city with an Asian majority. The sources of California's foreign-born, however, differ sharply from those of the rest of the country, with those from a single country, Mexico, exceeding totals for all of Europe and all of Asia. In Los Angeles, Hispanics, overwhelmingly Mexican, far outnumber other groups. In 2000, 64 percent of the Hispanics in Los Angeles were of Mexican origin, and 46.5 percent of Los Angeles residents were Hispanic, while 29.7 percent were non-Hispanic whites. By 2010, it is estimated that Hispanics will be 60 percent of the Los Angeles population.[9]

Most immigrant groups have higher fertility rates than natives, and hence the impact of immigration is heavily felt in schools. The highly diversified immigration into New York creates the problem of teachers dealing with students who may speak twenty different languages at home. In contrast, Hispanic children are substantial majorities of the students in the schools in many southwestern cities. "No school system in a major U.S. city," Katrina Burgess and Abraham Lowenthal said of Los Angeles in their scholarly 1993 study of Mexico-California ties, "has ever experienced such a large influx of students from a single foreign country. The schools of Los Angeles are becoming Mexican." By 2002, 71.9 percent of the students in the Los Angeles Unified School District were Hispanic, predominantly Mexican, with the proportion increasing steadily; 9.4 percent of schoolchildren were non-Hispanic whites. In 2003 for the first time since the 1850s a majority of newborn children in California were Hispanic.[10]

In the past, David Kennedy observes, "the variety and dispersal of the immigrant stream" facilitated assimilation. "Today, however, one large immigrant stream is flowing into a defined region from a single cultural, linguistic, religious, and national source: Mexico . . . the sobering fact is that the United States has had no experience comparable to what is now taking place in the Southwest."[11] It is also a sobering fact that the more highly concentrated immigrants are, the slower and less complete is their assimilation.

Persistence. Previous waves of immigration, we have seen, subsided and the proportions coming from individual countries fluctuated greatly. At the moment, however, the current wave shows no sign of ebbing and the conditions creating the large Mexican component of that wave are likely to endure for some while absent a major war or recession. In the longer term, Mexican immigration could decline when the economic well-being of Mexico approximates that of the United States. As of 2000, American per capita GDP was nine to ten times that of Mexico. If that difference were reduced to three to one, the economic incentives for migration might also drop substantially. To reach that ratio in any meaningful future, however, would require extremely rapid economic growth in Mexico, at a rate greatly exceeding that of the United States. Even if this occurred, economic development in itself need not reduce the impulse to emigrate. During the nineteenth century, when Europe was rapidly industrializing and per capita incomes rising significantly, 50 million Europeans emigrated to the Americas, Asia, and Africa. On the other hand economic development and urbanization may also lead to a decline in birth rates and thus reduce the numbers of people likely to move north. The Mexican birth rate has been declining. In 1970–1975 the total fertility rate was 6.5 percent; by 1995–2000, it had been more than halved to 2.8. Yet in 2001 the Mexican government's National Population Council predicted that these developments would not have any significant immediate impact and that total immigration was likely to average 400,000 to 515,000 a year until 2030.[12] By then, more than a half century of high-level migration will have drastically altered the demographic profile of the United States and the demographic relation between Mexico and the United States.

Sustained high levels of immigration have three important consequences. First, immigration builds on itself. "If there is a single 'law' in migration," Myron Weiner observed, "it is that a migration flow, once begun, induces its own flow. Migrants enable their friends and relatives back home to migrate by providing them with information about how to migrate, resources to facilitate movement, and assistance in finding jobs and housing." The result is "chain migration," with migration becoming easier for each subsequent group of migrants.[13]

Second, the longer migration continues, the more difficult politically it is to stop it. Immigrants often tend to favor closing the door behind them once they are in. At the organizational level, however, a different dynamic is at work. The views of immigrant group elites on this issue often differ significantly from those of their rank and file. Associations of immigrants are quickly formed, they lobby politically to expand immigrant rights and benefits, and hence they quickly develop an interest in enlarging their constituency by promoting more immigration. As the immigrant constituency grows, it becomes more difficult for politicians to oppose the wishes of its leaders. Representatives of different immigrant groups form coalitions that gather support from those favoring immigration for economic, ideological, or humanitarian reasons. The benefits of any legislative success these coalitions achieve redound most importantly, of course, to the biggest immigrant group, that is, Mexicans.

Third, sustained high-level immigration retards and can even obstruct assimilation. "A constant influx of new arrivals," Barry Edmonston and Jeffrey Passel conclude, "especially in predominantly immigration neighborhoods, keeps the language alive among immigrants and their children." As a result, Mark Falcoff observes, "the Spanish-speaking population is being continually replenished by newcomers faster than that population is being assimilated" and hence the widespread use of Spanish in the United States "is a reality that cannot be changed, even over the longer term."[14] As we have seen, the decline in the immigration of Irish and Germans after the Civil War and the drastic reduction in immigration of southern and eastern Europeans after 1924 facilitated their assimilation into American society. If current levels of immigration are sustained, no such transfer of loyalties, convictions, and identities can be expected with Mexican immigrants, and the great American assimilation success story of the past will not necessarily be duplicated for Mexicans.

Historical Presence. No other immigrant group in American history has asserted or has been able to assert a historical claim to American territory. Mexicans and Mexican-Americans can and do make that claim. Almost all of Texas, New Mexico, Arizona, California, Nevada, and Utah was part of Mexico until Mexico lost them as a result of the Texan War of Independence in 1835–1836 and the Mexican-American War of 1846–1848. Mexico is the only country that the United States has invaded, occupied its capital, placing the Marines in the "halls of Montezuma," and then annexed half its territory. Mexicans do not forget these events. Quite understandably, they feel that they have special rights in these territories. "Unlike other immigrants," Peter Skerry notes, "Mexicans arrive here from a neighboring nation that has suffered military defeat at the hands of the United States; and they settle predominantly in a region that was once part of their homeland. . . . Mexican Americans enjoy a sense of being on their own turf that is not shared by other immigrants." [15] That "turf" takes human form in the some twenty-five Mexican communities that have existed continuously since before the American conquest. Concentrated in the Mexican "homelands" of northern New Mexico and along the Rio Grande, their populations are more than 90 percent Hispanic with over 90 percent of the Hispanics speaking Spanish at home. One hundred and fifty years after these communities became part of the United States, "Hispanic cultural and demographic dominance of society and space has been maintained and Hispanic assimilation is weak." [16]

At times, scholars have suggested that the southwest could become America's Quebec. Both had Catholic populations and were conquered by Anglo-Protestant peoples, but otherwise they have little in common. Quebec is three thousand miles from France and each year several hundred thousand Frenchmen do not attempt to enter Quebec legally and illegally. History shows that serious potential for conflict exists when people in one country start to refer to territory in a neighboring country in proprietary terms and to assert special rights and claims to that territory.

Contiguity, numbers, illegality, regional concentration, persistence, and historical presence combine to make Mexican immigration different from other immigration and to pose problems for the assimilation of people of Mexican origin into American society.

HOW MEXICAN ASSIMILATION LAGS

The criteria that can be used to gauge assimilation of an individual, a group, or a generation include language, education, occupation and income, citizenship, intermarriage, and identity. With respect to almost all of these indices, Mexican assimilation lags behind that of contemporary non-Mexican immigrants and that of immigrants in the previous waves.

Language. Language assimilation historically has tended to follow a common pattern. The large majority of first-generation immigrants do not, unless they come from English-speaking countries, achieve fluency in English. The second generation, who either arrive as very young children with their parents or are born in the United States, have relatively high degrees of fluency in both English and their parents' language. The third generation is completely fluent in English and has little or no knowledge of their family's ancestral language, which creates a problem for communication with their grandparents, but is also often accompanied by a nostalgic interest in and expressed desire to learn the language of their ancestors.[17]

At the beginning of the twenty-first century, whether language assimilation by Mexicans would follow this pattern was unclear. The recency of this wave meant there was only a relatively small third generation. The evidence on English acquisition and Spanish retention also was limited and ambiguous. In 2000, over 26 million people spoke Spanish at home (10.5 percent of people over age five), and almost 13.7 million of these spoke English less than "very well," an increase of 65.5 percent over 1990. According to a Census Bureau survey, in 1990 about 95 percent of Mexican-born immigrants spoke Spanish at home; 73.6 percent of these did not speak English very well; and 43 percent of the Mexican foreign-born were "linguistically isolated."[18] For the second generation, born in the United States, the results were quite different. Only 11.6 percent spoke only Spanish or more Spanish than English, while 25 percent spoke both languages equally, 32.7 percent more English than Spanish, and 30.1 percent only English. Over 90 percent of the U.S.-born people of Mexican origin spoke English fluently.[19]

English language use and fluency for first- and second-generation Mexicans thus seem to follow the usual pattern. Two questions, however, remain. Have changes occurred over time in the acquisition or use of English by second-generation Mexican immigrants? One might suppose that with the rapid expansion of the Mexican immigrant community, people of Mexican origin would have less incentive to become fluent in and to use English in 2000 than they had in 1970. Second, will the third generation follow the classic pattern with fluency in English and little or no knowledge of Spanish or will it retain the second generation's fluency in both languages? Second-generation immigrants often look down on and reject their ancestral language and are intensely embarrassed by their parents' inability to communicate in English. Whether second-generation Mexicans share this attitude will, presumably, largely shape the extent to which the third generation retains any knowledge of Spanish. If the second generation does not reject Spanish out of hand, the third generation is also likely to be bilingual, and the maintenance of fluency in both languages is likely to become institutionalized in the Mexican-American community, reinforced by the continuing inflow of new immigrants speaking only Spanish.

Overwhelming majorities (66 percent to 85 percent) of Mexican immigrants and Hispanics have emphasized the need for their children to be fluent in Spanish. These attitudes contrast with those of other immigrant groups. "There appears," as one study concluded, "to be a cultural difference between the Asian and Hispanic parents with respect to having their children maintain their native language."[20] In part, this difference is undoubtedly a result of the size of Hispanic communities, which creates incentives for fluency in the ancestral language. Although second- and third-generation Mexican-Americans and other Hispanics acquire competence in English, they also appear to deviate from the usual pattern in maintaining their competence in Spanish. Second- or third-generation Mexican-Americans who were brought up speaking only English have learned Spanish as adults and are encouraging their children to become fluent in it. Spanish language competence, Professor F. Chris Garcia of the University of New Mexico has said, is "the one thing every Hispanic takes pride in, wants to protect and promote."[21]

Education. The education of Mexican-origin people differs significantly from the American norm. In 2000, 86.6 percent of native-born adults had graduated from high school. The rates for the foreign-born in the United States varied from 81.3 percent for Europeans, 83.8 percent for Asians, and 94.9 percent for Africans, down to 49.6 percent for all Latin Americans and only 33.8 percent for Mexicans. In 1990, the

Mexican rate of high school graduation was half the rate for the entire foreign-born population.[22] According to the 1986 and 1988 Current Population Survey, male Mexican immigrants had a mean value of 7.4 years of schooling compared to 11.2 for those of Cuban origin, 13.7 for Asians, and 13.1 for non-Hispanic white natives. Overall, Frank Bean and his associates concluded, Mexican immigrants averaged "about five fewer years of schooling compared to non-Hispanic immigrants or natives." Whether the educational level of Mexican immigrants is increasing appears uncertain. The Bean study found that between 1960 and 1988 later arrivals from Mexico had "lower education attainment than earlier migrants." A study by the Pew Hispanic Center, on the other hand, concluded that the educational level of Hispanic immigrants (Mexicans and others) improved significantly between 1970 and 2000 but still had "not yet produced a notable convergence with the level of education in the native-born U.S. population."[23]

What is clear is that the educational achievements of subsequent generations of Mexican-Americans continue to lag. Three comparisons are relevant. First, as James Smith has shown, third-generation Mexican-Americans descended from immigrants born in the late nineteenth and early twentieth centuries had on average four years more education than their parents. For the latest sequence of generations, however, his data show that while the educational level of third-generation Mexican-Americans (12.29 years) is almost double that of their first-generation ancestors (6.22 years), it is less than one year better than that of their parents (11.61 years).[24] Second, while Smith looked at successive generations over time, Rodolfo de la Garza and his associates compared different generations at a single point in time, 1989–1990. The results in Table 9.1 demonstrate a significant difference between first and second generations, but only modest improvement and some regression in the third and fourth generations.

Third, Table 9.1 shows that even fourth-generation educational achievement was significantly below the American norm in 1990. Other studies have also highlighted this gap. In 1998, the National Council of La Raza (a leading Hispanic organization in the United States) found that three out of ten Hispanic students drop out of school compared to one in eight blacks and one in fourteen whites. Among those aged eigh-

Table 9.1

Educational Level of Mexican-Americans and All Americans

	Mexican-Americans by Generation, 1989–1990				All Americans except Mexican-Americans, 1990
	First	Second	Third	Fourth	
No high school degree	69.9%	51.5%	33.0%	41.0%	23.5%
Only high school degree	24.7	39.2	58.5	49.4	30.4
Post–high school degree	5.4	9.3	8.5	9.6	45.1
College degree				3.5	19.9

Source: Rodolfo O. de la Garza, Angelo Falcon, P. Chris Garcia, John Garcia, "Mexican Immigrants, Mexican Americans, and American Political Culture," in Barry Edmonston and Jeffrey S. Passell, eds., *Immigration and Ethnicity: The Integration of America's Newest Arrivals* (Washington: Urban Institute Press, 1994), pp. 232–34; U.S. Census Bureau, 1990 Census of Population: Persons of Hispanic Origin in the United States, pp. 77–81.

teen to twenty-four in 2000, 82.4 percent of whites, 77 percent of blacks, and 59.6 percent of Hispanics had completed high school. Frank Bean and his associates conclude that "both second-and-third generation Mexican Americans have lower average educational levels than non-Hispanic whites and a much higher proportion of high school dropouts and a lower proportion of college attendees." The demographer William Frey has pointed out that between 1990 and 2000 high school dropout rates declined in forty-two states, and that the eight states where they increased, apart from Alaska, had a "common thread: significant increases in Latino populations." In addition, Bean et al. report that the "proportion of Hispanic high school graduates who had ever enrolled in college was much lower in 1990 than in 1973."[25]

At the start of the twenty-first century little progress had been made in the educational assimilation of Mexican-Americans.

Occupation and Income. The economic position of Mexican immigrants parallels, as one would expect, their educational attainment. In 2000, 30.9 percent of employed native-born Americans held professional and managerial positions. The extent to which immigrants from different countries approximated this norm varied greatly.[26]

Canada	46.3%
Asia	38.7
Europe	38.1
Africa	36.5
Latin America	12.1
Mexico	6.3

A survey of the immigrant children in South Florida and Southern California produced comparable results. The proportions of immigrant families of low socioeconomic status, that is, working as busboys, janitors, laborers, and comparable positions, were as follows.[27]

Cubans with children in private school	7.7%
Nicaraguans	23.8
Cubans with children in public school	25.8
Haitians	31.0
Vietnamese	45.3
Mexicans	66.9

Mexican immigrants have had low rates of self-employment or entrepreneurship. In 1990, over 20 percent of Armenian, Greek, Israeli, Russian (largely Jewish), and Korean male workers were self-employed. In this comparison of 60 ethnic groups, Mexican immigrants with 6.7 percent self-employment exceeded only Filipino, Central American, Laotian, and black immigrant groups.[28]

Mexican immigrants are more likely to live in poverty and to be on welfare than most other groups. In 1998, the poverty rates of the seven largest immigrant groups were.[29]

Mexicans	31%
Cubans	24
Salvadorans	21
Vietnamese	15
Chinese	10

| Filipinos | 6 |
| Indians | 6 |

In 1998, 15.4 percent of native households were on welfare. The welfare rates for national origin groups coming from countries that generated refugees were extremely high: Laotians 59.1 percent, Cambodians 47.9 percent, Soviet citizens 37.1 percent, Cubans 30.7 percent, and Vietnamese 28.7 percent. Apart from the Dominicans (54.9 percent on welfare), the proportion of Mexicans on welfare, 34 percent, exceeded that of all the national origin groups from the eighteen other countries in this analysis. An analysis of welfare use in 2001 by immigrants from a dozen regions and countries showed Mexican immigrant households ranking first, with 34.1 percent using welfare, compared to 22.7 percent of all immigrant households, and 14.6 percent of native American households.[30]

Overall, Mexican immigrants are at the bottom of the economic ladder. Do the next generations stay there? The evidence is spotty. The regional concentration of Mexican-Americans, which retards other forms of assimilation, may help their economic progress by fostering a relatively large enclave economy with a variety of businesses, occupations, and opportunities for upward economic mobility within that enclave. The argument has, however, been made that the pre–World War I economic success of Jewish immigrants and their offspring, along with that of Japanese, other Asian immigrants, and Florida Cubans, reflects economic success in their birth countries.[31] Few Mexican immigrants have been economically successful in Mexico; hence presumably relatively few are likely to be economically successful in the United States. In addition, any significant improvement in the economic status of Mexican-Americans depends on improvement of their educational level, and the ongoing influx of poorly educated people from Mexico makes that difficult. Joel Perlmann and Roger Waldinger are pessimistic about the economic prospects of second-generation Mexican-Americans:

While America's new immigrant population is extraordinarily diverse, its overwhelmingly largest component—the Mexicans—falls at the very bottom of the skill ladder; the Mexicans are even more heavily represented among the immigrants' children. Absent the Mexicans, today's second generation looks little different from the rest of the American population in socioeconomic characteristics. Those characteristics are not sufficient to guarantee satisfactory adjustment to the economy of the next generation; but the same can be said for young, third-generation-plus Americans of any ethnic stripe. The immigrant children most notably at risk are the Mexicans (most notable, surely, in numbers and as notable as any other immigrant group in the low level of economic well-being). It is the presence of a single large group, so far below the others in skills, that distinguishes today's from yesterday's second generation.[32]

These conclusions are supported by the analyses of James Smith and Rodolfo de la Garza and his associates. Smith's careful analysis shows a continuing lag in Mexican-American wage levels. He presents figures for the adjusted wage values of Mexican-American men as percentages of native white men's lifetime earnings. Those for the third-generation descendants of Mexican immigrants born in the 1860s were 74.5 percent. The adjusted wage values of third-generation Mexican-Americans whose immigrant parents were born between 1910 and 1920 had risen to only about 80 percent. The adjusted wage levels for all three generations of these latest birth cohorts for which he has data are:[33]

IMMIGRANT YEAR OF BIRTH	GENERATION		
	First	Second	Third
1910–1914	65.3%	81.2%	79.2%
1915–1919	65.3	83.8	83.2

As with educational levels, the second generation does markedly better than the first, but then progress falters. Using data from the 1989–1990 Latino National Political Survey, Garza and his associates found that on most socioeconomic indices the U.S.-born of Mexican origin did better than the Mexican-born. They also found, however, that the fourth generation of Mexican-origin people had, on most measures, not advanced much beyond the second generation and still remained distant from the

American norm. In addition, the rate of Mexican-American welfare use drops for second-generation Mexican-Americans but then rises again to 31 percent for the third generation. "The native-born," Garza et al. conclude, "do not significantly improve their socioeconomic position across generations. Thus, fourth generation Mexican Americans still do substantially worse on these . . . measures than Anglos."[34]

Table 9.2

Socioeconomic Characteristics of Mexican-Americans and All Americans

	Mexican-Americans by Generations, 1989–1990				All Americans 1990
	First	Second	Third	Fourth	
Home owner	30.6%	58.6%	55.1%	40.3%	64.1%*
Managerial or professional occupation	4.7	7.0	8.7	11.6	27.1†
Household income $50,000 or more	7.1	10.5	11.2	10.7	24.8†

Source: de la Garza et al., "Mexican Immigrants, Mexican Americans, and American Political Culture," pp. 232–34; U.S. Census Bureau, Current Population Survey, March 1990, and 1990 Census of Population: *Persons of Hispanic Origin in the United States*, pp. 115–19, 153–57.

* Includes Mexican-Americans.

† Excludes Mexican-Americans. Figures calculated by James Perry from census data.

Citizenship. Naturalization is the single most important political dimension of assimilation. Naturalization rates generally vary significantly in terms of income and occupation, education, age at entry, length of time in the United States, and propinquity of the country of origin. In the last decades of the twentieth century, Mexican naturalization was either the lowest or among the lowest of all immigrant groups. The naturalization rates in 1990, for instance, for Mexican immigrants who arrived before 1980 was 32.4 percent, lower than those of other immigrant groups, except Salvadorans, with a rate of 31.3 percent. In contrast, the rate for immigrants from the Soviet Union was 86.3 percent, Ireland 81.6 percent, Poland 81.6 percent, the Philippines 80.9 percent, Taiwan 80.5 percent, and Greece 78.3 percent.[35] Mexicans entering before 1965 and between 1965 and 1974 had the lowest rates of naturalization among the top fifteen sources of entry and the fifth lowest for those entering between 1975 and 1984. Leon Bouvier has constructed standardized 1990 naturalization rates that eliminate the effect of year of entry. His results for the top fifteen immigrant groups are as follows:

Filipinos	76.2%
Koreans	71.2
Chinese	68.5
Vietnamese	67.7
Poles	61.3
Indians	58.7
Italians	58.3
Jamaicans	57.5
Germans	51.8
Cubans	49.9
Britons	44.1
Dominicans	42.0
Canadians	40.0
Salvadorans	37.0
Mexicans	32.6

A *New York Times*/CBS poll similarly found that in 2003, 23 percent of Hispanic immigrants were citizens, compared to 69 percent of non-Hispanic immigrants. One important cause of this difference suggested by Roberto Suro, director of the Pew Hispanic Center, is his estimate that 35 percent to 45 percent of all Hispanic immigrants are in the United States illegally.[36]

Intermarriage. Data on the intermarriage of Mexican immigrants are not readily available. In 1998, however, Mexican-Americans were 63 percent of the Hispanic population in the United States. The rates for Hispanic intermarriage generally follow those of immigrants in previous waves, although they are lower than those for contemporary Asian immigrants. The percentages of married females in 1994 who had married outside their group were as follows.[37]

	ASIAN	HISPANIC
First Generation	18.6%	8.4%
Second Generation	29.2	26.4
Third Generation	41.5	33.2

Mexican intermarriage rates may not differ greatly from the Hispanic rates, but they are probably lower. Intermarriage is affected by group size, status, and dispersion. Members of small, widely dispersed groups often have little choice but to marry outside their group, as well as incentives to do so. Members of large, low-status, geographically concentrated groups, in contrast, are more likely to marry within the group. As the absolute number of Mexican immigrants increases and their high birth rate produces still larger numbers of offspring, one would expect the opportunities and incentives for them to marry each other to increase. This seems to be happening. In 1977, 31 percent of all marriages involving Hispanics were interethnic. In 1994, only 25.5 percent were, and in 1998, 28 percent of Hispanic marriages were out-marriages. As Gary D. Sandefur and his associates conclude in their 2001 National Research Council study, in contrast to "Blacks and Whites, levels of interracial marriage for Hispanics have changed little since 1970 and, if anything, have decreased." This overall out-marriage rate for Hispanics, Richard Alba notes, "is influenced especially by the high level of endogamy on the part of the largest Hispanic group, Mexican Americans."[38] Mexicans marry Mexicans.

In the past the marriages of newer immigrants and their offspring to Anglos or other native Americans have hastened the assimilation of the immigrants into mainstream American society and culture. With marriages between Hispanics and Anglos, Hispanic-American scholars have argued, this pattern is changing. "In fact, in many instances," William Flores and Rina Benmayor conclude, "assimilation is in the opposite direction. That is, the non-Latino spouse (who may or may not be Anglo) and children resulting from such marriages often identify as Latinos, even when they do not speak Spanish."[39] To the extent that this phenomenon exists, it represents a significant departure from the assimilation patterns of other immigrant groups.

Identity. The ultimate criterion of assimilation is the extent to which immigrants identify with the United States as a country, believe in its Creed, espouse its culture, and correspondingly reject loyalty to other countries and their values and cultures. The available evidence is limited, and, in some respects, contradictory. Unquestionably, a most significant manifestation of assimilation for Hispanic immigrants is conversion to evangelical Protestantism. This development parallels and is related to the dramatic increase in evangelical Protestants in many Latin American countries. Precise figures do not exist on the number of Protestant Hispanics in the United States, but Ron Unz has argued that "a quarter or more of Hispanics have shifted from their traditional Catholic faith to Protestant evangelical churches, a religious transformation of unprecedented speed, and one obviously connected partly to their absorption into American society."[40] The challenge posed by this defection has, in turn, stimulated intense counterefforts by the Catholic Church to induce Hispanic immigrants to assimilate into American society by becoming American Catholics. Competition for believers among American religions is a potent force for Americanization.

More detailed evidence suggests a weak identification with America on the part of Mexican immigrants and people of Mexican origin. The study of children of immigrants in Southern California and South Florida in 1992 asked the question: "How do you identify, that is, what do you call yourself?" The Latin American respondents were grouped into eight countries or groups of countries. None of the children born in Mexico answered "American" as compared with 1.9 percent to 9.3 percent of those born elsewhere in Latin America or the Caribbean. The largest number of Mexican-born children, 41.2 percent, identified themselves as "Hispanic" and the second largest, 32.6 percent, chose "Mexican." Among Mexican-American children born in the United States, only 3.9 percent responded "American" compared to 28.5 per-

cent to 50.0 percent of those born in America with parents from elsewhere in Latin America. The most numerous responses of these U.S.-
born children were "Mexican-American" 38.8 percent, "Chicano" 24.6
percent, and "Hispanic" 20.6 percent. Twice as many, 8.1 percent, chose
"Mexican" for their primary identification as the 3.9 percent who chose
"American." Whether born in Mexico or in America, Mexican-origin
children overwhelmingly did not choose "American" as their primary
identification.[41]

A different study analyzed the views of Mexican-origin respondents
to the Latino National Political Survey in 1989–1990. The authors of
this analysis tested the prediction of the "three generations model" that
assimilation would progress in linear fashion and be substantially completed by the third generation with the prediction of the "emergent ethnicity model" that "ethnic identities emerge in response to shared
experiences" of an immigrant group in the United States "such as
group-based discrimination." They analyzed the attitudes of Mexican-
Americans toward the use of English, political tolerance, and trust in
government. Overall the emergent ethnicity model had greater validity
than the three generations model. They found that "the longer the immigrants were in the United States, the less likely they were to agree
that everyone should learn English" and that "those more incorporated
into mainstream society, the native-born Mexican-Americans, are less
supportive of core American values than are the foreign-born." These
findings, as they point out, do not support the proposition that Mexican
culture "impedes support for the American creed."[42] They do, however,
document the failure of Mexican-Americans over several generations to
increase their identification with American values.

In 1994, Mexican-Americans vigorously demonstrated against California's Proposition 187, limiting welfare benefits to children of illegal
immigrants, by marching through the streets of Los Angeles waving
scores of Mexican flags and carrying American flags upside down. In
1998, as we saw, at a soccer game in Los Angeles between Mexican and
American teams, Mexican-Americans booed "The Star-Spangled Banner," assaulted the U.S. players, and attacked a spectator who waved an
American flag.[43] The limited quantitative data available suggest that

these dramatic rejections of America and assertions of Mexican identity were not limited to an extremist minority in the Mexican-American community. Many Mexican immigrants and their offspring do not appear to identify primarily with the United States. For them, as for Robin Fox's Hispanic student at Rutgers, "Uncle Sam no es mi tío." It is thus not surprising that in 1990 a representative sample of the American public viewed Hispanics as less patriotic than Jews, blacks, Asians, and Southern whites.[44]

Summary. The centrality of Mexico for immigration and assimilation in America becomes clearly visible if one assumes that other immigration continues as it has but that somehow Mexican immigration abruptly stopped. The flow of legal immigrants would be reduced by about 160,000, and hence be closer to the levels recommended by the Jordan Commission. Illegal entries would diminish dramatically and the total number of illegal immigrants in the United States would gradually decline. Agricultural and other businesses in the southwest would be disrupted, but the wages of low-income Americans would improve. Debates over the use of Spanish and whether English should be made the official language of state and national governments would fade away. Bilingual education and the controversies it spawns would decline. So also would controversies over welfare and other benefits for immigrants. The debate over whether immigrants were an economic burden on state and federal governments would be decisively resolved in the negative. The average education and skills of the immigrants coming to America and those continuing to come would rise to levels unprecedented in American history. The inflow of immigrants would again become highly diverse, which would increase incentives for all immigrants to learn English and absorb American culture. The possibility of a de facto split between a predominantly Spanish-speaking America and English-speaking America would disappear, and with it a major potential threat to the cultural and possibly political integrity of the United States.

INDIVIDUAL ASSIMILATION AND
ENCLAVE CONSOLIDATION

In the past, immigrants clustered with their own kind in neighborhood enclaves, and often concentrated in particular occupations. With the second and third generations, the members of each group gradually dispersed and became differentiated in terms of residence, occupation, income, education, and, with intermarriage, ancestry. The nature and extent of assimilation varied from person to person. For some it was rapid and pervasive, as they moved outward and upward from the immigrant enclave. Others were "left behind" in the enclave and in first-generation occupations. These variations reflected differences among individuals in terms of family, ability, energy, and motives. At its roots, assimilation takes place at the individual not the group level.

At the same time that various personal, economic, and social considerations encourage assimilation, other forces promote the expansion and consolidation of the immigrant community. The extent to which a cohesive community is maintained tends to be a function of its size and isolation. Small, isolated, rural communities may be able to maintain their social and cultural cohesiveness for several generations. Early-twentieth-century Jewish, Polish, and Italian communities in the northeastern and midwestern cities, in contrast, tended to melt into their urban environment in the course of two or three generations. The ability of an immigrant community to sustain itself in an urban society with a complex economy demanding multifarious interactions between individuals and groups depends in large part on the size of that community.

The processes of individual assimilation and community consolidation are complex, involve inherent contradictions, and ultimately are conflictual. They also can coexist and reinforce each other in specific ways. Development of a large, economically diversified immigrant community can provide opportunities for its individual members to assimilate economically through upward mobility into the American middle class. Also, however, more education and socioeconomic advancement often tend to encourage group consciousness and rejection of mainstream culture. Lower-class blacks continue to believe in the American dream, while middle-class blacks are more likely to reject it.[45] If Mexican-Americans achieve middle-class status within the Mexican-American community, their inclination to reject American culture and to adhere to and to attempt to propagate Mexican culture might be enhanced.

In addition, birth in the United States and naturalization make it easier for people to travel back and forth across the border and thus maintain contacts with and their identity with their place of origin.[46] Citizenship also facilitates expansion of the immigrant community by allowing the new citizens to bring in a wider range of relatives than they could as legal permanent residents. Also, of course, citizens can vote and participate in government and thus much more effectively promote the interests of their ethnic community.

In the past, individual assimilation has usually triumphed over enclave consolidation. Eventually, territorial dispersion, occupational and income differentiation, and intergroup marriage bring about increasing assimilation, although communal ties remain and later generations may attempt to revive communal consciousness. These forces may well work themselves out in a similar manner for Mexican-Americans. Given the distinctive characteristics of Mexican immigration, however, this cannot be assumed. "Mexican-Americans," as David Kennedy says, "will have open to them possibilities closed to previous immigrant groups. They will have sufficient coherence and critical mass in a defined region so that, if they choose, they can preserve their distinct culture indefinitely. They could also eventually undertake to do what no previous immigrant group could have dreamed of doing: challenge the existing cultural, political, legal, commercial, and educational systems to change fundamentally not only the language but also the very institutions in which they do business."[47]

In 1983, the distinguished sociologist Morris Janowitz already saw this happening. Pointing to the "strong resistance to acculturation among Spanish-speaking residents," he argued that "the Mexicans are unique as an immigrant group in the persistent strength of their communal bonds." As a result:

Mexicans, together with other Spanish-speaking populations, are creating a bifurcation in the social-political structure of the United States that approximates nationality divisions. . . .

[The] presence of Mexico at the border of the United States, plus the strength of Mexican cultural patterns, means that the "natural history" of Mexican immigrants has been and will be at variance with that of other immigrant groups. For sections of the Southwest, it is not premature to speak of a cultural and social irredenta—sectors of the United States which have in effect become Mexicanized and therefore, under political dispute.[48]

Others have voiced similar views. Mexican-Americans, in turn, argue that the Southwest was taken from them by military aggression in the 1840s, and that the time for *la reconquista* has arrived. Demographically, socially, and culturally that is well under way.

Conceivably this could lead to a move to reunite these territories with Mexico. That seems unlikely, but Professor Charles Truxillo of the University of New Mexico predicts that by 2080 the southwestern states of the United States and the northern states of Mexico will come together to form a new country, "La Republica del Norte." The basis for such a development exists in the surge of Mexicans northward and the increasing economic ties between communities on different sides of the border. Since September 11, the border has become more of a border, yet the forces eroding it are continuing and powerful. Scholars and observers have referred to this border as "melting," "becoming blurred," "moving" (northward, that is), and as "a sort of dotted line." This produces in the southwestern United States and to a limited extent also in northern Mexico what has been variously termed "MexAmerica," "Amexica," and "Mexifornia."[49] Commenting in 1997 on this trend, Robert Kaplan concluded that along the eastern segment of the border, "the reunification of the Lone Star State and northeastern Mexico is history quietly and boringly in the making." At the western end, opinion surveys and scholarly studies suggest that California's identity is rapidly becoming a Hispanic, that is, Mexican, identity. The *Economist* reported that in 2000 the populations of six of twelve important cities on the U.S. side of the border were over 90 percent Hispanic, three others were over 80 percent Hispanic, one between 70 percent and 79 percent, and only two (San Diego and Yuma) less than 50 percent Hispanic. "We are all Mexicans in this valley," a former county commissioner of El Paso (75 percent Hispanic) declared in 2001.[50]

If this trend continues, it could produce a consolidation of the Mexican-dominant areas into an autonomous, culturally and linguistically distinct, economically self-reliant bloc within the United States. Given "the unique coincidence of Hispanic ethnicity with specific regional territoriality and with an ideology of multiculturalism," Graham Fuller warns, "we may be building toward the one thing that will choke the melting pot: an ethnic area and grouping so concentrated that it will not wish, or need, to undergo assimilation into the mainstream of American multi-ethnic English-speaking life."[51] One prototype of such a development exists in Miami.

THE HISPANIZATION OF MIAMI

Miami is the most Hispanic large city in the fifty states. In the course of thirty years, Spanish speakers, overwhelmingly Cuban, established their dominance in virtually every aspect of the city's life and fundamentally changed its ethnic composition, its culture, its politics, and its language. The Hispanization of Miami is without precedent in the history of major American cities.

This process began in the early 1960s with the arrival of middle- and upper-class Cubans who did not want to live under the Castro regime. In the dozen years following Castro's victory, 260,000 Cubans fled the country, mostly to South Florida, which historically had always been the refuge for Cuban political exiles, including two Cuban presidents buried there. Cuban immigrants to the United States numbered 265,000 in the 1970s, 140,000 in the 1980s, and 170,000 in the 1990s. The U.S. government classified them as refugees and provided them special benefits, which aroused the resentment of other immigrant groups. In 1980, the Castro regime permitted and even encouraged the migration of 125,000

Cubans through the port of Mariél to Florida. These Marielitos were generally poorer, less-well-educated, younger, and more likely to be black than the earlier migrants. They had grown up under the Castro regime and their culture was the product of that regime. Castro also included some criminals and mentally retarded people.[52]

Meanwhile, the economic growth of Miami, led by the early Cuban immigrants, made it a magnet for migrants from other Latin American and Caribbean countries. By 2000, 96 percent of the foreign-born population of Miami was from Latin America and the Caribbean, almost all of whom were Spanish speakers except for the Haitians and Jamaicans. Two-thirds of Miami's people were Hispanic, and more than half of them were Cuban or of Cuban descent. In 2000, 75.2 percent of Miami city residents spoke at home a language other than English, compared to 55.7 percent of the residents of Los Angeles and 47.6 percent of New Yorkers. Of Miamians speaking a non-English language at home, 89.3 percent spoke Spanish. In 2000, 59.5 percent of the residents of Miami were foreign-born, compared to 40.9 percent in Los Angeles, 36.8 percent in San Francisco, and 35.9 percent in New York. In most other major cities less than 20 percent of the population was foreign-born. In 2000, 31.1 percent of adult Miami residents said they spoke English very well, compared to 39.0 percent in Los Angeles, 42.5 percent in San Francisco, and 46.5 percent in New York.[53]

The Cuban influx and takeover had major consequences for Miami. Traditionally Miami had been a somewhat somnolent place dependent on retirees and modest tourism. In the 1960s, the elite and entrepreneurial refugees from Castro started dramatic economic development. Unable to send money home, the Cubans invested in Miami. Personal income growth in Miami averaged 11.5 percent a year in the 1970s and 7.7 percent a year in the 1980s. Payrolls in Miami-Dade County tripled between 1970 and 1995. The Cuban economic drive made Miami an international economic dynamo, with expanding international trade and investment. The Cubans promoted international tourism, which, by the 1990s, exceeded domestic tourism and made Miami a leading center of the cruise ship industry. Major American corporations in manufacturing, communications, and consumer products moved their Latin American headquarters to Miami from other American and Latin American cities. A vigorous Spanish artistic and entertainment community emerged. The Cubans can legitimately claim that, in the words of Professor Damian Fernandez, "We built modern Miami," and made its economy larger than those of most Latin American countries.[54]

A key part of this development was the expansion of Miami's economic ties with Latin America. Brazilians, Argentines, Chileans, Colombians, Venezuelans flooded into Miami, bringing their money with them. By 1993, some $25 billion from foreign countries, mostly Latin American, had been deposited in Miami banks.[55] Throughout the hemisphere, Latin Americans concerned with investment, trade, culture, entertainment, holidays, drug smuggling, increasingly turned to Miami. It truly had become, in an oft-repeated phrase, "the capital of Latin America."

Achieving this eminence involved, of course, the transformation of Miami from a normal American city into a Cuban-led Hispanic city. By 2000 Spanish was not just the language spoken in most homes; it was also the principal language of commerce, business, and politics. The media and communications generally became increasingly Hispanic. In 1998, a Spanish language television station became the number one station watched by Miamians, the first time a foreign language station achieved that rating in a major American city. The changing linguistic and ethnic makeup of Miami was reflected in the troubled history in the 1980s and 1990s of the *Miami Herald*, one of the most respected papers in the United States and the winner of numerous Pulitzer Prizes. The owners of the *Herald* first attempted to maintain its traditional "Anglo focus," while appealing to Hispanic readers and advertisers with a Spanish supplement. This attempt to reach both Hispanics and Anglos failed. In 1960 the *Herald* was read in 80 percent of Miami households. In 1989, it was read in 40 percent. The paper antagonized the leaders of the Cuban community, who retaliated vigorously. Eventually the *Herald* had to set up a separate Spanish paper, *El Nuevo Herald*.[56]

The Cubans did not, in the traditional pattern, create an enclave immigrant neighborhood in Miami. They brought into existence an enclave city with its own cultural community and economy, in which assimilation and Americanization were unnecessary and in some measure undesired. By the late 1980s, "the Cubans had created in Miami their own banks, businesses, and voting blocs," which dominated the economy and politics and from which non-Hispanics were excluded. "They're outsiders," as one successful Hispanic put it. "Here we are members of the power structure," another boasted.[57]

Miami Hispanics had little or no incentive to assimilate into American mainstream culture. As one Cuban-born sociologist observed, "In Miami there is no pressure to be American. People can make a living perfectly well in an enclave that speaks Spanish." By 1987, Joan Didion comments, "an entrepreneur who spoke no English could still, in Miami, buy, sell, negotiate, leverage assets, float bonds, and, if he were so inclined, attend galas twice a week in black tie." By 1999 the heads of the largest bank, largest real estate development company, and the largest law firm were all Cuban-born or of Cuban descent. The Cubans also established their dominance in politics. By 1999, the mayor of Miami and the mayor, police chief, and state attorney of Miami-Dade County plus two thirds of Miami's congressmen and nearly one half of its state legislators were of Cuban origin. In the wake of the Elián González affair, the non-Hispanic city manager and police chief in Miami City were replaced by Cubans.[58]

The Cuban and Hispanic dominance of Miami left Anglos, as well as blacks, outside minorities that could often be ignored. Unable to communicate with government bureaucrats and discriminated against by store clerks, the Anglos came to realize, as one of them put it, "My God, this is what it's like to be the minority." The Anglos had three choices. They could accept their subordinate and "outsider" position. They could attempt to adopt the manners, customs, and language of the Hispanics and assimilate into the Hispanic community, "acculturation in reverse," as the scholars Alejandro Portes and Alex Stepick labeled it. Or, third, they could leave Miami, and between 1983 and 1993 about 140,000 did due to "the city's growing Hispanic character," their exodus reflected in a widely prevalent bumper sticker, "Will the last American to leave, please haul down the flag."[59]

The Cubanization of Miami coincided with high levels of crime. For each year between 1985 and 1993, Miami ranked among the top three large cities (over 250,000 people) in violent crime. Much of this was related to the growing drug trade but also to the intensity of Cuban immigrant politics. By the 1980s, Mimi Swartz reports, "anti-Castro political groups, race riots, and drug-related crime had made Miami a volatile and often dangerous place. Protests and bombings were frequent, and there was even an occasional assassination among feuding exile organizations." In 1992, the new publisher of the *Miami Herald*, David Lawrence, antagonized Jorge Mas Canosa, the right-wing leader of the Cuban community. "Lawrence suddenly found himself living in terror," Swartz says, from vandalism and anonymous death threats. In 2000, virtually all the top political leaders of the Cuban community defied the federal government and refused to cooperate with it in the Elián González case. By then Miami had taken on the characteristics, David Rieff argued, of "an out-of-control banana republic."[60]

In 2000, a *New York Times* story referred to the "virtual secession of Miami-Dade County," and to the "independent foreign policy" conducted by local politicians on behalf of the Cuban population. The Elián González controversy heightened talk of "virtual secession," with political leaders defying the federal government and protesters waving Cuban flags and burning the Stars and Stripes. "This is a city that is separate," as one Cuban scholar said. "We now have our own local foreign policy." The Elián affair highlighted the gap between the Miami Cuban community, overwhelmingly opposed to returning Elián to his father, and the 60 percent of the American people who believed the father should have custody and who approved the government's forceful action to give it to him.[61] The controversy also exposed the divisions between the older and younger generations within the Cuban community and between the Cubans and the rapidly increasing non-Cuban Hispanic population. If the migration of the latter continues, Miami will become less Cuban and more Hispanic in numbers but still be dominated by a Cuban establishment.

THE HISPANIZATION OF THE SOUTHWEST

Is Miami the future for Los Angeles and the southwest generally? In the end, the results could be similar: the creation of a large, distinct, Spanish-speaking community with economic and political resources sufficient to sustain its own Hispanic identity apart from the national identity of other Americans and also able to influence significantly American politics, government, and society. The processes by which this might come about, however, differ. The Hispanization of Miami has been rapid, explicit, and economically led from the top down. The Hispanization of the southwest has been slower, unrelenting, and politically driven from the bottom up. The Cuban influx into Florida was intermittent and heavily influenced by the policies of the Cuban government. It has been supplemented by the more sustained movement of people from throughout Latin America, attracted by the combination of Spanish culture and American prosperity. Mexican immigration, on the other hand, has been continuous, has included a large illegal component, and shows no signs of tapering off. The Hispanic, that is largely Mexican, population of Southern California far exceeds in numbers but has yet to reach the proportions of the Hispanic population of Miami, but it is increasing rapidly.

A second difference concerns the relations of Cubans and Mexicans with their countries of origin. The Cuban community has been united in its hostility to the Castro regime and in its efforts to punish and overthrow that regime. The Cuban government has responded in kind. The Mexican community has been more ambivalent and nuanced in its attitudes toward the Mexican government. That government has both encouraged emigration to the United States and encouraged Mexicans in the United States to maintain their ties with Mexico, to keep or acquire Mexican nationality, and, of course, to remit money to Mexico. For decades, the Cuban government has wanted to humiliate, contain, counter, and reduce the political power of the Cuban community in South Florida. The Mexican government wants to expand the numbers, wealth, and political power of the Mexican community in the southwest.

Third, the initial Cuban immigrants were largely middle- and upper-class. Their wealth, education, and abilities enabled them, in the course of a few decades, to establish their dominance in the economy, culture, and politics of Miami. Subsequent immigrants were more lower-class. In the southwest, the overwhelming bulk of Mexican immigrants have been poor, unskilled, and not well educated, and it appears that many of their offspring are likely to be similar. The pressures toward Hispanization in the southwest thus come from below, whereas those in South Florida came from above. In Los Angeles, as Joan Didion observed, Spanish has been "a language only barely registered by the Anglo population, part of the ambient noise, the language spoken by the people who worked in the car wash and came to trim the trees and cleared the tables in restaurants. In Miami Spanish was spoken by the people who ate in the restaurants, the people who owned the cars and trees, which made, on the socio-auditory scale, a considerable difference."[62] Undoubtedly it also makes considerable difference in the acquisition of political and economic power. In the long run, however, numbers are power, particularly in a multicultural society, a political democracy, and a consumer economy.

The persistence of Mexican immigration and the large and increasing absolute numbers of Mexicans reduce the incentives for cultural assimilation. Mexican-Americans no longer think of themselves as members of a small minority who must accommodate the dominant group and adopt its culture. As their numbers increase, they become more committed to their own ethnic identity and culture. Sustained numerical expansion promotes cultural consolidation, and leads them not to minimize but to glory in the differences between their culture and American culture. As the president of the National Council of La Raza said in 1995: "The biggest problem we have is a cultural clash, a clash between our values and the values in American society." He then went on to spell out the superiority of Hispanic values to American values. In similar fashion, Lionel Sosa, a successful Texas Mexican-American businessman, in 1998 hailed the emerging Hispanic middle-class professionals who look like Anglos, but whose "values remain quite different from an Anglo's."[63]

Mexican-Americans are more favorably disposed toward democracy than are Mexicans. Nonetheless, profound differences exist between Mexican and American values and culture, which impact Mexican-Americans and have been attested to by thoughtful Mexicans and Mexican-Americans. In 1997, Carlos Fuentes, Mexico's premier novelist, elaborated with Tocquevillean eloquence the distinction between

Mexico's combined Spanish-Indian heritage with its "culture of Catholicism" and America's Protestant culture descended "from Martin Luther." In 1994, Andres Rozental, a senior Mexican Foreign Ministry official, affirmed, "There's an inherent difference between our two cultures, and that is that the Mexican culture is more profoundly rooted than the American culture." In 1999, the Mexican philosopher Armando Cíntora explained the educational and other deficiencies of Mexican-Americans by their attitudes expressed in three sayings: *"Ahí se va"* ("Who cares? That is good enough"); *"Mañana se lo tengo"* ("Tomorrow it will be ready"); and *"El vale madrismo"* ("Nothing is really worthwhile"). In 1995, Mexico's future foreign minister, Jorge Casteñeda, referred to the "ferocious differences" between Mexico and America including differences in social and economic equality, institutions devoted to reducing inequality, beliefs about the unpredictability of events, concepts of time epitomized in the *mañana* syndrome, the ability to achieve results quickly, and attitudes toward history, expressed in "the cliché that Mexicans are obsessed with history, Americans with the future . . ." Lionel Sosa identifies several central Hispanic traits (different from Anglo-Protestant ones) that "hold us Latinos back": mistrust of people outside the family; lack of initiative, self-reliance, and ambition; low priority for education; acceptance of poverty as a virtue necessary for entrance into heaven. A "cultural revolution" is necessary, Armando Cíntora says, if Mexico is to join the modern world. While the values of Mexicans are undoubtedly evolving, helped by the spread of evangelical Protestantism, that revolution is unlikely to be completed soon or quickly. Over time the political values and culture of Mexican-Americans have come to resemble more closely those of other Americans. Expanding Mexican immigration, however, sustains and reinforces among Mexican-Americans the Mexican values that are the primary source of their lagging educational and economic progress and their slow assimilation into American society.[64]

As their numbers increase, Mexican-Americans feel increasingly comfortable with their own culture and often contemptuous of American culture. They demand recognition of their culture and the historic

Mexican identity of the American southwest. They increasingly call attention to and celebrate their Hispanic and Mexican past. What their growth in numbers has done, according to one 1999 report, "is help 'Latinize' many Hispanic people who are finding it easier to affirm their heritage . . . they find strength in numbers, as younger generations grow up with more ethnic pride and as a Latin influence starts permeating fields like entertainment, advertising, and politics." One index foretells the future: in 1998 José replaced Michael as the most popular name for newborn boys in both California and Texas.[65]

Compared to the American norm, Mexican-Americans are poor and are likely to remain so for some while. Nonetheless, the overall economic position of Hispanics is slowly improving as more of them move into the middle class. Although only some Hispanics are voters, all 38 million Hispanics are consumers. The annual buying power of Hispanics in 2000 was an estimated $440 billion.[66] In addition, the American economy is becoming one of highly segmented markets with sales appeals tailored to the specialized tastes and preferences of particular groups. These two trends have provided powerful incentives for American corporations to direct special appeals to the Hispanic market. These include products specially designed for Hispanics, most obviously Spanish language newspapers, periodicals, books, radio, and television, but also a much more diffuse range of products tailored for Hispanics and for particular segments, Mexican, Cuban, Puerto Rican, of that market. The size of the market encourages businesses to make their sales appeals increasingly in Spanish. As Lionel Sosa argues, companies must appeal to "ethnic customers" and "minority markets" in ways and language they find persuasive. In his words, *"El dinero habla."*[67]

Central to the emergence of the Hispanic community in the 1990s was Univision, the largest Spanish-language television network in the United States. Univision, it was alleged in 1996, could draw on "unlimited resources from its parent, Televisa, Mexico's most powerful multinational." Univision's nightly news audiences among people 18 to 34 years old in New York, Chicago, and Los Angeles reportedly rival or exceed those of ABC, CBS, NBC, CNN, and Fox.[68]

The continuation of high levels of Mexican and Hispanic immigration plus the low rates of assimilation of these immigrants into American society and culture could eventually change America into a country of two languages, two cultures, and two peoples. This will not only transform America. It will also have deep consequences for Hispanics, who will be in America but not of it. Lionel Sosa ends his book, *The Americano Dream*, of advice to aspiring Hispanic entrepreneurs, with the words: "The Americano dream? It exists, it is realistic, and it is there for all of us to share." He is wrong. There is no Americano dream. There is only the American dream created by an Anglo-Protestant society. Mexican-Americans will share in that dream and in that society only if they dream in English.

CHAPTER 10

Merging America
with the World

THE CHANGING ENVIRONMENT

In the last decades of the twentieth century, the end of the Cold War, the collapse of the Soviet Union, the transitions to democracy in scores of countries, plus the significant expansion of international trade, investment, transportation, and communication, usually labeled globalization, profoundly changed America's external environment and had at least three major consequences for American identity.

First, the collapse of the Soviet Union and of communism left America not only with no enemy, but also for the first time in its history without any clear "other" against which to define itself. For over two centuries the liberal, democratic principles of the American Creed had been a core component of American identity. American and European observers had often referred to this creedal component as the essence of "American exceptionalism." Now, however, exceptionalism was becoming universalism, as democracy became more and more accepted around the world, at least in theory, as the only legitimate form of government. No other secular ideology existed to challenge democracy as fascism and communism had in the twentieth century.

Second, the extensive international involvements of American business, academic, professional, media, nonprofit, and political elites lowered the salience of national identity for those elites, who now increasingly defined themselves, their interests, and their identities in terms of transnational and global institutions, networks, and causes. As we have seen, some American elites tended to attribute greater salience to subnational identities than did the American public. Many of these same elites also assigned greater salience to transnational identities than did the public, which remained highly nationalistic.

Third, the decline in the relevance of ideology increased the importance of culture as a source of identity. The collective counterpart to the growing number of individuals with dual identities, dual loyalties, and dual citizenships was the growing number and importance of diasporas. Diasporas are cultural communities cutting across the boundaries of two or more states, one of which is viewed as the homeland country of that community. Immigrant ethnic groups promoting their interests within American society have been a reality since the mid-nineteenth century. Immigrants now, however, can much more easily maintain ties, interactions, and communications with people in their origin country and thus see themselves as members of a diaspora. In addition, homeland governments now view their diasporas as key sources of financial and other support and as sources of influence on host country governments. Hence they promote the expansion, mobilization, and institutionalization of their diasporas.

The absence of an other until 2001, the spread of democracy, the denationalization of elites, and the rise of diasporas all blur the distinction between national and transnational identities.

THE SEARCH FOR AN ENEMY

In 1987, Georgiy Arbatov, a top adviser to Soviet President Mikhail Gorbachev, warned Americans: "We are doing something really terrible to you—we are depriving you of an enemy."[1] And they did, and that had important consequences for the United States, as Arbatov emphasized. What he did not mention, however, were the consequences for the Soviet Union. By depriving America of an enemy, the Soviets deprived themselves of an enemy, and the Soviet Union, as events a few years later demonstrated, needed an enemy far more than the United States did. From its beginning, Soviet officials had defined their country as the leader of world communism in the momentous struggle with world capitalism. Lacking that struggle, the Soviet Union had no identity, no raison d'être, and quickly dissolved into sixteen states, each with its own national identity defined largely by culture and history.

The loss of its enemy did not have the same impact on the United States. Soviet ideological identity was imposed on peoples of different nationality by a revolutionary dictatorship. American ideological identity was more or less freely accepted by Americans (except for the Tories of the Revolution and pre–Civil War Southerners) and was rooted in their common Anglo-Protestant culture. The Soviet collapse did, however, pose problems for American identity. In 84 B.C., when Rome defeated its last serious enemy, Mithradates, Sulla asked: "Now that the universe offers us no more enemies, what may be the fate of the Republic?" In 1997, the historian David Kennedy asked: "What happens to a nation's sense of identity when its enemies are utterly vanquished, and no longer provide the energizing force of a threat to that nation's very existence?" A few decades after Sulla voiced his worry, the Roman Republic collapsed into Caesarism. No similar fate is likely for the United States. For forty years, however, America was the leader of "the Free World" against "the evil empire." With the evil empire gone, how was America to define itself? Or, as John Updike put it, "Without the cold war, what's the point of being an American?"[2]

The Soviet collapse also affected America's allies and the institutions they had created to deal with the Soviet threat. In the early 1990s, speakers at NATO gatherings often quoted a poem by C. P. Cavafy about ancient Alexandria:

> *What are we waiting for, gathered in the market-place?*
> *The barbarians are to arrive today.* . . .
>
> *What does this sudden uneasiness mean,*
> *and this confusion? (How grave the faces have become!)*
> *Why are the streets and squares rapidly emptying,*
> *and why is everyone going back home so lost in thought?*

Because it is night and the barbarians have not come.
And some men have arrived from the frontiers
and they say that there are no barbarians any longer.

And now, what will become of us without barbarians?
Those people were a kind of solution.[3]

The question is: "a kind of solution" to what? External wars may stimulate controversies and disunity within countries and have other effects widely seen as dysfunctional. If, on the other hand, the "barbarians" fundamentally threaten or are perceived to threaten the existence of the country, more positive consequences may follow. "It is war," Heinrich von Treitschke said, "which turns a people into a nation." This is certainly true for America. The Revolution produced the American people, the Civil War the American nation, and World War II the epiphany of Americans' identification with their country. During major wars against major threats, the authority and resources of the state are strengthened. National unity is enhanced as potentially divisive internal antagonisms are suppressed in the face of a common enemy. Social and economic differences are reduced. Economic productivity, to the extent that it is not a casualty of physical destruction, tends to increase. As Robert Putnam and Theda Skocpol have shown, America's wars, especially World War II, stimulated civic engagement, volunteering for common causes, and the expansion of social capital, as well as a broader sense of national unity and commitment to the nation: "We are all in this together." Two of America's big wars are linked to the two major advances in racial equality in American history. The exigencies of the Cold War reinforced the drive to end racial discrimination and segregation.[4]

If war may, at least in some circumstances, produce positive results such as these, does peace lead to comparable negative consequences? Sociological theory and historical evidence suggest that the absence of an external enemy or other encourages internal disunity. It is thus not surprising that the waning and end of the Cold War increased the appeal of subnational identities in America as it did in many other countries. The absence of a significant external threat reduced the need for a strong national government and a coherent, unified nation. The end of the Cold War, two scholars warned in 1994, will "erode national political cohesiveness as ethnic and sectional differences come to the fore" and "make the achievement of internal social equity and welfare more difficult, reinvigorating class divisions."[5] In a similar vein, in 1996, Professor Paul Peterson saw the end of the Cold War leading to, among other things, an "ever more foggy sense of the national interest," "decreasing willingness to incur sacrifices for one's country," "dwindling trust in government," "softening of moral commitment," and "declining perceived need for experienced political leadership." In the absence of an external enemy, individual self-interest trumps national commitment. As Peterson went on to observe, "Ask not what your country can do for you but what you can do for your country. These words seem dated, almost chauvinist in an era when your country is no longer defending good from evil. . . ."[6]

The last major enemy Americans portrayed in racial terms was Japan in World War II. "The Japanese," John Dower observes, "were actually saddled with racial stereotypes that Europeans and Americans had applied to nonwhites for centuries . . . [including] the core imagery of apes, lesser men, primitives, children, madmen." The prevailing attitude was well expressed by a Pacific marine: "I wish we were fighting against Germans. They are human beings, like us. . . . But the Japs are like animals." Apart from this racial dimension in American perception of the Japanese, the enemies in America's twentieth-century wars, including the Japanese, were seen as ideological enemies. In all three of America's twentieth-century conflicts the enemy was defined as the opposite of the central principles of the American Creed. "Whether the enemy was German 'Kaiserism' in World War I, Japanese regimentation in World War II, or Russian collectivist communism in the Cold War," David Kennedy says, "a central component of the American definition of the adversary had to do with the enemy's embodiment of anti-individualist values."[7] The Cold War was the epitome of an ideological adversarial relationship. The Soviet Union was defined only by communism; its evil empire, and its goal to promote communism throughout the world, constituted the perfect ideological enemy for Americans.

At the end of the twentieth century, numerous nondemocratic regimes still existed, most importantly China, but none of them, including China, was attempting to promote nondemocratic ideologies in other societies. Democracy was left without a significant secular ideological rival, and the United States was left without a peer competitor. Among American foreign policy elites, the results were euphoria, pride, arrogance—and uncertainty. The absence of an ideological threat produced an absence of purpose. "Nations need enemies," Charles Krauthammer commented as the Cold War ended. "Take away one, and they find another."[8] The ideal enemy for America would be ideologically hostile, racially and culturally different, and militarily strong enough to pose a credible threat to American security. The foreign policy debates of the 1990s were largely over who might be such an enemy.

Participants in these debates came up with a variety of possibilities, none of which at the end of the century had won general acceptance. In the early 1990s, some foreign affairs specialists warned that the Soviet threat would reappear in a revived nationalistic, authoritarian Russia, with the natural resources, people, and nuclear weapons again to challenge American principles and threaten American security. By the end of that decade, however, Russian economic stagnation, demographic decline, conventional military weakness, pervasive corruption, and fragile political authority put a pause to images of Russia as America's possible other and/or enemy.

Small-time dictators like Slobodan Milosevic and Saddam Hussein were demonized as genocidal murderers, but it was hard persuasively to portray them as Hitler, Stalin, or even Brezhnev, in terms of constituting a formidable threat to America's principles or security. Recourse was often had to more nebulous groups of potential enemies, such as "rogue states," terrorists, or drug mafias, or to threatening processes, such as nuclear proliferation, cyberterrorism, and asymmetrical warfare. America's creedal identity leads it to grade and classify states by the extent to which they engage in evil behavior, such as suppressing human rights, supporting the drug trade, backing terrorist groups, and persecuting people because of their religion. Alone among states America publishes lists of its enemies: terrorist organizations (thirty-six listed in 2003), states sponsoring terrorism (seven in 2003), "rogue states" (a more informal category of varying numbers of states relabeled as "states of concern" in 2000), and the 2002 "axis of evil" of Iraq, Iran, and North Korea, to which the State Department added Cuba, Libya, and Syria.[9]

A plausible potential enemy was China, still communist in theory if not economic practice, clearly a dictatorship with no respect for political liberty, democracy, or human rights, with a dynamic economy, an increasingly nationalistic public, a strong sense of cultural superiority, and, among its military and some other elite groups, a clear perception of the United States as their enemy, all of which made it a rising hegemon in East Asia. The greatest threats to America in the twentieth century occurred when its fascist enemies, Germany and Japan, came together in the Axis of the 1930s and 1940s, and when its communist enemies, the Soviet Union and China, formed a coalition in the 1950s. If a comparable threat emerges, China will be at its core. Such a development, however, seems unlikely in the near future.

Some Americans came to see Islamic fundamentalist groups, or more broadly political Islam, as the enemy, epitomized in Iraq, Iran, Sudan, Libya, Afghanistan under the Taliban, and to a lesser degree other Muslim states, as well as in Islamic terrorist groups such as Hamas, Hezbollah, Islamic Jihad, and the Al Qaeda network. The attacks in the 1990s on the World Trade Center, the Khobar barracks, the U.S. embassies in Tanzania and Kenya, and the USS *Cole*, as well as other terrorist attempts that were successfully thwarted, certainly constituted an intermittent, low-level war against the United States. Five of the seven states the United States listed as supporting terrorism are Muslim. Muslim states and organizations threaten Israel, which many Americans see as a close ally. Iran and—until the 2003 war—Iraq pose potential threats to America's and the world's oil supplies. Pakistan acquired nuclear weapons in the 1990s and at various times Iran, Iraq, Libya, and Saudi Arabia have been reported to harbor nuclear weapons stockpiles, intentions, and/or programs. The cultural gap between Islam and America's Christianity and Anglo-Protestantism reinforces Islam's enemy qualifications. And on September 11, 2001, Osama bin Laden ended America's search. The attacks on New York and Washington followed by the wars with Afghanistan and Iraq and the more diffuse "war on terrorism" make militant Islam America's first enemy of the twenty-first century.

DEAD SOULS:
THE DENATIONALIZATION OF ELITES

In 1805 Walter Scott famously asked:

> *Breathes there the man with soul so dead*
> *Who never to himself hath said:*
> *"This is my own, my native Land!"*
> *Whose heart hath ne'er within him burned*
> *As home his footsteps he hath turned,*
> *From wandering on a foreign strand!*
>
> From *The Lay of the Last Minstrel*

One answer to his question today is: Yes, the number of dead or dying souls is small but growing among America's business, professional, intellectual, and academic elites. Possessing in Scott's words, "titles, power and pelf," they also have decreasing ties with the American nation. Coming back to America from a foreign strand, they are not likely to be overwhelmed with deep feelings of commitment to their "native land." Their attitudes and behavior contrast with the overwhelming patriotism and nationalistic identification with their country of the American public. And not only native Euro-Americans. As one Mexican-American said, "It's nice to visit my mother's country, but that's not my home; my home is here. When I get back here, I say, 'Thank God for America.' "[10] A major gap is growing in America between its increasingly denationalized elites and its "Thank God for America" public. This gap was temporarily obscured by the suspension of dissent and the patriotic rallying after September 11. In the absence of repeated comparable attacks, however, the pervasive and fundamental forces of economic globalization make it likely that the denationalizing of elites will continue.

Globalization involves: a huge expansion in the international interactions among individuals, corporations, governments, nongovernmental organizations (NGOs), and other entities; growth in number and size of multinational corporations investing, producing, and marketing globally; and the multiplication of international organizations, regimes, and regulations. The impact of these developments differs among groups and among countries. The involvement of individuals in globalizing processes varies almost directly with their socioeconomic status. Elites have more and deeper transnational interests, commitments, and identities than nonelites. American elites, government agencies, businesses, and other organizations have been far more important in the globalization process than those of other countries. Hence their commitments to national identities and national interests could be relatively weaker.

These developments resemble on a global basis what happened in the United States after the Civil War. As we have seen, when industrialization moved ahead, businesses had to go national in order to get the capital, the workers, and the markets they needed to succeed and expand. Ambitious individuals had to become geographically, organizationally, and to some extent, occupationally mobile, and pursue their careers on a national rather than a local basis. The growth of national corporations and other national associations promoted national viewpoints, national interests, and national power. National laws and standards took precedence over state ones. National consciousness and national identity became preeminent over state and regional identities.

The rise of transnationalism, although in its early stages, is somewhat similar. There are, however, two major differences. The technological developments of the late nineteenth century promoted the nationalization of American elites; those of the late twentieth century promote elite denationalization. Second, the triumph of nationalism over subnationalism was enhanced by the existence of external enemies, which reinforced national cohesion, national identity, and national institutions, particularly the presidency. The enemy of transnationalism, however, is nationalism, the populist appeal of which retards rather than enhances transnational trends.

Transnational ideas and people fall into three categories: universalist, economic, and moralist. The universalist approach is, in effect, American nationalism and exceptionalism taken to the extreme. In this view, America is exceptional not because it is a unique nation but because it has become the "universal nation." It has merged with the world through the coming to America of people from all other societies and through the widespread acceptance of American popular culture and values by other societies. The distinction between America and the world is disappearing because of the triumph of America as the only global superpower. The economic approach focuses on economic globalization as a transcendent force breaking down national boundaries, merging national economies into a single global whole, and rapidly eroding the authority and functions of national governments. This view is prevalent among executives of multinational corporations, large NGOs, and comparable organizations operating on a global basis and among individuals with skills, usually of a highly technical nature, for which there is a global demand and who are thus able to pursue careers moving from country to country. The moralistic approach decries patriotism and nationalism as evil forces and argues that international law, institutions, regimes, and norms are morally superior to those of individual nations. Commitment to humanity must supersede commitment to nation. This view is found among intellectuals, academics, and journalists. Economic transnationalism is rooted in the bourgeoisie, moralistic transnationalism in the intelligentsia.

In 1953, the head of General Motors, nominated to be secretary of defense, was widely criticized for allegedly saying, "What's good for General Motors is good for America," when he actually said, "What was good for our country was good for General Motors and vice versa." Either way, both he and his critics presumed some coincidence of interest between corporation and country. Now, however, large corporations often see their interests as increasingly distinct from America's interests. As their global operations expand, corporations founded and headquartered in the United States gradually become less American. As the responses of their executives to Ralph Nader (reported in the first chapter of this book) suggest, they reject expressions of patriotism and explicitly define themselves as multinational. Their attitude is reminiscent of Erie Railroad boss Jay Gould's response in the 1860s when asked if he was a Republican or a Democrat:

"In a Republican state, I am a Republican; in a Democratic state, I am a Democrat; in an independent state, I am independent; but I am always for Erie." America-based corporations operating globally recruit their workforce and their executives, including their top ones, without regard to nationality. In 2000, at least six major American-based corporations had non-American chairmen or CEOs: Alcoa; Becton, Dickinson; Coca-Cola; Ford; Philip Morris; Procter & Gamble. The CIA, one of its officials said in 1999, can no longer count on the cooperation of American corporations as it once was able to do, because the corporations view themselves as multinational and may think it not in their interests to help the U.S. government.[11]

Nationalism proved wrong Karl Marx's concept of a unified international proletariat. Globalization is proving right Adam Smith's observation that while "the proprietor of land is necessarily a citizen of the particular country in which his estate lies . . . the proprietor of stock is properly a citizen of the world, and is not necessarily attached to any particular country."[12] Smith's 1776 words describe the way contemporary transnational businessmen see themselves. Summarizing their interviews with executives of twenty-three American multinational corporations and nonprofit organizations, James Davison Hunter and Joshua Yates conclude: "Surely these elites *are* cosmopolitans: they travel the world and their field of responsibility is the world. Indeed, they see themselves as 'global citizens.' Again and again, we heard them say that they thought of themselves more as 'citizens of the world' who happen to carry an American passport than as U.S. citizens who happen to work in a global organization. They possess all that is implied in the notion of the cosmopolitan. They are sophisticated, urbane, and universalistic in their perspective and ethical commitments." Together with the "globalizing elites" of other countries, these American executives inhabit a "sociocultural bubble," apart from the cultures of individual nations, and communicate with each other in a social science version of English, which Hunter and Yates label "global speak."

The economic globalizers are fixated on the world as an economic unit. For them home is the global market, not the national community. As Hunter and Yates report, "All these globalizing organizations, and not just the multinational corporations, operate in a world defined by 'expanding markets,' the need for 'competitive advantage,' 'efficiency,' 'cost-effectiveness,' 'maximizing benefits and minimizing costs,' 'niche markets,' 'profitability,' and 'the bottom line.' They justify this focus on the grounds that they are meeting the need of consumers all over the world. That is their constituency." "One thing globalization has done," a consultant to Archer Daniels Midland said, "is to transfer the power of governments to the global consumer."[13] As the global market replaces the national community, the national citizen gives way to the global consumer.

Economic transnationals are the nucleus of an emerging global superclass. "As debates about global economic integration rage on, at least one of its effects has become clear," the Global Business Policy Council asserts. "The rewards of an increasingly integrated global economy have brought forth a new global elite. Labeled 'Davos Men,' 'gold-collar workers' or . . . 'cosmocrats,' this emerging class is empowered by new notions of global connectedness. It includes academics, international civil servants and executives in global companies, as well as successful high-technology entrepreneurs." Estimated to number about 20 million in 2000, of whom 40 percent were American, this elite is expected to double in size by 2010.[14] Less than 4 percent of the American people, these transnationals have little need for national loyalty, view national boundaries as obstacles that thankfully are vanishing, and see national governments as residues from the past whose only useful function now is to facilitate the elite's global operations. In the coming years, one corporate executive confidently predicted, "the only people who will care about national boundaries are politicians."[15]

Involvement in transnational institutions, networks, and activities not only defines the global elite but also is critical to achieving elite status within nations. Someone whose loyalties, identities, involvements are purely national is less likely to rise to the top in business, academia, the media, the professions, than someone who transcends these limits. Outside politics, those who stay home stay behind. Those who move ahead think and act internationally. As sociology professor Manuel Castells said, "Elites are cosmopolitan, people are local."[16] The opportunity to join this transnational world, however, is limited to a small minority of people in industrialized countries and to only a minuscule handful of people in developing countries.

The global involvements of the transnational economic elites erode their sense of belonging to a national community. An early 1980s poll showed that "The higher people's income and education . . . the more conditional the allegiance. . . . They were more likely than the poor and uneducated to say they would leave the country if they could double their income."[17] In the early 1990s, future Secretary of Labor Robert Reich reached a similar conclusion: "America's highest income earners . . . have been seceding from the rest of the nation. The secession has taken many forms, but it is grounded in the same emerging economic reality. This group of Americans no longer depends, as it once did, on the economic performance of other Americans. . . . [They] are linked instead to global webs of enterprise to which they add value directly as engineers, lawyers, management consultants, investment bankers, research scientists, corporate executives, and other deployers of abstract analysis." In 2001, Professor Alan Wolfe similarly argued: "The challenge to national citizenship posed by multiculturalism pales before the creation of truly global corporations that put their faith in the bottom line before their love of country." "The cosmocrats," John Micklethwait and Adrian Wooldridge say, "are increasingly cut off from the rest of society: Its members study in foreign universities, spend a period of time working abroad, and work for organizations that have a global reach. They constitute a world within a world, linked to each other by myriad global networks but insulated from the more hidebound members of their own societies. . . . They are more likely to spend their time chatting with their peers around the world—via phone or e-mail—than talking with their neighbors in the projects around the corner."[18]

In 1927 as class warfare and nationalism were reaching their apogee in Europe, Julian Benda, in his brilliant polemic *La Trahison des Clercs*, bitterly attacked intellectuals for betraying their commitment to disinterested truth and succumbing to the passions of nationalism. The *trahison* of contemporary intellectuals is different. They abandon commitment to their nation and their fellow citizens and argue the moral su-

periority of identifying with humanity at large. This proclivity flourished in the academic world in the 1990s. Professor Martha Nussbaum
of the University of Chicago denounced emphasis on "patriotic pride"
as "morally dangerous," urged the ethical superiority of cosmopolitanism over patriotism, and argued that people should direct their
"allegiance" to the "worldwide community of human beings." Professor
Amy Gutmann of Princeton argued that it was "repugnant" for American students to learn that they are, "above all, citizens of the United
States." The "primary allegiance" of Americans, she urged, "should not
be to the United States or to some other politically sovereign community," but to "democratic humanism." Professor Richard Sennett of
New York University denounced "the evil of a shared national identity"
and judged the erosion of national sovereignty "basically a positive phenomenon." Professor George Lipsitz of the University of California,
San Diego, argued that "in recent years refuge in patriotism has been
the first resort of scoundrels of all sorts." Professor Cecilia O'Leary of
American University saw the articulation of American patriotism as
right-wing, militaristic, male, white, Anglo, and repressive. Professor
Betty Jean Craige of the University of Georgia also attacked patriotism
because of its association with military prowess. Professor Peter Spiro of
Hofstra University approvingly concluded that it is "increasingly difficult to use the word 'we' in the context of international affairs." In the
past people used the word "we" with reference to the nation-state, but
now affiliation with the nation-state "no longer necessarily defines the
interests or even allegiances of the individual at the international
level." [19]

Moralist transnationals reject or are highly critical of the concept of
national sovereignty. In the past, this concept, dating back to the Treaty
of Westphalia, has been regularly affirmed in theory and regularly violated in practice. The moralists argue that it should be violated. They
agree with United Nations Secretary General Kofi Annan that national
sovereignty ought to give way to "individual sovereignty" so that the international community can act to prevent or stop gross violations by
governments of the rights of their citizens. This principle provides a basis for the United Nations to intervene militarily or otherwise in the do-

mestic affairs of states, a practice explicitly prohibited by the United Nations Charter. More generally, the moralists advocate the supremacy of international law over national law, the greater legitimacy of decisions made through international rather than national processes, and the expansion of the powers of international institutions compared to those of national governments. Moralist international lawyers have developed the concept of "customary international law," which, they say, is superior to national law.

A key step making this principle a reality in America was the 1980 decision by the Second Circuit Court of Appeals interpreting a 1789 statute designed to protect American ambassadors. In this case, *Filartiga v. Pena-Irala* (630 F.2d 876), the court held that Paraguayan citizens residing in the United States could bring civil action in American courts against a Paraguayan government official whom they accused of murdering a Paraguayan in Paraguay. This ruling led to a number of similar cases being filed in U.S. courts. In these cases, as in the action against General Augusto Pinochet by a Spanish judge, courts in one country transcend the territorial jurisdiction of their country and assert the authority to act on alleged human rights abuses by foreigners against foreigners in foreign countries.[20]

Moralist international lawyers argue that precedents in customary international law supersede previous federal and state laws. Since customary international law is not set forth in either statutes or treaties, it is, as Cornell Professor Jeremy Rabkin says, whatever experts persuade "a judge to think it may be. For that reason, it is likely to reach more and more deeply into domestic affairs. If a norm in customary international law exists against race discrimination, why not also against sex discrimination? And then why not also against discrimination on the basis of citizenship or language or sexual orientation?" Moralist international lawyers argue American law must meet international standards and approve unelected foreign judges, as well as American ones, defining the civil rights of Americans in terms of international rather than American norms.[21] In general, moralist transnationals believe that the United States should support the creation of tribunals such as the International Criminal Court and abide by its decisions as well as those of the International Court of Justice, the United Nations General Assembly, and comparable bodies. The international community, they hold, is morally superior to the national community.

The prevalence of anti-patriotic attitudes among liberal intellectuals led some of them to warn their fellow liberals of the consequences of such attitudes for the future not of America but of American liberalism. Most Americans, Professor Richard Rorty, a leading liberal philosopher, wrote, take pride in their country, but "Many of the exceptions to this rule are found in colleges and universities, in the academic departments that have become sanctuaries for left-wing political views." These leftists have done "a great deal of good for . . . women, African-Americans, gay men and lesbians. . . . But there is a problem with this left: it is unpatriotic." It "repudiates the idea of a national identity, and the emotion of national pride." If the left is to have influence, it must recognize that a "sense of shared national identity . . . is an absolutely essential component of citizenship." Without patriotism the left will be unable to achieve its goals for America. Professor Robert Bellah of the University of California, Berkeley, similarly argues, "That liberals have not found an effective way to appeal to the better instincts of American patriotism . . . is, in my opinion, both substantively unfortunate and tactically disastrous. . . . Somehow we must draw on deeper sources in our tradition if we are ever to build a public will for democratic change in America."[22] Liberals, in short, must use patriotism as a means to achieve liberal goals.

The scholars articulating anti-national views constituted a substantial portion of those people writing thoughtfully about the normative pros and cons of nationalism and the nation-state in the 1980s and 1990s. Serious defenses of patriotism and the primacy of national identity were rare. Suspicion of the nation-state also existed among people more directly concerned with public policy. In 1992, Strobe Talbott, then a journalist writing in *Time*, approvingly looked forward to a future when "nationhood as we know it will be obsolete; [and] all states will recognize a single global authority." Some months later he became a top official directing the foreign policy of the American nation he hoped would become obsolete.[23] Talbott's outlook arguably existed with others in the Clinton administration. Along with the Clinton policies on gays, it contributed to that administration's difficult relations with the military, for whom the American nation-state is the overriding loyalty. For America's 1990s elite transnationals, however, nationalism was evil, national identity suspect, and patriotism passé.

Such was far from the case with the American public.

THE PATRIOTIC PUBLIC

Nationalism is alive and well in most of the world. Whatever the disaffection of elites, most people in most countries are patriotic and identify strongly with their country. Americans have consistently and overwhelmingly been foremost among peoples in their patriotism and their commitment to their country. The extent of their identification varies, however, with race and place of birth.

Huge majorities of Americans claim to be patriotic and express great pride in their country. Asked in 1991, "How proud are you to be an American?," 96 percent of Americans said "very proud" or "quite proud." In 1994, in response to a similar question, 86 percent said they were "very" or "extremely" proud to be an American. In 1996 people were asked: "How important is being an American to you, where 0 is not at all important and 10 is the most important thing in your life?" Forty-five percent of the respondents chose 10; another 38 percent chose a number between 6 and 9; 2 percent chose 0. The September 11, 2001 attacks could not and did not have much effect on these high levels of patriotic assertion; in September 2002, 91 percent of Americans were "extremely" or "very" proud to be American.[24]

The extent to which Americans identify with their country appears to have increased toward the end of the twentieth century. Asked to choose the territorial entity to which they belonged "first of all"—locality or town, state or region of the country, the country as a whole, the North American continent, or the world as a whole—the proportions of Americans selecting America as a whole were 16.4 percent in 1981–1982, 29.6 percent in 1990–1991, and 39.3 percent in 1995–1997. The increase of 22.9 percent of Americans placing their nation first far exceeded the average increase in national identity of 5.6 percent for all countries in the world and of 3.4 percent for developed countries.[25] While elements of America's business and intellectual elites were identifying more with the world as a whole and defining themselves as "global citizens," Americans as a whole were becoming more committed to their nation.

These affirmations of patriotism and pride in country might be less meaningful if people in other countries responded similarly. By and large, they do not. America ranked first in national pride among the forty-one to sixty-five countries covered in each of the World Values Surveys of 1981–1982, 1990–1991, and 1995–1996, with 96 percent to 98 percent of Americans saying they were "very proud" or "quite proud" of their country.[26] A 1998 study of twenty-three countries asked people how much pride they had in their country in each of ten specific areas of achievement (e.g., arts, sports, economy) and how they generally viewed their country compared to other countries. The United States ranked second to Ireland in pride in specific achievements, second to Austria in general national pride, but first among the twenty-three countries when these two measures were combined. The positive responses to a mid-1980s poll in four Western countries asking people if they were proud of their nationality were: Americans 75 percent, British 54 percent, French 35 percent, West Germans 20 percent. Among youth, the responses were: Americans 97 percent, British 58 percent, French 80 percent, West Germans 65 percent.[27] Asked whether they wanted to do something to serve their country, the youth responses were:

	Yes	No
Americans	81%	18%
British	46	42
French	55	34
West Germans	29	40

A few population groups in the United States express less patriotic sentiment than Americans as a whole. In the 1990–1991 World Values Survey, over 98 percent of native-born Americans, immigrants, non-Hispanic whites, and blacks, and 95 percent of Hispanics said they were very proud or quite proud of their country. When asked about the priority of their national identity, however, differences appeared. Thirty-one percent of the native-born and of non-Hispanic whites said they identified primarily with America, but these proportions dropped to 25 percent for blacks, 19 percent for Hispanics, and 17 percent for immigrants. Asked whether they would be willing to fight for America, 81 percent of non-Hispanic whites and 79 percent of native-born Americans said yes, compared to 75 percent of immigrants, 67 percent of blacks, and 52 percent of Hispanics.[28]

As these figures suggest, recent immigrants and the descendants of people coerced into becoming part of American society, such as blacks, are likely to have more ambivalent attitudes toward that society than the descendants of settlers and earlier immigrants. Blacks and other minorities have fought valiantly in America's wars. Yet significantly fewer blacks than whites think of themselves as patriotic. In a 1983 poll, for instance, 56 percent of whites and 31 percent of blacks said they considered themselves "very" patriotic. In a 1989 poll, 95 percent of whites and 72 percent of blacks said that they considered themselves "very" or "somewhat" patriotic.[29] In a 1998 survey of the parents of schoolchildren, 91 percent of white, 92 percent of Hispanic, and 91 percent of immigrant parents strongly or somewhat agreed with the statement that "The U.S. is a better country than most other countries in the world." Among African-American parents, the proportion dropped to 84 percent. In other surveys, the difference in black and white pride in being American has been somewhat less, yet in a September 2002 Gallup poll for ABC News/*Washington Post*, 74 percent of whites and 53 percent of nonwhites said they were "extremely" proud to be American, a larger difference than between other major social-economic categories.[30]

Americans fought Indians fairly continuously for over two centuries; Indian tribes were recognized in American law as separate dependent nations; and they are, apart from the Puerto Ricans, the only ethnic groups that have been explicitly assigned pieces of territory as theirs. Indians thus face complex issues in separating, balancing, prioritizing, or amalgamating their tribal, Indian, and American identities. "We are Narragansetts first, and we are Americans when it is convenient," one

Indian historian proclaimed in 1993.[31] Evidence is lacking as to how many Indians share that view.

Overall, however, with only minor variations Americans overwhelmingly and intensely identify with their country, particularly compared to other peoples. Reviewing the relevant data, Russell Dalton observed: "National pride is exceptionally high in the United States. The chants of *USA! USA! USA!* are not limited to Olympic competition; they signify a persistent feeling among Americans. Most Europeans express their national pride in more moderate tones." Americans, the conductors of one comparative survey fittingly concluded, are "the world's most patriotic people."[32]

DIASPORAS, FOREIGN GOVERNMENTS, AND AMERICAN POLITICS

Diasporas are transnational ethnic or cultural communities whose members identify with a homeland that may or may not have a state. Jews were "the classic diaspora"; the term itself comes from the Bible and was for long primarily identified with Jews as a people who, following the destruction of Jerusalem in 586 B.C., were uniquely dispersed. They were the prototype of the "victim" diaspora, several of which exist in today's world. More important now, however, are migrant diasporas, people who voluntarily leave their homeland to live and work elsewhere but also identify primarily with a transnational ethnic-cultural community that encompasses their homeland. The essence of the diasporan mentality was well expressed in 1995 by the American Jewish Committee: "Although geographically dispersed and ideologically diverse, Jews are indeed one people, united by history, covenant, and culture. Together we must act to shape the Jewish destiny; let no one, in Israel, America or elsewhere, erect barriers among us."[33] Diasporans thus differ conceptually from ampersands. Ampersands have two national identities, diasporans one transnational identity. In practice, however, the two often merge and individuals easily shift from one to the other.

Diasporas differ from ethnic groups. An ethnic group is an ethnic or cultural entity that exists within a state. Diasporas are ethnic or cultural communities that cut across state boundaries. Ethnic groups have existed in America throughout the nation's history. They have promoted their economic, social, and political interests, including what they have seen as the interests of their ancestral country, and have competed with each other and with business, labor, agricultural, regional, and class groups. In so doing, they were engaging in national politics. Diasporas, on the other hand, form transnational alliances and engage in transnational conflicts. The central focus of diasporas is their homeland state. If that state does not exist, their overriding goal is to create one to which they can return. Irish and Jews have done this; Palestinians are in the process of doing so; Kurds, Sikhs, Chechens, and others aspire to do so. If a homeland state does exist, diasporas strive to strengthen it, improve it, and promote its interests in their host societies. In today's world, domestic ethnic groups are being transformed into transnational diasporas, which homeland states have increasingly seen as the communal and institutional extension of themselves and as a crucial asset of their country. This close relation and cooperation between state diasporas and homeland governments is a key phenomenon in contemporary global politics.

The new significance of diasporas is primarily the result of two developments. First, the large migrations from poor to rich countries have increased the numbers, wealth, and influence of diasporans with both their home and host countries. The Indian diaspora, it was estimated in 1996, consisted of 15 to 20 million people, with net assets of $40 billion to $60 billion and a "brain bank" of 200,000 to 300,000 highly skilled "doctors, engineers and other professionals, academics and researchers, managers and executives in multinational corporations (MNCs), high-tech entrepreneurs, and graduate students of Indian origin."[34] The 30 to 35 million members of the long-standing Chinese diaspora play key entrepreneurial roles in the economies of all East Asian countries except Japan and Korea and have been indispensable contributors to mainland China's spectacular economic growth. The rapidly growing Mexican diaspora of 20 to 23 million in the United States is, as we have seen, of increasing social, political, and economic importance to both countries.

The Filipino diaspora, largely in the Middle East and the United States, is crucial to the Philippine economy.

Second, economic globalization and the improvements in global communications and transportation make it possible for diasporas to remain in close contact economically, socially, and politically with their homeland governments and societies. In addition, the efforts of homeland governments, like those of China, India, and Mexico, to promote economic development, to liberalize their economies, and to become increasingly involved in the global economy all increase the importance to them of their diasporas and create a convergence of economic interests between diasporas and homelands.

As a result of these developments, the relations between homeland governments and diasporas have changed in three ways. First, governments increasingly view their diasporas not as reflections on but as important assets to their country. Second, diasporas make increasing economic, social, cultural, and political contributions to their homelands. Third, diasporas and homeland governments increasingly cooperate to promote the interests of the homeland country and government in the host society.

Historically, states have had varying attitudes toward their members who migrate elsewhere. In some cases they have attempted to prevent emigration and in others adopted ambivalent or permissive attitudes toward it. In the contemporary world, however, massive migration from poor to rich countries and the new means of maintaining contact with migrants have led homeland governments to view their diasporas as key contributors to the homeland and its goals. Governments see it in their interest to encourage emigration, to expand, mobilize, and organize their diasporas, and to institutionalize their homeland connections so as to promote homeland interests in host countries. Developed countries exert influence in world affairs through the export of capital, technology, economic aid, and military power. Poor overpopulated countries exert influence through the export of people.

Homeland government officials increasingly hail diasporans as vital members of the national community. Beginning in 1986 Philippine governments regularly encouraged Filipinos to migrate and become OFWs, "overseas Filipino workers," and as of 2002, up to 7.5 million had done so. "Educated families and young professionals—nurses, doctors, computer analysts" supplemented the poorly educated, manual workers who had dominated previous emigration. While in exile in the United States in the early 1990s, former President Jean-Bertrand Aristide, according to Yossi Shain, identified Haitian "diaspora members as Haiti's 'tenth department' (Haiti is divided into nine), to which they responded enthusiastically."[35] In the late 1990s a significant change occurred in the Israeli government attitude toward the Jewish diaspora. Earlier its policy had been, as J. J. Goldberg, author of the book *Jewish Power*, observes, "to replace Jewish life elsewhere, rather than reinforce it." In 1998, concerned about the worldwide erosion of Jewish culture and identity, the government of Benjamin Netanyahu adopted a new approach and launched efforts to revitalize Judaism outside Israel. Netanyahu became, in Goldberg's words, "the first Israeli prime minister to show an interest in supporting Jewish life in the Diaspora."[36] An even more dramatic indicator of the new importance of diasporas was the change in the policies of the Cuban government toward the overwhelmingly anti-Castro Cuban community in the United States. "Aware of the hostile attitudes, the government in the mid-1990s," Susan Eckstein reports, "modified its public stance toward the diaspora, facilitated transnational bonding, and more openly supported economically motivated migration. The émigrés whom Castro previously had pejoratively portrayed as *gusanos*, worms, to be spurned by good revolutionaries, were redefined as the 'Cuban community abroad.' "[37]

For most of the twentieth century, Mexicans, including government officials, also looked down on their countrymen who had migrated to the United States. They were disparaged as *pochos* or, in the term used by Octavio Paz, *pachucos*, who had lost their "whole inheritance: language, religion, customs, beliefs." Mexican officials rejected them as traitors to their country. By "imposing penalties," Yossi Shain says, "Mexico sought to warn its citizens against the perils of departing their native country and forsaking their culture in search of a better life in the United States." In the 1980s, that attitude changed dramatically. "The Mexican nation extends beyond the territory enclosed by its borders," President Ernesto Zedillo said in the 1990s. "Mexican migrants are an important, very important part of it." President Vicente Fox described himself as president of 123 million Mexicans, 100 million in Mexico and 23 million in the United States, a figure that includes Mexican-Americans not born in Mexico.[38] Homeland leaders drench with encomiums those who leave the homeland. "You yourselves are heroes," President Mohammad Khatami of Iran told eight hundred Iranian-Americans in September 1998. "We want to salute these heroes," President Fox of Mexico said in December 2000, who went to the United States searching "for a job, an opportunity they can't find at home, their community or their own country."[39]

Homeland governments encourage their people to leave their country and facilitate their doing so. Immediately after his election, Vicente Fox announced his long-term goal of an open border with the free movement of people between Mexico and the United States. As president, he supported legal status for the several million Mexicans who have entered the United States illegally, argued the need to provide "humane working conditions for Mexicans already in the United States," and urged the United States to provide up to $1 billion in Social Security benefits to Mexicans who had worked in the United States.[40] Homeland governments have developed formal institutions and informal processes to bolster their diasporas and link them more closely to their homelands. The countries to America's south, Columbia University Professor Robert C. Smith pointed out, "are the site of extremely interesting diasporaic experimentation, with Mexico, Colombia, Haiti, the Dominican Republic, and other states attempting to cultivate and institutionalize relations with what one Mexican official called their 'global nations.' "[41] In January 2003, the Indian government and the Federation of Indian Chambers of Commerce and Industry organized in New Delhi "the largest gathering of the Indian diaspora since independence in 1947." The two thousand "non-resident Indians" who came from sixty-three countries were "politicians, scholars, industrialists, and jurists," including the prime minister of Mauritius, the former prime minister of Fiji, and two Nobel Prize winners. Four hundred came from the United States, representing the 1.7 million Indian-Americans, who have an aggregate income equal to 10 percent of India's national income.[42]

In the last decade of the twentieth century, the Mexican government became a leader in developing intensive relations with its diaspora. President Carlos Salinas took the first major step by creating in 1990 the Program for Mexican Communities Abroad as a subsidiary of its foreign ministry. It was designed, in the words of Robert Leiken, "to build an institutional bridge between the Mexican government, on the one hand, and U.S. Mexicans and Mexican-Americans." The PCME carried out a widespread range of activities, sponsoring Mexican-American groups, promoting the interests of Mexican immigrants in the United States, enhancing their status in Mexico, founding cultural centers, and encouraging federations of the Mexican hometown associations in the United States. The personnel and budgets of Mexico's forty-two consulates in the United States were significantly expanded to carry out these functions. President Zedillo continued these activities. On taking office President Fox appointed a prominent state governor to a new post in his cabinet to coordinate activities relating to the U.S.-Mexican border. Six months later he laid out a six-year National Development Plan that included the goal of protecting Mexican immigrants in the United States and the creation of a special prosecutor's office for that purpose.[43]

The enhanced role of Mexican consulates was dramatically evident in Los Angeles with its huge Mexican population. In 2003 Consul General Martha Lara claimed, "I have more constituents than the mayor of Los Angeles." In one sense she is right: about 4.7 million Mexican-Americans live in greater Los Angeles, while the total population of the central city is 3.6 million. The consul general and her staff of seventy, according to the *New York Times*, provide "a range of services," which "often makes Ms. Lara seem more like a governor than a diplomat. She inaugurates immigrant-owned businesses, certifies births, marries lovers and crowns beauty queens."[44] The most significant "governing" role of the consulates, however, is providing certification to illegal Mexican immigrants that they are American residents.

September 11 reduced the salience to the United States of its relations with Mexico and the U.S. government did not move forward with the anticipated "normalization" of the several million Mexicans in the United States illegally. The Mexican government responded by promoting its own form of legalization: the issuance by its consulates of registration cards, the *matricula consular*, certifying that the bearer was a resident of the United States. Some 1.1 million of these were issued in 2002. Simultaneously Mexican agencies launched a major campaign to get general acceptance of these cards. By August 2003, they had succeeded with "more than 100 cities, 900 police departments, 100 financial institutions, and with thirteen states."[45]

Legal Mexican immigrants have no need for a *matricula consular*. Possession of such a card, consequently, is presumptive evidence that the bearer is in the United States illegally. Acceptance of that card by American public and private institutions cedes to the Mexican government the power to give to illegal immigrants the status and benefits normally available only to legal residents. A foreign government, in effect, determines who is an American. The success of the Mexican *matricula consular* prompted Guatemala to start issuing them in 2002, and other homeland governments have been rushing to follow.

As was documented in Chapter 8, ampersands promote dual citizenship laws to legitimate their dual loyalties and dual identities. Homeland governments also find it in their interest to allow diasporans to be homeland citizens as well as citizens of their host country. This establishes another tie to the homeland and also encourages them to promote homeland interests in their host country. In 1998, a Mexican law took effect that permitted Mexican migrants to retain their Mexican nationality while becoming U.S. citizens. "You're Mexicans—Mexicans who live north of the border," President Zedillo told Mexican-Americans. By 2001 as part of their extensive outreach to their diasporans, Mexican consulates were actively "encouraging Mexican nationals in the United States to naturalize as U.S. citizens, while keeping their nationality as Mexicans as well."[46] Candidates for political office in Mexico campaign in the United States to raise money, to induce diasporans to get their family and friends in Mexico to vote for them, and to get Mexican citizens to return to Mexico to vote. President Fox has supported Mexican citizenship for U.S. citizens of Mexican origin, including those born in the United States, which would enable them to vote in Mexican elections. They would constitute about 15 percent of all potential Mexican voters. If they can vote at their consulates in Los Angeles, Chicago, and elsewhere, the campaigns in these locations by candidates for office in Mexico are likely to be at least as, and possibly more, intense than the campaigns by candidates for office in America.

The promotion of their diasporas by homeland governments is paralleled by and has encouraged diasporas to contribute to and support their homeland. This takes many forms. Most obvious are huge remittances diasporans send home. Historically, emigrants have sent money back to their families and communities.[47] The extent and the institutionalization of these transfers took on new dimensions in the late twentieth century. In this process, diasporans as well as ampersands—and, of course, the two often overlap—have played active roles. The transfer of funds becomes not just an effort to help family and friends, but a collective effort to affirm a diasporan identity with the homeland and to support it because it is their homeland. Estimates of the global amount of migrant remittances vary from $63 billion in 2000, exceeding the $58 billion in official aid, to $80 billion in 2001, with $28.4 billion of this coming from the United States. Reportedly, Jewish Americans contribute $1 billion or more a year to Israel. Filipinos send more than $3.6 billion home. In 2000 Salvadorans in the United States sent $1.5 billion to their home country. Vietnamese diasporans reportedly send home $700 million to $1 billion a year. Even remittances from the United States to Cuba amounted to $720 million in 2000 and over $1 billion in 2002. The largest U.S. remittances, of course, are to Mexico, which have grown dramatically. The Mexican government estimated that they would increase by 35 percent in 2001, exceed $9 billion, and probably replace tourism as Mexico's second largest source of foreign exchange after oil exports. Estimates for 2002 and 2003 exceed $10 billion.[48]

Diasporas contribute to the economic well-being of their homelands not just through large numbers of small remittances to those they have left behind to be spent as the recipients wish, but also increasingly by substantial investments in particular projects, factories, and businesses, ownership of which they may share with indigenous partners. The Chinese government has encouraged such investments from Hong Kong, Taiwan, Singapore, Indonesia, and elsewhere. Indian, Mexican, and other successful immigrant entrepreneurs in the United States have been importuned for investments by their homeland governments. Beginning in the 1960s, some 25,000 Indian "top graduates" in engineering and related fields left for the United States, where many became extremely successful, among other things, running "more than 750 technology companies in California's Silicon Valley alone." They have responded positively to the Indian government's urging them to invest in educational programs, training institutes, and productive facilities in India. One 2002 survey found that half of foreign-born (largely Chinese and Indian) highly skilled technocrats and entrepreneurs in Silicon Valley had "set up subsidiaries, joint ventures, subcontracting arrangements, or other business operations in their native countries."[49] Successful entrepreneurs and professionals from Mexico and other countries have acted similarly, and the homeland governments vigorously attempt to direct such investments into projects that the governments deem essential.

Diasporas make noneconomic contributions to their homelands. Following the end of the communist regimes in eastern Europe, diasporans, many of them from the United States, provided presidents of Lithuania and Latvia, a prime minister of Yugoslavia, two foreign ministers, and a vice minister of defense who then became chief of the general staff in Lithuania, as well as numerous other lower officials in these countries. Support was expressed in Poland and the Czech Republic for Zbigniew Brzezinski and Madeleine Albright becoming presidents of these countries. Neither, however, evinced interest in that possibility, and Brzezinski commented that this suggestion forced him to examine his own identity and to conclude that while he was historically and culturally Polish, politically he was American. Diasporas also try to shape the policies of their homeland governments. As Yossi Shain has argued, on occasion they have attempted to "market the American Creed abroad," promoting American values of civil liberties, democracy, and free enterprise in their homelands. This certainly happens in some cases; nonetheless as critics like Rodolfo O. de la Garza point out, Shain did not convincingly demonstrate this to be the case for three most important diasporas in the United States: Mexican-Americans, Arab-Americans, and Chinese-Americans, all of which "act counter to

Shain's assertion regarding the promotion of democratic practices in the homeland."[50] It would appear, however, that in 2000 Mexican-Americans overwhelmingly supported the end after seven decades of the monopoly of power in their homeland by a single party.

Diasporas take positions on their homelands' foreign policy. In controversies involving the homeland country or homeland groups in conflict with other states or groups over the control of territory, diasporas have often, but not always, supported the more extremist of their homeland colleagues. Stateless diasporas, such as Chechens, Kosovars, Sikhs, Palestinians, Moros, and Tamils have provided money, weapons, military recruits, and diplomatic and political support to their compatriots fighting to create independent homelands. Without external diasporic support, such insurgencies are unsustainable. With that support, they end only when the insurgents achieve what they want. Diasporas are important to the maintenance of homeland states; they are indispensable to the creation of such states.

The third and in many ways the most significant new dimension of diasporas is the extent to which homeland governments have been able to mobilize and to establish close means of cooperation with them so as to promote homeland interests in host societies. This development is especially significant for the United States. First, America is the most powerful actor in global politics and is able to exercise some influence on events in almost every part of the world. Other governments hence have a special need to influence the policies and behavior of its government. Second, America is historically an immigrant society and in the late twentieth century opened its doors to tens of millions of new immigrants and thus became host to more and larger diasporic groups. It is clearly the world's number one diaspora hostland. Third, given the extent and variety of American power, foreign governments have only limited ability to affect American policies through conventional diplomatic, economic, and military means and hence must rely more on their diaspora. Fourth, the nature of American government and society enhances the political power of foreign governments and diasporas. Dispersion of authority among state and federal governments, three branches of government, and loosely structured and often highly autonomous bureaucracies provide them, as with domestic interest groups, multiple points of access for promoting favorable policies and blocking unfavorable ones. The highly competitive two-party system gives strategically placed minorities such as diasporas the opportunity to affect elections in the single-member districts of the House of Representatives and at times also in statewide Senate elections. In addition, multiculturalism and belief in the value of immigrant groups' maintaining their ancestral culture and identity provide a highly favorable intellectual, social, and political atmosphere, unique to the United States, for the exercise of diaspora influence.

Fifth, during the Cold War, as Tony Smith has pointed out, the interests of refugee diasporas from communist countries broadly corresponded with the goals of American foreign policy.[51] Eastern European diasporas promoted the liberation of their countries from Soviet rule; Russian, Chinese, and Cuban diasporas supported U.S. efforts to weaken or end communist control of their homelands. With the end of the Cold War, however, ideological opposition to homeland governments gave way (except for the Cubans) to renewed identification with and support for their homeland and its government, whose interests did not always coincide with American national interests. Sixth, during the decade between the end of the Cold War and the start of the war on terror, America had no overriding foreign policy goal, and hence the way was open for diasporas and economic interest groups to play more important roles in shaping American foreign policy. September 11 drastically reduced the power and status of Arab and Muslim groups and generated questioning attitudes toward immigrants generally. It is dubious, however, that in the absence of major additional attacks, it will have all that much of an effect in the longer run, given the powerful political, social, and intellectual forces deriving from both globalization and the nature of American society and politics that make the United States a fertile field for the exercise of influence by homeland governments and their diasporas.

As a result of these factors, in the late twentieth century, foreign governments greatly increased their efforts to affect American policies. These included expanding their lobbying efforts and public relations activity, providing support to think tanks and media, and mobilizing their diasporas to contribute funds and workers to political campaigns and to lobby congressional committees and bureaucratic agencies. These governments and their supporters also became much more sophisticated in their understanding of the dynamics of American government and the means of securing access to centers of power. The shift in the scale and sophistication of Mexico's efforts is one example of these changes.

In the mid-1980s Mexico was spending less than $70,000 a year on lobbying Washington, and President Miguel de la Madrid (a graduate of the Harvard Kennedy School of Government) lamented the difficulty he had getting his diplomats not just to deal formally with the State Department but to develop close relations with the congressmen who had the real power to affect Mexico's interests. In 1991 under President Carlos Salinas (also a Kennedy School alumnus), the Mexican embassy in Washington was doubled in size and its press attachés and congressional liaison officers expanded even further. By 1993 Mexico was spending $16 million on Washington lobbying, and Salinas was leading a multiyear $35 million campaign to get congressional approval of Mexico's joining the North American Free Trade Agreement. As has been pointed out, Mexican political and consular officials also began to make great efforts to mobilize and organize the Mexican diaspora to promote Mexico's agenda in Washington. In 1995 President Zedillo explicitly urged Mexican-Americans to become as effective in promoting Mexico's interests as the Jewish lobby was in promoting Israel's. As one State Department official commented: "The Mexicans used to be invisible here. Now they're all over the place."[52]

Mexico is a dramatic example of the intensified activity by foreign governments to influence American policy and to mobilize their diasporas for that purpose. Other governments making parallel efforts include those of Canada, Saudi Arabia, South Korea, Taiwan, Japan, Israel, Germany, the Philippines, and China, with annual spending by many of them reaching into tens of millions of dollars and in a few cases probably exceeding a hundred million dollars.

Homeland governments exploit their diasporas in various ways. One is as a source of agents for espionage and influence. Throughout history the desire for money has motivated people to turn against their country and to sell themselves to a foreign state. Americans working for the CIA, the FBI, and the military did this in the 1980s and 1990s. Spies also may have other motives. In the 1930s and 1940s, those who became Soviet agents, including U.S. officials, Los Alamos scientists, and the Cambridge coterie of diplomats, were motivated not by lucre but by ideology. In today's world, culture and ethnicity have replaced ideology. In America many different diasporan constituencies that can be exploited by many different foreign governments have replaced the single ideological constituency exploited by the Soviet Union. Immigrants whose primary loyalty is to America can provide and have provided important services, including espionage, to the United States in its relations with other governments. To the extent, however, that they see themselves as members of a diaspora encompassing their homeland society and its government, they also become a potential source of agents for that government. "Espionage," Senator Daniel Patrick Moynihan once observed, "is almost invariably associated with diaspora politics," and as the Department of Defense reported to Congress in 1996, "many foreign intelligence agencies attempt to exploit ethnic or religious ties" of American diasporans to their homelands.[53] Since the 1980s, the United States has successfully prosecuted Russian, Chinese, Cuban, South Korean, and Israeli diasporans as spies for their homelands.

Much more important than espionage and involving far more people are the efforts of diasporans to shape American policy to serve homeland interests. These efforts have been documented at length at a general level in studies by Tony Smith, Yossi Shain, Gabriel Sheffer, and others as well as in innumerable studies of specific diasporic groups.[54] In recent decades, diasporas have had a major impact on American policy toward Greece and Turkey, the Caucasus, recognition of Macedonia, support for Croatia, sanctions against South Africa, aid for black Africa, intervention in Haiti, NATO expansion, the controversy in Northern Ireland, and the relations between Israel and its neighbors. Diaspora-shaped policies may at times coincide with broader national interests, as could arguably be the case with NATO expansion, but they are also often pursued at the expense of broader interests and American relations with long-standing allies. It can hardly be otherwise when diasporans identify themselves completely with their homeland, as in the case of Elie Wiesel: "I support Israel—period. I identify with Israel—period. I never attack, never criticize Israel when I am not in Israel. . . . The role of a Jew is to be with our people."[55] Studies show, Tony Smith argues, that "the organized leadership" of the Jewish, Greek, Armenian, and other diasporas are "strongly influenced by foreign governments to take positions that may contradict American policy or interests in the region" and are unwilling "to concede that any voice but theirs should be authoritative with respect to the area of the world that concerns them." The claim of diasporas of the right to dominate the shaping of American policy toward their homeland area usually rests on an underlying assumption that no possible conflict could exist between homeland interests and American interests, an attitude succinctly expressed by convicted Israeli spy Jonathan Pollard: "I never thought for a second that Israel's gain would necessarily result in America's loss. How could it?"[56]

Diasporas achieve influence in Congress because they can affect elections to Congress by providing money and workers to their friends and campaigning vigorously against those opposed to their policies. The political action of the Jewish diaspora is credited with the defeat in 1982 of Representative Paul Findley (Rep.-Illinois), senior Republican on the Middle East Subcommittee of the House Foreign Affairs Committee, because of his support for the PLO, and in 1984 of Senator Charles Percy (Rep.-Illinois), chairman of the Senate Foreign Relations Committee, for his backing the sale of F-15s to Saudi Arabia. In 2002 Jewish diaspora groups were central to the primary defeats for reelection of Representatives Earl Hilliard (Dem.-Alabama) and Cynthia McKinney (Dem.-Georgia), because they had endorsed Palestinian and Arab causes. The Armenian National Committee of America gets some credit for the defeat in 1996 of two representatives whom it had labeled among the most pro-Turkish members of Congress: Jim Bunn (Rep.-Oregon) and Greg Laughlin (Dem.-Texas). Bunn's successful opponent, Darlene Hooley, praised the ANCA "for mounting a nationwide campaign in support of my candidacy."[57]

Countries such as Israel, Armenia, Greece, Poland, and India have obviously benefited from the efforts of their mostly small but well-placed, affluent, and articulate diasporas in the United States. Countries opposing these homelands have often lost out as a result. Increased and diversified immigration to America is multiplying, however, the numbers of diasporic communities and their actual and potential political influence. As a result, conflicts abroad between opposing homelands increasingly become conflicts in America between opposing diasporas. One Arab-American leader described the congressional contest in Georgia in 2002 as "a little, Middle East proxy war."[58] Such "proxy wars" fought politically between diasporas in America are tributes to America's power to influence the real wars between homelands abroad and also evidence of the extent to which homeland governments and their diasporas believe they can affect the course of American foreign policy. As the diaspora universe becomes more diverse, proxy wars are also likely to multiply and become more diverse. One particularly intense conflict was the 1996 senatorial contest in South Dakota. This was as much a contest between Indians and Pakistanis as between Republicans and Democrats. Each candidate ardently solicited the support of a diasporan constituency. Indian-Americans contributed about $150,000 to Senator Larry Pressler's reelection campaign because he supported limits on U.S. arms exports to Pakistan. Pakistani-Americans gave a similar amount to his opponent. Pressler's defeat produced elation in Islamabad and dejection in New Delhi. In 2003 a similar line-up and result occurred with the unsuccessful effort of an Indian-American, Bobby Jindal, to become governor of Louisiana. He was enthusiastically backed by Indians and Indian-Americans and vigorously opposed by Pakistani-Americans, who contributed substantial sums to his successful opponent.[59]

The increasing numbers of Arab-Americans and Muslim Americans and their growing political involvement also pose challenges to the influence of the Jewish diaspora on American Middle East policy. In the 2002 Democratic primary in Georgia, incumbent Representative Cynthia McKinney, who had been a major supporter of Palestinian causes, "received campaign contributions from Arab-Americans around the country," including "respectable lawyers, physicians and merchants" but also others who were "under scrutiny by the Federal Bureau of Investigation for possible terrorist links." McKinney's opponent, Denise Majette, was able to raise $1.1 million, almost twice what McKinney raised, with the help of "contributions from Jews outside Georgia." McKinney had other problems affecting her reelection campaign and lost by a vote of 58 percent to 42 percent. But as the *Economist* commented two years earlier on the growing political role of Arab-Americans, "The pro-Israel lobby is far better organized and financed than its putative rival. But now there is at least a putative rival—and that is quite a change in American politics."[60]

American politics is increasingly an arena in which homeland governments and their diasporas attempt to shape American policy to serve homeland interests. This brings them into battles with other homelands and their diasporas fought out on Capitol Hill and in voting precincts across America. An ineluctable dynamic is at work. The more power the United States has in world politics, the more it becomes an arena of world politics, the more foreign governments and their diasporas attempt to influence American policy, and the less able the United States is to define and to pursue its own national interests when these do not correspond with those of other countries that have exported people to America.

PART IV

Renewing
American Identity

CHAPTER 11

Fault Lines
Old and New

THE SHAPING TRENDS

The future substance and salience of American identity are being significantly shaped by four trends in American society:

- The virtual disappearance of ethnicity as a source of identity for white Americans;
- The slow blurring of racial distinctions and the fading salience of racial identities;
- The growing numbers and influence of the Hispanic community and the trend toward a bilingual, bicultural America; and
- The gap between the salience of national identity for many elites and its salience for the overall public.

Under some circumstances, these trends could provoke a nativist reaction, sharp polarization, and traumatic cleavages among Americans.

American identity will also be decisively shaped by the new realization of America's vulnerability to external attack and the impact of America's intensifying interactions with peoples of different cultures and religions. These external influences could promote the rediscovery and renewal by Americans of their historic religious identity and Anglo-Protestant culture.

THE ENDING OF ETHNICITY

In the late nineteenth century, Americans increasingly defined themselves racially. This was most obvious with respect to blacks and Asians, but white Americans also viewed Irish, Italian, Slavic, and Jewish immigrants as racially different from themselves. As the generations passed and assimilation proceeded, the descendants of these immigrants came to be accepted as white Americans, a process that has been spelled out in books with such titles as *How the Irish Became White, How Jews Became White Folks,* and *Whiteness of a Different Color: European Immigrants and the Alchemy of Race.* In order to become "white," the arriving "nonwhites" had to accept the racial distinctions prevalent in America and embrace the exclusion of Asians and the subordination of blacks.[1]

Racial assimilation was followed by ethnic differentiation. The economic and social progress of immigrants depended initially on their living with and cooperating with other immigrants like themselves. With the second and, more significantly, the third generation, however, structural assimilation got under way. Young people left the ethnic ghettos, attended multiethnic schools, colleges, and universities, obtained jobs in the new large, national corporations with multiethnic workforces, and moved to multiethnic suburbs. In due course, ethnic segregation and subordination gradually became history. By 1990 less than 6 percent of people with unmixed Irish ancestry in the New York metropolitan area lived in neighborhoods more than 40 percent Irish. Seventy-five percent of those with Irish ancestry lived in the suburbs, and less than 4 percent of the Irish total lived in primarily Irish neighborhoods in those suburbs. The Irish, Professor Reginald Byron concluded, are merging "into a broad category of middle-class European Americans who no longer have strongly marked ethnic characteristics associated with their old-country backgrounds."[2]

Structural assimilation in education, occupation, employment, and residence led to marital assimilation. In 1956, in an influential work, Will Herberg advanced the argument that, even then, ethnic intermarriages were the prevailing trend but that they occurred within religious communities. White America, he claimed, was developing three melt-

ing pots: Protestant, Catholic, and Jewish. English and Norwegian
Protestants married, as did Italian and Irish Catholics, and German and
Russian Jews. With only a tenuous, symbolic, ancestral ethnic identity,
the third generation, in a manifestation of "Hansen's Law" that the
third generation tries to remember what the second generation wanted
to forget, increasingly sought identity in religion. This process was reinforced by the fact that although assimilation into America involved sur-
rendering one's previous national loyalty and identity, it did not require
giving up one's religious commitment and identity.[3]

Other things being equal, the smaller a group the higher its intermarriage rate. Intermarriage between the largest religious communities in
the United States hence has lagged behind ethnic intermarriage. Since
the Census does not collect data on religion, religious marriage rates
have to be estimated from other sources and with less precision. In 1990,
however, between 80 percent and 90 percent of marriages involving one
Protestant involved two Protestants. The in-marriage rate for Catholics
was slightly lower, somewhere between 64 percent and 85 percent.
These figures are for all existing marriages, and the proportion of new
out-marriages was undoubtedly much higher. Catholic-Protestant intermarriages had "increased dramatically" by the 1980s, and people were
increasingly approving of marriages between people of different faiths.
Fifty percent of Italian-Americans born after World War II married non-
Catholic, mostly Protestant, spouses.[4]

Jews are both an ethnic and a religious group and very small in
number. At the start of the twentieth century, Jews had, nonetheless,
the lowest intermarriage rate of any European immigrant group. By the
1950s, their out-marriage rate was still only about 6 percent. With the
dramatic post–World War II increases in Jewish educational, occupational, and economic status, out-marriages proliferated. By the 1990s,
between 53 percent and 58 percent of new Jewish marriages were to
non-Jews. "Every year," as one Jewish observer commented, "the shock
Alan Dershowitz went through when his son told him that he planned
to marry a fine Irish Catholic girl is being duplicated in Jewish homes
across America." The increase in Jewish intermarriage could be reduced
if more American Jews become Orthodox Jews. The impact of inter-

marriage on the number of Jews could also be countered by the fact that Judaism is a religion as well as an ethnic identity, and non-Jewish spouses may convert to Judaism, converts mostly from this source constituting 3 percent of the American Jews in the 1990s.[5] In addition, the children of a mixed marriage may be raised as Jews.

In the latter part of the twentieth century, interethnic marriage among white Americans escalated. According to Richard Alba's analysis of the 1990 census, 56 percent of the marriages among whites were between people who had no overlap in their ethnic ancestry; roughly 25 percent were between people with a partial overlap in ethnic identity, that is, for example, when "a German-Irish groom takes an Irish-Italian bride," and 20 percent were marriages between people with identical ethnic backgrounds. For some ethnic groups, the proportion of entirely in-marriages for people born between 1956 and 1965 was extremely low: 7.6 for those of Polish ancestry, 7.0 for Scotch-Irish, 12.1 for French, 15.0 for Italian, and 12.7 for Irish.[6]

What is true with respect to interethnic marriages does not generally hold for interracial marriages, with one major exception. The overall out-marriage rate for those of Asian ancestry approximates that for those of European ancestry. Asian migrants include Japanese, Chinese, Koreans, Vietnamese, Filipinos, Indians, and others, who have little sense of a common Asian identity. As a result, while European ethnics marry other European ethnics, Asians in America rarely marry other Asians. In 1990, 50 percent of Asian-American men and 55 percent of the women between the ages of twenty-five and thirty-four were married to non-Asians. For those under twenty-five, these percentages went up to 54 percent for men and 66 percent for women.[7]

Even more dramatically than previous European ethnic groups, Asian-Americans are "becoming white," not necessarily because their skin color is whitening, although it is, but because they have, in varying degrees for different groups, brought with them values emphasizing work, discipline, learning, thrift, strong families, and in the case of Filipinos and Indians a knowledge of English. Because their values are similar to those of Americans and because of their generally high educational and occupational levels, they have been relatively easily absorbed into American society.

As white ethnics, once labeled "unmeltable," dissolve in America's white melting pot, what does ancestry mean for them as a source of identity? Consider two contemporary cases. In Family A, a Jewish-American marries a native of Korea. Their son marries an immigrant who is 100 percent Iranian. In terms of ancestry, the children of that marriage are one-quarter Jewish, one-quarter Korean, and one-half Iranian. In Family B, two native-born Americans marry, one of pure Armenian ancestry and one of pure Irish ancestry. Their daughter marries an immigrant who is 100 percent Egyptian. The child of that marriage is thus one-quarter Armenian, one-quarter Irish, and one-half Egyptian. The third generation in each family has three very different ethnic ancestries. What would then happen if members of the third generation in each family married each other? The offspring of that marriage would be one-quarter Iranian, one-quarter Egyptian, one-eighth Armenian, one-eighth Irish, one-eighth Jewish, and one-eighth Korean.

Intermarriage patterns like these fundamentally affect the nature of white America in two ways. First, the melting pot is working, but it is working at the individual, not the societal, level. Crèvecoeur and Zangwill were wrong. The tides of immigration are producing not one new American man but innumerable ethnically different ones. White America is changing from a multiethnic society of a few dozen ethnic groups into a nonethnic society of tens of millions of multiethnic individuals. In theory, the eventual result of sustained intermarriage would be a situation in which no two people except siblings had identical ethnic ancestries. Second, as individuals inherit more and more varied ancestries, ethnic identity becomes a matter of subjective choice. A member of the hypothetical fourth generation in the previous paragraph might choose to identify entirely and enthusiastically with his Irish heritage. His choice, however, would differ little from that of people with no Irish heritage who become enamored of Ireland and its culture, music, literature, history, language, and lore. Choosing an ethnic identity becomes like joining a club, and ethnic clubs might well compete throughout the white population to recruit people to share in their particular rituals, comradeship, and membership joys. Or, conceivably this fourth-generation person could embrace several of his ancestral ethnicities and join several clubs. Or he could consciously reject or simply forget about his ancestral ethnic identities.

Similar questions arise with respect to the identity of Asian-Americans. As one of them, citing their 50 percent out-marriage rate, asked:

> What will "Asian American" mean when a majority of the next generation is of mixed parentage? Will membership in the race depend more on heredity or on heritage? Chromosomes or culture? Will it be a matter of voluntary affiliation, a question of choice? Or will the "one-drop rule" that makes American blacks black make anyone with an Asian ancestor Asian? Who will pass for white—and who will want to? [8]

Being a hyphenated American becomes difficult as the hyphens multiply, and people may choose an ethnic identity randomly or arbitrarily. Alba's analysis of the 1980 and 1990 census forms shows that ancestry choices were significantly influenced simply by the order in which possible identities were listed as examples on the form. In 1980, English was close to the top of the list and was chosen by 49.6 million respondents. In 1990, English was not included as an example, and was chosen by only 32.7 million respondents. In 1980, German and Italian were low on the list of examples, but in 1990, they were the first two on the list, and the number choosing them increased by 20 percent. Perhaps one fifth of native-born whites, Alba concluded in 1990, "hold intensely to an ethnic identity." [9] Undoubtedly fewer do now.

Absent ethnicity, how will white Americans define themselves? Alba suggests the common ancestral immigration experience could be a source of identity. [10] Yet as white Americans think of themselves less and less in ethnic terms, it seems unlikely that they will turn to the rather abstract, historical, and increasingly remote immigration experience of their ancestors to find their identity. A related alternative is Euro-American or European-American, which several scholars have suggested. ("Euro" alone presumably has been preempted by the currency.) Alba, indeed, picks European-American as the label for those who identify with the immigrant experience. John Skrentny, David Hollinger, and Orlando Patterson also opt for Euro-American as a parallel to Afro-American.[11] This encompasses the ancestries of most non-Hispanic white Americans and highlights the swath of America's European cultural legacy. It also includes the descendants of both settlers and immigrants. Contemporary Americans apply the comparable umbrella label of Hispanic or Latino to immigrants from the several countries of Latin America. In some measure, however, it seems rather late to promote an umbrella European identity for white Americans. In the nineteenth century, settlers and their descendants did not apply this label to immigrants, and the arrivals from Europe were given hyphenated identities based on their perceived nationality. In May 1995, the Census Bureau polled non-Hispanic whites as to their "preference for racial or ethnic terminology." Only 2.35 percent chose European-American.[12]

If, as seems quite possible, culture emerges as a central fault line, the natural consequence would be for European Americans to define themselves in cultural terms. Hispanic Americans already define them this way, referring to non-Hispanic, nonblack Americans, including Asian-Americans, collectively as "Anglos." If this term is given only a cultural and not an ethnic meaning, it is not inappropriate. It affirms the centrality of America's Anglo-Protestant culture, the English language, and English political, legal, and social institutions and mores to American identity. Yet in the 1995 Census Bureau poll, less than one percent of non-Hispanic whites chose that label for themselves.

The most probable subnational identity for non-Hispanic, nonblack Americans to espouse is "white." In the 1995 poll, 61.7 percent chose that term, and an additional 16.5 percent preferred Caucasian. Three quarters of white Americans thus think of themselves primarily in racial terms. This could have serious implications for American society. Any identity requires an other, and "whiteness, to understand itself," as Karen Brodkin says, "depends upon an invented and contrasting blackness as its evil (and sometimes enviable) twin." Hence it is not surprising that in some situations whites of different backgrounds assert a "white ethnic pan-ethnicity" and cooperate with each other against non-whites.[13]

There is, however, another possibility that is the most inclusive of all.

White Americans could forgo subnational, communal identities and simply think of themselves as Americans. The descendants of pre-1800 settlers often chose this identity over other possibilities such as English-American, Scottish-American, German-American, and the like. In addition, as Stanley Lieberson notes, in the Current Population Surveys conducted in successive years, 1971, 1972, 1973, with the same people interviewed each year, only 64.7 percent of the respondents gave the response they had given the year before. The one third of Americans giving inconsistent responses were not randomly distributed. Consistency was roughly 80 percent to 95 percent for blacks, Hispanics, Italians, and eastern Europeans. It was "much lower for white groups from Northwestern Europe, the so-called 'old' European stocks who have many ancestors going back to a large number of generations in the United States." Only a little more than half those reporting English, Scottish, or Welsh ancestry in 1971 gave the same answer in 1972. In the early 1970s, roughly 57 percent of the U.S. population was at least fourth-generation, and 20 percent of the nonblack fourth generation did not name any ancestral country, contrasted with under one percent of first-, second-, or third-generation people.[14] By the fourth generation, in short, ancestral ethnicity faded fast. And now one more generation has matured.

The increase in the proportion of the population who does not identify an ethnic ancestry is paralleled by the rise in number who simply answer "American." The Census Bureau explicitly attempted to discourage this response in the 1979 Current Population Survey and the 1980 Census. Yet in 1980, 13.3 million people, or 6 percent of the population, chose this label, while another 23 million or about 10 percent did not report an ethnic ancestry. In the 2000 census, the "unhyphenating of America" continued. Compared to the 1990 census, the number of people reporting English ancestry dropped by 26 percent, Irish ancestry by 21 percent, and German ancestry by 27 percent. The number responding simply "American," on the other hand, rose 55 percent to about 20 million. These changes were most marked in the South, with 25 percent of Kentuckians, for instance, listing themselves as Americans.[15]

The identity white Americans choose to replace their fading ethnic identities has profound implications for America's future. If they define themselves primarily as Euro-American or Anglo in response to a perceived Hispanic challenge, the cultural divide in America will be formalized. If they think of themselves primarily as white in opposition to blacks and others, the historic racial fault line will be reinvigorated. On the other hand, national identity and national unity will be strengthened if white Americans echo Ward Connerly and conclude that their mixed ancestries make them "All American."

Which brings us to the issue of race.

RACE: CONSTANT, BLURRING, FADING

Individual humans are physically different. Groups of biologically related people have physical characteristics that differentiate them from other people. When these physical differences involve skin color, eye shape, hair, and facial features, people have for centuries labeled them differences in race. The physical differences exist; the identification of them as racial differences is a product of human perception and decision, and attributing significance to these racial differences is a result of human judgment.

Differences in height among humans are just as pronounced and even more obvious than differences in skin color and face. Except for pygmies, however, height differences, even though they may have socioeconomic consequences,[16] have not generally been the basis for differentiating among and categorizing people. Racism is a reality because people consider skin color differences important; heightism is not a similar reality because people usually do not, apart from basketball, consider differences in height very important. Hence individuals and groups classify themselves in racial terms and are classified by others in those terms. Unlike height, race is a social construction as well as a physical reality.

Race may also be a political construction. Governments classify people into different racial categories and assign rights, responsibilities, and obligations to these categories. For most of their histories the governments of South Africa and the United States placed their people in racial groupings, three such groupings in South Africa and from three to fifteen in the United States. South Africa stopped this practice, while the United States now requires people to classify themselves using a government-supplied list of races. In both South Africa and the United States, racial categories served as the basis for legal discrimination among races in government policy; in the United States they still do.

In the early twenty-first century, race and racial identities in America are evolving in three ways. First, differences in socioeconomic status and well-being among races are basically constant, although declining slightly in some areas. In these terms, America is still a racially divided society. Second, a slow process of racial blurring is occurring both biologically from intermarriage and symbolically and attitudinally, with individual multiracialism becoming a more widely accepted norm. Americans approve of their country moving from a multiracial society of racial groups to a nonracial society of multiracial individuals. Third, the overall salience of race compared to other elements of personal identity seems to be declining. Thus, while socioeconomic differences among races remain, a blurring and a fading of race are also occurring. These latter processes, however, could also contribute to the development of a new racial consciousness among whites, as they see America becoming increasingly nonwhite. (See below, "White Nativism.")

Major differences in socioeconomic status and political power among races have always existed and continue to exist in America. They include differences in wealth, income, education, power, residence, employment, health, crime (both as perpetrators and victims), and other markers of class and status. In most of these dimensions, the absolute levels of well-being for blacks and, to a lesser degree, Hispanics improved significantly in the last four decades of the twentieth century. These improvements did not, however, necessarily narrow significantly the gaps between blacks and Hispanics, on the one hand, and whites and Asians, on the other. Many of these gaps remain, as reflected in the continuing differences in family income over thirty years.

Differences between racial groups comparable to these in the United States have been prevalent in human societies throughout history. They are currently a global phenomenon within countries and between countries. In the modern world, whites almost always have been better off than other races and East Asians generally better off than brown and black peoples. These prevailing and persistent differences are presumably the result of a wide variety of factors including historical experience, culture, oppression, social institutions, geography, climate, genetic inheritance, and the ability of a group superior in one key dimension, such as wealth or military power, to extend its superiority to other dimensions. Reduction of racial differences in wealth, status, and power is difficult globally and within countries. The modest reductions that have been made in the United States probably exceed those in most other societies. Slow progress will undoubtedly continue to be made, but any major narrowing of these gaps deeply embedded in the history, culture, and institutions of American society will be a long-term process. Some socioeconomic differences between races are likely to exist as long as races exist.

Races will continue to exist, but not necessarily to the same degree or with the same significance that they have had in the past. The high rates of intermarriage among whites are ending ethnicity. The rates of intermarriage between the largest American racial groups are much lower, but they are high for Asians and increasing for blacks. Black outmarriage rates historically have been extremely low, bearing little relation to the proportions of America's black and white populations who have mixed ancestry. Yet, from its low base, the black out-marriage rate has increased dramatically. "In 1960 only 1.7% of all [new] marriages involving at least one black were mixed marriages, but by 1993, 12.1% of new marriages involving one black also included a white." In addition to varying with group size and income, interracial marriage rates vary inversely with age.[17]

To a small but growing extent, intermarriage is blurring the lines between races. Much more importantly, race and racial distinctions are losing significance in people's thinking. In the mid-1960s, nineteen states had anti-miscegenation laws on their books, and 42 percent of Northern whites and 72 percent of Southern whites endorsed such laws. In 1967, the Supreme Court declared these laws unconstitutional.[18] In the following decades, American opinion on intermarriage changed significantly, with majorities of every racial group coming to approve it. In a 1999 Pew Center poll, 63 percent of the respondents said interracial marriages were "good because they help break down racial barriers," while 26 percent said they were "bad because mixing races reduces the special talents or gifts of each individual race." A 1997 Gallup poll found that 70 percent of both black and white teenagers thought that interracial dating was "no big deal." In a 2001 Harvard/Kaiser Foundation/ *Washington Post* poll, 77 percent of blacks, 68 percent of Latinos, 67 percent of Asians, and 53 percent of whites said it made no difference whether people married someone of their race or of a different race. Forty percent of Americans reported dating someone of a different race. As one professor of sociology commented, "interracial marriages and their approval is increasing terribly fast. If you have hang-ups about interracial marriage, get over it. The train's left the station."[19]

Along with the approval of racial intermarriage has come the even more striking approval and, indeed, celebration of individual multiracialism. Americans have long viewed their country as a multiracial society composed of two or more racial groups. Americans now increasingly see and approve of their country becoming a nonracial society composed of multiracial individuals. In 2001, for instance, a CNN-sponsored poll asked whether it would be good or bad for the country if "more Americans think of themselves as multi-racial rather than as belonging to a single race." Sixty-four percent of the respondents said it would be good for the country; 24 percent said it would be bad. More and more Americans are identifying themselves as multiracial. In test runs leading up to the 2000 Census over 5 percent (almost triple what had been expected) of those polled chose two or more races; among those under eighteen years of age, over 8 percent did. In the 2000 Census itself, 14 percent of those who identified themselves as Asian also chose a second race, as did 6 percent of Hispanics, 5 percent of blacks, and 2.5 percent of whites. Overall, slightly fewer than seven million people (or 2 percent of the total U.S. population) made these double choices. Yet demographers estimate that by 2050 about 20 percent of Americans will be classifying themselves as multiracial.[20]

In the 1960s, the slogan was "Black is beautiful." By the 1990s, the equivalent slogan would be "Biracial (or multiracial) is beautiful." One oft-cited indicator of the changing attitudes is the cover of the 1993 special issue of *Time*, on "The New Face of America," which shows a highly attractive young woman, computer-generated from many races, and hailed by *Time* as the "new face" of America in the twenty-first century. By 1996 the face in the Betty Crocker ads had changed from a white-skinned blond-haired woman to one with olive skin and dark hair. In 1997 Tiger Woods famously described his race as "Cablinasian," that is, a mix of Caucasian, black, Indian, and Thai. Other prominent public figures similarly began to boast of their mixed-race heritages.[21] At the start of the twenty-first century, individual multi-racialism was chic and rewarding.

Americans are also paying increased attention to the extent to which they have been multiracial individuals in the past, when they had refused to recognize and accept that fact. Scholars now estimate that perhaps 75 percent of American blacks have nonblack ancestors, and one scholar concludes that in 1970 about 22 percent of American whites had non-white ancestors. Historically, Americans' subjective image of themselves as either black or white ran counter to objective reality. By the end of the twentieth century, Americans were bringing their subjective image more into accord with objective reality.

In keeping with this blurring of the black-white dichotomy, black leaders in 1988 expressed their preference for the term "African-American" instead of "black" because the former "deemphasizes race, focusing instead on culture and ethnicity." "African-American" was not racially polarizing, and instead identified blacks as simply one of many groups in American society, comparable to Irish-Americans, Italian-Americans, or Japanese-Americans. "To be called African-American," Jesse Jackson said, "has cultural integrity." The term rapidly caught on as a rival to black. In the 1995 Census Bureau poll, 44.2 percent of blacks said they preferred to be called black, but 40.2 percent chose African-American or Afro-American. The latter terms were particularly favored by younger blacks. In 1990 the people most likely to refer to themselves as African-Americans were "predominantly young, male, educated, and from the urban centers of the Northeast and Midwest."[22]

Given the pervasive penchant of Americans to prefer single-syllable over multisyllable names for almost everything, this high and growing popularity of a seven-syllable, two-word name over a one-syllable, one-word name is intriguing and perhaps significant.

The increased acceptance and, indeed, popularity of multiraciality manifested itself in the demands either to eliminate race from the 2000 census or to provide a "multiracial" alternative to the usual racial categories. Fifty-six percent of Americans polled in 1997 said the census should no longer ask about race, while 36 percent said it should continue to do so. Large numbers of Americans also supported adding a multiracial category to the questionnaire, with 49 percent of blacks and 36 percent of whites endorsing it in 1995. Mixed-race Americans and those with mixed-race children formed organizations to promote this cause, and a Multiracial Solidarity March took place in Washington in July 1996. Black interest groups, on the other hand, strongly opposed change, with four such groups, the NAACP, the National Urban League, the Lawyers' Committee for Civil Rights Under Law, and the Joint Center for Political and Economic Studies, urging the government not to "rush to institute the 'multiracial' category when there is this clear potential for increasing the racial segregation, discrimination and stigmatization of Black Americans."[23] Responding to this pressure, the Census Bureau did not add a multiracial category to the 2000 census. It did, however, permit respondents to check two of six standard racial categories. The seven million Americans who did so were almost three times those who identified themselves as "American Indian and Alaskan Native" and seventeen times those who chose "Pacific Islander," two of the listed racial categories. Census categories, as we have seen, generate identities. A "multiracial" option would undoubtedly have the effects black interest group leaders fear, as blacks and others realized they could legitimately affirm their multiracial heritage.

Racial perceptions and racial prejudices are and will remain facts of life in America. Yet the salience of race in people's perceptions and attitudes is clearly declining. Colin Powell once remarked, "In America, which I love from the depth of my heart and soul, when you look like me, you're black." Yes. When people look *at* Colin Powell, they may see a black, but they also see a secretary of state, a retired four-star general, the leader of America's military in a short, victorious war, and, if they are internationally oriented, the principal proponent in the Bush administration of multilateralism in American foreign policy. Powell's skin color fades into insignificance compared to these other components of his identity. In 1982 when Bryant Gumbel became the first black anchor on a major TV network, his skin color was important. Decades later when anchors, reporters, hosts, and commentators of all races come and go on the networks, who pays attention to their skin color? A half century after Jackie Robinson, when Americans look at a mixed group of baseball players, do they think skin colors or batting averages?

If the trends toward multiracialism continue, they will at some point, as Joel Perlmann and Roger Waldinger say, make government efforts to classify people by race "quaintly passé."[24] When it happens, the removal of race from census forms will signal a dramatic step toward the creation of a comprehensive American national identity. At present, race still matters in America, but in more and more segments of national life, it matters less and less, except for those who view its declining salience as a threat to the place of whites in America.

WHITE NATIVISM

In 1993 in *Newsweek*, David Gates described the film *Falling Down*, in which Michael Douglas plays a white former defense company employee reacting to the losses, defeats, aggravations, and humiliations that he sees imposed on him by a multiethnic, multiracial, and multicultural society. These "annoyances and menaces," Gates says, "are a cross-section of white-guy grievances. From the get-go, the film pits Douglas—the picture of obsolescent rectitude with his white shirt, tie, specs, and astronaut haircut—against a rainbow coalition of Angelenos. It's a cartoon vision of the beleaguered white male in multicultural America."[25]

But is it just a cartoon? Consider the comments of a distinguished sociologist seven years later about the vote in the Judiciary Committee of the House of Representatives on impeaching President Clinton. "On the Republican side, voting for, was a group composed exclusively of WASPs, almost all from the South, and all but one male. On the Democratic side, voting against, were Catholics, Jews, Blacks, women, a gay, and one male Southern WASP. Is it so difficult to see in this passion the rebellion of the male WASPs against what they perceive as their diminished role in U.S. society?"[26]

It should not be difficult to see that "rebellion" and the reasons for it. It would, indeed, be extraordinary and possibly unprecedented in human history if the profound demographic changes occurring in America did not generate reactions of various sorts. One very plausible reaction would be the emergence of exclusivist sociopolitical movements composed largely but not only of white males, primarily working-class and middle-class, protesting and attempting to stop or reverse these changes and what they believe, accurately or not, to be the diminution of their social and economic status, their loss of jobs to immigrants and foreign countries, the perversion of their culture, the displacement of their language, and the erosion or even evaporation of the historical identity of their country. Such movements would be both racially and culturally inspired and could be anti-Hispanic, anti-black, and anti-immigration. They would be the heir to the many comparable exclusivist racial and anti-foreign movements that helped define American identity in the past. Social movements, political groups, intellectual currents, dissidents of various sorts who share these characteristics differ in many ways, but still have enough in common to be brought together under the label "white nativism."

The term "white" in this label does not mean that people of other races would not be involved in such movements or that these movements are focused exclusively on racial issues. It does mean that their members are likely to be overwhelmingly white and that the preservation or restoration of what they see as "white America" is a central goal. The term "nativism" has acquired pejorative connotations among denationalized elites on the assumption that it is wrong vigorously to defend one's "native" culture and identity and to maintain their purity against foreign influences. In his classic study of American reactions to foreigners, however, John Higham defines nativism more neutrally as the "intense opposition to an internal minority on the ground of its foreign (i.e., 'un-American') connections."[27] It is in this neutral sense that the term is used here, but with two modifications so as to include, first, opposition to groups, such as blacks, that lack "foreign connections" but are nonetheless seen as not a true part of American society and, second, to include "opposition to an internal minority" that is perceived as becoming a majority.

White nativism of this sort should not be confused with extremist fringe groups, such as the militia movements that flourished briefly during the 1990s in Michigan and several Western states or the perennial "hate groups" who are simply and exclusively anti-Jewish or anti-black and reflect prejudice inherited from the Ku Klux Klan. These groups typically have paranoid fantasies and imagine dire conspiracies, including the existence of a "Zionist Occupied Government" in America or the takeover of the United States by a secret United Nations cabal. Groups like these always exist on the fringes of American society, with their numbers and strength varying from time to time. The Waco attack and other incidents apparently produced a substantial growth in active militia movements in the mid-1990s, but they then dwindled in number from 858 in 1996 to 194 in 2000. In April 2001 the leader of one such group in Michigan announced its disbanding because, according to the *New York Times*, "membership had plummeted and it no longer had any members with enough military experience to lead training exercises in the woods."[28] People associated with these groups have plotted to attack government officials and facilities, and like Timothy McVeigh, some of them may be successful in the future. Although they may be able to point to specific governmental actions, such as those in Waco, to buttress their case, their overall image of American society is far removed from reality.

The broad-gauged nativist movements that could emerge, in contrast, would be reactions to the new realities of American society. The leaders of such movements would have little in common with those of the fringe groups. Many of them would be what Carol Swain terms "the new white nationalists." "Cultured, intelligent, and often possessing impressive degrees from some of America's premier colleges and universities, this new breed of white racial advocate is a far cry from the populist politicians and hooded Klansmen of the Old South." These new white nationalists do not advocate white racial supremacy. They do believe in "racial self-determination and self-preservation" and that America "is fast becoming a nation dominated by non-white people." Most importantly, they follow in the tradition of Horace Kallen, the multiculturalists, and those adhering to the dichotomous concept of national identity, and link race, ethnicity, and culture together in a single package. For them, race is the source of culture, and since a person's race is fixed and unchangeable, so also is a person's culture. Hence the shifting racial balance in the United States means a shifting cultural balance and the replacement of the white culture that made America great by black or brown cultures that are different and, in their view, intellectually and morally inferior.[29] This mixing of races and hence cultures is the road to national degeneration. For them, to keep America America, it is necessary to keep America white.

White nativist movements are likely to include people with differing priorities concerning racial balance, "white" culture, immigration, racial preferences, language, and other issues. Underlying these specific concerns, however, is the fundamental question of the racial balance in America, most importantly, the declining proportion of non-Hispanic whites. This trend received much publicity from the 2000 census figures reporting a drop to 69.1 percent from 75.6 percent in 1990. Most dramatic was the evidence that in California, like Hawaii, New Mexico, and the District of Columbia, non-Hispanic whites are a minority. The decline was particularly marked in the nation's cities. In 1990 non-Hispanic whites were a minority in thirty of the one hundred largest cities and constituted 52 percent of the total population of those cities. In 2000 they were a minority in forty-eight of these cities and made up only 44 percent of their population. In 1970 non-Hispanic whites made up an overwhelming 83 percent majority of the American people. Demographers predict that by 2040 they could be a minority of Americans.

The effects of these demographic shifts are reinforced by the ending of ethnicity, which had provided most whites one long-standing and comforting subnational source of identity. In addition, for several decades interest groups and nonelected governmental elites have promoted racial preferences, affirmative action, and minority language and cultural maintenance programs, which violate the American Creed and serve the interests of blacks and nonwhite immigrant groups. The globalization policies of business elites have shifted jobs overseas and contributed to growing income inequality and a decline in real wages of working-class Americans. The liberal establishment media is seen by some whites as using double standards in reporting crimes against blacks, gays, and women, as compared to those against white males. The large and continuing influx of Hispanics threatens the preeminence of white Anglo-Protestant culture and the place of English as the only national language. White nativist movements are a possible and plausible response to these trends, and in situations of serious economic downturn and hardship they could be highly probable. The possibility of their occurring is heightened by several factors.

The actual and prospective continuing loss in power, status, and numbers by any social, ethnic, racial, or economic group almost always leads to efforts by that group to stop or reverse those losses. In 1961 in Bosnia-Herzegovina, the population was 43 percent Serb and 26 percent Muslim. In 1991 it was 31 percent Serb and 44 percent Muslim. The Serbs reacted with ethnic cleansing. In 1990 the population of California was 57 percent white and 26 percent Hispanic. In 2040 it is predicted to be 31 percent white and 48 percent Hispanic. The probability that, in this comparable situation, California whites will react like Bosnia Serbs is about zero. The probability that they will not react at all is also about zero. Indeed, that reaction has already begun with the overwhelming referenda votes against benefits for illegal immigrants, affirmative action, and bilingual education, and the movement of whites out of the state. As the racial balance continues to shift and more Hispanics become citizens and politically active, white groups may look for other means of protecting their interests.

In the 1990s, anti-immigrant nativist political parties emerged in several western European countries, often polled 20 percent of the vote, and in Austria and the Netherlands participated in governing coalitions. In America white nativism is likely to materialize not in a new political party but in a new political movement that will aim to influence the choice of candidates and policies by the two dominant parties. Industrialization in the late nineteenth century produced losses for American farmers and led to the formation of numerous agrarian protest groups, including the Populist movement, the Grange, the Non-Partisan League, and the American Farm Bureau Federation. Comparable organizations promoting white interests could emerge in the coming years. In 2000 in California, the *Economist* reported, "whites, who were once so generous to newcomers, are beginning to behave like a minority under pressure."[30] Whites nationally are likely to react in similar fashion.

As we have seen, the ending of ethnicity creates an identity vacuum that a broader white racial identity could fill. Espousal of such an identity could be legitimated by the racial identities embraced by minority groups in the 1980s after race was formally eliminated from national identity. Nativist whites could ask: If blacks and Hispanics organize and lobby for special government-sponsored privileges, why not whites? If the National Association for the Advancement of Colored People and La Raza are legitimate organizations, why not a national organization to promote white interests?

White elites dominate all major American institutions, yet millions of nonelite whites have very different attitudes from those of the elites, lack their assurance and security, and think of themselves as losing out in the racial competition to other groups favored by the elites and supported by government policy. Their losses do not have to exist in reality; they only have to exist in their minds to generate fear and hatred of the rising groups. In 1997, for instance, in a national survey of whites, 15 percent estimated that blacks were more than 40 percent of Americans, 20 percent estimated blacks as between 31 percent and 40 percent, 25 percent said between 21 percent and 30 percent. Sixty percent of whites thus saw blacks as more than 20 percent of the American people, although at that time, they actually constituted 12.8 percent. In similar fashion, 43 percent of whites estimated Latinos as more than 15 percent, although they actually were 10.5 percent. A majority of white Americans also see themselves as relatively poorer and blacks as relatively richer than is the case. As the sociologist Professor Charles Gallagher of Georgia State University explains:

Like it or not, middle-class and lower middle-class whites see themselves as a minority and have adopted a posture of being the victims.
Most of them feel they have no real culture. They might have a grand-
mother who was Italian and a grandfather who was French, but by
now they are so hybridized that they have no ethnic identity.

Ethnicity used to fill a vacuum as people assimilated. The only
thing that is filling the void now is victimization.[31]

The late 1990s saw the emergence of an academic movement that argued white consciousness was necessary for whites to understand other
races. "We want to racialize whites," one advocate said. "How can you
build a multiracial society if one of the groups is white and it doesn't
identify itself as a race." Whiteness no longer defines America; hence
whites should think of themselves as just another racial group, like the
others. The bulk of the authors of "whiteness studies" in the 1990s were
virulently anti-white. "Treason to whiteness," as one of them said, "is
loyalty to humanity."[32] Their views undoubtedly did not reach many
middle-class and working-class whites, but to the extent they did, they
could only reinforce the tendency of many whites to see themselves as a
victimized minority in a country that once was theirs.

The makings of serious white nativist movements and of intensified
racial conflict exist in America. Carol Swain probably overdramatizes
the possibility, but her eloquent warning deserves serious thought. We
are witnessing, she says, "the simultaneous convergence of a host of
powerful social forces." These include "changing demographics, the
continued existence of racial preference policies, the rising expectations
of ethnic minorities, the continued existence of liberal immigration
policies, growing concerns about job losses associated with globalization, the demands for multiculturalism, and the Internet's ability to enable like-minded individuals to identify with each other and to share
mutual concerns and strategies for impacting the political system."
These factors can only serve "to nourish white racial consciousness and
white nationalism, the next logical stage for identity politics in America." As a result, America is "increasingly at risk of large-scale racial
conflict unprecedented in our nation's history."[33]

The most powerful stimulus to white nativism, however, is likely to be the threat to their language, culture, and power that whites see coming from the expanding demographic, social, economic, and political roles of Hispanics in American society.

BIFURCATION:
TWO LANGUAGES AND TWO CULTURES?

The continuing growth of Hispanic numbers and influence has led some Hispanic advocates to set forth two goals. The first is to prevent the assimilation of Hispanics into America's Anglo-Protestant society and culture, and instead create a large, autonomous, permanent, Spanish-speaking, social and cultural Hispanic community on American soil. Advocates, such as William Flores and Rina Benmayor, reject the idea of a "single national community," attack "cultural homogenization," and castigate the effort to promote the use of English as a manifestation of "xenophobia and cultural arrogance." They also attack multiculturalism and pluralism because these concepts relegate "different cultural identities" to "private lives" and assume that "in the public sphere, except in those sanctioned displays of ethnicity, we must put aside those identities and interact instead in a culturally neutral space as 'Americans.'" Hispanics, they argue, should not espouse an American identity but embrace an "emerging Latino identity and political and social consciousness." They should claim and are claiming a separate "cultural citizenship" involving "a distinct social space for Latinos in this country."[34]

The second goal of these Hispanic advocates follows from the first. It is to transform America as a whole into a bilingual, bicultural society. America should no longer have the core Anglo-Protestant culture plus the ethnic subcultures that it has had for three centuries. It should have two cultures, Hispanic and Anglo, and, most explicitly, two languages, Spanish and English. A choice must be made "about the future of America," the Duke professor Ariel Dorfman declares: "Will this country speak two languages or merely one?" And his answer, of course, is that it should speak two. This is increasingly the case, not only in Miami and the southwest. "New York," Flores and Benmayor claim, already "is a bilingual city, as Spanish is daily currency in street life, in business, in public and social services, in schools, and in the home."[35] "Nowadays," Professor Ilan Stavans observes, "you can open a bank account, get medical care, watch soap operas, file your taxes, love and die in America without a single word 'en inglés.' In short, we are witnessing a reshaping of the nation's linguistic identity."[36] The driving force behind this Hispanization, the Mexican influx, shows no signs of weakening.

On July 2, 2000, Vicente Fox Quesada became the first opposition candidate to be elected president of Mexico in a relatively free and competitive election. Americans hailed this triumph of democracy south of their border. On July 4, 2000, in almost his first statement as president-elect, Fox advocated the end of controls on the movement of his people north. In the past, "Mexico's goal," he said, "has been to open an escape valve, allowing 350,000 young people to cross the border each year and washing its hands of any responsibility." The goal of the United States "has been to put up walls, police and soldiers to fight immigration. That can't work."[37] Hence, he argued, the two countries must move toward an open border, allowing for the unrestricted movement of money, goods, and people. What he did not say is that without border controls, goods would flow in both directions, money flow south, and people flood north. A decade earlier Vicente Fox's predecessor Carlos Salinas de Gortari had campaigned across the United States arguing for NAFTA because reducing trade barriers would reduce immigration: "You must take our goods or our people." Vicente Fox says: "You must take both."

Immigration, Jorge Castañeda said, before becoming Fox's foreign minister, "has not been a problem in binational relations but, rather, has been part of the solution to other, graver problems." These graver problems are, of course, Mexico's problems and, Castañeda argued, "forcing Mexico to deter its citizens from emigrating . . . will make social peace in the barrios and pueblos of Mexico untenable."[38] Mexico, in his view, should not try to solve its problems; it should export them.

If each year a million Mexican soldiers attempted to invade the United States and more than 150,000 of them succeeded, established themselves on American territory, and the Mexican government then demanded that the United States recognize the legality of this invasion, Americans would be outraged and would mobilize whatever resources were necessary to expel the invaders and to establish the integrity of their borders. Yet an illegal demographic invasion of comparable dimensions occurs each year, the president of Mexico argues that it should be legalized, and, at least before September 11, American political leaders more or less ignored it or implicitly accepted elimination of the border as a long-term goal.

In the past, Americans have taken actions that drastically affected the identity of their country without realizing that they were doing so. As we have seen, the 1964 Civil Rights Act was explicitly intended to remove racial preferences and quotas, but federal officials administered it so as to produce exactly the opposite. The 1965 immigration law was not intended to produce a massive wave of immigration from Asia and Latin America, but it did. These changes came about as a result of inattention to possible consequences, bureaucratic arrogance and subterfuge, and political opportunism. Something similar is happening with respect to Hispanization. Without national debate or conscious decision, America is being transformed into what could be a very different society from what it has been.

When Americans talk about immigration and assimilation, they have tended to generalize about immigrants without discriminating among them. They have thus hidden from themselves the peculiar characteristics, challenge, and problems posed by Hispanic, primarily Mexican, immigration. By avoiding, at least until 2004, the issue of Mexican immigration and treating the overall relationship with their neighbor as if it did not differ from that with other countries, they also avoided the issue of whether America will continue to be a country with a single national language and a common Anglo-Protestant mainstream culture. To ignore that question, however, is also to answer it and acquiesce in the eventual transformation of Americans into two peoples with two languages and two cultures.

If this happens and America ceases to be a "Babel in reverse" in which almost 300 million people share one and only one common language, it could become divided into a large number of people who know English and little or no Spanish and hence are limited to America's English world, a smaller number of people who know Spanish and little or no English, and hence can function only in the Hispanic community, and an indeterminate number of people fluent in both languages and hence much more able than the monolinguists to operate on a national basis. For over three hundred years, fluency in English has been a prerequisite to moving ahead in America. Now, however, fluency in both English and Spanish is becoming increasingly important for success in key sectors of business, academia, the media, and, most importantly, politics and government.

America appears to be moving in that direction through a process of creeping bilingualism. Hispanics numbered 38.8 million in June 2002, growing 9.8 percent since the 2000 census compared to 2.5 percent for Americans as a whole, and accounting for half of the American population growth in those two and one third years. The combination of sustained high immigration and high reproduction rates means their numbers and influence on American society will continue to increase. In 2000, 47 million people (18 percent of those age five and older) spoke a non-English language at home; 28.1 million of these spoke Spanish. The proportion of Americans aged five and over speaking English less than "very well" grew from 4.8 percent in 1980 to 8.1 percent in 2000.[39]

The leaders of Hispanic organizations have been continuously active in promoting their language. Starting in the 1960s, Jack Citrin and his colleagues observe, "Hispanic activists articulated the concept of language rights as a constitutional entitlement."[40] They pressured government agencies and the courts to interpret laws prohibiting discrimination on the basis of national origin to require education of children in the language of their parents. Bilingual education has become Spanish language education, with the demand for teachers fluent in Spanish leading California, New York, and other states actively to recruit teachers from Spain and Puerto Rico.[41] With one carefully planned exception (*Lau v. California*), the principal court cases involving language rights have Spanish names: Gutiérrez, García, Yniguez, Jurado, Serna, Ríos, Hernández, Negrón, Soberal-Pérez, Castro.

Hispanic organizations have played a central role in persuading Congress to authorize cultural maintenance programs in bilingual education, with the result that children are slow to join mainstream classes. In New York in 1999, it was reported that "ninety percent of the students in Spanish bilingual programs fail to make it into mainstream classes after three years, as guidelines stipulate they should."[42] Many children have spent as many as nine years in these essentially Spanish language classes. This inevitably affects the speed and the extent to which they achieve command of English. Most second- and subsequent-generation Spanish-speaking immigrants acquire enough English to function in an English environment. As a result of the continuing huge inflow of migrants, however, Spanish speakers in New York, Miami, Los Angeles, and elsewhere are increasingly able to live normal lives without knowing English. Sixty-five percent of the children in bilingual education in New York City are in Spanish classes, and hence have little need or opportunity to use English in school. And apparently, unlike the mothers in Los Angeles, in New York, according to the *New York Times*, "Spanish-speaking parents [are] generally more receptive to having their children in such classes, and Chinese and Russian parents more resistant."[43] A person can, James Traub reported,

> live in an all-Spanish-speaking world in New York. "I try to tell the kids at least to watch TV in English," [the middle school teacher] Jose García said. "But these kids go home and speak Spanish; they watch TV and listen to music in Spanish; they go to the doctor, and the doctor speaks Spanish. You can go down the street here to the Chinese fruit store, and the Chinese grocer speaks Spanish." Spanish-speaking children don't ever have to break out of their enclosed world: New York has high schools that are virtually all Spanish and even a bilingual community college. Only when students leave school do they discover that their English isn't up to the demands of the job market.[44]

Bilingual education has been a euphemism for teaching students in Spanish and immersing them in Hispanic culture. The children of past generations of immigrants did not have such programs, became fluent in English, and absorbed America's culture. The children of contemporary non-Hispanic immigrants by and large learn English and assimilate into American society faster than those of Hispanic immigrants. Quite apart from the controversies over its impact on students' academic progress, bilingual education has clearly had a negative impact on the integration of Hispanic students into American society.

Hispanic leaders have actively pushed the desirability of all Americans being fluent in both English and at least one other language, meaning Spanish. A persuasive case can be made that in a shrinking world all Americans should know at least one important foreign language—Chinese, Japanese, Hindi, Russian, Arabic, Bahasa Malay, French, German, Spanish—so as to be able to understand one foreign culture and communicate with its people. It is quite different to argue that Americans should know a non-English language in order to communicate with their fellow Americans. Yet that is what the Spanish advocates have in mind. "English is not enough," argues Osvaldo Soto, president of the Spanish American League Against Discrimination (SALAD). "We don't want a monolingual society."[45] The English Plus Information Clearing House, formed in 1987 by a coalition of Hispanic and other organizations, argued that all Americans should "acquire strong English language proficiency *plus* mastery of a second or multiple languages."

In dual language programs students are taught in both English and Spanish on an alternating basis. Their purpose is to make Spanish the equal of English in American society. "The dual language approach," two advocates argue, "has English-speaking children learn a new language while NES [non-English-speaking] children learn English. As children learn the languages, they also learn about the two cultures involved. Thus, all children are acquiring a second language and facing similar problems. This minimizes the inferiority felt by members of the minority group." In March 2000, in his speech "Excelencia para Todos—Excellence for All," U.S. Secretary of Education Richard Riley endorsed dual language education and predicted that by 2050 one quarter of the U.S. population and a larger proportion of young people would be Spanish-speaking.[46]

The impetus toward bilingualism is supported not just by Hispanic groups but also by some liberal and civil rights organizations, church leaders, particularly Catholic ones, who see a growing constituency of communicants, and politicians, both Republican and Democratic, responding to the growing numbers and slowly rising naturalization rates of Hispanic immigrants. Also of central importance are business concerns that appeal to the Hispanic market. Official English was opposed not only by "Univision, the Spanish-language television network that stood to lose viewers if students began learning English," but also by Hallmark, "which owns the Spanish language broadcast network SIN" and hence saw official English "as a threat to their ability to serve customers who speak languages other than English."[47]

The orientation of businesses to Hispanic customers means that they increasingly need bilingual employees. This was a central factor behind the 1980 official English referendum in Miami. As the sociologist Max Castro observes:

> Probably the single most resented consequence of the ethnic transformation was the increasing number of jobs in Miami that required bilingual skills. In this arena bilingualism had real, not just symbolic, consequences for non-Hispanic Miamians. But for many it also symbolized a reversal of the expectation that the newcomers must adjust to the dominant language and culture. Even worse, it conferred upon immigrants a labor market advantage based on a need that had been created by their own presence.[48]

Something similar occurred in the small town of Doraville, Georgia. The influx of Hispanics led the local supermarket owner to change his goods, signs, advertising, and language. It also forced him to change his employment policies. After making the switch, he said, "we wouldn't hire anybody unless they were bilingual." Then when it became difficult to find such people "we decided we had to hire people who are pretty much Spanish-only." Bilingualism also affects earnings. Bilingual police officers and firemen in southwestern cities such as Phoenix and Las Vegas are paid more than those who only speak English. In Miami, one study found, families that spoke only Spanish had average incomes of

$18,000, English only families had average incomes of $32,000, while bilingual families averaged $50,376.[49] For the first time in American history, increasing numbers of Americans will not be able to get the jobs or the pay they would otherwise get because they can speak to their countrymen only in English.*

In the debates over language policy, Senator S. I. Hayakawa highlighted the unique role of Hispanics in opposing English:

> Why is it that no Filipinos, no Koreans object to making English the official language? No Japanese have done so. And certainly not the Vietnamese, who are so damn happy to be here. They're learning English as fast as they can and winning spelling bees all across the country. But the Hispanics alone have maintained there is a problem. There [has been] considerable movement to make Spanish the second official language.[50]

The spread of Spanish as America's second language may or may not continue. If it does, this could, in due course, have significant consequences. In many states, those aspiring to political office might have to be fluent in both languages. Bilingual candidates for president and appointed national offices could have an advantage over English-only speakers. If dual-language education, that is, teaching children equally in English and Spanish, becomes prevalent in elementary and secondary schools, teachers would increasingly be expected to be bilingual. Government documents and forms could routinely be published in both languages. The use of both languages could become acceptable in congressional hearings and debates and in the general conduct of government business. Since most of those whose first language is Spanish will also probably have high fluency in English, English speakers lacking fluency in Spanish are likely to be at a disadvantage in the competition for jobs, promotions, and contracts.

---

* At some point in the bilingualization process, incentives give way to sanctions: in April 2003 the Canadian government announced that it was dismissing, demoting, or transferring two hundred senior civil servants who had not become sufficiently bilingual in English and French. *New York Times*, 3 April 2003, p. A8.

In 1917 Theodore Roosevelt said: "We must have but one flag. We must also have but one language. That must be the language of the Declaration of Independence, of Washington's Farewell address, of Lincoln's Gettysburg speech and second inaugural." On June 14, 2000, President Clinton said, "I very much hope that I'm the last President in American history who can't speak Spanish." On May 5, 2001, President Bush celebrated Mexico's Cinco de Mayo national holiday by inaugurating the practice of delivering the weekly presidential radio address to the American people in both English and Spanish.[51] On March 1, 2002, the two candidates, Tony Sanchez and Victor Morales, for the Democratic nomination to be governor of Texas, held a formal public debate in Spanish. On September 4, 2003, the first debate among the Democratic candidates for president was conducted in both English and Spanish. Despite the opposition of large majorities of Americans, Spanish is joining the language of Washington, Jefferson, Lincoln, Roosevelts, and Kennedys as the language of America. If this trend continues, the cultural division between Hispanics and Anglos will replace the racial division between blacks and whites as the most serious cleavage in American society. A bifurcated America with two languages and two cultures will be fundamentally different from the America with one language and one core Anglo-Protestant culture that has existed for over three centuries.

UNREPRESENTATIVE DEMOCRACY:
ELITES VS. THE PUBLIC

The views of the public on issues of national identity differ significantly from those of many elites. These differences reflect the underlying contrast, spelled out in Chapter 10, between the high levels of national pride and commitment to the nation on the part of the public and the extent to which elites have been denationalized and favor transnational and subnational identities. The public, overall, is concerned with societal security, which, we have noted, involves "the sustainability, within acceptable conditions for evolution, of traditional patterns of language, culture, association, and religious and national identity and custom." For many

elites, these concerns are secondary to participating in the global economy, supporting international trade and migration, strengthening international institutions, promoting American involvement abroad, and
encouraging minority identities and cultures.

The differences between a "patriotic public" and "denationalized
elites" parallel other differences in values and philosophy. Growing differences between the leaders of major institutions and the public on domestic and foreign policy issues affecting national identity form a major
cultural fault line cutting across class, denominational, racial, regional,
and ethnic distinctions. In a variety of ways, the American establishment, governmental and private, has become increasingly divorced
from the American people. Politically America remains a democracy
because key public officials are selected through free and fair elections.
In many respects, however, it has become an unrepresentative democracy because on crucial issues, especially involving national identity, its
leaders pass laws and implement policies contrary to the views of the
American people. Concomitantly, the American people have become
increasingly alienated from politics and government.

Overall, American elites are not only less nationalistic but are also
more liberal than the American public. This is revealed by twenty public
opinion surveys from 1974 to 2000, in which people were asked to identify themselves as liberal, moderate, or conservative. Consistently, about
one quarter identified themselves as liberal, about one third as conservative, and 35 percent to 40 percent as moderate. The attitudes of elites
were quite different. Surveys between 1979 and 1985 of elites in a dozen
occupations and institutions asked the same question used in the public
opinion surveys. The proportions of the elites in these groups identifying themselves as liberal were as follows, together with the public's
choice in 1980.[52]

Public interest groups	91%
Television	75
Labor	73
Movies	67
Religion	59
Bureaucrats	56

Media	55
Judges	54
Congressional aides	52
Lawyers	47
The public	25
Business	14
Military	9

Apart from business and the military, these elites were almost twice to more than three times as liberal as the public as a whole. Another survey similarly found that on moral issues leaders are "consistently more liberal" than rank-and-file Americans. Governmental, nonprofit, and communications elites in particular are overwhelmingly liberal in their outlooks. So also are academics. In a 1969 survey, 79 percent of faculty at high-quality schools considered themselves liberal compared to 45 percent of those at low-quality schools. In a 2001–2002 UCLA survey of 32,000 full-time faculty, 48 percent of faculty said they were "liberal" or "far left," 18 percent said they were "conservative" or "far right." The radical students of the 1960s, as Stanley Rothman had observed, had become tenured professors, particularly in elite institutions. "Social science faculties at elite institutions are overwhelmingly liberal and cosmopolitan or on the Left. Almost any form of civic loyalty or patriotism is considered reactionary."[53]

Liberalism tends to go with irreligiosity. In a 1969 study by Seymour Martin Lipset and Everett Ladd, the percentages of academics who identified themselves as liberal were as follows:[54]

Table 11.1

Liberalism and Religion of Academics

Religious Commitment	Religious Background		
	Jewish	Catholic	Protestant
Deeply religious	48%	33%	31%
Largely indifferent to religion	75	56	50
Basically opposed to religion	82	73	71

These differences in ideology, religion, and nationalism generate differences on domestic and foreign policy issues related to national identity. As the analysis in Chapter 7 makes clear, elites and the public have differed fundamentally on the salience of two central elements of American identity, the Creed and the English language. There is, Jack Citrin observes, a "gulf between elite advocacy of multiculturalism and stubborn mass support of assimilation to a common national identity."[55] The parallel gap between the nationalist public and cosmopolitan elites has its most dramatic impact on the relation between American identity and foreign policy. As Citrin and his colleagues concluded in their 1994 study, "the dwindling of consensus about America's international role follows from the waning of agreement on what it means to be an American, on the very character of American nationalism. The domestic underpinnings for the long post–World War II hegemony of cosmopolitan liberalism and internationalism have frayed, quite apart from the fact that the United States no longer confronts a powerful military adversary."[56]

Publics and elites have had similar views on many important foreign policy issues. Substantial and continuing differences, however, have existed on questions affecting American identity and the American role in the world.* The public is overwhelmingly concerned with the protection of military security, societal security, the domestic economy, and sovereignty. Foreign policy elites are more concerned with U.S. promotion of international security, peace, globalization, and the economic development of foreign nations than is the public. In 1998 the public and the leaders differed by 22 percent to 42 percent on thirty-four major foreign policy issues. The American public is also more pessimistic than its elites. In 1998, 58 percent of the public and only 23 percent of the leaders thought there would be more violence in the twenty-first century than in the twentieth, while 40 percent of the leaders and 19 percent of the public thought there would be less. Three years before

---

* The quadrennial polls of the Chicago Council on Foreign Relations starting in 1974 are an indispensable source of the views on foreign policy of both the public and foreign policy leaders. Unless otherwise cited the data used here come from these reports.

September 11, 84 percent of the public but only 61 percent of the leaders saw international terrorism as a "critical threat" to the United States.

Public nationalism and elite transnationalism are evident on a variety of issues. In six polls from 1978 to 1998, 96 percent to 98 percent of the foreign policy elites favored the United States taking an active part in world affairs, but only 59 percent to 65 percent of the public did. With a few exceptions the public has been much more reluctant than the leaders to use U.S. military force to defend other countries against invasion. In 1998, for instance, minorities of the public ranging from 27 percent to 46 percent and majorities of the leaders ranging from 51 percent to 79 percent favored the use of military forces in response to hypothetical invasions of Saudi Arabia by Iraq, Israel by Arabs, South Korea by North Korea, Poland by Russia, and Taiwan by China. On the other hand, the public is more concerned with upheavals closer to home. In 1998, 38 percent of the public and only 18 percent of the leaders supported U.S. military intervention if the Cuban people attempted to overthrow Castro, and in 1990, 54 percent of the public and 20 percent of the leaders favored the use of U.S. military force if Mexico were threatened by revolution. While the public is reluctant to support U.S. military action to defend other countries against invasion, a substantial majority, 72 percent, said the United States should not act alone in international crises without support from its allies, as compared to 48 percent of the leaders saying it should not do so. The public's backing for collaborative action was also reflected in their 57 percent approval of the United States taking part "in U.N. international peacekeeping forces in troubled parts of the world."

The public has been much less favorable than the leaders toward American economic involvement in the world. In 1998, 87 percent of foreign policy leaders and 54 percent of the public thought economic globalization was mostly good for the United States, while 12 percent of the leaders and 35 percent of the public thought it mostly bad or equally good and bad. In seven polls from 1974 to 1998, no more than 53 percent of the public and no less than 86 percent of the leaders supported giving economic aid to other nations. In four polls from 1980 to 1998, 50 percent to 64 percent of the public and 18 percent to 32 percent of the leaders favored cutting back economic aid. Similarly, in 1998, 82 percent of the leaders and only 25 percent of the public thought the United States should join other countries and "contribute more money to the IMF to meet world financial crises," while 51 percent of the public and 15 percent of the leaders thought the United States should not do this.

Despite the arguments of elites and government leaders in favor of reducing obstacles to international trade, the American public has remained stubbornly protectionist. In 1986, 66 percent of the public but only 31 percent of the leaders thought tariffs were necessary. In 1994, 40 percent of the public and 79 percent of the leaders were sympathetic to eliminating tariffs. In 1998, 40 percent of the public and 16 percent of the leaders thought that economic competition from low-wage countries was "a critical threat" to America. In the 1986, 1994, and 1998 polls, 79 percent to 84 percent of the public and 44 percent to 51 percent of the leaders thought that protecting American jobs should be a "very important goal" of the American government. In a 1998 multination poll, the American public ranked eighth among twenty-two peoples in its support for protection with 56 percent of Americans saying they thought protectionism best for the American economy, while 37 percent said free trade was. In April 2000, 48 percent of Americans said they thought international trade was bad for the American economy compared to 34 percent who viewed it positively.[57] During those years, both Democratic and Republican administrations pursued free trade policies reflecting elite preferences opposed by majorities or substantial pluralities of the American people.

Although Americans like to think of their country as a nation of immigrants, it seems probable that at no time in American history has a majority of Americans favored the expansion of immigration. This is clearly the case since the 1930s when survey evidence became available. In three 1938 and 1939 polls, 68 percent, 71 percent, and 83 percent of Americans opposed altering existing law to allow more European refugees into America. In subsequent years, the extent and intensity of public opposition to immigration varied with the state of the economy and the sources of immigrants, but high immigration has never been popular overall. In nineteen polls from 1945 to 2002, the proportion of the public favoring increased immigration never rose above 14 percent and was less than 10 percent in fourteen polls. The proportion wanting less immigration was never less than 33 percent, rose to 65 percent to 66 percent in the 1980s and early 1990s, and dropped to 49 percent in 2002. In the 1990s, large majorities of the public ranked large numbers of immigrants and nuclear proliferation as "critical threats" to America, with international terrorism coming in a close third. In the 1995–1997 World Values Survey, the United States ranked fifth (behind the Philippines, Taiwan, South Africa, and Poland) out of forty-four countries in the proportion, 62.3 percent, of its population that wanted to prohibit or put strict limits on immigration.[58] The people of this "nation of immigrants" have been more hostile to immigration than those of most other countries.

Prior to World War II, American business, social, and political elites often opposed immigration, and, of course, were responsible for the 1921 and 1924 laws restricting it. In the late twentieth century, however, elite opposition decreased markedly. Adherents of neo-liberal economics, such as Julian Simon and the *Wall Street Journal*, argued that the free movement of people was as essential to globalization and economic growth as the free movement of goods, capital, and technology. Business elites welcomed the depressing effect immigration would have on the wages of workers and the power of unions. Leading liberals supported immigration for humanitarian reasons and as a way of reducing the gross inequalities between rich and poor countries. Restrictions on the immigration of any particular nationality were viewed as politically incorrect, and efforts to limit immigration generally were at times thought to be inherently suspect as racist attempts to maintain white dominance in America. By 2000 even the leadership of the AFL-CIO was modifying its previously staunch objections to immigration.[59]

This shift in elite opinion produced a major gap between elite and public attitudes, and meant, of course, that government policy would continue to reflect the former rather than the latter. In the 1994 and 1998 Chicago Council polls, 74 percent and 57 percent of the public and 31 percent and 18 percent of foreign policy leaders thought that large numbers of immigrants were a "critical threat" to the United States. In these same years, 73 percent and 55 percent of the public and 28 percent and 21 percent of the leaders thought that reducing illegal immigration should be "a very important goal" for America. In a 1997 poll asking to what extent the federal government had been successful in achieving sixteen policy goals, "controlling illegal immigration" came in next to the last (reducing drug abuse), with 72 percent of the public saying it had been fairly or very *un*successful.[60]

The persistent and pervasive anti-immigration attitudes often reflect a door-closing approach: "It's great we got in, but any more will be disastrous." A 1993 *Newsweek* poll asked people whether immigration had been "a good thing or a bad thing for this country in the past." Fifty-nine percent said a good thing and 31 percent a bad thing. Asked whether immigration was "a good thing or a bad thing for this country today," the proportions were exactly reversed: 29 percent good, 60 percent bad. The American public was thus divided almost equally: one third for past and present immigration, one third against past and present immigration, and one third door-closers approving past immigration and against it now. Immigrants often are door-closers too. A Latino National Political Survey in 1992 found that 65 percent of American citizens or legal residents of Mexican, Puerto Rican, and Cuban descent thought there were "too many immigrants in this country," a skepticism also manifested in answers to a 1984 survey of Texas Mexican-Americans by Rodolfo de la Garza.[61]

The differences between elites and the public produced a growing gap between the preferences of the public and policies embodied in law. One study of whether changes in public opinion on a wide range of issues were followed by comparable changes in public policy showed a steady decline from the 1970s when there was a 75 percent congruence between public opinion and government policy to 67 percent in 1984–1987, 40 percent in 1989–1992, and 37 percent in 1993–1994. "The evidence, overall," the authors of this study concluded, "points to a persistent pattern since 1980: a generally low and at times declining level of responsiveness to public opinion especially during the first two years of the Clinton presidency." Hence, they said, there is no basis for thinking that Clinton or other political leaders were "pandering to the public." Another study showed that policy outcomes were consistent with the majority preferences of the public 63 percent of the time between 1960 and 1979 but dropped to 55 percent between 1980 and 1993. Somewhat similarly, the Chicago Council on Foreign Relations reports that the number of issues on which public and elite views on foreign policy differed by more than 30 percent increased from nine in 1982 and six in 1986 to twenty-seven in 1990, fourteen in 1994, and fifteen in 1998. The issues where the public-elite difference was 20 percent or more rose from twenty-six in 1994 to thirty-four in 1998. "A disturbing gap is growing," one analyst of these surveys concluded, "between what ordinary Americans believe is the proper role of the United States in world affairs and the views of leaders responsible for making foreign policy."[62] Governmental policy at the end of the twentieth century was deviating more and more from the preferences of the American public.

The failure of political leaders to "pander" to the public had predictable consequences. When government policies on important issues deviate sharply from the views of the public, one would expect the public to lose trust in government, to reduce its interest and participation in politics, and to turn to alternative means of policymaking not controlled by political elites. All three happened in the late twentieth century. All three undoubtedly had many causes, which social scientists have explored at length, and one trend, decline in trust, occurred in most industrialized democracies. Yet at least for the United States, it can be assumed that the growing gap between public preferences and government policies contributed to all three trends.

First, public confidence in and trust in government and the major private institutions of American society declined dramatically from the 1960s to the 1990s. The decline in trust in government is shown in Figure 11.1. As Robert Putnam, Susan Pharr, and Russell Dalton point out, on every question asked concerning confidence in their government, roughly two thirds of the public expressed confidence in the 1960s and only about one third in the 1990s. In April 1966, for instance, "with the Vietnam War raging and race riots in Cleveland, Chicago, and Atlanta, 66 percent of Americans *rejected* the view that 'the people running the

Figure 11.1

Public Confidence in Government

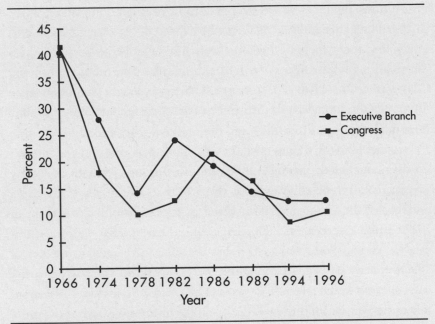

Percent expressing "a great deal" of confidence in the executive branch and Congress.

Source: Louis Harris Poll, 1996. Reprinted with permission from Joseph S. Nye, Jr., Philip D. Zelikow, David C. King, eds., *Why People Don't Trust Government* (Cambridge: Harvard University Press reprint, 1997), p. 207.

country don't really care what happens to you.' In December 1997, in the midst of the longest period of peace and prosperity in more than two generations, 57 percent of Americans *endorsed* that same view."[63] Similar declines occurred over these decades in the degree that the public had confidence in major public and private institutions. Beginning in 1973, Americans were asked every year or two whether they had "a great deal," "some," or "hardly any" confidence in the leaders of these institutions. Subtracting the "hardly any" responses from the "a great deal" responses produces a rough index of confidence. In 1973 the leaders of organized labor and television had negative indices of -10 and -3 respectively. All the others were positive, ranging from +8 for the press to +48 for medicine. By 2000 the confidence indices for the leaders of all these institutions, except two, had declined, most of them quite significantly. Five had negative indices. As might be expected, the changes were dramatic for the two policymaking branches of government, Congress dropping 25 points from +9 to -16 and the executive branch dropping 31 points from +11 to -20. In contrast, the two increases in confidence involved the nonelected institutions of government, the Supreme Court, rising from +16 to +19, and the military, from +16 to +28.[64]

Second, as many studies have shown, public participation and interest in the major governmental and private institutions of American society declined fairly consistently from the 1960s to the 1990s. Sixty-three percent of the adult population voted in 1960, but only 49 percent in 1996 and 51 percent in 2000. In addition, as Thomas Patterson observes, "Since 1960, participation has declined in virtually every area of election activity, from the volunteers who work on campaigns to the viewers who watch televised debates. The United States had 100 million fewer people in 1960 than it did in 2000 but, even so, more viewers tuned in to the October presidential debates in 1960 than did so in 2000." In the 1970s, one in three taxpayers allocated a dollar from their tax payments to the fund created by Congress to support political campaigns. In 2000, one in eight did so.[65]

The third consequence of the gap between leaders and the public was the dramatic proliferation of initiatives on major policy issues, including those relating to national identity. Initiatives had been an instrument of Progressive reform before World War I. Their use, however, then declined steadily from fifty per two-year election cycle to twenty in the early 1970s. As legislatures neglected the concerns of their constituents, initiatives regained popularity, beginning in June 1978, when 65 percent of California voters approved Proposition 13, drastically limiting taxes, despite the opposition of virtually all the state's political, business, and media establishment. This started a tripling of initiatives to an average of sixty-one per two-year election cycle from the late 1970s to 1998. Fifty-five initiatives were voted on in 1998, sixty-nine in 2000, and forty-nine in 2002. As we have seen, elite attitudes on issues such as racial preferences and bilingual education were effectively challenged by economic and political entrepreneurs such as Ward Connerly and Ron Unz, who used the initiative process to compel referenda on these issues. Surveying this record, David Broder concluded, "The trust between governors and governed on which representative government depends has been badly depleted."[66]

As the twentieth century ended, major gaps existed between America's elites and the general public over the salience of national identity compared to other identities and over the appropriate role for America in the world. Substantial elite elements were increasingly divorced from their country, and the American public was increasingly disillusioned with its government.

CHAPTER 12

Twenty-first Century America: Vulnerability, Religion, and National Identity

THE CREED IN AN AGE OF VULNERABILITY

American identity began a new phase with the new century. Its salience and substance in this phase are being shaped by America's new vulnerability to external attack and by a new turn to religion, a Great Awakening in America that parallels the resurgence of religion in most of the world.

With the end of the Soviet Union, the United States became the world's only superpower, holding a commanding lead in virtually every dimension of global power. September 11 demonstrated, however, that it also was more vulnerable to attack than it had been for almost two hundred years. The last time that something like September 11 happened in the continental United States was on August 25, 1814, when the British burned the White House. After 1815 Americans came to assume that security and invulnerability were inherent and lasting characteristics of their nation. Their twentieth-century wars were fought across thousands of miles of ocean, behind which they sat safe and free. Geographical security provided the context for how they defined themselves as a nation.

September 11 brutally awakened Americans to the new reality that distance no longer meant invulnerability. Americans found themselves in a new war fought on many fronts, the most important of which was right at home. After September 11, President Bush said: "We refuse to live in fear." But this new world is a fearful world, and Americans have no choice but to live *with* fear if not *in* fear. Coping with these new threats requires difficult trade-offs between the preservation of what Americans have assumed to be their traditional freedoms and the preservation now of that most important freedom which they had taken for granted: the freedom to be safe at home from violent enemy assaults on their lives, property, and institutions.

This vulnerability is central to how Americans define themselves in this new phase in the evolution of their national identity. In the past, when Americans spoke of their "homeland" they usually meant the country from which they or their ancestors had come to America. The new vulnerability made it clear to Americans, as Rachel Newman explained in Chapter 1, that America is their homeland, and that the security of that homeland has to be the primary function of government. Vulnerability gives new salience to national identity. Vulnerability does not, however, end the identity trends or conflicts of the previous half century.

As a result, at the end of the twentieth century the Creed was the principal source of national identity for most Americans. Two factors enhanced its importance. First, as ethnicity and race lost salience and Anglo-Protestant culture came under serious attack, the Creed was left as the only unchallenged survivor of the four major historical components of American identity. Second, the Creed had acquired renewed status, comparable to what it had in the Revolution, as the defining characteristic distinguishing America from the ideologies of its German, Japanese, and Soviet enemies. Hence many Americans came to believe that America could be multiracial, multiethnic, and lack any cultural core, and yet still be a coherent nation with its identity defined solely by the Creed. Is this, however, really the case? Can a nation be defined only by a political ideology?

Several considerations suggest the answer is no. A creed alone does not a nation make.

Historically, American identity has involved three other major components as well as the Creed. For the Creed to become the sole source of national identity would be a sharp break from the past. In addition, few nations have ever been defined only by an ideology or set of political principles. The most notable modern cases involve communist states where that ideology was used either to unite people of different cultures and nationalities, as with the Soviet Union, Yugoslavia, and Czechoslovakia, or to separate some people from other people of the same nationality, as with East Germany and North Korea. These creedal or ideologically defined states were the result of coercion. When communism lost its appeal and the incentive to maintain these entities ended with the Cold War, they all, except for North Korea, disappeared and were replaced by countries defined by nationality, culture, and ethnicity. The fading of communist ideology in China, in contrast, has posed no threat to the unity of a country with a core Han culture going back thousands of years and, to the contrary, has spurred a new Chinese nationalism. In France also, a set of political principles has been a component of national identity, but never the sole component. The French identify France as a nation going far back into history: "Notre ancestres, les Gaulois," and the religious component of their identity was reinforced by recurring wars with the English. The ideological component only came with the Revolution, and whether it should be accepted as part of French identity was hotly disputed well into the twentieth century.

People can with relative ease change their political ideologies. Communists have become fervent anti-communists; democratic liberals have embraced Marxism; socialists have adopted capitalism. In 2000, there could well have been in Dresden people in their eighties who in their youth were sincere Nazis, then became sincere communists, and after 1989 were sincere democrats. Throughout the former communist world in the 1990s, former communist elites regularly redefined themselves as liberal democrats, free marketers, or fervent nationalists. They did not abandon their identity as Hungarians, Poles, or Ukrainians. A nation defined only by political ideology is a fragile nation.

The principles of the Creed—liberty, equality, democracy, civil rights, nondiscrimination, rule of law—are markers of how to organize a society. They do not define the extent, boundaries, or composition of that society. Some proponents of a creedal concept of America argue that the Creed's political principles are in theory applicable to people everywhere. If this is the case, however, they cannot be the only basis for distinguishing Americans from other peoples. Democracy in various forms has spread to many more countries, and no significant other secular ideology exists. Russians, Chinese, Indians, and Indonesians who subscribe to the creedal principles share something with Americans but they do not thereby become Americans so long as they stay in their homeland, remain committed to that homeland and its culture, and identify primarily with their fellow Russians, Chinese, Indians, and Indonesians. They become Americans only if they also migrate to America, participate in American life, learn America's language, history, and customs, absorb America's Anglo-Protestant culture, and identify primarily with America rather than with their country of birth.

People are not likely to find in political principles the deep emotional content and meaning provided by kith and kin, blood and belonging, culture and nationality. These attachments may have little or no basis in fact but they do satisfy a deep human longing for meaningful community. The idea that "We are all liberal democratic believers in the American Creed" seems unlikely to satisfy that need. A nation, Ernest Renan said, may be "a daily plebiscite," but it is a plebiscite on whether or not to maintain an existing inheritance. It is, as Renan also said, "the culmination of a long past of endeavors, sacrifice, and devotion."[1] Without that inheritance, no nation exists, and if the plebiscite rejects that inheritance, the nation ends. America is "a nation with the soul of a church." The soul of a church, however, does not exist solely or even primarily in its theological dogma, but in its rituals, hymns, practices, moral commandments and prohibitions, liturgy, prophets, saints, gods, and devils. So also a nation may, as America does, have a creed, but its soul is defined by the common history, traditions, culture, heroes and villains, victories and defeats, enshrined in its "mystic chords of memory."

The Creed was the product of people with a distinct Anglo-Protestant culture. Although other peoples have embraced elements of this creed, the Creed itself is the result, as Myrdal argued, of the English traditions, dissenting Protestantism, and Enlightenment ideas of the eighteenth-century settlers. "The customs of the Americans of the United States are, then," Tocqueville said, "the peculiar cause which renders that people the only one of the American nations that is able to support a democratic government." Their democratic institutions are the product "of the practical experience, the habits, the opinions, in short, of the customs of the Americans."[2] "We the people of the United States" had to exist with common ethnicity, race, culture, language, and religion before we could "ordain and establish this Constitution of the United States of America." The Creed is unlikely to retain its salience if Americans abandon the Anglo-Protestant culture in which it has been rooted. A multicultural America will, in time, become a multicreedal America, with groups with different cultures espousing distinctive political values and principles rooted in their particular cultures.

September 11 dramatically symbolized the end of the twentieth century of ideology and ideological conflict, and the beginning of a new era in which people define themselves primarily in terms of culture and religion. The real and potential enemies of the United States now are religiously driven militant Islam and entirely nonideological Chinese nationalism. For Americans the religious component of their identity takes on new relevance in this environment.

AMERICANS TURN TO RELIGION

In 1984, the Reverend Richard John Neuhaus published a book, *The Naked Public Square: Religion and Democracy in America*, in which he decried the absence of religious influences, perspectives, and groups from American public life. A decade later the square was filling up rapidly. In the 1990s, religious ideas, concerns, issues, groups, and discourse underwent a dramatic resurgence, and the presence of religion in public life far exceeded what it had been earlier in that century. "One of the most striking and unexpected features of late-20th-century American life," Patrick Glynn observed, "has been the re-emergence of religious feeling as a major force in politics and culture."[3] By the end of the century, the religious resurgence had become sufficiently extensive to generate alarm among secularists who had thought history was on their side. "Religion is intruding in areas that are very disturbing," as the chairman of one secular humanist group complained in 2002.[4]

Two aspects of this development were of crucial importance. First, the numbers and proportions of Americans who were evangelical Protestants or who identified themselves as "born-again Christians" increased significantly in the latter decades of the century, as did the number and activities of evangelical organizations. Second, large numbers of Americans became concerned about what they saw as the decline in values, morality, and standards in American society and also came to feel personal needs for believing and belonging that secular ideologies and institutions did not satisfy. The interaction of the proselytizing and institutional dynamism of the Christian conservatives and the spiritual needs and moral concerns of large numbers of Americans made religion a key factor in public life and Christianity again a central feature of American identity.

The Rise of Conservative Christianity. Between 1990 and 2000, the fastest growing denominations in terms of adherents were the Mormons (with a 19.3 percent increase) and the conservative evangelical Christian Churches and Churches of Christ (18.6 percent increase) and the Assemblies of God (18.5 percent increase), followed by the Catholic Church (16.2 percent increase). The membership of the Southern Baptist Convention increased by 17 percent between 1973 and 1985, while mainline Protestant groups declined. The Presbyterian Church lost 11.6 percent of its members and the United Church of Christ 14.8 percent.[5] Simultaneous with the growth in adherents, the evangelical movement generated a huge number of organizations with differing creeds, purposes, and supporters, giving institutional form and strength to a subculture that appealed to 30 percent or more of the American people. The first effort to organize this constituency comprehensively was the Moral Majority, founded by Jerry Falwell in 1979. It faded in the late 1980s and was superseded by the Christian Coalition, established by Pat Robertson in 1989, which by 1995 reportedly involved roughly 1.7 million people. Other evangelical organizations included

Focus on the Family, with two million supporters, the American Family Association, with 600,000 members, the Promise Keepers, involving hundreds of thousands of men, and Concerned Women for America, which with 600,000 members was purportedly the largest women's organization in the country.[6] Christian media multiplied in number and circulation. By 1995, some 130 publishers were bringing out Christian books, and forty-five others were focusing on textbooks and other school materials. The sales of Christian books, marketed by seven thousand Christian book retailers, tripled to $3 billion a year between 1980 and 1995. Christian novels were best-sellers, with the *Left Behind* series by Tim LaHaye and Jerry B. Jenkins selling 17 million copies by 2001. Five million copies of Frank Paretti's three religious novels had been sold by 1995. As of 1995, there were more than 1,300 religious radio stations and 163 television stations. By the late 1990s, a huge network of Christian retail stores had come into existence selling a variety of products with Christian themes and doing billions of dollars' worth of business a year. Evangelicals also made up most of the members of the six hundred or more mega-churches with congregations of two thousand to twenty thousand that had emerged by 2002.

In the 1990s, extending their reach beyond their core constituency, evangelical organizations, most notably the Christian Coalition, moved into politics and elections. They focused on grassroots organizing, local issues, and raising funds in small amounts from large numbers of supporters. Numerous in the south, evangelicals traditionally voted Democratic. As they became more politically conscious, however, their partisan loyalties changed dramatically. Fifty-one percent of evangelicals voted for Jimmy Carter in 1976, but Ronald Reagan successfully appealed to them in 1980, and by 1988 they were solidly Republican. In 2000, George W. Bush received 84 percent of the votes of white evangelical Protestants who attended church regularly, and evangelicals made up perhaps 40 percent of his total vote.[7] Evangelicals had become a key force within the Republican Party.

The Christian Coalition and other groups were much less successful in appealing to the general public on particular issues. Their drive to remove Clinton from office failed in the Senate and was not endorsed by the American public. Their efforts to prohibit abortion and to promote other policies that challenged centrist opinion came to naught. Their substantial electoral activities in 1998, including the Christian Coalition's distribution of 45 million voter guides, did not produce the gains they had hoped for. Following that election, some conservative Christians were ready to give up politics and concentrate on promoting their values at the individual and community level. The "political mobilization of conservative Christians has stalled," Andrew Kohut and his associates concluded in 2000. Two years later, it was reported that many of them had become "disillusioned with the world of Caesar," and the Christian Coalition was but "a shadow of its former self."[8]

The limited success of the Christian conservatives in pushing particular items on their political agenda was overshadowed by their success in responding to the psychological and moral needs of Americans. They advanced a compelling argument that morality and values, which ultimately derive from religion and which had faded in the 1970s and 1980s, must be reasserted in social and political life. The "religious-conservative movement," as David Shribman said in 1999, was comparable to the civil rights and women's movements of the mid-twentieth century in the impact it has had on American thought, values, and discourse. "Religious conservatives have changed the American conversation. They have changed who participates in that conversation, they have changed the assumptions brought to bear on that conversation, they have changed the tone of that conversation, and they have changed the content of it. They may even eventually change the conclusion of it." Carole Shields, president of People for the American Way, a leading organization opposed to the Christian right, regretfully agreed. "They've changed the rules. What's bad is good, what's good is bad. All of what they have done changes how we think about democracy."[9]

The Public and Religion. The religious conservatives were able to bring religion back into the public square only because vast numbers of Americans were eager to welcome it there. In the 1980s, Americans increasingly and overwhelmingly focused on issues that could be interpreted as evidence of moral decay: tolerance of sexual behavior previously considered unacceptable, teenage pregnancy, single-parent families, mounting divorce rates, high levels of crime, widespread drug use, pornography and violence in the media, and the perception that large numbers of people were living the easy life on the welfare rolls funded by hardworking taxpayers. More broadly, there seemed to be feelings, first, that more meaningful forms of community and civil society had disappeared, and, as Robert Putnam demonstrated, Americans were bowling alone rather than coming together; and, second, that the prevailing intellectual mode, deriving from the 1960s, held there were no absolute values or moral principles and everything was relative. Hence educational and behavioral standards in schools had eroded, and America was, as Daniel Patrick Moynihan said, "defining delinquency down," and all forms of belief and behavior, short of the clearly criminal, could be tolerated.

Facing these challenges, Americans increasingly turned to religion and religious concepts to meet what Michael Sandel called "the vague but pervasive hunger for a public life of larger meanings."[10] As the sponsors of a 2000 poll on religion in American life concluded: "One message arrived loud and clear: Americans strongly equate religion with personal ethics and behavior, considering it an antidote to the moral decline they perceive in our nation today. Crime, greed, uncaring parents, materialism—Americans believe that all these problems would be mitigated if people were more religious. And to most citizens, it doesn't matter which religion is involved."[11] Between 1987 and 1997, Kohut and his colleagues demonstrate, increases of 10 percent or more occurred in the proportions of Americans who "strongly agreed" that there was no doubt God existed, that inevitably they would have to answer for their sins before God on Judgment Day, that God performed miracles in today's world, that prayer was an important part of their daily life, and that clear guidelines distinguishing good from evil apply to everyone everywhere. These increases took place in every major religious category: evangelical, mainline, and black Protestants, Catholics, and even seculars. In 2002, after the attacks on America, 59 percent of Americans believed that the apocalyptic prophecies of the Book of Revelation would come true.[12]

The need of Americans to secure moral reassurance and psychological security from religion took popular form in the extraordinary angel craze that swept the country in the 1990s. In 1993, 69 percent of Americans said they believed in angels, stimulating CBS to launch *Touched by an Angel,* which by 1998 had become one of TV's most watched programs, with 18 million viewers. It "touched a chord," one CBS executive accurately observed, "which America desperately wants."[13] Evangelical preachers and writers also responded to that want. As the sociologist James Davison Hunter has shown, the best-selling works of evangelical ministers such as James Dobson, head of Focus on the Family, were a "breathtaking" combination of modern psychology and traditional biblical teaching. The evangelicals sought "to co-opt psychology for their own purposes, making therapeutic concepts subordinate to biblical wisdom. The premise is that psychology provides tools that are, by themselves, theologically and morally neutral but useful all the same when linked to the truths of the Christian faith."[14]

The turn to religion was evident in the corporate world. "Driven by a search for meaning, unsatisfied by bigger paychecks or lofty promotions, and a desire to reconnect with their faith," it was reported in 1998, "white-collar workers are crowding breakfast prayer meetings and lunchtime Bible studies in conference rooms and university clubs." Reportedly the number of workplace Christian groups doubled to ten thousand between 1987 and 1997, at which time there also were an estimated one thousand Torah and two hundred Muslim study groups in the American corporate world. These groups, it was argued, provided an antidote to the "rampant ambition, cut-throat competition, and greed" prevalent in business.[15]

Major denominations also tended to return to or to adopt more traditional religious practices. In the 1970s, the country's largest Protestant denomination, the Southern Baptist Convention, with 16 million members, had moved in a conservative direction, endorsing "biblical inerrancy," the belief that the Bible is the very word of God, completely without error. In subsequent years, it affirmed its opposition to abortion and homosexuality and its approval of the submission of women to their husbands, the latter stance causing it to lose one of its more prominent members, Jimmy Carter. In 1999, the leaders of Reform Judaism overwhelmingly voted to approve many of the rituals and practices associated with Orthodox Judaism, including wearing of the yarmulke and expanded use of Hebrew. During the 1990s the number of Catholic dioceses permitting masses in Latin or in English and Latin increased from six to 131, or 70 percent of the total.[16]

By the 1990s, Americans overwhelmingly supported a greater role for religion in American public life. In a 1991 survey, 78 percent of the respondents favored allowing children on school grounds to say prayers, to have voluntary Bible classes, and to hold meetings of voluntary Christian fellowship groups. Some 67 percent favored the display of nativity scenes or menorahs on government property; 73 percent approved prayers before athletic games; and 74 percent opposed removing all references to God from oaths of public office. In this same poll, 55 percent said they thought religion had too little influence in American life, while 30 percent thought it had the right amount, and 11 percent (roughly equal to the proportion who say they are agnostic or atheist) thought it had too much.[17] Americans also viewed more favorably the role of churches in public affairs. In the 1960s, 53 percent of Americans thought that churches should not be involved in politics, while 40 percent thought it was acceptable. By the mid-1990s, the proportions had reversed: 54 percent thought that churches should speak out on political and social issues, 43 percent thought they should not.[18]

Religion in Politics. The activities of the religious conservatives and the sentiments of the public made religion a key element of American politics. In 2000, the moderate Republican governor of Kansas, Bill Graves, referring to the religious conservatives, said that in 1990 "you talked about economic issues 90 percent of the time and some of their kinds of things 10 percent of the time. Now you're talking about their issues 50 percent of the time and my kind of issues 50 percent of the time." Following the Christian conservatives and Republicans, Democrats and other groups rushed to enlist in the crusade for values, particularly "family values." "No wound has afflicted the Democratic Party so deeply," Joel Kotkin wrote in *The New Democrat*, "as its divorce from religious experience and community. In the name of opposing religious dogmatism, it has embraced a morally relative dogma that many Americans find shallow and uninspiring." A Democratic legislator agreed, "These are not issues that only Republicans should talk about. The Democrats cannot afford to ignore these things."[19] And they didn't. Beginning in 1988, the amount of space devoted to values and cultural issues in the platforms of the major parties increased dramatically (although still less than 10 percent of the total platforms), with the Democratic platforms of 1988 and 1996 devoting about twice as much space to these issues as the Republican ones. And in 1999 Al Gore declared that with respect to government support for religion, "The moment has come for Washington to catch up with the rest of America."[20]

Washington was already beginning to catch up with America. Following World War II, the idea had become widely prevalent that the Constitution required the total separation of government and religion. Governments should not provide support of any sort for religious groups or activities and should not allow religious groups to use public facilities. Federal courts held that it was illegal to invoke God in public school ceremonies, to require prayer in class, and to have Bible readings in school. Governmental agencies went to considerable lengths to avoid any form of engagement with churches and religious organizations. The latter were, in effect, excluded from forms of participation in society and public life open to most other private organizations.

The religious surge of the 1980s and 1990s challenged this exclusion of religion from public life, and Congress, the executive branch, and, most importantly, the courts began to respond positively. In 1971, in an opinion outlawing state subsidies for the salaries of parochial schoolteachers, the Supreme Court held that to be constitutional, government actions had to have a secular purpose, could not advance or inhibit religion, and could not create "excessive entanglement" of government with religion. With the appointments to the federal bench by the Reagan and first Bush administrations, however, the courts began to become more tolerant of religion in the public square. Signaling this shift, Chief Justice William Rehnquist argued in 1985, "The wall of separation between church and state is a metaphor based on bad history. It should be frankly and explicitly abandoned."[21] And slowly but surely the wall was breached if not abandoned. According to Kenneth Wald's careful analysis building on that of Joseph Kobylka, between 1943 and 1980, thirteen of twenty-three Supreme Court cases involving church-state issues were separationist in their outcome, eight were accommodationist, and two were mixed. Between 1981 and 1995, the balance shifted dramatically: out of a total of thirty-three cases, the decisions were separationist in twelve, accommodationist in twenty, and in one mixed.[22] The issues that came up were hotly contested by religious and secular groups, the battles taking place on three fronts.

First, to what extent could government provide financial or other support to educational and charitable activities carried out by religious organizations? Many private groups, some religious, some not, argued that churches and other religious organizations were peculiarly suited to cope with the problems of crime, drugs, delinquency, teenage pregnancy, single-parent families prevalent in America's inner cities. Responding to these arguments, in 1996 Congress passed and Clinton signed a welfare reform act with a "charitable choice" provision that authorized states to contract with religious organizations to support welfare and community development programs. This option, however, was not extended to other social programs, and bureaucratic resistance limited the funds that actually went to religious organizations. As governor of Texas, George W. Bush actively promoted charitable choice and government support for social services provided by religious organizations, including Christian ministries to those in Texas prisons. Reliance on faith-based organizations became a central theme of his presidential campaign, and in 1999 Al Gore endorsed this cause: "If you elect me president, the voices of faith-based organization will be integral to the policies set forth in my administration." "We must dare to embrace faith-based approaches that advance our shared goals as Americans," he told the Salvation Army.[23]

Ten days after his inauguration, President Bush set forth his program for federal support for religious groups performing societal services, including the creation of a White House Office of Faith-Based and Community Initiatives and centers in five cabinet departments to facilitate this program. Congress did not approve legislation to implement it and, as a result, in December 2002, Bush issued a broad executive order prohibiting federal agencies from excluding religious organizations from receiving funds for community programs and social services. "The days of discriminating against religious groups just because they are religious," Bush declared, "are coming to an end." His statement, according to the *New York Times*, was "infused with references to faith and was built around the idea that religion can and should occupy a central place in public and private life."[24]

The biggest step toward government support for religion, however, was the Supreme Court's 5-to-4 decision in June 2002 authorizing parents to use government-issued vouchers to pay for the tuition of their children in church-run schools. The decision was both hailed and denounced as the most important court decision on state-church relations in the forty years since it outlawed mandatory school prayer. The general proposition that seemed to emerge from this and other decisions is that government may give aid to religious organizations and use them, like other private organizations, to promote accepted public and social purposes, provided it does not discriminate among religious groups.

The second area of conflict and change concerned the use of government property or facilities, particularly schools, by religious groups or for religious purposes. In 1962 the Supreme Court had prohibited compulsory prayers in schools. This holding has not met any real challenge, but efforts have been made to explore what other religious activities might be permissible in government facilities. In 1983, Congress passed the Equal Access Act, requiring schools to permit the use of their facilities by religious groups on the same basis they did for secular groups. The Supreme Court's decision in 1990 upholding its constitutionality was followed by the proliferation of student religious clubs and prayer groups in the south and west. In 1995, the Clinton administration issued guidelines prohibiting school officials from preventing students praying or discussing religion at school. The Constitution, Clinton said, "does not require children to leave their religion at the schoolhouse door." Two years later, Adam Meyerson reports, the administration issued rules for the federal workplace that required "government supervisors to respect individual expressions of faith by federal employees. Christians will be able to keep Bibles on their desks. Muslim women will be able to wear headscarves. Jewish workers who want to honor their high holy days will have to be accommodated as much as possible. No one will be able to stop a federal worker from talking about or arguing about religion during coffee breaks and lunch." These actions led one conservative critic of Clinton to suggest that his "greatest legacy" could be "his leadership in reducing the bigotry against religion that has been expressed in recent decades by much of the Democratic Party and American liberalism."[25]

The third group of contentious church-state issues concerned government restrictions on religious activities and hence the free exercise clause rather than the establishment clause of the First Amendment. In the past, legislation prohibiting polygamy had been upheld against the Church of Latter Day Saints, while the right to object to compulsory military service on religious grounds was accepted. In the 1990s Congress acted to limit other government restrictions on religion. In 1993 almost unanimously it passed the Religious Freedom Restoration Act to overturn a ban on the use of peyote in Amerindian religious ceremonies. The Supreme Court, however, ruled that this was an unconstitutional restriction on the power of the states. In 2000 Congress passed, again almost unanimously, the Religious Land Use and Institutionalized Persons Act designed to prevent local zoning boards from forbidding the construction of churches in residential areas and to require prisons to provide religious services for their inmates.[26]

The Religious Election. Religion was a central factor in the 2000 presidential election and quite possibly more central than it had been in any other election in American history. Four aspects of its role are of special importance.

First, the election brought into power a president, an attorney general, and an administration determined to emphasize the importance of religion in American life and to expand significantly government support for activities by religious organizations that served useful social purposes. The creation in the White House of an Office for Faith-Based and Charitable Initiatives was an unprecedented action unthinkable in previous administrations. Religion became a legitimate element in the functioning of the federal government in a way in which it had never been before.

Second, the booming economy of the late 1990s and the absence of serious foreign threats opened the way for morality to play a central role in the political battles leading up to the election. In a March 1998 survey, 49 percent of the public said that America was confronting a moral crisis and another 41 percent said the decline in morality was a major problem. Asked in February 1999 whether they were more concerned with the moral or economic problems facing the country, 58 percent of Americans chose moral problems and 38 percent economic ones. Fourteen percent of the electorate in 2000 identified abortion as the number one issue; school prayer, government support for faith-based charities, and gay rights also were on the agenda. As one observer commented, in contrast to 1992, "It's no longer the economy, stupid." Concern with morality led to a focus on religion. In a poll taken immediately after the election, 69 percent of Americans said that "more religion is the best way to strengthen family values and moral behavior in America," and 70 percent said they wanted the influence of religion in America to increase.[27]

Third, the belief that religion was the antidote to moral decline naturally made the religious views and commitment of people highly relevant to how they voted. Denominational membership has always been related to partisan choice. In the mid-twentieth century, mainline Protestants tended to vote Republican, while Southern, mostly evangelical, white Protestants, large majorities of Jews, and lesser majorities of Catholics normally voted Democratic. In the last decades of the century white evangelical Protestants, as we have seen, shifted overwhelmingly to the Republican side, black Protestants voted overwhelmingly Democratic, mainline Protestants tended to move in the Democratic direction, while non-Hispanic Catholics shifted toward the Republicans. Voting in 2000 confirmed these shifting patterns.

Overlying these denominational differences, however, was a new development involving differences in religiosity. Beginning in the 1970s, the differences between the two major parties over religion and cultural issues increased significantly. Between 1972 and 1992, as Geoffrey Layman has shown, delegates to Democratic national conventions who attended church weekly or more never exceeded 40 percent and by 1992 had dropped below 30 percent. The percentage of Democratic delegates who said religion provided them with a great deal of guidance in their lives never went above 30 percent and in 1992 was 25 percent. The proportion of Republican delegates who regularly attended church, in contrast, rose from about 43 percent in 1972 to 50 percent in 1992, with 55 percent of the 1992 first-time delegates falling in that category. The proportion of Republican delegates for whom religion provided a great deal of guidance went from 35 percent in 1976 to 44 percent in 1992 and to 49 percent for first-time delegates. Democratic Party activists, in short, consistently had low levels of religious activity and commitment, while the religious involvement of Republican activists increased significantly over two decades. A new "great divide" over religion had emerged. "Religious conservatives from most of the major Christian traditions," Layman concludes, "but particularly among evangelical Protestants, tend to support the Republican party, while the Democratic party draws its support disproportionately from the ranks of religious liberals in the major faith traditions and secularists."[28]

These tendencies became dramatically evident among voters in 2000. Frequency of church attendance rivaled income and class, although not race, as a predictor of voting behavior (see Table 12.1). The differences between the more and less religiously committed existed within denominations. The proportions voting for Bush among the following groups were:

	More observant	Less observant
Catholics	57%	41%
White mainline Protestants	66	57
White evangelical Protestants	84	55

These differences coincided with growing differences between the party activists on cultural issues such as abortion, the Equal Rights Amendment, gun control, gay rights. Fifty-six percent of the 1996 Republican

Table 12.1

Votes for President, 2000

Frequency of religious service attendance	Bush	Gore
More than weekly	63%	36%
Weekly	57	40
Monthly	46	51
Seldom	42	54
Never	32	61

Source: Exit poll by Voter News Service reported by CNN at http://www.cnn.com/ELECTION/2000/epolls/US/P000.html.

and only 27 percent of the Democratic delegates said the government should do more to promote traditional values, while school prayer was endorsed by 57 percent of the Republican and 20 percent of the Democratic delegates.[29]

Fourth, the election also witnessed a totally new level of discussion of their religious beliefs by candidates for national office. Like these other trends, this too had been developing during the previous two decades. John F. Kennedy had tried to separate his religious beliefs from his political role, saying he favored "a president whose views on religion are his own private affairs." Jimmy Carter started a different pattern, articulating and explaining his religious beliefs, as did his successors except for the first Bush. "Ever since the election of Jimmy Carter in 1976," Wilfred McClay noted in 2000, "the taboo on the expression of religious sentiments by American political leaders seems to have been steadily eroding, to the extent that the presidential candidates in the current campaign have been invoking God and Jesus Christ at a pace not seen since the days of William Jennings Bryan." With the lone exception of Bill Bradley, all the 2000 national candidates responded to what they saw as the public's interest in and endorsement of religion by setting forth and discussing their own religious beliefs in an unprecedented way. Probably the most articulate candidate was Joseph Lieberman, who referred regularly to his religious convictions and his belief in God, cited the Old Testament, and argued that "there must be a place for faith in America's public life. As a people, we need to reaffirm our faith and renew the dedication of our nation and ourselves to God and God's purpose."[30]

The comments by the other candidates were notable because, unlike previous religious statements by political leaders, they expressed a belief not only in the abstract God of America's currency and civil religion but also in Jesus Christ and the Christian God. Candidates for the Republican nomination went on "national television to declare their belief in Jesus Christ." Asked who his favorite political philosopher was, George W. Bush said: "Christ, because he changed my heart. . . . When you turn your heart and your life over to Christ, when you accept Christ as the Savior, it changes your heart. It changes your life. And that's what happened to me." Steve Forbes said: "I do believe that Jesus Christ is my Lord and savior. And I believe God created the world." Like Bush, Orrin Hatch and Gary Bauer said Christ was the historical figure they most admired. Alan Keyes went them one better: "I don't admire Christ. I worship him. He is the living son of the living God." On the Democratic side, Al Gore described how he had spent a year in divinity school to explore "the most important questions about what's the purpose of life, what's our relationship to the Creator, what's our spiritual obligation to one another," and concluded that "the purpose of life is to glorify God. I turn to my faith as the bedrock of my approach to any important question in my life." Faced with a difficult decision, he would ask himself "What would Jesus do?"[31]

In this first election with a Jewish candidate for national office, the other candidates thus shifted from "God talk" to "Christ talk" and from generalized statements of religious piety to explicit affirmations of Christian identity. Implicitly they seemed to agree with the majority of the public that the United States is a Christian country. These statements marked a high point in America's religious surge and the reentry of religion into the public square. Whether religion would remain there is not certain. In an election where the voters are more concerned with the economy than with morality, candidates are more likely to profess their belief in jobs than their belief in Christ. Given the overall religiosity of Americans, however, no candidate for national office will want to appear irreligious. In addition, powerful forces outside the country are increasing the salience of religion for American identity and the likelihood that Americans will continue to think of themselves as a religious and a Christian people.

THE GLOBAL RESURGENCE OF RELIGION*

For almost three centuries religion was a declining factor in human affairs. In the seventeenth century, after more than a hundred years of bloody religious war, the leaders of Europe in the Treaty of Westphalia attempted to reduce and contain the influence of religion in politics. In the following century, Enlightenment thinkers exalted reason over faith as a source of human understanding. The nineteenth century saw increasing confidence that science would dethrone religion. Mankind, it was widely believed, was moving into a new phase of rationalism, pragmatism, and secularism. Religious beliefs, Freud argued (in *The Future of an Illusion*), were "insusceptible to proof . . . incompatible with everything we have discovered about the reality of the world." They were, in short, "delusions."[32]

Modernization and modernity appeared to be undermining religion, which was held to be a dark holdover from the past. Outside the United States fewer people in the Western world practiced religion, churches were increasingly empty, and religious beliefs and religious institutions came to play a minor and peripheral role in most Western societies. In the public arena, religion gave way to ideology. People, governments, social movements were defined by their identification with one of the major secular ideologies: liberalism, socialism, communism, fascism, authoritarianism, corporatism, democracy. These ideologies dominated political debate, shaped domestic and international alignments and conflicts, and provided models for how countries could organize their politics and economies.

* Portions of this section are taken from my essay "The Religious Factor in World Politics," Swiss Institute of International Studies, University of Zurich, 24 January 2001.

In the last quarter of the twentieth century, however, the march toward secularism was reversed. An almost global resurgence of religion got under way, manifest in almost every part of the world—except in western Europe. Elsewhere in countries all over the world, religious political movements gained supporters. And in these countries, the most religious people have not been elderly, but young, and not poor peasants but upwardly mobile, well-educated white-collar workers and professional people, epitomized by the female medical school students in Turkey who defied their secular government by wearing Islamic headdress to class. The two great missionary religions, Islam and Christianity, are competing worldwide for converts and gaining them, most notably in Muslim fundamentalist movements and evangelical Protestantism, which has had a tremendous impact in Latin America and is now influencing Africa, Asia, and the former Soviet world. An exhaustive quantitative report on global religion in the late twentieth century concluded bluntly: "the majority of countries in the world, with a majority of the global population, are in the midst of a religious resurgence. The resurgence is most strongly affecting former Communist countries of Eastern Europe, Central Asia, and the Caucasus, as well as Latin America, the Middle East, Africa, China, and South East Asia. . . . [In contrast] Within the developed world, religion seems to be on the decline in most countries, with the most notable exception being the United States."[33] The resurgence has been duly noted by scholars, who published books titled *La Revanche de Dieu, The Questioning of the Secular State*, and *Secularism in Retreat*.

The twenty-first century is beginning as an age of religion. Western secular models of the state are being challenged and replaced. In Iran, the shah's effort to create a modernizing, secular, Western state fell victim to the Iranian Revolution. In Russia, Lenin's secular and antireligious Soviet state has given way to a Russian state that terms Orthodoxy central to "the establishment and development of Russia's spirituality and culture." In Turkey, Ataturk's vision of a Westernized, secular nation state has been under challenge from an increasingly powerful Islamist political movement, and a religiously defined political party won an election and formed a government in 2002. Nehru's concept of India as a secular, socialist, parliamentary democracy came under attack by several political and religious movements and their affiliate, the BJP, scored an electoral victory and took control of the government. Ben-Gurion's image of Israel as a secular Jewish social democracy has been repudiated by Orthodox Jewish groups. In the Arab world, Kiren Chaudhry has shown that a "new nationalism" is emerging, fusing the formerly antagonistic old nationalism of the Nasser era and the now increasingly powerful currents of political Islam.[34] Where elections have been held in the Arab world, Islamist political parties almost consistently increased their strength around the start of the new century. Throughout the world, political leaders, as Mark Juergensmeyer put it, have been "striving for new forms of national order based on religious values."[35] The United States has not been alone in filling its naked public square.

The increased salience of religion to the identity of nations and peoples also meant the increased association of religion with conflicts in many parts of the world. These conflicts often have political or economic origins in disputes over territory or resources. Politicians, however, find it in their interest to exploit and intensify the religious passions. Once the conflict becomes focused on religious issues, it tends to become zero sum and difficult to compromise: either a temple or a mosque is built at Ayodhya; either Jews or Muslims control the Temple Mount. "Religion is often at the heart of conflict," Jonathan Sacks, chief rabbi of the United Hebrew Congregations of the British Commonwealth, observed in 2000. "Religion has been particularly acute in conflict zones such as Bosnia, Kosovo, Chechnya, Kashmir and the rest of India and Pakistan, Northern Ireland, the Middle East, sub-Saharan Africa, and parts of Asia."[36] The following year America also became a conflict zone.

MILITANT ISLAM VS. AMERICA

When Osama bin Laden attacked America and killed several thousand people, he also did two other things. He filled the vacuum created by

Gorbachev with an unmistakably dangerous new enemy, and he pinpointed America's identity as a Christian nation. Those attacks were the most destructive of a series of attacks dating back to the 1980s by Al Qaeda and other militant groups against American and other targets. Bin Laden justified these attacks in his formal declaration of war in February 1998 calling for a "jihad against the Jews and the Crusaders" and declaring that killing "Americans and their allies, civilians and military, is an individual duty for every Muslim who can do it in any country in which it is possible to do it."[37] America was targeted as the enemy because it was powerful, because it was Christian, and because it was deploying its military forces in the holy land of Islam and sustaining a corrupt Saudi regime, which was but "a branch or an agent of the U.S."[38]

Americans do not see Islam, its people, its religion, or its civilization as America's enemy. Islamic militants, both religious and secular, do see America, its people, its religion, and its civilization as Islam's enemy, and Americans can only view these Islamic militants similarly. This new war between militant Islam and America has many similarities to the Cold War. Muslim hostility encourages Americans to define their identity in religious and cultural terms, just as the Cold War promoted political and creedal definitions of that identity. George Kennan's 1946 words on the Soviet threat could well describe America's new Islamic enemies:

> We have here a political force committed fanatically to the belief that with [the] U.S. there can be no permanent modus vivendi, that it is desirable and necessary that the internal harmony of our society be disrupted, our traditional way of life be destroyed, the international authority of our state be broken.[39]

As the Communist International once did, militant Muslim groups maintain a network of cells in countries throughout the world. Like the communists, they organize peaceful protests and demonstrations, and Islamist parties compete in elections. They sponsor organizations pursuing legitimate religious, charitable, and civic goals, from whose members individuals are recruited for more violent purposes. The Muslim migrant communities in western Europe and the United States provide a nonthreatening and often sympathetic environment comparable to that provided by left-wing admirers of the Soviet Union. Mosques can serve as a base and a cover, and the struggles between moderates and militants to control them duplicate struggles between pro- and anti-communists in American unions in the 1930s and 1940s. President Reagan's reference to the Soviet Union as "the evil empire" has its parallel in President Bush's terming two Muslim states, Iraq and Iran, plus North Korea "the axis of evil." The rhetoric of America's ideological war with militant communism has been transferred to its religious and cultural war with militant Islam.

Two crucial differences, however, exist between the communist movements against Western democracies in the twentieth century and contemporary Islamist movements. First, a single major state supported the communist movements. Islamist movements are supported by a variety of competing states, religious organizations, and individuals, and Islamist political parties and terrorist groups have many different and often conflicting objectives. Second, the communists wanted to mobilize a mass movement of workers, peasants, intellectuals, and disaffected middle-class people in order to fundamentally change the democratic political and capitalist economic systems of Western societies into communist systems. Militant Islamist groups, in contrast, do not expect to convert Europe and America into Islamic societies. Their principal aim is not to change those societies but to inflict serious damage on them. Their activists do not go to union halls to urge workers to go out on strike but instead go underground to plan violent terrorist attacks on people, structures, and institutions.

In recent decades, Muslims have fought Protestant, Catholic, and Orthodox Christians, Hindus, Jews, Buddhists, and Han Chinese. In Bosnia, Kosovo, Chechnya, Kashmir, Xingjian, Palestine, and the Philippines, Muslims fought for independence or autonomy from rule by non-Muslims; in Nagorno-Karabakh and Sudan, Orthodox and Western Christians fought against Muslim rule. Superimposed on these local wars, however, has been a broader conflict between Islamist governments in Iran and Sudan, militant non-Islamist regimes (Iraq, Libya), and Muslim terrorist organizations, most notably Al Qaeda and its affiliates, on the one hand, and the United States, Israel, plus, on occasion, Britain and other Western countries, on the other. This series of conflicts escalated from a quasi-war in the 1980s and 1990s, to the "war on terrorism" after September 11 to a full-scale conventional war against Iraq in 2003. This escalation fueled the increasing hostility of Muslims, particularly Arabs, to the United States. What Americans see as a war on terrorism, Muslims see as a war on Islam.

The negative feelings and hostile attitudes of Muslims toward America gathered force in the 1990s and became dramatically evident after September 11. Muslims generally expressed horror and sympathy at what happened that day, but many quickly embraced theories that the attacks had been organized by the CIA or by the Israeli security agency, Mossad. They overwhelmingly opposed U.S. military action against Al Qaeda in Afghanistan and the Taliban regime that provided Al Qaeda with a base of operations. The sponsors of a survey of ten thousand respondents in nine Muslim countries in December 2001–January 2002 reported that the interviewees thought America to be "ruthless, aggressive, conceited, arrogant, easily provoked and biased in its foreign policy."[40] The following year a Pew Research Center poll found that 56 percent to 85 percent of the people in Egypt, Jordan, Indonesia, Lebanon, Senegal, Turkey, and Indonesia opposed the U.S. war on terror. Majorities had a "somewhat/very unfavorable" view of America in Turkey and Lebanon. In Egypt, Jordan, and Pakistan, majorities of the people had a "very unfavorable" view of America. Of the Muslim countries surveyed, only in Bangladesh and Indonesia did less than a majority of the people have an unfavorable view of the United States.[41]

The antagonism of Muslims toward the United States stems in part from American support for Israel. It also has deeper roots in the fear of American power, envy of American wealth, resentment of what is perceived as American domination and exploitation, and hostility to American culture, secular and religious, as the antithesis of Muslim culture. Attitudes such as these are propagated in thousands of the religious madrassas and other schools, supported by the Saudi and other Muslim governments, and by individuals and charitable foundations from

Southeast Asia to North Africa. The sermons delivered to the two million Muslims at the annual *haj* in Mecca in February 2003 were, the *Economist* reported, sermons that resound with "the clash of civilizations."[42] Muslims increasingly see America as their enemy. If that is a fate Americans cannot avoid, their only alternative is to accept it and to take the measures necessary to cope with it.

Recent history suggests that America is likely to be involved in various sorts of military conflicts with Muslim countries and groups, and possibly others, in the coming years. Will these wars unite or divide America? The historical experiences of both America and Britain, as persuasively analyzed by Arthur Stein, show that the degree of coherence or disunity wars produce, and hence their impact on national identity, are shaped largely by two factors. First, the greater the perceived threat from the enemy, the greater the unity of the country. Second, the greater the mobilization of resources needed to fight the war, the greater the disunity that is likely to occur, because of the different degrees of sacrifices that people will be asked to make.[43] These propositions have the following implications for recent American wars:

Level of Perceived Threat	Level of Mobilization	
	High	Low
High	A. Initial unity, developing disunity (World War II)	D. Sustained unity (War on Terrorism)
Low	B. Initial and continued disunity (Vietnam War)	C. Slowly developing disunity (Gulf War I)

A war (Box A) in which there is a high level of threat at the start produces a high level of unity, but if the war also involves high mobilization of people, goods, productive capacity, and taxes, disunity increases during the course of the war, as happened in World War II. A war (Box B) with a low level of threat and substantial mobilization produces considerable disunity from the start, which the government may attempt to reduce by lowering the level of mobilization, as the Nixon administration did by reducing the American forces in Vietnam and ending the draft. A war (Box C) involving low threat and low mobilization means initial low disunity but this is likely to expand if the war goes on for a long period of time. Finally, a war (Box D) with high threat but very low mobilization means the country will probably stay reasonably united in the pursuit of the war. This has been the situation with the post–September 11 "war on terrorism." The dramatic images of the planes going into the World Trade Center towers and their collapse embedded in Americans a profound and lasting sense of threat. The Bush administration then maximized national unity and support for the war by not asking people to pay higher taxes, endure shortages, or suffer any except minor inconveniences. With acute political sense it maintained support for the war by not demanding the sacrifices that some people thought it should demand in order to make the war a "real" war.

Recurring terrorist attacks on the United States without substantial mobilization are likely to maintain the salience of national identity and reasonably high levels of national unity. An extended war against one or more hostile states that had not attacked America directly and yet which did require high levels of mobilization could generate disunity and opposition. Throughout 2003, the Bush administration attempted to persuade the American public that the war in Iraq was part of the war on terrorism and belonged in Box D: Iraq posed serious threats to American security and the administration was responding efficiently and economically. Critics argued in effect that the war belonged in Box B: Iraq had not attacked America, posed no serious threat to America or its vital interests, and the war against it was requiring escalating resources in money (the $87 billion Congress approved in November 2003) and manpower (extended tours of duty in Iraq, call-ups of National Guard and Reserves), while American soldiers were being killed almost daily.

AMERICA IN THE WORLD: COSMOPOLITAN, IMPERIAL, AND/OR NATIONAL?

How Americans define themselves determines their role in the world, but how the world views that role also shapes American identity. In this new phase, three broad concepts exist of America in relation to the rest of the world. Americans can embrace the world, that is, open their country to other peoples and cultures, or they can try to reshape those other peoples and cultures in terms of American values, or they can maintain their society and culture distinct from those of other peoples.

The first, or cosmopolitan, alternative involves a renewal of the trends dominating pre–September 11 America. America welcomes the world, its ideas, its goods, and, most importantly, its people. The ideal would be an open society with open borders, encouraging subnational ethnic, racial, and cultural identities, dual citizenship, diasporas, and led by elites who increasingly identified with global institutions, norms, and rules rather than national ones. America should be multiethnic, multi-racial, multicultural. Diversity is a prime if not the prime value. The more people who bring to America different languages, religions, and customs, the more American America becomes. Middle-class Americans would identify increasingly with the global corporations for which they worked rather than with the local communities in which they lived and the people whose occupations or lack of skills tied them to those com-munities. The activities of Americans would more and more be gov-erned not by the federal and state governments, but by rules set by international authorities, such as the United Nations, the World Trade Organization, the World Court, customary international law, and global treaties and regimes. National identity loses salience compared to other identities.

In the cosmopolitan alternative, the world reshapes America. In the imperial alternative, America remakes the world. The end of the Cold War eliminated communism as the overriding factor shaping America's role in the world. It thus enabled liberals to pursue their foreign policy goals without having to confront the charge that those goals compro-mised national security and hence to promote nation building, humani-tarian intervention, and "foreign policy as social work." The emergence of the United States as the world's only superpower had a parallel im-pact on American conservatives. During the Cold War America's ene-mies denounced it as an imperial power. At the start of the new millennium conservatives accepted and endorsed the idea of an American empire and the use of American power to reshape the world according to American values.

The imperial impulse was thus fueled by beliefs in the supremacy of American power and the universality of American values. America's power, it was argued, far exceeded that of other individual nations and groupings of nations, and hence America had the responsibility to create order and confront evil throughout the world. According to the universalist belief, the people of other societies have basically the same values as Americans, or if they do not have them, they want to have them, or if they do not want to have them, they misjudge what is good for their society, and Americans have the responsibility to persuade them or to induce them to embrace the universal values that America espouses. In such a world America loses its identity as a nation and becomes the dominant component of a supranational empire.

Neither the supremacy assumption nor the universalist assumption accurately reflects the state of the early-twenty-first-century world. America is the only superpower, but there are other major powers: Britain, Germany, France, Russia, China, Japan at a global level, and Brazil, India, Nigeria, Iran, South Africa, Indonesia within their regions. America cannot achieve any significant goal in the world without the cooperation of at least some of these countries. The culture, values, traditions, and institutions of other societies are also often not compatible with reconfiguring those societies in terms of American values. Their peoples normally feel deeply committed to their indigenous cultures, traditions, and institutions, and hence fiercely resist efforts to change them by outsiders from alien cultures. In addition, whatever the goals of U.S. elites, the American public has consistently ranked the promotion of democracy abroad as a low-priority foreign policy goal. In accordance with "the paradox of democracy," the introduction of democracy in other societies also often stimulates and provides access to power for anti-American forces, such as nationalistic populist movements in Latin America and fundamentalist movements in Muslim countries.

Cosmopolitanism and imperialism attempt to reduce or to eliminate the social, political, and cultural differences between America and other societies. A national approach would recognize and accept what distinguishes America from those societies. America cannot become the world and still be America. Other peoples cannot become American and still be themselves. America is different, and that difference is defined in large part by its Anglo-Protestant culture and its religiosity. The alternative to cosmopolitanism and imperialism is nationalism devoted to the preservation and enhancement of those qualities that have defined America since its founding.

Religiosity distinguishes America from most other Western societies. Americans are also overwhelmingly Christian, which distinguishes them from most non-Western peoples. Their religiosity leads Americans to see the world in terms of good and evil to a much greater extent than others do. The leaders of other societies often find this religiosity not only extraordinary but also exasperating for the deep moralism it engenders in the consideration of political, economic, and social issues.

Religion and nationalism have gone hand in hand in the history of the West. As Adrian Hastings has shown, the former often defined the content of the latter: "Every ethnicity is shaped significantly by religion just as it is by language. . . . [In Europe] Christianity has shaped national formation."[44] The connection between religion and nationalism was alive and well at the end of the twentieth century. Those countries that are more religious tend to be more nationalist. A survey of forty-one countries found that those societies in which more people gave a "high" rating to the importance of God in their life were also those in which more people were "very proud" of their country (see Figure 12.1).[45]

Within countries, individuals who are more religious also tend to be more nationalist. A 1983 survey of fifteen, mostly European, countries found that "in every country surveyed, those who said they were not religious are less likely to be proud of their country." On average, the difference is 11 percent.[46] Most European peoples rank low in their belief in God and their pride in country. America ranks with Ireland and Poland close to the top on both dimensions. Catholicism is essential to Irish and Polish national identity. Dissenting Protestantism is central to America's. Americans are overwhelmingly committed to both God and country, and for Americans they are inseparable. In a world in which religion shapes the allegiances, the alliances, and the antagonisms of peo-

Figure 12.1

National Pride and the Importance of God

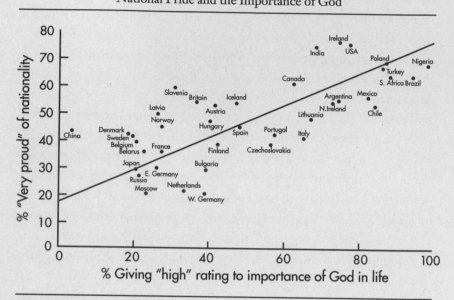

Source: 1990–1991 World Values Survey, Ronald Inglehart and Marita Carballo, "Does Latin America Exist? (And Is There a Confucian Culture?): A Global Analysis of Cross-Cultural Differences," *PS: Political Science and Politics*, 30 (March 1997), p. 38.

ple on every continent, it should not be surprising if Americans again turn to religion to find their national identity and their national purpose.

Significant elements of American elites are favorably disposed to America becoming a cosmopolitan society. Other elites wish it to assume an imperial role. The overwhelming bulk of the American people are committed to a national alternative and to preserving and strengthening the American identity that has existed for centuries. America becomes the world. The world becomes America. America remains America. Cosmopolitan? Imperial? National? The choices Americans make will shape their future as a nation and the future of the world.

NOTES

Chapter 1. The Crisis of National Identity

1. Luntz Research Co. survey of 1,000 adults, 3 October 2001, reported in *USA Today*, 19–21 October 2001, p. 1.

2. *New York Times*, 23 September 2001, p. B6.

3. Rachel Newman, "The Day the World Changed, I Did Too," *Newsweek*, 1 October 2001, p. 9.

4. *Los Angeles Times*, 16 February 1998, pp. B1, C1; John J. Miller, "Becoming an American," *New York Times*, 26 May 1998, p. A27.

5. Joseph Tilden Rhea, *Race Pride and the American Identity* (Cambridge: Harvard University Press, 1997), pp. 1–2, 8–9; Robert Frost, *Selected Poems of Robert Frost* (New York: Holt, Rinehart and Winston, 1963), pp. 297–301, 422; Maya Angelou, "On the Pulse of Morning," *New York Times*, 21 January 1993, p. A14.

6. Ward Connerly, "Back to Equality," *Imprimis*, 27 (February 1998), p. 3.

7. Correspondence supplied by Ralph Nader; Jeff Jacoby, "Patriotism and the CEOs," *Boston Globe*, 30 July 1998, p. A15.

8. Robert D. Kaplan, "Fort Leavenworth and the Eclipse of Nationhood," *Atlantic Monthly*, 278 (September 1996), p. 81; Bruce D. Porter, "Can American Democracy Survive?" *Commentary*, 96 (November 1993), p. 37.

9. Mehran Kamrava, *The Political History of Modern Iran: From Tribalism to Theocracy* (London: Praeger, 1992), p. 1; James Barber, "South Africa: The Search for Identity," *International Affairs*, 70 (January 1994); Lowell Dittmer and Samuel S. Kim, *China's Quest for National Identity* (Ithaca: Cornell University Press, 1993); Timothy Ka-Ying Wong and Milan Tung-Wen Sun, "Dissolution and Reconstruction of National Identity: The Experience of Subjectivity in Taiwan," *Nations and Nationalism*, 4 (April 1998); Gilbert Rozman, "A Regional Approach to Northeast Asia," *Orbis*, 39 (Winter 1995); Robert D. Kaplan, "Syria: Identity Crisis," *Atlantic Monthly*, 271 (February 1993); *New York Times*, 10 September 2000, p. 2, 25 April 2000, p. A3; Conrad Black, "Canada's Continuing Identity Crisis," *Foreign Affairs*, 74 (March/April 1995), pp. 95–115; "Algeria's Destructive Identity Crisis," *Washington Post National Weekly Edition*, 31 January–6 February 1994, p. 19; *Boston Globe*, 10 April 1991, p. 9; Anthony DePalma, "Reform in Mexico: Now You See It," *New York Times*, 12 September 1993, p. 4E; Bernard Lewis, *The Multiple Identities of the Middle East* (New York: Schocken, 1998).

10. Gilles Kepel, *The Revenge of God: The Resurgence of Islam, Christianity, and Ju-*

daism in the Modern World (University Park: Pennsylvania State University Press, 1994). See also Mark Juergensmeyer, *The New Cold War? Religious Nationalism Confronts the Secular State* (Berkeley: University of California Press, 1993); Peter L. Berger, ed., *The Desecularization of the World: Resurgent Religion and World Politics* (Grand Rapids, MI: William B. Eerdmans, 1999); David Westerlund, ed., *Questioning the Secular State: The Worldwide Resurgence of Religion in Politics* (London: Hurst, 1996).

11. Ivor Jennings, *The Approach to Self-Government* (Cambridge: Cambridge University Press, 1956), p. 56, quoted in Dankwart A. Rustow, "Transitions to Democracy: Toward a Dynamic Model," *Comparative Politics*, 2 (April 1970), p. 351.

12. Charles Tilly, "Reflections on the History of European State-Making," in Tilly, ed., *The Formation of National States in Western Europe* (Princeton: Princeton University Press, 1975), p. 42.

13. Peter Wallensteen and Margareta Sollenberg, "Armed Conflict, 1989–99," *Journal of Peace Research*, 39 (September 2000), p. 638.

14. Bill Clinton, quoted in *The Tennessean*, 15 June 1997, p. 10.

Chapter 2. Identities: National and Other

1. Karmela Liebkind, *Minority Identity and Identification Processes: A Social Psychological Study: Maintenance and Reconstruction of Ethnolinguistic Identity in Multiple Group Allegiance* (Helsinki: Societas Scientiarium Fennica, 1984), p. 42; Erik H. Erikson, *Identity: Youth and Crisis* (New York: Norton, 1968), p. 9, and quoted by Leon Wieseltier, "Against Identity," *New Republic*, 28 November 1994, p. 24; Wieseltier, *Against Identity* (New York: W. Drenttel, 1996), and *Kaddish* (New York: Knopf, 1998).

2. Ronald L. Jepperson, Alexander Wendt, and Peter J. Katzenstein, "Norms, Identity, and Culture in National Security," in Peter J. Katzenstein, ed., *The Culture of National Security: Norms and Identity in World Politics* (New York: Columbia University Press, 1996), p. 59.

3. Liebkind, *Minority Identity and Identification Processes*, p. 51, citing Henri Tajfel, "Interindividual Behaviour and Intergroup Behaviour" in Tajfel, ed., "Differentiation Between Social Groups: Studies in the Social Psychology of Intergroup Relations," *European Monographs in Social Psychology*, 14 (London: Academic Press, 1978), pp. 27–60.

4. Committee on International Relations, Group for the Advancement of Psychiatry, *Us and Them: The Psychology of Ethnonationalism* (New York: Brunner/Mazel, 1987), p. 115.

5. Ibid.; Jonathan Mercer, "Anarchy and Identity," *International Organization*, 49 (Spring 1995), p. 250.

6. Josef Goebbels, quoted in Jonathan Mercer, "Approaching Hate: The Cognitive Foundations of Discrimination," CISAC (Stanford University, January 1994),

p. 1; André Malraux, *Man's Fate* (New York: Random House, 1969), p. 3, cited by Robert D. Kaplan, "The Coming Anarchy," *Atlantic Monthly*, 273 (February 1994), p. 72; Albert Einstein and Sigmund Freud, "Why War?," in *The Standard Edition of the Complete Psychological Works of Sigmund Freud* (London: Hogarth Press, 1964), pp. 199–215.

7. Vamik D. Volkan, "The Need to Have Enemies and Allies: A Developmental Approach," *Political Psychology*, 6 (June 1985), pp. 219, 243, 247; Volkan, *The Need to Have Enemies and Allies: From Clinical Practice to International Relationships* (Northvale, N.J.: J. Aronson, 1994), p. 35; Francis Fukuyama, *The End of History and the Last Man* (New York: Free Press, 1992), pp. 162–77.

8. Mercer, "Anarchy and Identity," p. 242; Volkan, "The Need to Have Enemies and Allies," p. 231; Dennis Wrong, *The Problem of Order: What Unites and Divides Society* (New York: Free Press, 1994), pp. 203–4; *Economist*, 7 July 1990, p. 29. The form this discrimination takes may, however, be shaped by culture. Mercer, "Approaching Hate," pp. 4–6, 8, 11, citing Margaret Wetherell, "Cross-Cultural Studies of Minimal Groups: Implications for the Social Identity Theory of Intergroup Relations," in Henri Tajfel, ed., *Social Identity and Intergroup Relations* (Cambridge: Cambridge University Press, 1982), pp. 220–21; Robert Axelrod, *The Evolution of Cooperation* (New York: Basic Books, 1984), pp. 110–12; Michael A. Hogg and Dominic Abrams, *Social Identifications: A Social Psychology of Intergroup Relations and Group Processes* (New York: Routledge, 1988), p. 49.

9. Volkan, "The Need to Have Enemies and Allies," pp. 243–44.

10. Committee on International Relations, *Us and Them*, p. 119. See also Volkan, *The Need to Have Enemies and Allies*, pp. 88, 94–95, 103.

11. Michael Howard, "War and the Nation-State," *Daedalus*, 108 (Fall 1979), p. 102.

12. R. R. Palmer, "Frederick the Great, Guibert, Bülow: From Dynastic to National War," in Peter Paret, ed., *Makers of Modern Strategy from Machiavelli to the Nuclear Age* (Princeton: Princeton University Press, 1986), p. 18.

13. Linda Colley, *Britons: Forging the Nation, 1707–1837* (New Haven: Yale University Press, 1992), p. 5.

14. For statements of these distinctions, see William B. Cohen, "Nationalism in Europe," in John Bodnar, *Bonds of Affection: Americans Define Their Patriotism* (Princeton: Princeton University Press, 1996), pp. 323–38; Thomas M. Franck, "Tribe, Nation, World: Self-Identification in the Evolving International System," *Ethics and International Affairs*, 11 (1997), pp. 151–69; Anthony D. Smith, *National Identity* (London: Penguin, 1991), pp. 11–14, 79ff; Hans Kohn, *Nationalism, Its Meaning and History* (Princeton: Van Nostrand, 1965); Alan Patten, "The Autonomy Argument for Liberal Nationalism," *Nations and Nationalism*, 5 (January 1999), p. 1ff; Maurizio Viroli, *For Love of Country: An Essay on Patriotism and Nationalism* (Oxford: Clarendon Press, 1995), Introduction; Tom Nairn, "Breakwaters of 2000: From Ethnic to Civic Nationalism," *New Left Review*, 214 (November/December 1995), pp. 91–103; Bernard Yack, "The Myth of the Civil Nation," *Critical Review*,

10 (Spring 1996), p. 193ff; Volkan, *The Need to Have Enemies and Allies*, p. 85, who summarizes Orwell's view as nationalism is "patriotism turned sour."

A 2003 sophisticated empirical study provides convincing evidence that national pride comes in two forms: "patriotism," which is defined in civic terms as "self-referential," noncompetitive love of country, and "beliefs in the *social system* and *values* of one's country," and "nationalism," defined as "inherently *comparative*—and almost exclusively downwardly comparative." Rui J. P. de Figueiredo, Jr., and Zachary Elkins, "Are Patriots Bigots? An Inquiry into the Vices of In-Group Pride," *American Journal of Political Science*, 47 (January 2003), pp. 171–88. This study does not provide evidence as to how those who are patriotic feel when they compare, as they must, their country to other countries. Nor does it come to grips with the fact that in a globalizing world intercountry interactions and comparisons are increasingly frequent and unavoidable. Annual surveys now regularly rate countries on the extent to which they are free, have a free press, are corrupt, are productive, are globalized, provide effective schooling, and on other dimensions. How much national pride does a "patriot" have if his country ranks badly on most of these?

15. Horace M. Kallen, *Culture and Democracy in the United States* (New York: Boni & Liveright, 1924), p. 94.

Chapter 3. Components of American Identity

1. Gunnar Myrdal, *An American Dilemma: The Negro Problem and Modern Democracy* (New York: Harper, 1962), vol. 1, p. 3; Stanley Hoffmann, "More Perfect Union: Nation and Nationalism in America," *Harvard International Review* (Winter 1997/1998), p. 72.

2. Franklin D. Roosevelt, quoted in John F. Kennedy, *A Nation of Immigrants* (New York: Harper & Row, 1986), p. 3; Robert N. Bellah, *The Broken Covenant: American Civil Religion in a Time of Trial* (Chicago: University of Chicago Press, 2nd ed., 1992), p. 88; Oscar Handlin, *The Uprooted* (Boston: Little, Brown, 2nd ed., 1973), p. 3.

3. Wilbur Zelinsky, *The Cultural Geography of the United States* (Englewood Cliffs, NJ: Prentice Hall, 1992), pp. 23–24.

4. John Higham, *Send These to Me: Jews and Other Immigrants in Urban America* (New York: Atheneum, 1975), p. 6.

5. Herman Merivale, *Lectures on Colonization and Colonies Delivered Before the University of Oxford in 1839, 1840, and 1841* (London: Oxford University Press, 1928); Albert Galloway Keller, *Colonization: A Study of the Founding of New Societies* (Boston: Ginn, 1908).

6. John Porter, *The Vertical Mosaic: An Analysis of Social Class and Power in Canada* (Toronto: University of Toronto Press, 1965), p. 60, quoted in Jack P. Green and J. R. Pole, eds., *Colonial British America: Essays in the New History of the Early Modern Era* (Baltimore: Johns Hopkins University Press, 1984), p. 205; Zelinsky, *The Cul-*

tural Geography of the United States, pp. 13–14; Michael Lind, *Vietnam: The Necessary War* (New York: Free Press, 1999), pp. 122–23.

7. Ronald Syme, *Colonial Elites: Rome, Spain and the Americas* (London: Oxford University Press, 1958), p. 18; Alexis de Tocqueville, letter to Abbé Lesueur, 7 September 1831, quoted in George W. Pierson, *Tocqueville and Beaumont in America* (New York: Oxford University Press, 1938), p. 314.

8. David Hackett Fischer, *Albion's Seed: Four British Folkways in America* (New York: Oxford University Press, 1989), pp. 6–7; J. Rogers Hollingsworth, "The United States," in Raymond Grew, ed., *Crises of Political Development in Europe and the United States* (Princeton: Princeton University Press, 1978), p. 163.

9. Louis Hartz, *The Founding of New Societies* (New York: Harcourt Brace Jovanovich, 1964). For reconsiderations of the reconsiderations of Hartz's thesis of the pervasiveness and stability of the American consensus, see John Gerring, "The Perils of Particularism: Political History After Hartz," *Journal of Policy History*, 11 (1999), pp. 313–22; Leo P. Ribuffo, "What Is Still Living in 'Consensus' History and Pluralist Social Theory," *American Studies International*, 38 (February 2000), pp. 42–60.

10. George Peabody Gooch, *English Democratic Ideas in the Seventeenth Century* (New York: Harper, 1959), p. 71.

11. Frederick Jackson Turner, *The Frontier in American History* (New York: Henry Holt, 1920), p. 1.

12. Peter D. Salins, *Assimilation, American Style* (New York: Basic Books, 1997), p. 23; U.S. Immigration and Naturalization Service, *2000 Statistical Yearbook of the Immigration and Naturalization Service*, p. 18.

13. Richard T. Gill, Nathan Glazer, and Stephan A. Thernstrom, *Our Changing Population* (Englewood Cliffs, N.J.: Prentice Hall, 1992); Paul Johnson, *A History of the American People* (New York: HarperCollins, 1997), p. 283; Jim Potter, "Demographic Development and Family Structure," in Jack P. Greene and J. R. Pole, eds., *Colonial British America: Essays in the New History of the Early Modern Era* (Baltimore: Johns Hopkins University Press, 1984), p. 149; Congressman Glover quoted in D. W. Meinig, *The Shaping of America* (New Haven: Yale University Press, 1993), vol. 2, p. 222.

14. Campbell Gibson, "The Contribution of Immigration to the Growth and Ethnic Diversity of the American Population," *Proceedings of the American Philosophical Society*, 136 (June 1992), p. 166.

15. Richard Hofstadter, quoted in Hans Kohn, *American Nationalism: An Interpretive Essay* (New York: Macmillan, 1957), p. 13; Samuel P. Huntington, *American Politics: The Promise of Disharmony* (Cambridge: Harvard University Press, 1981), pp. 24, 23.

16. Benjamin Franklin quoted in Kohn, *American Nationalism*, p. 7.

17. Jürgen Heideking, "The Image of an English Enemy During the American Revolution," in Ragnhild Fiebig-von Hase and Ursula Lehmkuhl, eds., *Enemy Images in American History* (Providence, RI: Berghahn Books, 1997), pp. 104, 95.

18. John M. Owen IV, *Liberal Peace, Liberal War: American Politics and International Security* (Ithaca: Cornell University Press, 1997), p. 130 and passim.

19. Rogers M. Smith, "The 'American Creed' and American Identity: The Limits of Liberal Citizenship in the United States," *Western Political Quarterly*, 41 (June 1988), p. 226; Michael Lind, *The Next American Nation: The New Nationalism and the Fourth American Revolution* (New York: Free Press, 1995), p. 46.

20. Herbert C. Kelman, "The Role of Social Identity in Conflict Resolution: Experiences from Israeli-Palestinian Problem-Solving Workshops," paper presented at the Third Biennial Rutgers Symposium on Self and Social Identity: Social Identity, Intergroup Conflict, and Conflict Resolution (April 1999), p. 1.

21. George W. Pierson, *The Moving American* (New York: Knopf, 1973), p. 5; Jason Schacter, "Geographical Mobility: Population Characteristics," *Current Population Reports* (U.S. Census Bureau, P 20-538, 2001), pp. 1–2; Stephen Vincent Benét, *Western Star* (New York: Farrar & Rinehart, 1943), p. 3.

22. Alexander Mackey quoted in John Higham, "Hanging Together: Divergent Unities in American History," *The Journal of American History*, 61 (June 1974), p. 17; Gabriel A. Almond and Sidney Verba, *The Civic Culture: Political Attitudes and Democracy in Five Nations* (Boston: Little, Brown, 1965), p. 64.

23. Frederick Jackson Turner, *Frontier and Section: Selected Essays* (Englewood Cliffs, NJ: Prentice Hall, 1961), p. 37; Roger Finke and Rodney Stark, *The Churching of America, 1776–1990: Winners and Losers in Our Religious Economy* (New Brunswick: Rutgers University Press, 1992), p. 290, n. 3; Lord Dunmore quoted in Pierson, *Moving America*, p. 5. See generally Henry Nash Smith, *Virgin Land: The American West as Symbol and Myth* (Cambridge: Harvard University Press, 1978).

24. Arthur M. Schlesinger, Jr., *The Disuniting of America* (New York: Norton, rev. ed., 1998), p. 18.

25. Russell Bourne, *The Red King's Rebellion: Racial Politics in New England, 1675–1678* (New York: Atheneum, 1990), pp. 23–26; James D. Drake, *King Philip's War: Civil War in New England, 1675–1676* (Amherst: University of Massachusetts Press, 1999), pp. 36–37.

26. Alan Taylor, "In a Strange Way," *New Republic*, 13 April 1998, pp. 39–40; Jill Lepore, *The Name of War: King Philip's War and the Origins of American Identity* (New York: Knopf, 1998), p. 240; Eric B. Schultz and Michael J. Tougias, *King Philip's War: The History and Legacy of America's Forgotten Conflict* (Woodstock, VT: Countryman Press, 1999), pp. 4–5.

27. Richard Slotkin, *Regeneration Through Violence: The Mythology of the American Frontier, 1600–1860* (Middletown, CT: Wesleyan University Press, 1973), p. 79; Alexis de Tocqueville, *Democracy in America* (New York: Vintage, 1945), vol. 1, p. 352. Tocqueville follows this with an unusually vivid and emotional description of the forced movement of the Choctaws, which he witnessed in Memphis in 1831.

28. James H. Kettner, *The Development of American Citizenship, 1608–1870* (Chapel Hill: University of North Carolina Press, 1978), pp. 288–300; Peter H. Schuck and Rogers M. Smith, *Citizenship Without Consent: Illegal Aliens in the Ameri-*

can Polity (New Haven: Yale University Press, 1985), p. 63ff; Chief Justice John Marshall, *The Cherokee Nation v. The State of Georgia*, 30 U.S. 1 (1831).

29. Edmund Randolph, *History of Virginia* (Charlottesville: University Press of Virginia, 1970), p. 253; Thomas Jefferson, "The Autobiography of Thomas Jefferson," in Adrienne Koch and William Peden, eds., *The Life and Selected Writings of Thomas Jefferson* (New York: Modern Library, 1944), p. 51; John Patrick Doggins, *On Hallowed Ground: Abraham Lincoln and the Foundations of American History* (New Haven: Yale University Press, 2000), pp. 175–76.

30. Reginald Horsman, *Race and Manifest Destiny: The Origins of American Racial Anglo-Saxonism* (Cambridge: Harvard University Press, 1981), p. 134.

31. Lind, *Next American Nation*, pp. 43, 68; Smith, " 'The American Creed' and American Identity," pp. 233, 235; Horsman, *Race and Manifest Destiny*; Hazel M. McFerson, *The Racial Dimension of American Overseas Colonial Policy* (Westport, CT: Greenwood Press, 1997).

32. David Heer, *Immigration in America's Future: Social Science Findings and the Policy Debate* (Boulder: Westview Press, 1996), p. 37.

33. Justice Stephen J. Field, *Chae Chang Ping v. United States*, 130 U.S. 581 (1889); Smith, " 'The American Creed' and American Identity," p. 244.

34. Philip Gleason, "American Identity and Americanization," in Stephen Thernstrom, ed., *Harvard Encyclopedia of American Ethnic Groups* (Cambridge: Belknap Press of Harvard University Press, 1981), p. 46.

35. Immigration Restriction League, quoted in Maldwyn Allen Jones, *American Immigration* (Chicago: University of Chicago Press, 2nd ed., 1992), p. 222.

36. William S. Bernard, "Immigration: History of U.S. Policy," in Thernstrom, ed., *Harvard Encyclopedia of American Ethnic Groups*, p. 493.

37. Gleason, "American Identity and Americanization," p. 47.

Chapter 4. Anglo-Protestant Culture

1. Alden T. Vaughan, "Seventeenth Century Origins of American Culture," in Stanley Coben and Lorman Ratner, eds., *The Development of an American Culture* (New York: St. Martin's, 2nd ed., 1983), pp. 30–32; Arthur M. Schlesinger, Jr., *The Disuniting of America* (New York: Norton, rev. ed., 1998), p. 34.

2. James A. Morone, "The Struggle for American Culture," *PS: Political Science and Politics*, 29 (September 1996), pp. 428–29; John Higham, *Send These to Me: Jews and Other Immigrants in Urban America* (New York: Atheneum, 1975), p. 180.

3. Samuel P. Huntington, *Political Order in Changing Societies* (New Haven: Yale University Press, 1968), p. 93ff.

4. Anthony D. Smith, *National Identity* (Reno: University of Nevada Press, 1991), p. 150; Michael Novak, *Further Reflections on Ethnicity* (Middletown, PA: Jednota Press, 1977), p. 26; Will Kymlicka, *Multicultural Citizenship: A Liberal Theory of Minority Rights* (New York: Oxford University Press, 1995), p. 14, who levels

the same charge against Canada and Australia; Robert N. Bellah, *The Broken Covenant: American Civil Religion in Time of Trial* (Chicago: University of Chicago Press, 1992), p. 93, quoting from Harold Cruse, *The Crisis of the Negro Intellectual* (New York: Morrow, 1967), p. 256.

5. Benjamin C. Schwarz, "The Diversity Myth," *Atlantic Monthly*, 275 (May 1995), p. 62.

6. Adrian Hastings, *The Construction of Nationhood: Ethnicity, Religion and Nationalism* (New York: Cambridge University Press, 1997), p. 187, and Chapter 8 generally; Samuel P. Huntington, *American Politics: The Promise of Disharmony* (Cambridge: Harvard University Press, 1981), p. 154; Philip Schaff, *America: A Sketch of Its Political, Social, and Religious Character* (Cambridge: Harvard University Press, 1961), p. 72.

7. Louis Hartz, *The Liberal Tradition in America* (New York: Harcourt, Brace, 1955); William Lee Miller, "Religion and Political Attitudes," in James Ward Smith and A. Leland Jamison, eds., *Religious Perspectives in American Culture* (Princeton: Princeton University Press, 1961), p. 85; Huntington, *American Politics: The Promise of Disharmony*, p. 154.

8. Jon Butler, *Awash in a Sea of Faith: Christianizing the American People* (Cambridge: Harvard University Press, 1990), pp. 38–66.

9. Sacvan Bercovitch, *The Puritan Origins of the American Self* (New Haven: Yale University Press, 1975), p. 144ff; Hastings, *The Construction of Nationhood*, pp. 74–75; Morone, "The Struggle for American Culture," p. 426.

10. Edmund Burke, *Reflections on the Revolution in France* (Chicago: Regnery, 1955), pp. 125–26, and "Speech on Moving Resolutions for Conciliation with the Colonies," in Ross J. S. Hoffman and Paul Levack, eds., *Burke's Politics* (New York: Knopf, 1949), pp. 69–71.

11. Morone, "The Struggle for American Culture," p. 429; Alexis de Tocqueville, *Democracy in America* (New York: Vintage, 1945), vol. 2, p. 32; Huntington, *American Politics*, p. 153; James Bryce, *The American Commonwealth* (London: Macmillan, 1891), vol. 2, p. 599.

12. David Hackett Fischer, *Albion's Seed: Four British Folkways in America* (New York: Oxford University Press, 1989), p. 787; Kevin P. Phillips, *The Cousins' Wars: Religion, Politics, and the Triumph of Anglo-America* (New York: Basic Books, 1999), p. xv and passim.

13. John C. Green et al., *Religion and the Culture Wars: Dispatches from the Front* (Lanham, MD: Rowman & Littlefield, 1996), pp. 243–44.

14. George M. Marsden, *Fundamentalism and American Culture: The Shaping of Twentieth Century Evangelicalism, 1870–1925* (New York: Oxford University Press, 1982), p. 6; Garry Wills, *Under God: Religion and American Politics* (New York: Simon & Schuster, 1990), p. 19.

15. Nathan O. Hatch, *The Democratization of American Christianity* (New Haven: Yale University Press, 1989), p. 4; William McLoughlin, ed., *The American Evangelicals, 1800–1900: An Anthology* (New York: Harper & Row, 1968), p. 26, quoted in Bellah, *Broken Covenant*, p. 46.

16. George Gallup, Jr., and Jim Castelli, *The People's Religion: American Faith in the 90's* (New York: Macmillan, 1989), p. 93. For other estimates, see Cullen Murphy, "Protestantism and the Evangelicals," *The Wilson Quarterly* (Autumn 1981), p. 107ff; Marsden, *Fundamentalism and American Culture*, p. 228; *Boston Sunday Globe*, 20 February 2000, p. A1.

17. Alexis de Tocqueville, *Democracy in America* (New York: Vintage, 1954), vol. 1, p. 409; Bryce, *American Commonwealth*, vol. 2, pp. 417–18; Gunnar Myrdal, *An American Dilemma* (New York: Harper, 1944), vol. 1, p. 3; Daniel Bell, "The End of American Exceptionalism," in Nathan Glazer and Irving Kristol, eds., *The American Commonwealth 1976* (New York: Basic Books, 1976), p. 209; Seymour Martin Lipset, *American Exceptionalism: A Double-Edged Sword* (New York: Norton, 1996), pp. 63–64.

18. Seymour Martin Lipset, *The First New Nation: The United States in Historical and Comparative Perspective* (New York: Norton, 1973), p. 103.

19. William Lee Miller, "Religion and Political Attitudes," in James Ward Smith and A. Leland Jamison, eds., *Religion in American Life* (Princeton, NJ: Princeton University Press, 1961), pp. 98–99; John Higham, "Hanging Together: Divergent Unities in American History," *Journal of American History*, 61 (June 1974), p. 15; Jeff Spinner, *The Boundaries of Citizenship* (Baltimore: Johns Hopkins University Press, 1994), pp. 79–80.

20. Lipset, *American Exceptionalism*, pp. 63–64.

21. Francis J. Grund, *The Americans in Their Moral, Social and Political Relations* (New York: Johnson Reprint, 1968), pp. 355–56.

22. Geert Hofstede, *Culture's Consequences: International Differences in Work-Related Values* (Beverly Hills: Sage, 1980), p. 222; Henry van Loon, "How Cadets Stack Up," *Armed Forces Journal International* (March 1997), pp. 18–20; Ronald Inglehart et al., *World Values Survey and European Values Survey 1995–1997* (Ann Arbor, MI: Inter-University Consortium for Political and Social Research, 2000); Lipset, *American Exceptionalism*, p. 218; Charles Hampden-Turner and Alfons Trompenaars, *The Seven Cultures of Capitalism* (New York: Doubleday, 1993), pp. 48, 57. See also Harry C. Triandis, "Cross-Cultural Studies of Individualism and Collectivism," *Nebraska Symposium on Motivation 1989* (Lincoln: University of Nebraska Press, 1990), vol. 37, pp. 41–133.

23. Bellah, *Broken Covenant*, p. 76; John G. Cawelti, *Apostles of the Self-Made Man* (Chicago: University of Chicago Press, 1965), p. 39ff; Bill Clinton, remarks to Democratic Leadership Council, 1993, quoted in Jennifer L. Hochschild, *Facing Up to the American Dream*, p. 18.

24. Judith N. Shklar, *American Citizenship: The Quest for Inclusion* (Cambridge: Harvard University Press, 1991), pp. 1–3, 67, 72–75.

25. Schaff, *America*, p. 29; Michel Chevalier, *Society, Manners and Politics in the United States; Letters on North America* (Gloucester, MA: Peter Smith, 1967), pp. 267–68.

26. Roger M. Smith, "The 'American Creed' and American Identity: The Limits

of Liberal Citizenship in the United States," *Western Political Quarterly*, 41 (June 1988), p. 239, citing Eric Foner, *Free Soil, Free Labor, Free Men: The Ideology of the Republican Party Before the Civil War* (New York: Oxford University Press, 1970); Cawelti, *Apostles of the Self-Made Man*, esp. p. 39ff.

27. Cindy S. Aron, *Working at Play: A History of Vacations in the United States* (New York: Oxford University Press, 1999), p. 236; International Labor Organization, study, September 1999, cited in *The Daily Yomiuri*, 7 September 1999, p. 12; *Prospect*, 49 (February 2000), p. 7, citing *Boston Review*, December 1999–January 2000.

28. Daniel Yankelovich, "What's Wrong—And What's Right—With U.S. Workforce Performance," *The Public Perspective*, 3 (May/June 1992), pp. 12–14 and the accompanying insert; "American Enterprise Public Opinion and Demographic Report"; Jack Citrin et al., "Is American Nationalism Changing? Implications for Foreign Policy," *International Studies Quarterly*, 38 (March 1994), p. 13.

29. *New York Times*, 9 May 1999, p. WK5; Shklar, *American Citizenship*, p. 98.

30. Schaff, *America*, p. 29; Hochschild, *Facing Up to the American Dream*, pp. 228–29; *New York Times*, 11 February 1999, p. A1.

31. Bellah, *Broken Covenant*, p. 179; Wills, *Under God*, p. 25.

32. Alan Heimert, *Religion and the American Mind: From the Great Awakening to the Revolution* (Cambridge: Harvard University Press, 1966), pp. 14, 19; Ruth H. Bloch, *Visionary Republic: Millennial Themes in American Thought*, 1756–1800 (Cambridge: Cambridge University Press, 1985), p. xiv.

33. John Adams, letter to Hezekiah Niles, 13 February 1818, in Adrienne Koch and William Peden, eds., *The Selected Writings of John and John Quincy Adams* (New York: Knopf, 1946), p. 203.

34. Bellah, *Broken Covenant*, pp. 44–45.

35. William W. Sweet, *Revivalism in America: Its Origin, Growth, and Decline* (New York: Scribners, 1944), pp. 159–61.

36. Alan P. Grimes, *The Puritan Ethic and Woman Suffrage* (New York: Oxford University Press, 1967), p. 102.

37. Sidney Ahlstrom, "National Trauma and the Changing Religious Values," *Daedalus*, 107 (Winter 1978), pp. 19–20.

38. Al Haber quoted in Edward J. Bacciocco, Jr., *The New Left in America* (Stanford: Hoover Institution Press, 1974), pp. 228–29.

39. Walter A. McDougall, *Promised Land, Crusader State: The American Encounter with the World Since 1776* (Boston: Houghton Mifflin, 1997); and for a somewhat different view, James Kurth, "The Protestant Reformation and American Foreign Policy," *Orbis*, 42 (Spring 1998), pp. 221–39.

Chapter 5. Religion and Christianity

1. *Newsweek*, 8 July 2002, pp. 23–25; *New York Times*, 27 June 2002, pp. A1, A21.

2. *New York Times*, 27 June 2002, p. A21, 1 July 2002, p. A8, 1 March 2003, p. A2.

3. *New York Times*, 29 November 1999, p. A14.

4. Gaines M. Foster, "A Christian Nation: Signs of a Covenant," in John Bodnar, ed., *Bonds of Affection: Americans Define Their Patriotism* (Princeton: Princeton University Press, 1996), pp. 121–22; Nathan O. Hatch, *The Sacred Cause of Liberty: Republican Thought and the Millennium in Revolutionary New England* (New Haven: Yale University Press, 1977), p. 22; Robert Middlekauff, "The Ritualization of the American Revolution," in Stanley Coben and Lormon Ratner, eds., *The Development of an American Culture* (New York: St. Martin's, 2nd ed., 1983), pp. 50–53; Rogers M. Smith, *Civic Ideals: Conflicting Visions of Citizenship in U.S. History* (New Haven: Yale University Press, 1997), p. 75; Michael Novak, *God's Country or Taking the Declaration Seriously* (Washington, D.C.: American Enterprise Institute, 1999 Francis Boyer Lecture, 2000), pp. 12–17.

5. Quotations from Walter A. McDougall, *Promised Land, Crusader State: The American Encounter with the World Since 1776* (Boston: Houghton Mifflin, 1997), p. 38; Robert N. Bellah, *The Broken Covenant: American Civil Religion in Time of Trial* (Chicago: University of Chicago Press, 2nd ed., 1992), pp. 180–82; Jon Butler, *Awash in a Sea of Faith: Christianizing the American People* (Cambridge: Harvard University Press, 1990), p. 214; Novak, *God's Country*, pp. 25–26; Alexis de Tocqueville, *Democracy in America* (New York: Vintage, 1945), vol. 1, p. 316.

6. Sidney E. Mead, *The Nation with the Soul of a Church* (New York: Harper & Row, 1975), p. 78ff.

7. Butler, *Awash in a Sea of Faith*, p. 268.

8. Roger Finke and Rodney Stark, *The Churching of America: 1776–1990: Winners and Losers in Our Religious Economy* (New Brunswick: Rutgers University Press, 1992), pp. 16–21 and passim.

9. Tocqueville, *Democracy in America*, vol. 1, pp. 45, 316, 319; Philip Schaff, *America: A Sketch of Its Political, Social, and Religious Character* (Cambridge: Harvard University Press, 1961), pp. 14, 75–76.

10. James Bryce, *The American Commonwealth* (London: Macmillan, 1891), vol. 2, pp. 278, 577, 583; Gunnar Myrdal, *An American Dilemma: The Negro Problem and Modern Democracy* (New York: Harper, 1962), vol. 1, p. 11; Paul Johnson, "Writing *A History of the American People*" (lecture, American Enterprise Institute, Washington, D.C., 13 March 1998), p. 6; Paul Johnson, "The Almost-Chosen People," *The Wilson Quarterly*, 9 (Winter 1985), pp. 85–86.

11. Gallup/CNN/*USA Today* poll, 9–12 December 1999, 17–19 February 2003, 9–10 December 2002, 2–4 September 2002; Quinnipiac University poll, 4–9 June 2003; *General Social Survey 2002*, 6 February–26 June 2002, National Opinion Research Center, Q0118; *The National Election Studies* (Ann Arbor: University of

Michigan, Center of Political Studies, 1995–2000), V850; Jack Citrin, Ernst B. Haas, Christopher Muste, and Beth Reingold, "Is American Nationalism Changing? Implications for Foreign Policy," *International Studies Quarterly*, 38 (March 1994), p. 13, citing 1992 National Election Study.

12. Quinnipiac University poll, 4–9 June 2003; Gallup poll, 17–19 February 2003, 18–20 March 2002, 22–24 July 2002, 17–29 June 2002; Gallup/CNN/*USA Today* poll, 17–19 February 2003, 9–10 December 2002, 3–6 October 2002, 2–4 September 2002, 28–30 June 2002, 21–23 June 2002; CBS News poll, 28 April–1 May 2003; Time/CNN/Harris Interactive poll, 27 March 2003; *Investor's Business Daily/Christian Science Monitor* poll, 3–8 September 2002; *Boston Globe*, 16 January 1999, p. A3, citing C. Kirk Hadaway and Penny Long Marler, "Did You Really Go to Church This Week? Behind the Poll Data," *Christian Century*, 6 May 1998, pp. 472–75, and Andrew Walsh, *Religion in the News*, Fall 1998; Lipset, *American Exceptionalism*, p. 278; *Wall Street Journal*, 9 November 1990, p. A8; *Economist*, 29 May 1999, p. 29.

13. Krister Stendhal quoted in William G. McLoughlin and Robert N. Bellah, *Religion in America* (Boston: Beacon Press, 1968), p. xv; The Gallup Organization, *The Gallup Poll: Public Opinion 1999* (Wilmington: Scholarly Resources, 2000), pp. 50–55.

14. Kenneth D. Wald, *Religion and Politics in the United States* (New York: St. Martin's, 1987).

15. George Bishop, "What Americans Really Believe," *Free Inquiry*, 19 (Summer 1999), pp. 38–42.

16. Ronald Inglehart, Miguel Basanez, and Alejandro Moreno, *Human Values and Beliefs: A Cross-Cultural Sourcebook: Political, Religious, Sexual, and Economic Norms in 43 Societies: Findings from the 1990–1993 World Values Survey* (Ann Arbor: University of Michigan Press, 1998), V9, V20, V38, V143, V146, V147, V151, V166, V176.

17. Smith, *Civic Ideals*, pp. 55–56, 56–57; Kettner, *The Development of American Citizenship*, pp. 66–69; Linda Colley, *Britons: Forging the Nation, 1707–1837* (New Haven: Yale University Press, 1992), pp. 5–6, 11–54.

18. Smith, *Civic Ideals*, p. 57; Ernest Lee Tuveson, *Redeemer Nation: The Idea of America's Millennial Role* (Chicago: University of Chicago Press, 1968), Chapter 5; Ruth H. Bloch, *Visionary Republic: Millennial Themes in American Thought, 1756–1800* (Cambridge: Cambridge University Press, 1985), p. 12; Hatch, *The Sacred Cause of Liberty*, pp. 36–44; Kettner, *The Development of American Citizenship*, p. 114.

19. Hatch, *The Sacred Cause of Liberty*, pp. 75–76, 131; Cushing Strout, *The New Heavens and New Earth: Political Religion in America* (New York: Harper & Row, 1974), p. 71; Kevin P. Phillips, *The Cousins' Wars: Religion, Politics and the Triumph of Anglo-America* (New York: Basic Books, 1999), pp. 91–100; McDougall, *Promised Land, Crusader State*, p. 18; Garry Wills, *Under God: Religion and American Politics* (New York: Simon & Schuster, 1990), pp. 360–62; Bloch, *Visionary Republic*, pp. 58–59.

20. Ray Allen Billington, *The Protestant Crusade, 1800–1860* (New York: Macmillan, 1938), pp. 3–21; Theodore Maynard, *The Story of American Catholicism* (New York: Macmillan, 1941), p. 115.

21. Will Herberg, *Protestant, Catholic, Jew: An Essay in American Religious Sociology* (Garden City: Doubleday, 1955), pp. 151–52, 186–87; Schaff, *America*, p. 73. On the effects of intermarriage on the Catholic community, including the family of Bishop John Carroll, see Joseph Agonito, *The Building of an American Catholic Church: The Episcopacy of John Carroll* (New York: Garland, 1988), pp. 171–77.

22. Heer, *Immigration in America's Future*, pp. 35–37, 85–86; Billington, *Protestant Crusade*, Chapters 15–16; Perry Miller, *The Life of the Mind in America* (New York: Harcourt, Brace & World, 1965), p. 56.

23. Ivan Musicant, *Empire by Default: The Spanish-American War and the Dawn of the American Century* (New York: Holt, 1998), p. 17; Philip Gleason, "American Identity and Americanization," in Stephan Thernstrom, ed., *Harvard Encyclopedia of American Ethnic Groups* (Cambridge: Harvard University Press, 1980), pp. 31–38.

24. Quoted in Johnson, "The Almost-Chosen People," p. 88.

25. Edward Wakin and Joseph F. Scheuer, *The De-Romanization of the American Catholic Church* (New York: Macmillan, 1966), pp. 15–16 and passim; Maynard, *The Story of American Catholicism*, p. 502; Dorothy Dohen, *Nationalism and American Catholicism* (New York: Sheed & Ward, 1967), p. 71.

26. Peter Steinfels, "Parish Politics," *New York Times Book Review*, 17 August 1997, p. 20.

27. Ronald Inglehart and Marita Carballo, "Does Latin America Exist? (And Is There a Confucian Culture?): A Global Analysis of Cross-Cultural Differences," *PS: Political Science and Politics*, 30 (March 1997), p. 44; Inglehart, "The Clash of Civilizations? Empirical Evidence from 61 Societies" (paper presented at Annual Meeting of the Midwest Political Science Association, Chicago, 23–25 April 1998), pp. 9–10.

28. Dohen, *Nationalism and American Catholicism*, p. 171; Schaff, *America*, pp. 72–73; Herberg, *Protestant, Catholic, Jew*, pp. 100, 152–54.

29. John Ireland, *The Church and Modern Society: Lectures and Addresses* (St. Paul: Pioneer Press, 1905), p. 58, quoted in Dohen, *Nationalism and American Catholicism*, pp. 109 and 165.

30. Kwame Anthony Appiah, "The Multiculturist Misunderstanding," *New York Review of Books*, 9 October 1997, p. 31.

31. Tocqueville, *Democracy in America*, vol. 1, pp. 314–15; Bryce, *The American Commonwealth*, vol. 2, pp. 576–77.

32. *The People v. Ruggles*, 8 Johns. 295 (1811); Wills, *Under God*, p. 424; David J. Brewer, *The United States: A Christian Nation* (Philadelphia: John C. Winston, 1905); Justice Sutherland, *U.S. v. Macintosh*, 283 U.S. 605 (1931), 633–34; Justice David J. Brewer, *Church of the Holy Trinity v. U.S.*, 143 U.S. 457 (1892), 465, 471; Justice William O. Douglas, *Zorach v. Clauson*, 343 U.S. 306 (1952), 312; Foster, "A Christian Nation: Signs of a Covenant," pp. 122, 134–35; Thomas C. Reeves, "The Col-

lapse of the Mainline Churches," in Robert Royal, ed., *Reinventing the American People: Unity and Diversity Today* (Washington, D.C.: Ethics and Public Policy Center, 1995), pp. 204–5.

33. Quoted in Marsden, *Fundamentalism and American Culture*, p. 12.

34. Russell Shorto, "Belief by the Numbers," *New York Times Magazine*, 7 December 1997, p. 60; Barna Research Group results in *The American Enterprise*, 6 (November/December 1995), pp. 12, 19; CUNY survey, *New York Times*, 10 April 1991, p. A1; *National Election Studies*, University of Michigan, 1995–2000.

35. Diana Eck, "Neighboring Faiths: How Will Americans Cope with Increasing Religious Diversity?" *Harvard Magazine* (September/October 1996), p. 40; *New York Times*, 29 January 2000, p. A11.

36. Will Kymlicka, *Multicultural Citizenship: A Liberal Theory of Minority Rights* (New York: Oxford University Press, 1995), pp. 114–15, 223; Jeff Spinner, *The Boundaries of Citizenship: Race, Ethnicity, and Nationality in the Liberal State* (Baltimore: Johns Hopkins University Press, 1994), pp. 174–75.

37. *New York Times*, 10 April 1991, pp. A1, A16, 24 April 2000, p. A11; *New York Times Magazine*, 7 December 1997, p. 60; Philip Jenkins, *The Next Christendom: The Coming of Global Christianity* (New York: Oxford University Press, 2002), pp. 102–5.

38. Trollope quoted in Seymour Martin Lipset, *The First New Nation: The United States in Historical and Comparative Perspective* (New York: Norton, 1979), p. 156; Eisenhower quoted in Johnson, "Almost-Chosen People," p. 87, citing *Christian Century* magazine interview.

39. Irving Kristol, "On the Political Stupidity of the Jews," *Azure: Ideas for the Jewish Nation* (Autumn 5760/1999), p. 60, cited by *The Wilson Quarterly*, 24 (Winter 2000), p. 87.

40. Karl Zinsmeister, "Indicators," *American Enterprise*, 9 (November/December 1998), p. 19ff.; George Gallup, Jr., and Jim Castelli, *The People's Religion: American Faith in the 90s* (New York: Macmillan, 1989), pp. 18, 91.

41. Wills, *Under God*, p. 388, n.28; Andrew M. Greeley, *Religious Change in America* (Cambridge: Harvard University Press, 1989), pp. 8, 44–50, 115–16; Gallup and Castelli, *The People's Religion*, p. 36.

42. Gallup and Castelli, *The People's Religion*, pp. 6, 11–13, 30, 31, 36; Gallup/CNN/*USA Today* poll, 9–10 December 2002, 2–4 September 2002; Andrew M. Greeley, "American Exceptionalism: The Religious Phenomenon," in Byron E. Shafer, ed., *Is America Different?: A New Look at American Exceptionalism* (New York: Oxford University Press, 1991), p. 99.

43. Butler, *Awash in a Sea of Faith*, pp. 238, 268–70; Finke and Stark, *The Churching of America*, pp. 15–16.

44. Tocqueville, *Democracy in America*, vol. 2, p. 6; Robert N. Bellah, *Varieties of Civil Religion* (San Francisco: Harper & Row, 1980), p. 17.

45. Justice Douglas, *Zorach v. Clawson*, 343 U.S. 306 (1952), 313; Eisenhower quoted in Mead, *The Nation with the Soul of a Church*, p. 25.

46. Conrad Cherry, "Two American Sacred Ceremonies: Their Implications for the Study of Religion in America," *American Quarterly*, 21 (Winter 1969), p. 748.

47. W. Lloyd Warner, "An American Sacred Ceremony," in Russell E. Richey and Donald G. Jones, eds., *American Civil Religion* (New York: Harper & Row, 1974), pp. 89–111.

48. Peter Steinfels, "Beliefs: God at the Inauguration: An Encounter That Defies American Notions About Church and State," *New York Times*, 23 January 1993, p. 7.

49. D. W. Brogan, *The American Character* (New York: Vintage, 1959), p. 164.

50. Bellah, *Varieties of Civil Religion*, pp. 11–13; Cherry, "Two American Sacred Ceremonies," pp. 749–50.

Chapter 6. Emergence, Triumph, Erosion

1. Isaiah Berlin, "Nationalism: Past Neglect and Present Power," *Partisan Review*, 46 (no. 3, 1979), p. 348, quoted in John Mack, "Nationalism and the Self," *The Psychohistory Review*, 2 (Spring 1983), pp. 47–48; Anthony D. Smith, *National Identity* (Reno: University of Nevada Press, 1991), p. 143; Wilbur Zelinsky, *Nation into State: The Shifting Symbolic Foundations of American Nationalism* (Chapel Hill: University of North Carolina Press, 1988), p. 1.

2. Benjamin Franklin quoted in Max Savelle, "Nationalism and Other Loyalties in the American Revolution," *American Historical Review*, 67 (July 1962), p. 903.

3. S. M. Grant, " 'The Charter of Its Birthright': The Civil War and American Nationalism," *Nations and Nationalism*, 4 (April 1998), p. 163.

4. Richard L. Merritt, *Symbols of American Community, 1735–1775* (New Haven: Yale University Press, 1966), pp. 174, 180.

5. John M. Murrin, "A Roof Without Walls: The Dilemma of American National Identity," in Richard Beeman, Stephen Botein, Edward C. Carter II, eds., *Beyond Confederation: Origins of the Constitution and American National Identity* (Chapel Hill: University of North Carolina Press, 1987), p. 339; Merritt, *Symbols of American Community*, p. 58.

6. Albert Harkness, Jr., "Americanism and Jenkins' Ear," *Mississippi Valley Historical Review*, 37 (June 1950), p. 88; E. McClung Fleming, "Symbols of the United States: From Indian Queen to Uncle Sam," in Ray B. Browne, Richard H. Crowder, Virgil L. Lokke, and William T. Stafford, eds., *Frontiers of American Culture* (Lafayette, IN: Purdue University Studies, 1968), p. 4.

7. Merritt, *Symbols of American Community*, pp. 56, 125, 144, Table 8-2.

8. Fisher Ames quoted in Daniel J. Boorstin, *The Americans: The National Experience* (New York: Random House, 1966), pp. 403, 416; Elbridge Gerry quoted in Max Farrand, ed., *The Records of the Federal Convention of 1787: Proceedings*, vol. 1 (New Haven: Yale University Press, 1966), p. 552; Anders Stephanson, *Manifest Destiny: American Expansion and the Empire of Right* (New York: Hill & Wang, 1995), p. 30; Henry Steele Commager, *Jefferson, Nationalism, and the Enlightenment* (New York: George Braziller, 1975), p. 162; John Marshall quoted in Paul Johnson, *A History of the American People* (New York: HarperCollins, 1997), p. 423; John Calhoun, letter to Oliver Dyer, 1 January 1849; John Bodnar, *Remaking America: Public Mem-*

ory, Commemoration, and Patriotism in the Twentieth Century (Princeton: Princeton University Press, 1992), p. 21ff; Zelinsky, *Nation into State*, p. 218.

9. Commager, *Jefferson, Nationalism, and the Enlightenment*, p. 159.

10. Seymour Martin Lipset, *The First New Nation: The United States in Historical and Comparative Perspective* (New York: Norton, 1979), p. 18ff.

11. Zelinsky, *Nation into State*, p. 218.

12. Boorstin, *The Americans*, pp. 362–65.

13. Ibid., pp. 370, 373, 367.

14. Bodnar, *Remaking America*, pp. 21, 26; Stuart McConnell, "Reading the Flag: A Reconsideration of the Patriotic Cults of the 1890's," in John Bodnar, ed., *Bonds of Affection: Americans Define Their Patriotism* (Princeton: Princeton University Press, 1996), p. 107; Lyn Spillman, *Nation and Commemoration: Creating National Identities in the United States and Australia* (New York: Press Syndicate of the University of Cambridge, 1997), p. 24; Zelinsky, *Nation into State*, pp. 218–19.

15. Abraham Lincoln, "The Perpetuation of Our Political Institutions," speech, 27 January 1837, Springfield, IL, in *The Speeches of Abraham Lincoln* (New York: Chesterfield Society, 1908), pp. 9–10.

16. Merle Curti, *The Roots of American Loyalty* (New York: Columbia University Press, 1946), pp. 169–70.

17. Boorstin, *The Americans*, p. 402; Gaines M. Foster, "A Christian Nation: Signs of a Covenant," in Bodnar, ed., *Bonds of Affection*, p. 123; Spillman, *Nation and Commemoration*, pp. 24–25.

18. Morton Keller, *Affairs of State: Public Life in Late Nineteenth Century America* (Cambridge: Belknap Press of Harvard University Press, 1977), p. 39; Oliver Morton quoted in Keller, *Affairs of State*, p. 69.

19. John Higham, *Strangers in the Land: Patterns of American Nativism, 1860–1925* (New Brunswick: Rutgers University Press, 1988), p. 344.

20. Robert D. Putnam, *Bowling Alone: The Collapse and Revival of American Community* (New York: Simon & Schuster, 2000), p. 384ff, citing Theda Skocpol, "How Americans Became Civic," in Theda Skocpol and Morris P. Fiorina, eds., *Civic Engagement in American Democracy* (Washington, D.C.: Brookings Institution Press, 1999).

21. Cecilia Elizabeth O'Leary, *To Die For: The Paradox of American Patriotism* (Princeton: Princeton University Press, 1999), p. 49.

22. Zelinsky, *Nation into State*, pp. 105–6; McConnell, "Reading the Flag," p. 113.

23. Higham, *Strangers in the Land*, pp. 75–76.

24. Cecilia Elizabeth O'Leary, " 'Blood Brotherhood'. The Racialization of Patriotism, 1865–1918," in Bodnar, ed., *Bonds of Affection*, pp. 54, 73, 75–76; Curti, *The Roots of American Loyalty*, p. 192; Higham, *Strangers in the Land*, pp. 170–71.

25. O'Leary, " 'Blood Brotherhood,' " in Bodnar, ed., *Bonds of Affection*, pp. 57–58, 64; Higham, *Strangers in the Land*, pp. 170–71.

26. Zelinsky, *Nation into State*, p. 144, citing Boyd C. Shafer, *Faces of Nationalism: New Realities and Old Myths* (New York: Harcourt Brace Jovanovich, 1972), p. 203;

O'Leary, " 'Blood Brotherhood,' " p. 65, citing Bessie Louise Pierce, *Public Opinion and the Teaching of History in the United States* (New York: Knopf, 1926), pp. 13–16.

27. Curti, *The Roots of American Loyalty*, p. 190.

28. Zelinsky, *Nation into State*, pp. 29, 56, 150; Bessie Louise Pierce, *Civic Attitudes in American School Textbooks* (Chicago: University of Chicago Press, 1930), p. 254.

29. Zelinsky, *Nation into State*, pp. 86–88.

30. Curti, *The Roots of American Loyalty*, p. 136.

31. Catherine Albanese, "Requiem for Memorial Day: Dissent in the Redeemer Nation," *American Quarterly*, 26 (1974), p. 389; Zelinsky, *Nation into State*, p. 74.

32. Zelinsky, *Nation into State*, pp. 204–5.

33. Ibid., pp. 202–3; O'Leary, *To Die For*, pp. 20–24; Boleslaw Mastai and Marie-Louise D'Orange, *The Stars and Stripes: The American Flag As Art and As History from the Birth of the Republic to the Present* (New York: Knopf, 1973), p. 130, quoted in Zelinsky, *Nation into State*, pp. 202–3.

34. O'Leary, *To Die For*, pp. 233–34, citing *Halter v. Nebraska* 205 U.S. 34–46 and quoting *Halter et al. v. State* 105 *Northwestern Reporter*, pp. 298–301.

35. J. Hector St. John de Crèvecoeur, *Letters from an American Farmer and Sketches of 18th-Century America* (New York: Penguin, 1981), pp. 68, 70; Israel Zangwill, *The Melting Pot: A Drama in Four Acts* (New York: Arno Press, 1975), p. 184.

36. Milton M. Gordon, *Assimilation in American Life: The Role of Race, Religion, and National Origin* (New York: Oxford University Press, 1964), p. 89; Michael Novak, *Further Reflections on Ethnicity* (Middletown, PA: Jednota Press, 1977), p. 59.

37. Horace M. Kallen, *The Structure of Lasting Peace: An Inquiry into the Motives of War and Peace* (Boston: Marshall Jones Company, 1918), p. 31; Kallen, *Cultural Pluralism and the American Ideal: An Essay in Social Philosophy* (Philadelphia: University of Pennsylvania Press, 1956); Kallen, *Culture and Democracy in the United States: Studies in the Group Psychology of the American Peoples* (New York: Boni & Liveright, 1924).

38. Philip Gleason, *Speaking of Diversity: Language and Ethnicity in Twentieth-Century America* (Baltimore: Johns Hopkins University Press, 1992), p. 51.

39. Randolph Bourne quoted in T. Alexander Aleinikoff, "A Multicultural Nationalism," *American Prospect*, 36 (January/February 1998), p. 81.

40. Arthur Mann, *The One and the Many: Reflections on the American Identity* (Chicago: University of Chicago Press, 1979), pp. 137, 142–47.

41. Theodore Roosevelt quoted in Gordon, *Assimilation in American Life*, p. 122, from Edward N. Saveth, *American Historians and European Immigrants, 1875–1925* (New York: Columbia University Press, 1948), p. 121.

42. Robert A. Carlson, *The Quest for Conformity: Americanization Through Education* (New York: John Wiley, 1975), pp. 6–7.

43. Louis Brandeis, address, Faneuil Hall, Boston, July 4, 1915, in Solomon Goldman, ed., *The Words of Justice Brandeis* (New York: Henry Schuman, 1953), p. 29.

44. John F. McClymer, "The Federal Government and the Americanization

Movement, 1915–1924," *Prologue*, 10 (Spring 1978), p. 24; Ronald Fernandez, "Getting Germans to Fight Germans: The Americanizers of World War I," *The Journal of Ethnic Studies*, 9 (Summer 1981), p. 61.

45. Carlson, *The Quest for Conformity*, p. 113; Edward George Hartmann, *The Movement to Americanize the Immigrant* (New York: Columbia University Press, 1948), p. 92; Henry Ford, quoted in Otis L. Graham and Elizabeth Koed, "Americanizing the Immigrant, Past and Future," *The Social Contract*, 4 (Winter 1993–1994), p. 101; Gerd Korman, *Industrialization, Immigrants and Americanization* (Madison: State Historical Society of Wisconsin, 1967), pp. 147, 158–59; Higham, *Strangers in the Land*, pp. 244–45.

46. Higham, *Strangers in the Land*, p. 249.

47. Carlson, *The Quest for Conformity*, pp. 89–90.

48. John F. McClymer, "The Americanization Movement and the Education of the Foreign-Born Adult, 1914–25," in Bernard J. Weiss, ed., *American Education and the European Immigrant*, 1840–1940 (Urbana: University of Illinois Press, 1992), p. 98; Hartmann, *The Movement to Americanize the Immigrant*, p. 64ff.

49. Miller, *The Unmaking of Americans*, pp. 221, 223; McClymer, "The Federal Government and the Americanization Movement, 1915–1924," p. 40.

50. Carl F. Kaestle, *Pillars of the Republic: Common Schools and American Society, 1780–1860* (New York: Hill & Wang, 1983), pp. 161–62.

51. Stephen Steinberg, *The Ethnic Myth: Race, Ethnicity, and Class in America* (New York: Atheneum, 1981), p. 54.

52. Joel M. Roitman, *The Immigrants, the Progressives, and the Schools* (Stark, KS: De Young Press, 1996), p. 1; McClymer, "The Americanization Movement," p. 103; Miller, *The Unmaking of Americans*, p. 49; Roitman, *The Immigrants, the Progressives, and the Schools*, pp. 51–52; Carlson, *The Quest for Conformity*, p. 114; Reed Ueda, "When Assimilation Was the American Way," *Washington Post*, 2 April 1995, p. R10.

53. Curti, *Roots of American Loyalty*, p. 223ff; Paul C. Stern, "Why Do People Sacrifice for Their Nations?," *Political Psychology*, 16 (no. 2, 1995), pp. 223–24.

54. Robin M. Williams, Jr., *American Society: A Sociological Interpretation* (New York: Knopf, 1952), p. 527, quoted in Gleason, *Speaking of Diversity*, p. 175.

55. Gleason, *Speaking of Diversity*, p. 175; Arthur A. Stein, *The Nation at War* (Baltimore: Johns Hopkins University Press, 1980), p. 92; Philip Gleason, "American Identity and Americanization," in Stephan Thernstrom, ed., *Harvard Encyclopedia of American Ethnic Groups* (Cambridge: Belknap Press of Harvard University Press, 1980), p. 47; Albert O. Hirschman, *Journeys Toward Progress* (New York: Twentieth Century Fund, 1963), p. 137. See also J. M. Winter, *The Great War and the British People* (Cambridge: Harvard University Press, 1986).

56. Hedrick Smith, *The Russians* (New York: Quadrangle/New York Times Books, 1976), pp. 302–3.

57. Jack Citrin, Ernst B. Haas, Christopher C. Muste, Beth Reingold, "Is American Nationalism Changing? Implications for Foreign Policy," *International Studies Quarterly*, 38 (March 1994), pp. 3–5.

58. Robert D. Kaplan, "Fort Leavenworth and the Eclipse of Nationhood," *Atlantic Monthly*, 278 (September 1996), p. 75ff; Diana Schaub, "On the Character of Generation X," *The Public Interest*, 137 (Fall 1999), p. 23; George Lipsitz, "Dilemmas of Beset Nationhood: Patriotism, the Family, and Economic Change in the 1970s and 1980s," in Bodnar, ed., *Bonds of Affection*, p. 251ff; Walter Berns, "On Patriotism," *The Public Interest*, 127 (Spring 1997), p. 31; Peter H. Schuck, *Citizens, Strangers, and In-Betweens: Essays on Immigration and Citizenship* (Boulder: Westview Press, 1998), p. 163ff.

Chapter 7. Deconstructing America: The Rise of Subnational Identities

1. Horace Kallen, quoted in Arthur Mann, *The One and the Many: Reflections on the American Identity* (Chicago: University of Chicago Press, 1979), pp. 143–44; Michael Walzer, *What It Means to Be an American* (New York: Marsilio, 1992), p. 62.

2. Arthur M. Schlesinger, Jr., *The Disuniting of America* (New York: Norton, rev. ed., 1992), p. 43; Nathan Glazer, *We Are All Multiculturalists Now* (Cambridge: Harvard University Press, 1997).

3. Gunnar Myrdal, *An American Dilemma: The Negro Problem and Modern Democracy* (New York: Harper, 1944), p. 4.

4. Ralph Waldo Emerson, "Lecture on the Times," in Emerson, *Prose Works* (Boston: Fields, Osgood, 1870), vol. 1, p. 149.

5. Andrew Kull, *The Color-Blind Constitution* (Cambridge: Harvard University Press, 1992), pp. 1–2, 146–48; U.S. Commission on Civil Rights, *Equal Protection of the Laws in Higher Education, 1960* (Washington, D.C.: U.S. Government Printing Office, 1960), p. 148.

6. Senator Hubert Humphrey, 110 *Congressional Record*, 1964, pp. 6548–49, quoted in Edward J. Erler, "The Future of Civil Rights: Affirmative Action Redivivus," *Notre Dame Journal of Law, Ethics, and Public Policy*, 11 (1997), p. 26.

7. Kull, *The Color-Blind Constitution*, p. 202; Hugh Davis Graham, *The Civil Rights Era: Origins and Development of National Policy, 1960–1972* (New York: Oxford University Press, 1990), p. 150; Herman Belz, *Equality Transformed: A Quarter Century of Affirmative Action* (New Brunswick, NJ: Transaction, 1991), p. 25; Nathan Glazer, *Ethnic Dilemmas, 1964–1982* (Cambridge: Harvard University Press, 1983), p. 162.

8. Bayard Rustin, "From Protest to Politics: The Future of the Civil Rights Movement," *Commentary*, 39 (February 1965), p. 27; Glazer, *Ethnic Dilemmas*, pp. 161–62.

9. Graham, *The Civil Rights Era*, p. 250; Glazer, *Ethnic Dilemmas*, p. 262; Kull, *The Color-Blind Constitution*, pp. 200–3, quoting Labor Department regulations.

10. Kull, *The Color-Blind Constitution*, pp. 204–5; Belz, *Equality Transformed*, pp. 51, 55.

11. Kull, *The Color-Blind Constitution*, pp. 214–16.

12. Jack Citrin, "Affirmative Action in the People's Court," *The Public Interest*, 122 (Winter 1996), p. 46; Seymour Martin Lipset, "Affirmative Action and the American Creed," *The Wilson Quarterly*, 16 (Winter 1992), p. 59.

13. Richard Kahlenberg, "Bob Dole's Colorblind Injustice," *Washington Post National Weekly Edition*, 10–16 June 1996, p. 24; Stephan Thernstrom and Abigail Thernstrom, *America in Black and White: One Nation, Indivisible* (New York: Simon & Schuster, 1997), p. 452; *New York Times*, 1 June 2001, p. A17.

14. Lieberman quoted in *New York Times*, 10 March 1995, p. A16; John Fonte, "Why There Is a Culture War: Gramsci and Tocqueville in America," *Policy Review*, 104 (December 2000/January 2001), p. 21.

15. Connerly quoted in Fonte, "Why There Is a Culture War," p. 21; Ward Connerly, *Creating Equal: My Fight Against Race Preferences* (San Francisco: Encounter Books, 2000), p. 228.

16. Seymour Martin Lipset, "Equal Chances Versus Equal Results," *Annals of the American Academy of Political and Social Science*, 523 (September 1992), pp. 66–67.

17. Lipset, "Affirmative Action and the American Creed," p. 58; *Washington Post*, 11 October 1995, p. A11; Citrin, "Affirmative Action in the People's Court," p. 43; William Raspberry, "What Actions Are Affirmative?" *Washington Post National Weekly Edition*, 28 August–3 September, 1995, p. 28; Citrin, "Affirmative Action in the People's Court," p. 41.

18. Citrin, "Affirmative Action in the People's Court," p. 43.

19. Ibid., *Boston Globe*, 30 April 1997, p. A19.

20. Thernstrom and Thernstrom, *America in Black and White*, p. 437; *City of Richmond v. J. A. Croson Company*, 488 U.S. 469 (1989).

21. Thernstrom and Thernstrom, *America in Black and White*, pp. 456–59.

22. *Washington Post*/Kaiser Family Foundation/Harvard University, "Race and Ethnicity in 2001: Attitudes, Perceptions, and Experiences" (August 2001); Princeton Survey Research Associates poll, January 2003; Jennifer Barrett, "*Newsweek* Poll: Bush Loses Ground," *Newsweek*, 14 February 2003, online; Jonathan Chait, "Pol Tested," *New Republic*, 3 February 2003, p. 14.

23. Belz, *Equality Transformed*, pp. 66–67; Daniel Bell, *The Coming of Post-Industrial Society: A Venture in Social Forecasting* (New York: Basic Books, 1973), p. 417; Thernstrom and Thernstrom, *America in Black and White*, p. 492.

24. Martinez in *Miami Herald*, 12 October 1988, cited in Raymond Tatalovich, *Nativism Reborn?: The Official English Language Movement and the American States* (Lexington: University Press of Kentucky, 1995), p. 99.

25. Tatalovich, *Nativism Reborn?*, pp. 1–2.

26. Unamuno quoted in Carlos Alberto Montaner, "Talk English—You Are in the United States," in James Crawford, ed., *Language Loyalties* (Chicago: University of Chicago Press, 1992), p. 164; Karl W. Deutsch, *Nationalism and Social Communication* (Cambridge: MIT Press, 1966).

27. Immigration and Nationality Act, Title III, Chapter 2, Section 312 (8 U.S.C. 1423).

28. 42 U.S.C. 1973b (f), Pub. L. 94-73, 89 Stat. 400; Tatalovich, *Nativism Reborn?*, p. 105; James Crawford, *Hold Your Tongue: Bilingualism and the Politics of "English Only"* (Reading, MA: Addison-Wesley, 1992), p. 272, n. 13; *Washington Post*, 14 November 2002, p. T3; *Chicago Sun-Times*, 2 May 1996, p. 29, 5 August 2002, p. 1.

29. *Asian American Business Group v. City of Pomona*, in Crawford, *Language Loyalties*, pp. 284–87; *Wall Street Journal*, 21 August 1995, p. A8; *Alexander v. Sandoval*, 532 U.S. 275 (2001); *New York Times*, 25 April 2001, p. A14.

30. *Ruiz et al. v. Hull et al.*, 191 Ariz. 441, 957 P.2d 984 (1998); cert. denied, 11 January 1999.

31. Edward M. Chen, "Language Rights in the Private Sector" in Crawford, ed., *Language Loyalties*, pp. 276–77.

32. James Crawford, *Bilingual Education: History, Politics, Theory, and Practice* (Trenton, NJ: Crane, 1989), p. 33; J. Stanley Pottinger, Office for Civil Rights, memorandum, 25 May 1970; *Serna v. Portales Municipal Schools*, 351 F. supp. 1279 (1972); *Lau v. Nichols*, 414 U.S. 563 (1974).

33. Crawford, *Bilingual Education*, p. 39; William J. Bennett, "The Bilingual Education Act: A Failed Path," in Crawford, ed., *Language Loyalties*, p. 361.

34. *Time*, 8 July 1985, pp. 80–81.

35. Scheuer quoted in Bennett, "The Bilingual Education Act: A Failed Path," in Crawford, ed., *Language Loyalties*, p. 361.

36. Badillo quoted in *New York Post*, 17 October 2000, p. 16.

37. Carol Schmid, "The English Only Movement: Social Bases of Support and Opposition Among Anglos and Latinos," in Crawford, ed., *Language Loyalties*, p. 202.

38. Jack Citrin, Donald Philip Green, Beth Reingold, Evelyn Walters, "The 'Official English' Movement and the Symbolic Politics of Language in the United States," *Western Political Quarterly*, 43 (September 1990), pp. 540–41; Camilo Pérez-Bustillo, "What Happens When English Only Comes to Town?: A Case Study of Lowell, Massachusetts," in Crawford, ed., *Language Loyalties*, pp. 194–201.

39. Citrin et al., "The 'Official English' Movement," pp. 548–52; Zogby International poll, 15–17 November and 10–13 December 1998.

40. Tatalovich, *Nativism Reborn?*, pp. 85–88.

41. Ibid., pp. 114–22.

42. Ibid., pp. 136–48, 150–60.

43. Geoffrey Nunberg, "Linguists and the Official Language Movement," *Language*, 65 (September 1989), p. 581.

44. *Boston Globe*, 6 November 2002, p. A1.

45. *Rocky Mountain News*, 6 November 2002, p. 29A; *Boston Globe*, 10 November 2002, p. 10.

46. Schmid, "The English Only Movement," in Crawford, ed., *Language Loyalties*, pp. 203–5; Max J. Castro, "On the Curious Question of Language in Miami," in ibid., p. 179; Peter Skerry, *Mexican Americans: The Ambivalent Minority* (Cambridge:

Harvard University Press, 1993), p. 285; Jack Citrin, "Language Politics and American Identity," *The Public Interest*, 99 (Spring 1990), p. 104.

47. Steve Farkas, ed., *A Lot to Be Thankful For* (New York: Public Agenda, 1998).

48. *Boston Globe*, 31 August 1997, p. A12; *New York Times*, 15 August 1997, p. A39; *New York Times*, 5 June 1998, p. A12; Glenn Garvin, "Loco, Completamente Loco: The Many Failures of 'Bilingual Education,' " *Reason*, 29 (January 1998), p. 20.

49. James Counts Early, "Affirmations of a Multiculturalist," in Robert Royal, ed., *Reinventing the American People: Unity and Diversity Today* (Grand Rapids: William B. Eerdmans, 1995), p. 58; Clifford Orwin, "All Quiet on the (Post)Western Front," *The Public Interest*, 123 (Spring 1996), p. 10.

50. Pamela L. Tiedt and Iris M. Tiedt, *Multicultural Teaching: A Handbook of Activities, Information, and Resources* (Boston: Allyn and Bacon, 3rd ed., 1990), p. 7.

51. Mikulski quoted in Mann, *The One and the Many*, p. 29; Nathan Glazer and Daniel Patrick Moynihan, *Beyond the Melting Pot* (Cambridge: MIT Press, 1963), pp. 16–17, 290.

52. Mann, *The One and the Many*, pp. 37, 38–39.

53. Stephen Steinberg, *The Ethnic Myth: Race, Ethnicity, and Class in America* (New York: Atheneum, 1981), p. 51.

54. Thaddeus V. Gromada, "Polish Americans and Multiculturalism," 4 January 1997, presidential address at meeting of Polish American Historical Association, in conjunction with American Historical Association, New York Hilton Hotel, New York City.

55. Betty Jean Craige, *American Patriotism in a Global Society* (Albany: State University of New York Press, 1996), pp. 65–66.

56. Lilia I. Bartolome, "Introduction," in Alfonso Nava et al., *Educating Americans in a Multicultural Society* (New York: McGraw-Hill, 2nd ed., 1994), p. v.

57. James A. Banks, *Multiethnic Education: Theory and Practice* (Boston: Allyn & Bacon, 1994), p. 3.

58. Tiedt and Tiedt, *Multicultural Teaching*, p. xi.

59. Sandra Stotsky, *Losing Our Language* (New York: Free Press, 1999), pp. 59–62, reporting the research of Charlotte Iiams, "Civic Attitudes Reflected in Selected Basal Readers for Grades One Through Six Used in the United States from 1900–1970" (Unpublished doctoral dissertation, University of Idaho, 1980).

60. Paul Vitz, *Censorship: Evidence of Bias in Our Children's Textbooks* (Ann Arbor: Servant Books, 1986), pp. 70–71, 75; Nathan Glazer and Reed Ueda, *Ethnic Groups in History Textbooks* (Washington, D.C.: Ethics and Public Policy Center, 1983), p. 15.

61. Robert Lerner, Althea K. Nagai, Stanley Rothman, *Molding the Good Citizen: The Politics of High School History Texts* (Westport, CT: Praeger, 1995), p. 153, citing the study by Diana Ravitch and Chester E. Finn, *What Do Our 17-Year-Olds Know?* (New York: Harper & Row, 1987), pp. 270–72; Stotsky, *Losing Our Language*, pp. 72–74, 86–87, 90, 294, n. 20.

62. Glazer, *We Are All Multiculturalists Now*, p. 83; Schlesinger, *The Disuniting of*

America, p. 123; American Council of Trustees and Alumni, *Inside Academe*, 8 (Fall 2002), pp. 1, 3, citing the council's report, *Restoring America's Legacy: The Challenge of Historical Literacy in the 21st Century (2002)*.

63. Lerner et al., *Molding the Good Citizen*, p. 153, citing *U.S. News & World Report*, 12 April 1993, p. 63; American Council of Trustees and Alumni, *Newsletter*, 18 December 2000, citing the council's report, *Losing America's Memory: Historical Illiteracy in the 21st Century (2000)*.

Chapter 8. Assimilation: Converts, Ampersands, and the Erosion of Citizenship

1. U.S. Immigration and Naturalization Service, *2000 Statistical Yearbook of the Immigration and Naturalization Service* (unpublished, selections available online at http://uscis.gov/graphics/shared/aboutus/statistics/yearbook2000.pdf.

2. *Economist*, 24 June 2000, p. 63.

3. Organization for Economic Cooperation and Development, *Trends in International Migration: Continuous Reporting System on Migration*, 2000 ed. (Paris, France: OECD, 2001).

4. *World Population Prospects: The 2000 Revision—Highlights*, Annex Tables, 28 February 2001 (United Nations Population Division).

5. National Institute of Population and Social Security Research, *Population Projections for Japan: 1996–2100* (1997).

6. Ole Waever et al., *Identity, Migration and the New Security Agenda in Europe* (London: Pinter, 1993), p. 23.

7. Organization for Economic Cooperation and Development, *Trends in International Migration*, p. 304.

8. U.S. Immigration and Naturalization Service, *2000 Statistical Yearbook*.

9. Milton M. Gordon, *Assimilation in American Life* (New York: Oxford University Press, 1964), pp. 70–71.

10. Peter D. Salins, *Assimilation, American Style* (New York: Basic Books, 1997), pp. 6, 48–49.

11. Gordon, *Assimilation in American Life*, pp. 127, 244–45.

12. Will Herberg, *Protestant Catholic Jew* (Garden City: Doubleday, 1955), pp. 33–34; George R. Stewart, *American Ways of Life* (New York: Doubleday, 1954), p. 23, cited in Gordon, *Assimilation in American Life*, pp. 127–28.

13. Thomas Jefferson, *Notes on Virginia* (Chapel Hill: University of North Carolina Press, 1954), pp. 84–85.

14. Michael Piore, *Birds of Passage: Migrant Labor and Industrial Societies* (Cambridge: Cambridge University Press, 1979), p. 151.

15. Gordon, *Assimilation in American Life*, p. 190; Thomas Sowell, *Migrations and Cultures: A World View* (New York: Basic Books, 1996), p. 48. For an excellent overview and analysis of the successful assimilation of pre–World War II immigrants

and their descendants, see Richard Alba and Victor Nee, *Remaking the American Mainstream: Assimilation and Contemporary Immigration* (Cambridge: Harvard University Press, 2003), Chapter 3.

16. Samuel P. Huntington, *The Clash of Civilizations and the Remaking of World Order* (New York: Simon & Schuster, 1996), p. 264.

17. American Muslim Council, Zogby poll, released 28 August 2000, reported in *Pittsburgh Post-Gazette*, 29 August 2000, p. A5.

18. Kambiz Ghanea Bassiri, *Competing Visions of Islam in the United States: A Study of Los Angeles* (Westport, CT: Greenwood Press, 1997), pp. 43–49.

19. Corey Michael Spearman, "The Clash of Civilizations in Dearborn, Michigan" (term paper, Kalamazoo College, Michigan, March 2000), p. 7, quoting Abu Mustafa Al-Bansilwani, "There Has to Be a Better Way—and There Is!," *Ummah*, 1 (no. 1, 1999), pp. 1–2.

20. Daniel Patrick Moynihan, "The Sonnet About the Statue of Liberty," *New York*, 19 (May 1986), p. 58.

21. Sowell, *Migrations and Cultures*, pp. 39–40; John C. Harles, *Politics in the Lifeboat: Immigrants and the American Democratic Order* (Boulder: Westview Press, 1993), p. 99.

22. Henri Wéber, quoted in *Economist*, 12 February 2000, p. 20.

23. Oscar Handlin, *The Uprooted* (Boston: Little, Brown, 2nd ed., 1973), p. 272; Arthur M. Schlesinger, Jr., *The Disuniting of America: Reflections on a Multicultural Society* (New York: Norton, rev. ed., 1998), p. 17; Harles, *Politics in the Lifeboat*, p. 4.

24. Salins, *Assimilation, American Style*, pp. 48–49; Josef Joffe, personal conversation.

25. Piore, *Birds of Passage*, p. 149ff.

26. Roberto Suro, *Strangers Among Us* (New York: Knopf, 1998), p. 325.

27. Washington, Jefferson, Franklin quoted in Matthew Spalding, "From Pluribus to Unum," *Policy Review*, 67 (Winter 1994), pp. 39–40.

28. Gordon, *Assimilation in American Life*, pp. 132–33; Marcus Lee Hansen, *The Immigrant in American History* (Cambridge: Harvard University Press, 1940), p. 132; Heinz Kloss, *The American Bilingual Tradition* (Rowley, MA: Newbury House, 1977), p. 128; Will Kymlicka, *Multicultural Citizenship* (Oxford: Clarendon Press, 1998), pp. 28–29.

29. Samuel Lubell, *The Future of American Politics* (New York: Harper, 1951), p. 58ff.

30. *New York Times*, 9 December 1999, pp. 1, 20, 5 March 2000, pp. A1, A20; *Washington Post*, 18 September 1993, p. A1; New York City Department of City Planning, *The Newest New Yorkers: 1995–1996: An Update of Immigration to NYC in the Mid '90s* (8 November 1999).

31. James Dao, "Immigrant Diversity Slows Traditional Political Climb," *New York Times*, 28 December 1999, p. A1; John J. Miller, *The Unmaking of Americans* (New York: Free Press, 1998), pp. 218–19; Edward P. Lazear, *Culture Wars in America* (Stanford: Hoover Institution, Essays in Public Policy, no. 71, 1996), p. 9, citing 1990 census data.

32. Nathan Glazer, "Immigration and the American Future," *The Public Interest*, 118 (Winter 1995), p. 51; "Issue Brief: Cycles of Nativism in U.S. History," *Immigration Forum*, 19 May 2000, p. 1.

33. Robert William Fogel, *The Fourth Great Awakening and the Future of Egalitarianism* (Chicago: University of Chicago Press 2000), p. 60; Barry Edmonston and Jeffrey P. Passel, "Ethnic Demography: U.S. Immigration and Ethnic Variations," in Edmonston and Passel, eds., *Immigration and Ethnicity* (Washington, D.C.: Urban Institute Press 1994), p. 8; Campbell J. Gibson and Emily Lennon, *Historical Census Statistics on the Foreign Born Population of the United States, 1850–1990* (Washington, D.C.: Census Bureau Population Division, Working Paper 29, February 1999).

34. Richard Alba and Victor Nee, "Rethinking Assimilation Theory for a New Era of Immigration," *International Migration Review*, 31 (Winter 1997), pp. 842–43; Douglas Massey, "The New Immigration and Ethnicity in the United States," *Population and Development Review*, 21 (September 1995), p. 645, quoted in Peggy Levitt, *The Transnational Villagers* (Berkeley: University of California Press, 2001), p. 18.

35. U.S. Immigration and Naturalization Service, *1999 Statistical Yearbook of the Immigration and Naturalization Service* (Washington, D.C.: U.S. Government Printing Office, March 2002), p. 19; U.S. Census Bureau, *Statistical Abstract of the United States: 2001*, p. 45.

36. Stephen A. Camarota, *Immigrants in the United States—2002: A Snapshot of America's Foreign-Born Population* (Washington, D.C.: Center for Immigration Studies, backgrounder, November 2002), p. 1; *Boston Globe*, 10 March 2003, p. A3, citing William Frey's analysis of Census Bureau figures.

37. Frederick Douglass, quoted in Judith N. Shklar, *American Citizenship* (Cambridge: Harvard University Press, 1991), pp. 48, 52.

38. Ronald Takaki, *Double Victory: A Multicultural History of America* (Boston: Little, Brown, 2000), p. 82.

39. John Higham, *Strangers in the Land* (New Brunswick: Rutgers University Press, 1988), p. 12ff; Kevin Phillips, *The Cousins' Wars* (New York: Basic Books, 1999), p. 543ff.

40. John A. Hawgood, *The Tragedy of German-America* (New York: G. P. Putnam's Sons, 1940), pp. 291–301; Ronald Fernandez, "Getting Germans to Fight Germans: The Americanizers of World War I," *Journal of Ethnic Studies*, 9 (1981), pp. 64–66; Higham, *Strangers in the Land*, pp. 216–17.

41. *New York Times*, 5 July 1918, pp. 1, 6; John J. Miller, "Americanization Past and Future," *Freedom Review*, 28 (Fall 1997), p. 11.

42. Nathan Glazer and Daniel Patrick Moynihan, *Beyond the Melting Pot* (Cambridge: MIT Press, 1970), p. 20; Mary C. Waters, "Ethnic and Racial Identities of Second-Generation Black Immigrants in New York City," *International Migration Review*, 28 (Winter 1994), p. 799.

43. Michael Walzer, *What It Means to Be an American* (New York: Marsilio, 1992), p. 49.

44. *Boston Globe*, 27 May 2002, p. A1, 15 August 2002, p. A3, 23 November 2002, p. A15.

45. Miller, *The Unmaking of Americans*, pp. 219–21.

46. Marilyn Halter, *Washington Post*, 16 July 2000, p. B3.

47. See Peter Skerry, *Mexican Americans: The Ambivalent Minority* (Cambridge: Harvard University Press, 1993), passim; and Michael Jones-Correa, *Between Two Nations: The Political Predicament of Latinos in New York City* (Ithaca: Cornell University Press, 1998), pp. 5, 69–90.

48. Calculated by James Perry from U.S. Census Bureau, *Profile of the Foreign-Born Population in the United States: 2000* (Washington: Government Printing Office, 2001), p. 24; Miller, *The Unmaking of Americans*, pp. 120, 134–35, 221–23; James R. Edwards and James G. Gimbel, "The Immigration Game," *American Outlook*, Summer 1999, p. 43; Linda Chavez, "Multilingualism Getting Out of Hand," *USA Today*, 14 December 1994, p. A13.

49. Mark Krikorian, "Will Americanization Work in America?" *Freedom Review*, 28 (Fall 1997), pp. 51–52; Rubén G. Rumbaut, *Achievement and Ambition Among Children of Immigrants in Southern California* (Jerome Levy Economics Institute, Working Paper 215, November 1997), pp. 14–15; Peter Skerry, "Do We Really Want Immigrants to Assimilate?" *Society*, 37 (March/April 2000), p. 60, citing University of California Diversity Project, *Final Report: Recommendations and Findings* (Berkeley: Graduate School of Education, 2000).

50. Fernando Mateo, quoted in *New York Times*, 19 July 1998, p. 1; Levitt, *Transnational Villagers*, pp. 3–4, 239–40; Jones-Correa, *Between Two Nations*, pp. 5–6, 191–93; Robert S. Leiken, *The Melting Border: Mexico and Mexican Communities in the United States* (Washington, D.C.: Center for Equal Opportunity, 2000), pp. 4–5.

51. Suro, *Strangers Among Us*, p. 124.

52. Levitt, *Transnational Villagers*, p. 219, citing 1990 census data.

53. Ibid., pp. 2–3.

54. Deborah Sontag and Celia W. Dugger, "The New Immigrant Tide: A Shuttle Between Worlds," *New York Times*, 19 July 1998, p. 26; *New York Times*, 17 June 2001, p. 1; Levitt, *Transnational Villagers*, p. 16, citing Lars Schoultz, "Central America and the Politicization of U.S. Immigration Policy," in Christopher Mitchell, ed., *Western Hemisphere Immigration and United States Foreign Policy* (University Park: Pennsylvania State University Press, 1992), p. 189.

55. Ryan Rippel, "Ellis Island or Ellis Farm" (term paper, Government 1582, Harvard University, Spring 2002), pp. 14, 28.

56. Leiken, *The Melting Border*, pp. 6, 13, 12–15; Levitt, *Transnational Villagers*, p. 180ff.

57. Stanley A. Renshon, *Dual Citizens in America* (Washington, D.C.: Center for Immigration Studies, backgrounder, July 2000), p. 3, and *Dual Citizenship and American National Identity* (Washington, D.C.: Center for Immigration Studies, Paper 20, October 2001), p. 15.

58. Renshon, *Dual Citizens in America*, p. 6; Aleinikoff, "Between Principles and Politics: U.S. Citizenship Policy," in T. Alexander Aleinikoff and Douglas Klus-

meyer, eds., *From Migrants to Citizens: Membership in a Changing World* (Washington, D.C.: Carnegie Endowment for International Peace, 2000), pp. 139–40.

59. Michael Jones-Correa, "Under Two Flags: Dual Nationality in Latin America and Its Consequences for Naturalization in the United States," *International Migration Review*, 35 (Winter 2001), p. 1010.

60. Ibid., pp. 1016–17.

61. Yasemin Soysal, *Limits of Citizenship: Migrants and Postnational Membership in Europe* (Chicago: University of Chicago Press, 1994), p. 205; Nathan Glazer, estimate, Harvard University, Globalization and Culture Seminar, 16 February 2001.

62. Jones-Correa, "Under Two Flags," p. 1024; *Boston Globe*, 20 December 1999, p. B1, 13 May 2000, p. B3.

63. Jones-Correa, "Under Two Flags," pp. 1004, 1008.

64. *New York Times*, 19 June 2001, p. A4, 3 July 2001, p. A7; Levitt, *Transnational Villagers*, p. 19.

65. For a balanced assessment of the costs and benefits of dual citizenship, see Peter H. Schuck, "Plural Citizenships," in Noah M. J. Pickus, ed., *Immigration and Citizenship in the Twenty-first Century* (Lanham, MD: Rowman and Littlefield, 1998), pp. 162–76.

66. James H. Kettner, *The Development of American Citizenship, 1608–1870* (Chapel Hill: University of North Carolina Press, 1978), pp. 55, 267–69, 281–82, 343ff.

67. Arthur Mann, *The One and the Many: Reflections on the American Identity* (Chicago: University of Chicago Press, 1979), p. 178.

68. Aleinikoff, "Between Principles and Politics," p. 137.

69. Peter H. Schuck and Rogers M. Smith, *Citizenship Without Consent: Illegal Aliens in the American Polity* (New Haven: Yale University Press, 1985), p. 167, n. 31.

70. Renshon, *Dual Citizenship and American National Identity*, p. 6; Renshon, *Dual Citizens in America*, p. 3.

71. See Schuck, "Plural Citizenships," pp. 149–51, 173ff.; Renshon, *Dual Citizenship and American National Identity*, pp. 11–12.

72. Aristotle, *The Politics*, 1275a, 1278a, quoted in Michael Walzer, *Spheres of Justice: A Defense of Pluralism and Equality* (New York: Basic Books, 1983), pp. 53–54. See pp. 92–113 of Ernest Barker's translation (Oxford: Clarendon Press, 1946) for Aristotle's extensive discussion of citizenship and its relation to different constitutions.

73. Schuck, "Plural Citizenships," p. 169.

74. Soysal, *Limits of Citizenship*, p. 1.

75. Joseph H. Carens, "Why Naturalization Should Be Easy: A Response to Noah Pickus," in Pickus, *Immigration and Citizenship*, p. 143.

76. Deborah J. Yashar, "Globalization and Collective Action," *Comparative Politics*, 34 (April 2002), p. 367, citing Soysal, *Limits of Citizenship*, p. 119ff.; Schuck and Smith, *Citizenship Without Consent*, p. 107.

77. Aleinikoff, "Between Principles and Politics," p. 150.

78. Peter J. Spiro, "Questioning Barriers to Naturalization," *Georgetown Immi-*

gration Law Journal, 13 (Summer 1999), p. 517; Aleinikoff, "Between Principles and Politics," p. 154.

79. Jones-Correa, *Between Two Nations*, p. 198, n. 11; Leticia Quezada, quoted in *Washington Post National Weekly Edition*, 11–17 July 1994, p. 23.

80. David Jacobson, *Rights Across Borders: Immigration and the Decline of Citizenship* (Baltimore: Johns Hopkins University Press, 1996), pp. 8–9; Sarah V. Wayland, "Citizenship and Incorporation: How Nation-States Respond to the Challenges of Migration," *Fletcher Forum of World Affairs*, 20 (Summer/Fall 1996), p. 39; Irene Bloemraad, "The North American Naturalization Gap: An Institutional Approach to Citizenship Acquisition in the United States and Canada," *International Migration Review*, 36 (Spring 2002), pp. 193–228, especially p. 209, and "A Macro-Institutional Approach to Immigrant Political Incorporation: Comparing the Naturalization Rates and Processes of Portuguese Immigrants in the US and Canada" (paper, annual meeting, American Sociological Association, August 1999, Chicago).

81. Maria Jiminez, quoted in *New York Times*, 13 September 1996, p. A16; Jones-Correa, *Between Two Nations*, p. 200.

82. Department of Homeland Security, Office of Immigration Statistics, *2002 Yearbook of Immigration Statistics* (October 2003), pp. 159, 163.

83. Spiro, "Questioning Barriers to Naturalization," pp. 492, 518.

84. Schuck and Smith, *Citizenship Without Consent*, p. 108.

85. Carens, "Why Naturalization Should Be Easy," p. 146.

86. Waters, "Ethnic and Racial Identities," pp. 797, 800, citing Tekle Mariam Woldemikael, *Becoming Black American: Haitians and American Institutions in Evanston, Illinois* (New York: AMS Press, 1989), pp. 81, 94.

Chapter 9. Mexican Immigration and Hispanization

1. David M. Kennedy, "Can We Still Afford to Be a Nation of Immigrants?" *Atlantic Monthly*, 278 (November 1996), p. 67.

2. Roger Daniels, *Coming to America: A History of Immigration and Ethnicity in American Life* (New York: HarperCollins, 1990), pp. 129, 146.

3. Campbell J. Gibson and Emily Lennon, "Historical Census Statistics on the Foreign-Born Population of the United States, 1850–1990" (Population Division Working Paper 29, U.S. Census Bureau, February 1999), Table 3; U.S. Census Bureau, March 2000 Current Population Survey, *Profile of the Foreign-Born Population in the United States 2000* (PPL-145, 2001), Tables 1-1, 3-1, 3-2, 3-3, and 3-4.

4. *Economist*, 24 August 2002, pp. 21–22; U.S. Department of Homeland Security, Office of Immigration Statistics, *2002 Yearbook of Immigration Statistics* (Washington, forthcoming, 2003), Table 2; *New York Times*, 19 June 2003, p. A22.

5. Mark Krikorian, "Will Americanization Work in America?" *Freedom Review*, 28 (Fall 1997), pp. 48–49.

6. Barry Edmonston and Jeffrey S. Passel, "Ethnic Demography: U.S. Immigration and Ethnic Variations," in Edmonston and Passell, eds., *Immigration and*

Ethnicity: The Integration of America's Newest Arrivals (Washington, D.C.: Urban Institute Press, 1994), p. 8.

7. *Economist*, 20 May 1995, p. 29; *New York Times*, 3 January 1995, p. B2; Immigration and Naturalization Service study, reported in *New York Times*, 8 February 1997, p. 9; INS study, reported in *Boston Globe*, 1 February 2003, p. A8; Census Bureau figure reported in *Washington Post*, 25 October 2001, p. A24; Office of Immigration Statistics, Department of Homeland Security, *2002 Yearbook of Immigration Statistics* (October 2003), p. 213.

8. Michael Fix and Wendy Zimmermann, "After Arrival: An Overview of Federal Immigrant Policy in the United States," in Edmonston and Passel, eds., *Immigration and Ethnicity*, pp. 257–58; Frank D. Bean et al., "Educational and Sociodemographic Incorporation Among Hispanic Immigrants to the United States," in Edmonston and Passell, eds., *Immigration and Ethnicity*, pp. 80–82; George J. Borjas, *Heaven's Door: Immigration Policy and the American Economy* (Princeton: Princeton University Press, 1999), p. 118; "U.S. Survey," *Economist*, 11 March 2000, p. 12; *New York Times*, 1 February 2000, p. A12; *Economist*, 18 May 1996, p. 29.

9. Bean et al., "Educational and Sociodemographic Incorporation," pp. 80–82; "US Survey," *Economist*, p. 12; James Sterngold, "A Citizenship Incubator for Immigrant Latinos," *New York Times*, 1 February 2000, p. A12; "Where Salsa Meets Burger," *Economist*, 18 May 1996, p. 29.

10. "US Survey," *Economist*, p. 15, citing *Los Angeles Times;* Abraham F. Lowenthal and Katrina Burgess, eds., *The California-Mexico Connection* (Stanford: Stanford University Press, 1993), p. 256; *New York Times*, 17 February 2003, p. A13.

11. Kennedy, "Can We Still Afford to Be a Nation of Immigrants?," p. 68.

12. Summary of Mexican report in David Simcox, *Backgrounder: Another 50 Years of Mass Mexican Immigration* (Washington, D.C.: Center for Immigration Studies, March 2002).

13. Myron Weiner, *The Global Migration Crisis: Challenge to States and to Human Rights* (New York: HarperCollins, 1995), p. 21ff.; David M. Heer, *Immigration in America's Future: Social Science Findings and the Policy Debate* (Boulder: Westview Press, 1996), p. 147.

14. Edmonston and Passel, "Ethnic Demography," p. 21; Mark Falcoff, *Beyond Bilingualism* (Washington, D.C.: American Enterprise Institute, On the Issues Release, August 1996), p. 4.

15. Peter Skerry, *Mexican Americans: The Ambivalent Minority* (Cambridge: Harvard University Press, 1993), p. 289, also pp. 21–22.

16. Terrence W. Haverluk, "Hispanic Community Types and Assimilation in Mex-America," *Professional Geographer,* 50 (November 1998), p. 467.

17. Stephen Steinberg, *The Ethnic Myth: Race, Ethnicity, and Class in America* (New York: Atheneum, 1981), pp. 45–46.

18. Tech Paper 29, Table 5, *Language Spoken at Home for the Foreign-Born Population 5 Years and Over: 1980 and 1990*, U.S. Bureau of the Census, 9 March 1999; *We the American Foreign Born*, U.S. Bureau of the Census, September 1993, p. 6; Census Bureau figures reported in *Miami Herald*, 6 August 2002, p. 4A.

19. Heer, *Immigration in America's Future*, pp. 197–98.

20. Skerry, *Mexican Americans*, pp. 286, 289.

21. *Washington Post Weekly Edition*, 1–14 July 2002, p. 13.

22. Census Bureau, *We the American Foreign Born*, p. 6.

23. U.S. Census Bureau, *Profile of the Foreign-Born Population of the United States 2000* (Washington: Government Printing Office, 2001), p. 37; Bean et al., "Educational and Sociodemographic Incorporation," pp. 79, 81, 83, 90–93; Lindsay Lowell and Roberto Suro, *The Improving Educational Profile of Latino Immigrants* (Washington: Pew Hispanic Center, 4 December 2002), p. 1.

24. James P. Smith, "Assimilation Across the Latino Generations," *American Economic Review*, 93 (May 2003), pp. 315–19. I am deeply grateful to James Perry for his help in analyzing Smith's data.

25. *Washington Post Weekly Edition*, 10 August 1998, p. 33; Bean et al., "Educational and Sociodemographic Incorporation," pp. 94–95; American Council on Education, Minorities in Higher Education 19th annual report, 1999–2000, reported in *Boston Globe*, 23 September 2002, p. A3; William H. Frey, "Chanticle," *Milken Institute Review* (3rd quarter, 2002), p. 7.

26. U.S. Census Bureau, Profile of the Foreign-Born Population of the United States 2000 (December 2001), p. 41.

27. M. Patricia Fernandez Kelly and Richard Schauffler, "Divided Fates: Immigrant Children and the New Assimilation," in Alejandro Portes, ed., *The New Second Generation* (New York: Russell Sage Foundation, 1996), p. 48.

28. Robert W. Fairlie and Bruce D. Meyer, "Ethnic and Racial Self-Employment Differences and Possible Explanations," *Journal of Human Resources*, 31 (September 1996), pp. 772–73, citing 1990 census data.

29. U.S. Census Bureau, Current Population Survey, March 1998; Steven A. Camarota, *Immigrants in the United States—1998: A Snapshot of America's Foreign-Born Population* (Washington, D.C.: Center for Immigration Studies), pp. 6, 9. Two smaller immigrant groups had poverty rates above the Mexicans: Dominicans, 38 percent, and Haitians, 34 percent.

30. Borjas, *Heaven's Door*, pp. 110–11; Steven A. Camarota, *Immigration from Mexico: Assessing the Impact on the United States* (Washington, D.C.: Center for Immigration Studies, July 2001), p. 55; Camarota, *Back Where We Started: An Examination of Trends in Immigrant Welfare Use Since Welfare Reform* (Washington, D.C.: Center for Immigration Studies, March 2003), p. 13.

31. Steinberg, *The Ethnic Myth*, pp. 272–73.

32. Joel Perlmann and Roger Waldinger, "Are the Children of Today's Immigrants Making It?" *The Public Interest*, 132 (Summer 1998), p. 96.

33. Smith, "Assimilation Across the Latino Generations," p. 317.

34. Rodolfo O. de la Garza, Angelo Falcon, F. Chris Garcia, John Garcia, "Mexican Immigrants, Mexican Americans, and American Political Culture," in Edmonston and Passel, eds., *Immigration and Ethnicity*, pp. 232–35.

35. Leon Bouvier, *Embracing America: A Look at Which Immigrants Become Citizens*

(Washington, D.C.: Center for Immigration Studies Center Paper 11, 1996), p. 14, Table 4.3.

36. Ibid., pp. 32–33, Tables 9.2, 9.4; *Washington Post Weekly Edition*, 25 October 1999, pp. 30–31, citing U.S. census study; *New York Times*, 6 August 2003, pp. A1, A14.

37. Gregory Rodriguez, *From Newcomers to Americans: The Successful Integration of Immigrants into American Society* (Washington, D.C.: National Immigration Forum, 1999), p. 22, citing Current Population Survey, June 1994.

38. Calculations by Tammy Frisby from U.S. census data: U.S. Bureau of the Census, *Current Population Reports*, Special Studies Series, P-23, No. 77, "Perspectives on American Husbands and Wives," 1978; U.S. Bureau of the Census, *Current Population Reports*, P-20-483, "Household and Family Characteristics," March 1994, Table 13; U.S. Bureau of the Census, *Statistical Abstract of the United States 1999* (119th edition), Washington, D.C., 1999; Gary D. Sandefur, Molly Martin, Jennifer Eggerling-Boeck, Susan E. Mannon, Ann M. Meier, "An Overview of Racial and Ethnic Demographic Trends," in Neil J. Smelser, William Julius Wilson, Faith Mitchell, eds., *America Becoming: Racial Trends and Their Consequences* (Washington, D.C.: National Academy Press, 2001), vol. 1, pp. 74–75; Richard Alba, "Assimilation's Quiet Tide," *The Public Interest*, 119 (Spring 1995), pp. 3–18.

39. William V. Flores and Rina Benmayor, *Latino Cultural Citizenship: Claiming Identity, Space, and Rights* (Boston: Beacon Press, 1997), p. 11, citing a study by Renato Rosaldo.

40. Ron Unz, "The Right Way for Republicans to Handle Ethnicity in Politics," *The American Enterprise*, 11 (April/May 2000), p. 35.

41. Rubén G. Rumbaut, "The Crucible Within: Ethnic Identity, Self-Esteem, and Segmented Assimilation Among Children of Immigrants," in Portes, ed., *The New Second Generation*, pp. 136–37.

42. De la Garza et al., "Mexican Immigrants, Mexican Americans, and American Political Culture," pp. 231, 241, 248.

43. John J. Miller, "Becoming an American," *New York Times*, 26 May 1998, p. A27.

44. Robin Fox, "Nationalism: Hymns Ancient and Modern," *The National Interest*, 35 (Spring 1994), p. 56; de la Garza et al., "Mexican Immigrants, Mexican Americans, and American Political Culture," p. 229, citing Tom Smith, "Ethnic Survey," Topical Report 19 (Chicago: National Opinion Research Center, University of Chicago).

45. Jennifer L. Hochschild, *Facing Up to the American Dream: Race, Class, and the Soul of the Nation* (Princeton: Princeton University Press, 1995), passim, especially Chapter 4.

46. Susan Gonzales Baker et al., "U.S. Immigration Policies and Trends: The Growing Importance of Migration from Mexico," in Marcelo M. Suarez-Orozco, ed., *Crossings: Mexican Immigration in Interdisciplinary Perspectives* (Cambridge: Harvard University Press, 1998), pp. 99–100.

47. Kennedy, "Can We Still Afford to Be a Nation of Immigrants?," p. 68.

48. Morris Janowitz, *The Reconstruction of Patriotism: Education for Civic Consciousness* (Chicago: University of Chicago Press, 1983), pp. 128–29, 137.

49. "U.S. Survey," *Economist*, p. 13; *Rocky Mountain News*, 6 February 2000, p. 2Aff; Robert S. Leiken, *The Melting Border: Mexico and Mexican Communities in the United States* (Washington, D.C.: Center for Equal Opportunity, 2000); Lowenthal and Burgess, *The California-Mexico Connection*, p. vi; Council on Foreign Relations, *Defining the National Interest: Minorities and U.S. Foreign Policy in the 21st Century* (New York: Council on Foreign Relations, 1996), p. 12; Lester Langley, *MexAmerica, Two Countries, One Future* (New York: Crown, 1988); "Welcome to Amexica," *Time*, special issue, 11 June 2001; Victor Davis Hanson, *Mexifornia: A State of Becoming* (San Francisco: Encounter Books, 2003).

50. Robert D. Kaplan, "History Moving North," *Atlantic Monthly*, 279 (February, 1997), p. 24; *New York Times*, 17 February 2003, p. A13; *Economist*, 7 July 2001, p. 29; *New York Times*, 10 February 2002, Section 4, p. 6.

51. Graham E. Fuller, "Neonationalism and Global Politics: An Era of Separatism," *Current* 344 (July/August 1992), p. 22.

52. *Economist*, 8 April 2000, pp. 28–29; Joan Didion, "Miami," *New York Review*, 28 May 1987, p. 44; *Boston Globe*, 21 May 2000, p. A7.

53. U.S. Census Bureau, 2000 Census of Population and Housing, *Summary Social, Economic and Housing Characteristics*, PHC-2-1 (2003), pp. 27–29; U.S. Census Bureau, 2000 Census of Population and Housing, *Summary Population and Housing Characteristics*, PHC-1-1 (2001), pp. 32, 34, 36.

54. Fix and Zimmermann, "After Arrival: An Overview of Federal Immigrant Policy in the United States," pp. 256–58; *New York Times*, 1 April 2000, p. 1A, *Economist*, 8 April 2000, p. 27.

55. Cathy Booth, "The Capital of Latin America: Miami," *Time* (Fall 1993), p. 82.

56. Booth, "The Capital of Latin America," p. 84; Mimi Swartz, "The Herald's Cuban Revolution," *New Yorker*, 7 June 1999, p. 39.

57. Swartz, "The Herald's Cuban Revolution," p. 37; Booth, "The Capital of Latin America, p. 84.

58. Booth, "The Capital of Latin America," p. 84; *New York Times*, 11 February 1999, p. A1; *New York Times*, 10 May 2000, p. A17; Didion, "Miami," p. 47.

59. Swartz, "The Herald's Cuban Revolution," *The New Yorker*, 7 June 1999, p. 37, citing Alejandro Portes and Alex Stepick, *City on the Edge: The Transformation of Miami* (Berkeley: University of California Press, 1993); Booth, "The Capital of Latin America," p. 85; Didion, "Miami," p. 48.

60. Booth, "The Capital of Latin America," p. 82; Swartz, "The Herald's Cuban Revolution," pp. 39–40; David Rieff, quoted in *Economist*, 8 April 2000, p. 27.

61. *New York Times*, 1 April 2000, p. A1; *New York Times*, 2 April 2000, p. A22.

62. Didion, "Miami," p. 47.

63. *Boston Globe*, 24 July 1995, p. 11; Lionel Sosa, *The Americano Dream* (New York: Plume, 1998), p. 210.

64. Roderic Ai Camp, "Learning Democracy in Mexico and the United States,"

Mexican Studies, 19 (Winter 2003), p. 13; Carlos Fuentes, "Conversations with Rose Styron," *New Perspectives Quarterly*, Special Issue 1997, pp. 59–61; Andres Rozental quoted in Yossi Shain, *Marketing the American Creed Abroad* (Cambridge: Cambridge University Press, 1999), p. 189; Armando Cíntora, "Civil Society and Attitudes: The Virtues of Character," *Annals AAPSS*, 565 (September 1999), pp. 145–146; Jorge Casteñeda, "Ferocious Differences," *Atlantic Monthly*, 276 (July 1995), pp. 71–76; Sosa, *Americano Dream*, chaps. 1, 6.

65. *New York Times*, 3 May 1998, p. 26; *New York Times*, 19 September 1999, p. 18.

66. *New York Times*, 17 July 2000, p. A20.

67. Sosa, *Americano Dream*, pp. 205–7, 211.

68. *Washington Post*, 8 September 1996, p. X03; *Washington Post*, 17 August 2000, p. C4; *Houston Chronicle*, 23 June 2002, p. A1.

Chapter 10. Merging America with the World

1. Georgiy Arbatov, "Preface," in Richard Smoke and Andrei Kortunov, eds., *Mutual Security: A New Approach to Soviet-American Relations* (New York: St. Martin's, 1991), p. xxi; the original version of this quotation was slightly different, *New York Times*, 8 December 1987, p. 38.

2. David M. Kennedy, "Culture Wars: The Sources and Uses of Enmity in American History," in Ragnhild Fiebig-von Hase and Ursula Lehmkuhl, eds., *Enemy Images in American History* (Providence, RI: Berghahn, 1997), p. 355; John Updike, *Rabbit at Rest* (New York: Knopf, 1990), pp. 442–43.

3. "Waiting for the Barbarians," by C. P. Cavafy, from *Six Poets of Modern Greece*, edited by Edmund Keeley and Philip Sherrard (New York: Knopf, 1968). Reprinted with permission from Thames & Hudson, London. For one typical use of this poem, see Colonel S. Nelson Drew, USAF, *NATO from Berlin to Bosnia: Trans-Atlantic Security in Transition* (Washington, D.C.: National Defense University, Institute for National Strategic Studies, McNair Paper 35, January 1995), p. 36.

4. Bruce D. Porter, "Can American Democracy Survive?" *Commentary*, 96 (November 1993), pp. 37–40; Robert Putnam, *Bowling Alone: The Collapse and Revival of American Community* (New York: Simon & Schuster, 2000), pp. 272, 267–68; Philip A. Klinker and Rogers M. Smith, *The Unsteady March: The Rise and Decline of Racial Equality in America* (Chicago: University of Chicago Press, 1999); Michael C. Desch, "War and Strong States, Peace and Weak States?," *International Organization*, 50 (Spring 1996), pp. 237–68.

5. Daniel Deudney and G. John Ikenberry, "After the Long War," *Foreign Policy*, 94 (Spring 1994), p. 29.

6. Paul E. Peterson, "Some Political Consequences of the End of the Cold War" (Cambridge: Harvard University, Center for International Affairs, Trilateral Workshop on Democracy, Memorandum, 23–25 September 1994), pp. 4–9.

7. John W. Dower, *War Without Mercy: Race and Power in the Pacific War* (New

York: Pantheon, 1986), p. 10; John Hersey, *Into the Valley: A Skirmish of the Marines* (New York: Knopf, 1943), p. 56; Kennedy, "Culture Wars," in *Enemy Images*, pp. 354–55.

8. Charles Krauthammer, "Beyond the Cold War," *New Republic*, December 19, 1988, p. 18.

9. U.S. Department of State, Office of Counterterrorism, "Foreign Terrorist Organizations," 23 May 2003, and "Overview of State-Sponsored Terrorism," 30 April 2003; *Boston Globe*, 7 May 2002, p. A19.

10. Steve Farkas et al., *A Lot to Be Thankful For: What Parents Want Children to Learn About America* (New York: Public Agenda, 1998), p. 10.

11. "How Global Is My Company?" *Communiqué*, Global Business Policy Council, A.T. Kearny, no. 2 (fourth quarter, 2000), p. 3; statement by John Davey, Directorate of Intelligence Analysis, television interview, 11 March 1999.

12. Adam Smith, *An Inquiry into the Nature and Cause of the Wealth of Nations* (Chicago: University of Chicago, 1976), vol. 2, pp. 375–76, quoted in Walter Berns, *Making Patriots* (Chicago: University of Chicago Press, 2001), pp. 59–60.

13. James Davison Hunter and Joshua Yates, "In the Vanguard of Globalization: The World of American Globalizers," in Peter L. Berger and Samuel Huntington, eds., *Many Globalizations: Cultural Diversity in the Contemporary World* (New York: Oxford University Press, 2000), pp. 352–57, 345.

14. John Micklethwait and Adrian Wooldridge, *A Future Perfect: The Challenge and Hidden Promise of Globalization* (New York: Crown Business, 2000), p. 235; *"How Global Is My Company?"* p. 4.

15. Quoted in Hunter and Yates, "In the Vanguard of Globalization," in *Many Globalizations*, p. 344.

16. Manuel Castells, *The Rise of the Network Society*, 1 (Cambridge: Blackwell, 1996), p. 415, quoted in Micklethwait and Wooldridge, *A Future Perfect*, p. 242.

17. Adam Clymer, "The Nation's Mood," *New York Times Magazine*, December 11, 1983, p. 47.

18. Robert B. Reich, "What Is a Nation?," *Political Science Quarterly*, 106 (Summer 1991), pp. 193–94; Alan Wolfe, "Alien Nation," *New Republic*, 26 March 2001, p. 36; Micklethwait and Wooldridge, *A Future Perfect*, pp. 241–42.

19. Martha Nussbaum, "Patriotism and Cosmopolitanism," in Martha C. Nussbaum et al., *For Love of Country: Debating the Limits of Patriotism* (Boston: Beacon Press, 1996), pp. 4–9; Amy Gutmann, "Democratic Citizenship," in ibid., pp. 68–69; Richard Sennett, "America Is Better Off Without a 'National Identity,'" *International Herald Tribune*, 31 January 1994, p. 6; George Lipsitz, "Dilemmas of Beset Nationhood: Patriotism, the Family, and Economic Change in the 1970s and 1980s," in John Bodnar, ed., *Bonds of Affection: Americans Define Their Patriotism* (Princeton: Princeton University Press, 1996), p. 256; Cecilia E. O'Leary, " 'Blood Brotherhood': The Racialization of Patriotism, 1865–1918," in Bodnar, ed., *Bonds of Affection*, p. 55ff; Betty Jean Craige, *American Patriotism in a Global Society* (Albany: State University of New York Press, 1996), pp. 35–36; Peter Spiro, "New

Global Communities: Non-Governmental Organizations in International Decision-Making Institutions," *Washington Quarterly* (18 Winter 1995), p. 45.

20. See Jeremy A. Rabkin, *Why Sovereignty Matters* (Washington, D.C.: AEI Press, 1998), p. 51ff; *Filartiga v. Pena-Irala*, 630 F.2d 876 (2nd Cir., 1980).

21. Rabkin, *Why Sovereignty Matters*, pp. 56–58, 138.

22. Richard Rorty, *Achieving Our Country: Leftist Thought in Twentieth-Century America* (Cambridge: Harvard University Press, 1998), p. 15; Richard Rorty, "The Unpatriotic Academy," *New York Times*, 13 February 1994, p. E15; Robert Bellah, *The Broken Covenant: American Civil Religion in Time of Trial* (Chicago: University of Chicago Press, 1992), pp. xii–xiii.

23. Strobe Talbott, "The Birth of the Global Nation," *Time*, 20 July 1992, p. 70.

24. *Washington Post*, 16–20 June 1989, ABC/*Washington Post* poll, September 2002, reported in *New York Times*, 6 July 2003, Section 4, p. 1.

25. Ronald Inglehart et al., *World Values Surveys and European Values Surveys, 1981–1984, 1990–1993, and 1995–1997*, ICPSR version (Ann Arbor: Institute for Social Research, 2000).

26. Ibid.

27. Tom W. Smith and Lars Jarkko, *National Pride: A Cross-National Analysis* (Chicago: University of Chicago/National Opinion Research Center, GSS Cross National Report 19, May 1998), pp. 3–4; Elizabeth Hann Hastings and Phillip K. Hastings, *Index to International Public Opinion, 1988–89* (New York: Greenwood, 1990), p. 612; Seymour Martin Lipset, *American Exceptionalism: A Double-Edged Sword* (New York: Norton, 1996), p. 51; Richard Rose, "National Pride in Cross-National Perspective," *International Social Science Journal*, 37 (1985), pp. 86, 93–95.

28. Pippa Norris, ed., *Critical Citizens: Global Support for Democratic Government* (New York: Oxford University Press, 1999), pp. 38–42.

29. *New York Times* poll, *New York Times Magazine*, 11 December 1983, p. 89; *Washington Post Weekly Edition*, 16–20 June 1989.

30. Farkas et al., *A Lot to Be Thankful For*, p. 35; *New York Times*, 6 July 2003, Section 4, p. 5.

31. Ella Sekatu, quoted in Jill Lepore, *The Name of War: King Philip's War and the Origins of American Identity* (New York: Knopf, 1998), p. 240.

32. Russell Dalton, *Citizen Politics: Public Opinion and Political Parties in Advanced Industrial Democracies* (Chatham, NJ: Chatham House, 1996), pp. 275–76; Pippa Norris, ed., *Critical Citizens*, pp. 38–42; Smith and Jarkko, *National Pride*, pp. 3–4.

33. Deuteronomy 27:25; Daniel J. Elazar, "The Jewish People as the Classical Diaspora: A Political Analysis," in Gabriel Sheffer, ed., *Modern Diasporas in International Politics* (London: Croom Helm, 1986), p. 212ff; Robin Cohen, "Diasporas and the Nation-State: from Victims to Challengers," *International Affairs*, 72 (July 1996), pp. 507–9; American Jewish Committee, "Beyond Grief," *New York Times*, 3 December 1995, p. E15.

34. Institute of Southeast Asian Studies, "Trends," *The Business Times* (Singapore), 27–28 July 1996, p. 2.

35. *New York Times*, 8 April 2002, p. A11; Yossi Shain, *Marketing the American Creed Abroad: Diasporas in the U.S. and Their Homelands* (Cambridge: Cambridge University Press, 1999), pp. 71–72.

36. J. J. Goldberg quoted in *Boston Globe*, 18 August 1998, p. A6.

37. Susan Eckstein, "Diasporas and Dollars: Transnational Ties and the Transformation of Cuba" (Massachusetts Institute of Technology Center for International Studies, Rosemarie Rogers Working Paper 16, February 2003), p. 19.

38. Yossi Shain, "Marketing the American Creed Abroad: U.S. Diasporic Politics in the Era of Multiculturalism," *Diaspora*, 3 (Spring 1994), p. 94; Shain, *Marketing the American Creed Abroad*, pp. 181–82; Octavio Paz, *The Labyrinth of Solitude: Life and Thought in Mexico* (New York: Grove, 1961), pp. 13–19; Ernesto Zedillo, quoted in "Immigration and Instability," *American Outlook*, Spring 2002, p. 15; Vicente Fox reported in *New York Times*, 13 October 2002, p. 4.

39. Khatami quoted in *New York Times*, 23 September 1998, p. A7; Fox quoted in *New York Times*, 14 December 2000, p. A14.

40. *New York Times*, 25 August 2000, p. A25; *Washington Post Weekly Edition*, 23 December 2002–5 January 2003, p. 17.

41. Robert C. Smith, Review of Robin Cohen, *Global Diaspora: An Introduction*, *Political Science Quarterly*, 114 (Spring 1999), p. 160.

42. *New York Times*, 12 January 2003, p. 4; Jagdish Bhagwati, "Borders Beyond Control," *Foreign Affairs*, 82 (January/February 2003), p. 102.

43. Robert S. Leiken, *The Melting Border: Mexico and Mexican Communities in the United States* (Washington, D.C.: Center for Equal Opportunity, 2000), p. 10; *New York Times*, 30 May 2001, p. A12.

44. *New York Times*, 15 March 2003, p. A12.

45. *New York Times*, 13 October 2002, p. 4; *New York Times*, 25 August 2003, pp. A1, A14.

46. *New York Times*, 10 December 1995, p. 16.

47. John C. Harles, *Politics in the Lifeboat: Immigrants and the American Democratic Order* (Boulder: Westview Press, 1993), p. 97.

48. *Economist*, 6 January 2001, p. 32; *New York Times*, 8 April 2002, p. A11; Lorena Barberia, "Remittances to Cuba: An Evaluation of Cuban and U.S. Government Policy Measures" (Massachusetts Institute of Technology Center for International Affairs: Rosemarie Rogers Working Paper No. 15, September 2002), p. 11; *Economist*, 2 August 2003, p. 37; *New York Times*, 2 November 2001, p. A8, 9 January 2002, p. A8.

49. *New York Times*, 29 February 2000, p. A1; Public Policy Institute of California survey as reported by Moisés Naim, "The New Diaspora," *Foreign Policy*, 131 (July/August 2002), p. 95.

50. Rodolfo O. de la Garza, review of Yossi Shain, *Marketing the American Creed Abroad*, *American Political Science Review*, 95 (December 2001), p. 1045, and similar comments by Gary P. Freeman in his review, *Political Science Quarterly*, 115 (Fall 2000), pp. 483–85.

51. Tony Smith, *Foreign Attachments: The Power of Ethnic Groups in the Making of American Foreign Policy* (Cambridge: Harvard University Press, 2000), pp. 47–48, 54–64.

52. *New York Times*, 20 December 1991, pp. A1, A4; Todd Eisenstadt, "The Rise of the Mexico Lobby in Washington: Even Further from God, and Even Closer to the United States," in Rodolfo O. de la Garza and Jesus Velasco, eds., *Bridging the Mexican Border: Transforming Mexico–U.S. Relations* (New York: Rowman and Littlefield, 1997), pp. 89, 94, 113; Carlos Salinas de Gortari, *Mexico: The Policy and Politics of Modernization* (New York: Random House, 2002); *New York Times*, 10 December 1995, p. 16.

53. Daniel Patrick Moynihan, "The Science of Secrecy" (address, Massachusetts Institute of Technology, Cambridge, 29 March 1999), p. 8; *Washington Post*, 26 September 1996, p. A15.

54. See Smith, *Foreign Attachments*; Shain, *Marketing the American Creed Abroad*; Sheffer, *Modern Diasporas in International Politics*.

55. Elie Wiesel, quoted in Smith, *Foreign Attachments*, p. 147, and in Noam Chomsky, *The Fateful Triangle* (Boston: South End Press, 1983), p. 16, citing *Jewish Post-Opinion*, 19 November 1982; J. J. Goldberg, *Jewish Power: Inside the American Jewish Establishment* (Reading, PA: Addison-Wesley, 1996), p. 70; Smith, *Foreign Attachments*, p. 161.

56. Jonathan Pollard, quoted in Seymour M. Hersh, "The Traitor," *The New Yorker*, 18 January 1999, p. 26.

57. *Washington Post*, 24 March 1997, p. A1ff.

58. Khalil E. Jahshan, quoted in *New York Times*, 19 August 2002, p. A10.

59. *Washington Post*, 24 March 1997, p. A1ff.; *Times-Picayune*, 7 November 2003, p. 2; Associated Press file 14 November 2003; *The Times of India*, 7 November 2003.

60. *New York Times*, 19 August 2002, p. A10; *Economist*, 14 October 2000, p. 41.

Chapter 11. Fault Lines Old and New

1. Noel Ignatiev, *How the Irish Became White* (New York: Routledge, 1995); Karen Brodkin, *How Jews Became White Folks and What That Says About Race in America* (New Brunswick: Rutgers University Press, 1998); Matthew Frye Jacobson, *Whiteness of a Different Color: European Immigrants and the Alchemy of Race* (Cambridge: Harvard University Press, 1998).

2. Reginald Byron, *Irish America* (Oxford: Clarendon Press, 1999), p. 273.

3. Will Herberg, *Protestant, Catholic, Jew: An Essay in American Religious Sociology* (Garden City: Doubleday, 1955), pp. 43–44; Philip Gleason, *Speaking of Diversity: Language and Ethnicity in Twentieth-Century America* (Baltimore: Johns Hopkins University Press, 1992), p. 175; Marcus Lee Hansen, *The Problem of the Third Generation Immigrant* (Rock Island, IL: Augustana Historical Society, 1938), p. 12; Nathan Glazer and Daniel Patrick Moynihan, *Beyond the Melting Pot: The Negroes*,

Puerto Ricans, Jews, Italians, and Irish of New York City (Cambridge: Harvard University Press, 1963), pp. 313–14; Herberg, *Protestant, Catholic, Jew*, p. 40, citing George Rippey Stewart, *American Ways of Life* (Garden City: Doubleday, 1954).

4. Matthijs Kalmijn, "Shifting Boundaries: Trends in Religious and Educational Homogamy," *American Sociological Review*, 56 (December 1991), pp. 786–800; Stephen Steinberg, *The Ethnic Myth* (New York: Atheneum, 1981), pp. 70–71; Robert Christopher, *Crashing the Gates: The De-WASPing of America's Power Elite* (New York: Simon & Schuster, 1989), pp. 52–54.

5. Arthur Mann, *The One and the Many: Reflections on the American Identity* (Chicago: University of Chicago Press, 1979), p. 121; Alan M. Dershowitz, *The Vanishing American Jew: In Search of Jewish Identity for the Next Century* (Boston: Little, Brown, 1997), p. 16; Richard D. Alba, "Assimilation's Quiet Tide," *Public Interest*, 119 (Spring 1995), p. 15; Ari Shavit, "Vanishing," *New York Times Magazine*, 8 June 1997, p. 52; Gustav Niebuhr, "For Jews, a Little Push for Converts, and a Lot of Angst," *New York Times*, 13 June 1999, p. WE3.

6. Alba, "Assimilation's Quiet Tide," p. 13.

7. Eric Liu, *The Accidental Asian: Notes of a Native Speaker* (New York: Random House, 1998), p. 188.

8. Ibid.

9. Richard D. Alba, *Ethnic Identity: The Transformation of White America* (New Haven: Yale University Press, 1990), p. 294; Alba, "Assimilation's Quiet Tide," p. 5.

10. Alba, *Ethnic Identity*, pp. 313–15.

11. John David Skrentny, *Color Lines: Affirmative Action, Immigration, and Civil Rights Options for America* (Chicago: University of Chicago Press, 2001), p. 23; David A. Hollinger, *Postethnic America: Beyond Multiculturalism* (New York: Basic Books, 1995), pp. 30–31; Orlando Patterson, *The Ordeal of Integration: Progress and Resentment in America's "Racial" Crisis* (Washington, D.C.: Civitas/Counterpoint, 1997), p. xi.

12. Bureau of the Census/Bureau of Labor Statistics, "A CPS Supplement for Testing Methods of Collecting Racial and Ethnic Information: May 1995" (Washington, D.C.: Bureau of Labor Statistics, October 1995), Table 4.

13. Alba, *Ethnic Identity*, pp. 316–17; Brodkin, *How Jews Became White Folks*, p. 151.

14. Alba, *Ethnic Identity*, p. 315; Stanley Lieberson, "Unhyphenated Whites in the United States," *Ethnic and Racial Studies*, 8 (January 1985), pp. 173–75.

15. Lieberson, "Unhyphenated Whites," pp. 171–72; *Boston Globe*, 31 May 2002, p. A1; *New York Times*, 9 June 2002, p. 19.

16. *Economist*, 28 February 1998, p. 83.

17. "Interracial Marriage," *Vital STATS*, August 1997, http://www.stats.org/newsletters/9708/interrace2.htm.

18. Douglas J. Besharov and Timothy S. Sullivan, "One Flesh: America Is Experiencing an Unprecedented Increase in Black-White Intermarriage," *New Democrat*, 8 (July/August 1996), p. 19.

19. Pew Research Center for the People and the Press poll, *1999 Millenium Survey*, April 6–May 6, 1999 polling, released October 24, 1999, http://people-press.org/reports/display.php3?ReportID=51; Karlyn Bowman, "Getting Beyond Race," *American Enterprise Institute Memo*, January 1999, earlier version in *Roll Call*, November 5, 1998; Frank D. Bean, quoted in *Boston Globe*, 6 July 2001, p. A5.

20. Gallup/CNN/*USA Today* poll, 9–11 March 2001, released March 13, 2001; *New York Times*, 13 March 2001, p. A1; *Boston Sunday Globe*, 18 February 2001, p. D8.

21. *Time*, 142 (Special Issue, fall 1993); *Boston Sunday Globe*, 18 February 2001, p. D8.

22. Gina Philogène, *From Black to African-American: A New Social Representation* (Westport, CT: Praeger, 1999), pp. 16–17, 34, 51, 83.

23. Karl Zinsmeister, "Indicators," *American Enterprise*, 9 (November/December 1998), p. 18, citing Penn, Schoen, and Berland 1997 poll; *Newsweek* poll, February 1995, cited in Michael K. Frisby, "Black, White or Other," *Emerge* (December 1995/January 1996), http://www.usus.usemb.se/sft/142/sf14211.htm.

24. Joel Perlmann and Roger Waldinger, "Are the Children of Today's Immigrants Making It?" *The Public Interest*, 132 (Summer 1998), pp. 86–87.

25. David Gates, "White Male Paranoia," *Newsweek*, 29 March 1993, p. 48.

26. Immanuel Wallerstein, "The Clinton Impeachment," Online Commentary, no. 10, February 15, 1999, http://fbc.binghamton.edu/10en.htm.

27. John Higham, *Strangers in the Land: Patterns of American Nativism, 1860–1925* (New Brunswick: Rutgers University Press, 1988), p. 4.

28. *Time*, 14 May 2001, p. 6; *New York Times*, 30 April 2001, p. A17.

29. Carol M. Swain, *The New White Nationalism in America: Its Challenge to Integration* (New York: Cambridge University Press, 2002), pp. 15–17.

30. *Economist*, 11 March 2000, p. 4.

31. *Boston Globe*, 21 December 1997, p. A40, citing 1997 *Boston Globe*/WBZ-TV survey conducted by KRC Communications.

32. Professor Charley Flint, quoted in *Boston Globe*, 21 December 1997, p. A40; Noel Ignatiev, quoted in ibid. For a brief overview of whiteness studies as of 2003, see Darryl Fears, "Seeing Red Over 'Whiteness Studies,' " *Washington Post Weekly Edition*, 30 June–13 July 2003, p. 30.

33. Swain, *The New White Nationalism*, p. 423.

34. William V. Flores and Rina Benmayor, *Latino Cultural Citizenship: Claiming Identity, Space, and Rights* (Boston: Beacon Press, 1997), pp. 3, 5, 9–10.

35. Dorfman quoted in *New York Times*, 24 June 1998, p. A31; Flores and Benmayor, *Latino Cultural Citizenship*, p. 7.

36. *Boston Globe*, 8 January 1995, p. A31.

37. *New York Times*, 5 July 2000, p. A5.

38. Jorge G. Castañeda, "Ferocious Differences," *Atlantic Monthly*, 276 (July 1995), p. 76.

39. Hyon B. Shin with Rosalind Bruno, *Language Use and English-Speaking Ability* (U.S. Census Bureau, October 2003), pp. 2–3; U.S. Newswire, "Hispanic Popula-

tion Reaches All-Time High New Census Bureau Estimates Show" (Medialink Worldwide Release, 18 June 2003).

40. Jack Citrin, Donald Philip Green, Beth Reingold, Evelyn Walters, "The 'Official English' Movement and the Symbolic Politics of Language in the United States," *Western Political Quarterly*, 43 (September 1990), p. 537.

41. *Christian Science Monitor*, 15 September 1998, p. B1.

42. James Traub, "The Bilingual Barrier," *New York Times Magazine*, 31 January 1999, p. 35.

43. *New York Times*, 16 December 2000, p. A15.

44. Traub, "The Bilingual Barrier," p. 35.

45. Quoted in James Crawford, *Bilingual Education: History, Politics, Theory, and Practice* (Los Angeles: Bilingual Educational Services, 1995), p. 65.

46. Quoted in Raymond Tatalovich, *Nativism Reborn?: The Official English Language Movement and the American States* (Lexington: University Press of Kentucky, 1995), p. 17; Pamela L. Tiedt and Iris M. Tiedt, *Multicultural Teaching: A Handbook of Activities, Information, and Resources* (Boston: Allyn & Bacon, 2nd ed., 1986), p. 15; Richard W. Riley, remarks, Bell Multicultural High School, Washington, D.C., 15 March 2000.

47. *New York Times*, 16 August 1999, p. B1; Geoffrey Nunberg, "Linguists and the Official Language Movement," *Language*, 65 (September 1989), p. 586.

48. Max J. Castro, "On the Curious Question of Language in Miami," in James Crawford, ed., *Language Loyalties* (Chicago: University of Chicago Press, 1992), p. 183.

49. *Washington Post*, 6 February 1999, p. A4; Domenico Maceri, "Americans Are Embracing Spanish," *International Herald Tribune*, 24 June 2003, p. 6.

50. S. I. Hayakawa quoted in James Crawford, *Hold Your Tongue: Bilingualism and the Politics of "English Only"* (Reading, MA: Addison-Wesley, 1992), pp. 149–50.

51. Theodore Roosevelt, "One Flag, One Language (1917)," in Crawford, ed., *Language Loyalties*, p. 85; *New York Times*, 6 May 2001, p. 25; *Boston Globe*, 6 May 2001, p. A6; *Financial Times*, 23 June 2000, p. 15.

52. Robert Lerner, Althea K. Nagai, Stanley Rothman, *American Elites* (New Haven: Yale University Press, 1996), p. 50; General Social Survey 1980.

53. Everett Carll Ladd, Jr., and Seymour Martin Lipset, *The Divided Academy: Professors and Politics* (New York: McGraw-Hill, 1975), pp. 141–46; Jennifer A. Lindholm et al., *The American College Teacher: National Norms for the 2001–2002 HERI Faculty Survey* (Los Angeles: UCLA Higher Education Research Institute, 2002); Stanley Rothman, "Academics on the Left," *Society*, 23 (March/April 1986), p. 6; Connecticut Mutual Life Insurance Co., *Report on American Values in the 80's: The Impact of Belief* (New York: Research & Forecasts, 1986), pp. 27–28.

54. Ladd and Lipset, *Survey of the Social, Political, and Educational Perspectives*, p. 163.

55. Jack Citrin, "The End of American Identity?" in Stanley A. Renshon, ed., *One America? Political Leadership, National Identity, and the Dilemmas of Diversity* (Washington, D.C.: Georgetown University Press, 2001), p. 303.

56. Jack Citrin et al., "Is American Nationalism Changing? Implications for Foreign Policy," *International Studies Quarterly*, 38 (March 1994), pp. 26–27.

57. *Economist*, 2 January 1999, p. 59; *International Herald Tribune*, 17–18 March 2001, p. 10; David Broder, citing NBC News/*Wall Street Journal* poll *Washington Post Weekly Edition*, 2–8 April 2001, p. 4.

58. Rita J. Simon, "Old Minorities, New Immigrants: Aspirations, Hopes, and Fears," *Annals of the American Academy of Political and Social Science*, 530 (November 1993), pp. 63, 68; *The American Enterprise*, Public Opinion and Demographic Report, referring to series of polls from different sources, 5 (January/February 1994), p. 97; *World Values Survey*, 1995–1997.

59. See Vernon M. Briggs, Jr., *American Unionism and U.S. Immigration Policy* (Washington, D.C.: Center for Immigration Studies, August 2001).

60. Everett Carll Ladd, Jr., and Karlyn H. Bowman, *What's Wrong: A Survey of American Satisfaction and Complaint* (Washington, D.C.: AEI Press, 1998), pp. 92–93.

61. *Newsweek*, 9 August 1993, p. 19; Simon, "Old Minorities, New Immigrants," pp. 62, 64; *Time*, 1 March 1993, p. 72.

62. Lawrence R. Jacobs and Robert Y. Shapiro, "Debunking the Pandering Politician Myth," *Public Perspective*, 8 (April/May 1997), pp. 3–5; Alan D. Monroe, "Public Opinion and Public Policy, 1980–1993," *Public Opinion Quarterly*, 62 (Spring 1998), p. 6; Richard Morin, "A Gap in Worldviews," *Washington Post Weekly Edition*, 19 April 1999, p. 34.

63. Susan J. Pharr, Robert D. Putnam, Russell J. Dalton, "What's Troubling the Trilateral Democracies," in Susan J. Pharr and Robert D. Putnam, eds., *Disaffected Democracies: What's Troubling the Trilateral Countries?* (Princeton: Princeton University Press, 2000), pp. 9–10.

64. James Allan Davis and Tom W. Smith, *General Social Surveys, 1972–2000* [machine-readable data file] (Storrs, CT: Roper Center for Public Opinion Research).

65. Thomas E. Patterson, *The Vanishing Voter: Public Involvement in an Age of Uncertainty* (New York: Knopf, 2002), pp. 4–5.

66. David S. Broder, *Democracy Derailed: Initiative Campaigns and the Power of Money* (New York: Harcourt, 2000), pp. 3, 6–7; *Economist*, 9 November 2002, p. 30.

Chapter 12. Twenty-first Century America: Vulnerability, Religion, and National Identity

1. Ernest Renan, "What is a Nation?" in Geoff Eley and Ronald Gripor Suny, eds., *Becoming National: A Reader* (New York: Oxford University Press, 1996), pp. 41–55. See also Bernard Yack's discussion in "The Myth of the Civic Nation," *Critical Review*, 10 (Spring 1996), pp. 197–98.

2. Alexis de Tocqueville, *Democracy in America* (New York: Vintage, 1954), vol. 1, pp. 334–335.

3. Patrick Glynn, "Prelude to a Post-Secular Society," *New Perspectives Quarterly*, 12 (Spring 1995), p. 17.

4. Paul Kurtz, Chairman of the Center for Inquiry, quoted in *New York Times*, 24 August 2002, p. A17.

5. *Religious Congregations and Membership in the United States* (Nashville: Glenmary Research Center, 2002), issued September 2000; *New York Times*, 18 September 2002, p. A16; *Economist*, 16 May 1987, p. 24.

6. Doug Bandow, "Christianity's Parallel Universe," *The American Enterprise*, 6 (November/December 1995), pp. 58–60; Kenneth D. Wald, *Religion and Politics in the United States* (Washington, D.C.: CQ Press, 3rd ed., 1997), pp. 234–35; Janet Elder, "Scandal in the Church: American Catholics," *New York Times Magazine*, 21 April 2002, p. 36.

7. David M. Shribman, "One Nation Under God," *Boston Globe Magazine*, 10 January 1999, p. 29; Andrew Kohut et al., *The Diminishing Divide: Religion's Changing Role in American Politics* (Washington, D.C.: Brookings Institution Press, 2000), p. 82; John Green et al., "Faith in the Vote: Religiosity and the Presidential Election," *Public Perspective*, 12 (March/April 2001), pp. 33–35.

8. *New York Times*, 29 October 1998, p. 21; Kohut, *The Diminishing Divide*, pp. 126–127; *Economist*, 2 November 2003, p. 33.

9. Shribman, "One Nation Under God," pp. 20–21.

10. Michael J. Sandel, "The State and the Soul," *The New Republic*, 10 June 1985, p. 38.

11. Public Agenda Online Special Edition, *For Goodness' Sake: Why So Many Want Religion to Play a Greater Role in American Life*, 17 January 2003, p. 1, http://www.publicagenda.org/specials/religion/religion.html.

12. Kohut, *The Diminishing Divide*, pp. 26–27, pp. 28–29; *Economist*, 24 August 2002, p. 27, citing *Time* poll.

13. *Time*, 27 December 1993, pp. 56–65; Ruth Shalit, "Angels on Television, Angels in America: Quality Wings," *The New Republic*, 20–27 July 1998, p. 24.

14. James Davison Hunter, "When Psychotherapy Replaces Religion," *Public Interest*, 139 (Spring 2000), p. 14.

15. *Boston Globe*, 12 January 1998, pp. A1, A11.

16. *Time*, 7 June 1999, p. 65; R. Albert Mohler, Jr., "Against an Immoral Tide," *New York Times*, 19 June 2000, p. A23.

17. *Time*, 9 December 1991, p. 64.

18. Kohut, *The Diminishing Divide*, pp. 4–5; *New York Times*, 24 August 2002, citing Professor Hugh Heclo of George Mason University.

19. Quoted in Shribman, "One Nation Under God," p. 28; quoted in David Broder, *Boston Globe*, 3 January 1996, p. 11; Charles Alston and Evan Jenkins, quoted in Shribman, "One Nation Under God," p. 21.

20. Joel Kotkin, "In God We Trust Again," *The New Democrat*, 8 (January–February 1996), p. 24; Geoffrey C. Layman, *The Great Divide: Religious and Cultural Conflict in American Party Politics* (New York: Columbia University Press, 2001), p. 114; *Boston Globe*, 27 June 1999, p. F1.

21. Ibid., p. 64; quoted in ibid., p. 63.

22. Wald, *Religion and Politics in the United States*, pp. 94–96.

23. See "Compassionate Conservatism Ahead," *American Enterprise*, 11 (June 2000), p. 26ff.; "Religious Discrimination Slowly Ending," *American Enterprise*, 11 (March–April 2000), pp. 15–16; *Boston Globe*, 27 June 1988, p. F1.

24. *New York Times*, 13 December 2000, p. A1, 30 January 2001, p. A18.

25. Adam Meyerson, quoted in E. J. Dionne, Jr., *International Herald Tribune*, 20 August 1997, p. 8.

26. *Wall Street Journal*, 22 January 2003, p. A14.

27. Gertrude Himmelfarb, "Religion in the 2000 Election," *The Public Interest*, 143 (Spring 2001), p. 23; Pew Charitable Trusts, *For Goodness' Sake*, pp. 10–11; *New York Times*, 31 August 1999, p. A14; CNN-*USA Today*/Gallup survey, 16 March 1998; *Washington Post Weekly Edition*, 28 August 2000, p. 21; Richard John Neuhaus, "The Public Square: A Survey of Religion and Public Life," *First Things*, 126 (October 2002), p. 107; Steve Farkas, ed., *A Lot to be Thankful For* (New York: Public Agenda, 1998).

28. Layman, *The Great Divide*, pp. 16, 107–10.

29. Ibid., pp. 110–11.

30. *New York Times*, 15 December 1999, p. A31; Wilfred McClay, "Two Concepts of Secularism," *Wilson Quarterly*, 24 (Summer 2000), p. 57; *New York Times*, 29 August 2000, p. A17; *Boston Globe*, 29 August 2000, p. A12.

31. *New York Times*, 19 December 1999, Section 4, p. 5; *Boston Globe*, 23 December 1999, pp. A1, A14; *New York Times*, 29 May 1999, p. A11; *Economist*, 23 December 1999, p. 18.

32. Sigmund Freud, *The Future of an Illusion* (New York: W.W. Norton, 1961), p. 31.

33. Assaf Moghadam, *A Global Resurgence of Religion?* (Cambridge: Harvard University Weatherhead Center for International Affairs, Paper No. 03-03, August 2003), pp. 65, 67.

34. Kiren Aziz Chaudhry, "Templates of Despair, Visions of Redemption: A New Arab Nationalism for a New International Order," unpublished paper in Harvard Academy for International and Area Studies, *Conflict or Convergence: Global Perspectives on War, Peace, and International Order* (Cambridge: Weatherhead Center for International Affairs, 1997).

35. Mark Juergensmeyer, *The New Cold War? Religious Nationalism Confronts the Secular State* (Berkeley: University of California Press, 1993), pp. 1–3.

36. Jonathan Sacks, "The Dignity of Difference: Avoiding the Clash of Civilizations," *Foreign Policy Research Institute Wire*, vol. 10, no. 3, July 2002, p. 1.

37. Rohan Gunaratna, *Inside Al Qaeda: Global Network of Terror* (New York: Columbia University Press, 2002), pp. 45–47.

38. Interview with Peter Arnett, quoted in Gunaratna, *Inside Al Qaeda*, p. 90.

39. George Kennan, "The Long Telegram," February 22, 1946, in Thomas Etzold and John Lewis Gaddis, *Containment: Documents on American Policy and Strategy, 1945–1950* (New York: Columbia University Press, 1978), p. 61.

40. Gallup press release, 27 February 2002.

41. *New York Times*, 5 December 2002, p. A11.

42. *Economist*, 15 February 2003, p. 41.

43. Arthur A. Stein, *The Nation at War* (Baltimore: Johns Hopkins University Press, 1980).

44. Adrian Hastings, *The Construction of Nationhood: Ethnicity, Religion, and Nationalism* (New York: Cambridge University Press, 1997), pp. 185–87, 205.

45. Ronald Inglehart and Marita Caballo, "Does Latin America Exist?," *PS: Political Science and Politics*, 30 (March 1997), p. 38.

46. Richard Rose, "National Pride in Cross-National Perspectives," *International Social Science Journal*, 37 (1985), p. 89.

INDEX

Abkhazians, 13
abolitionist movement, 117, 119
Academy Awards, 96
Acehans, 13
Adams, John, 77, 84, 113, 115, 142
Adarand Contractors v. Pena (1995), 155
Addams, Jane, 133
Aetna, 7
affirmative action, 19, 144, 148–57, 313
Afghanistan, 263; U.S. war on, 199, 264
AFL-CIO, 167, 330
African-Americans, *see* blacks
African race, 55
Africans, 180–82, 232, 235
Agriculture, U.S. Department of, 122
Ahlstrom, Sidney, 78
Alabama, 226
Alba, Richard, 195, 240, 298, 300
Albanians, 14, 24, 180, 222
Albright, Madeleine, 284
Alcoa, 267
Aleinikoff, Alexandre, 216–17
Alexander, Lamar, 177
Algeria, 12, 209
Al Qaeda, 263, 358, 360
Alvarez, Alex, 75
American Broadcasting Company (ABC), 275
American Colonization Society, 55
American Council of Trustees and Alumni, 177
American Creed, xix–xxi, 11, 37–38, 41, 46–49, 66–69, 105, 141, 242, 327; in age of vulnerability, 336–40; assimilation of immigrants to, 178, 183, 241; challenges to, 17–20, 142, 145–58, 176, 177, 313; diasporas and, 284; enemies defined in

opposition to, 257, 261; naturalization and, 215, 219; Protestantism and, 62, 63, 106; reform ethic in, 75
American Express, 156
American Family Association, 342
American Farm Bureau Federation, 314
American Institutes for Research, 164
American International College, 133
American Jewish Committee, 276
American Legion, 122
American National Election Studies, 153
American Revolution, 18, 48, 76, 77, 83, 93, 108, 113, 115, 116, 118, 174–76, 214, 259, 260, 337, 338; *see also* Declaration of Independence; Founding Fathers
Americanization, 18, 131–35, 142, 183–85, 192, 199–203, 220, 241, 249; of Catholicism, 95–98, 133–35
Ames, Fisher, 114
Anderson, Benedict, 22, 115
Angelou, Maya, 6
Anglicans, 64, 68
Anglo-conformity, 130, 145, 173
Anglo-Protestant culture, xix–xxi, 17–20, 30, 28, 49, 58–80, 141, 221, 259, 295, 365, 337; American Creed and, 66–69; assimilation of immigrants to, 41, 128–31, 134, 183, 190, 192, 339; challenge of multiculturalism to, 171–77; dissidence of dissent in, 62–66; Hispanics and, 254, 256, 301, 313, 316, 318, 324; individualism in, 69–70; gap between Islam and, 263;

411